CASE CLOSED

VOLUME 18

Gosho Aoyama

Case Briefing:

Subject:
Occupation:
Special Skills:
Equipment:

Jimmy Kudo, a.k.a. Conan Edogawa
High School Student/Detective
Analytical thinking and deductive reasoning, Soccer
Bow Tie Voice Transmitter, Super Sneakers,
Homing Glasses, Stretchy Suspenders

The subject is hot on the trail of a pair of suspicious men in black when he is attacked from behind and administered a strange substance which physically transforms him into a first grader. When the subject confides in the eccentric inventor Dr. Agasa, they decide to keep the subject's true identity a secret for the safety of everyone around him. Assuming the new identity of first-grader Conan Edogawa, the subject continues to assist the police force on their most baffling cases. The only problem is that most crime-solving professionals won't take a little kid's advice!

Table of Contents

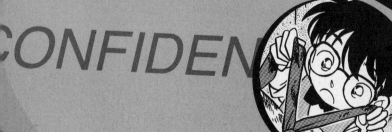

CONFIDEN

CASE CLOSED

Volume 18 • VIZ Media Edition

GOSHO AOYAMA

Translation
Naoko Amemiya

Touch-up & Lettering
Walden Wong

Cover & Graphics Design
Andrea Rice

Editor
Shaenon K. Garrity

Editor in Chief, Books **Alvin Lu**
Editor in Chief, Magazines **Marc Weidenbaum**
VP of Publishing Licensing **Rika Inouye**
VP of Sales **Gonzalo Ferreyra**
Sr. VP of Marketing **Liza Coppola**
Publisher **Hyoe Narita**

© 1998 Gosho AOYAMA/Shogakukan Inc.
First published by Shogakukan Inc. in Japan as "Meitantei Conan."
All rights reserved.
The stories, characters and incidents mentioned in this publication are entirely fictional.

store.viz.com

www.viz.com

Printed in the U.S.A.
Published by VIZ Media, LLC
P.O. Box 77010
San Francisco, CA 94107

10 9 8 7 6 5 4 3 2
First printing, July 2007
Second printing, October 2007

FILE 1: THE SAME?

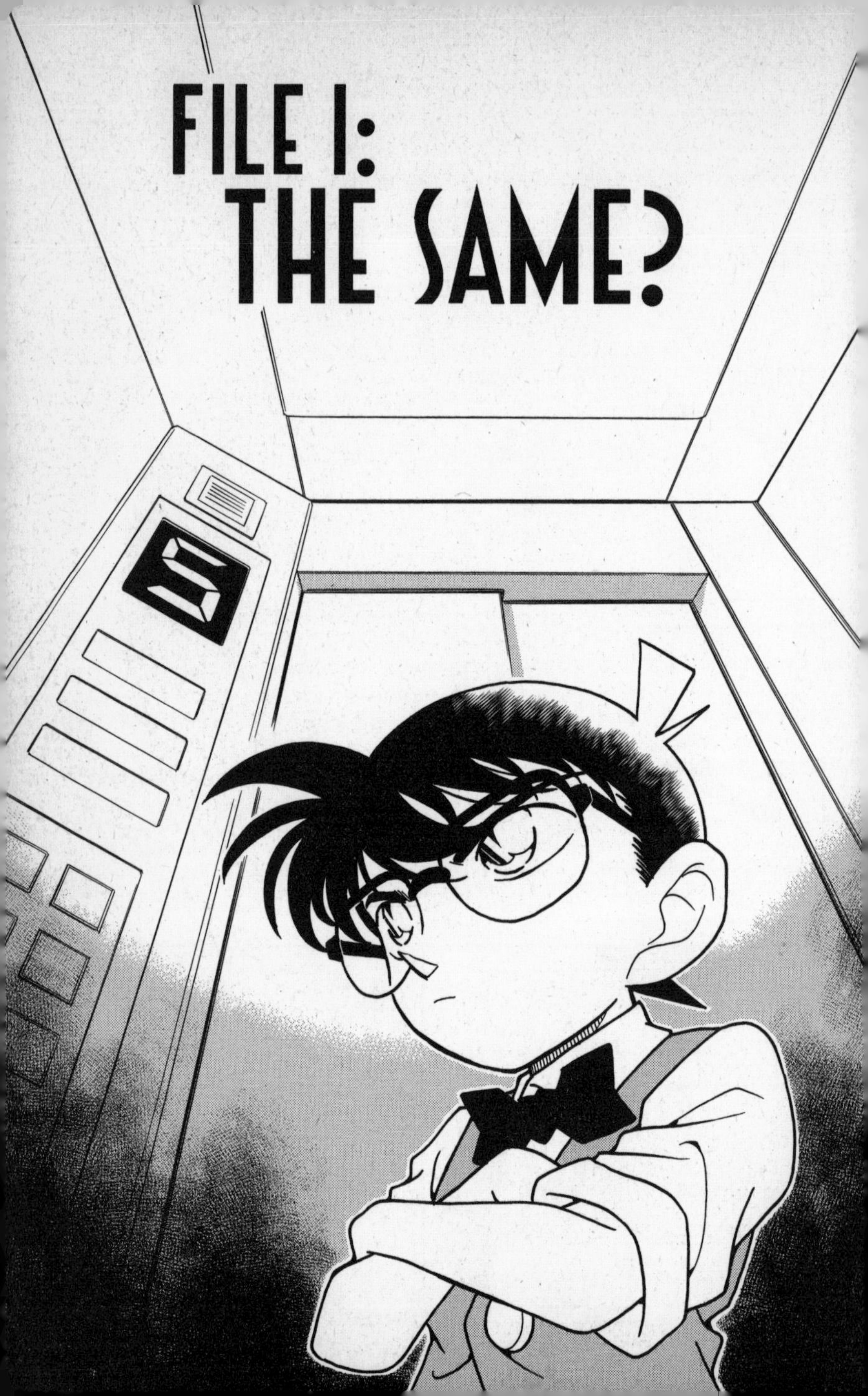

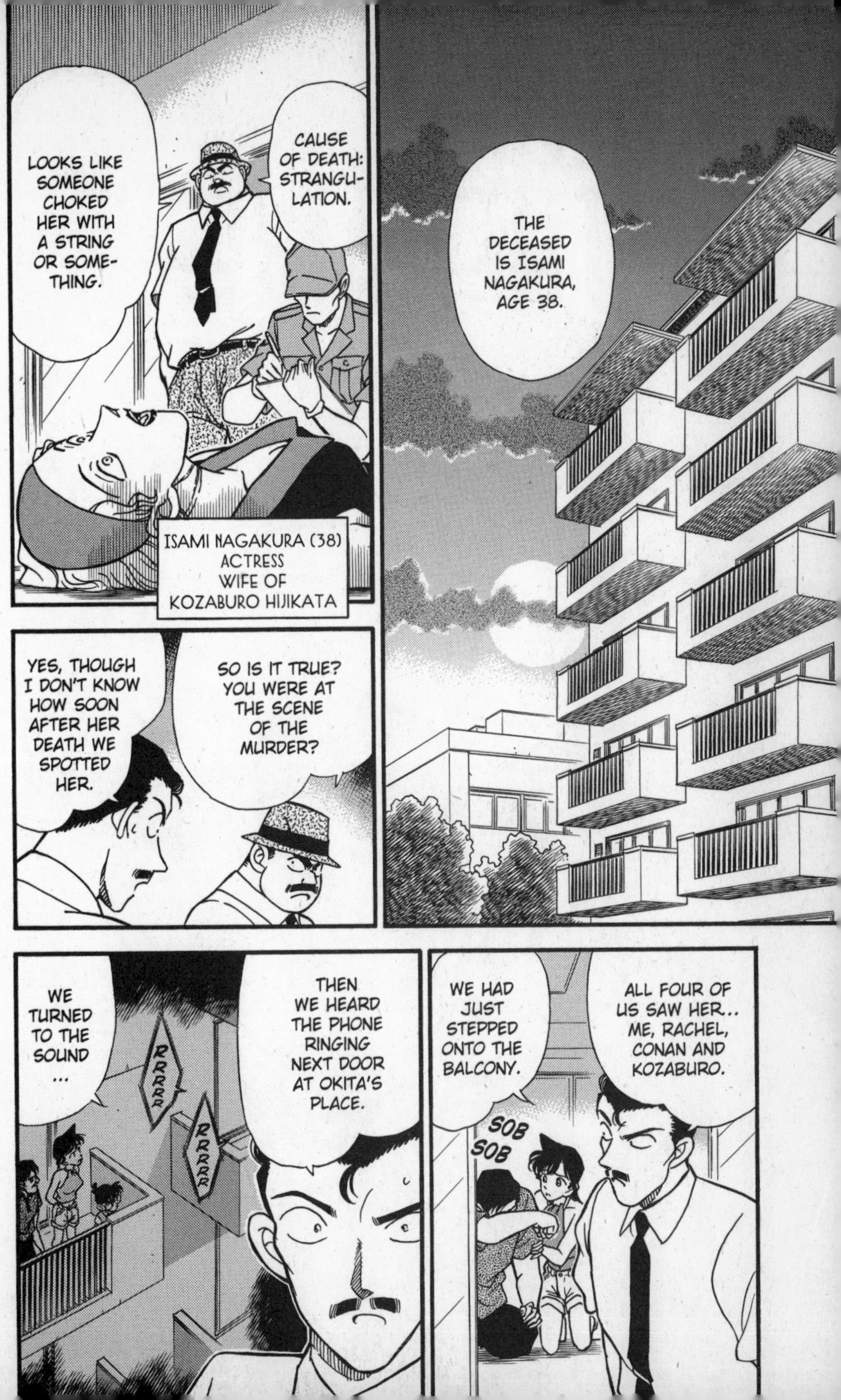
THE DECEASED IS ISAMI NAGAKURA, AGE 38.
CAUSE OF DEATH: STRANGULATION.
LOOKS LIKE SOMEONE CHOKED HER WITH A STRING OR SOMETHING.
ISAMI NAGAKURA (38) ACTRESS WIFE OF KOZABURO HIJIKATA
SO IS IT TRUE? YOU WERE AT THE SCENE OF THE MURDER?
YES, THOUGH I DON'T KNOW HOW SOON AFTER HER DEATH WE SPOTTED HER.
ALL FOUR OF US SAW HER... ME, RACHEL, CONAN AND KOZABURO.
WE HAD JUST STEPPED ONTO THE BALCONY.
SOB SOB
THEN WE HEARD THE PHONE RINGING NEXT DOOR AT OKITA'S PLACE.
WE TURNED TO THE SOUND ...
RRRRR
RRRRR

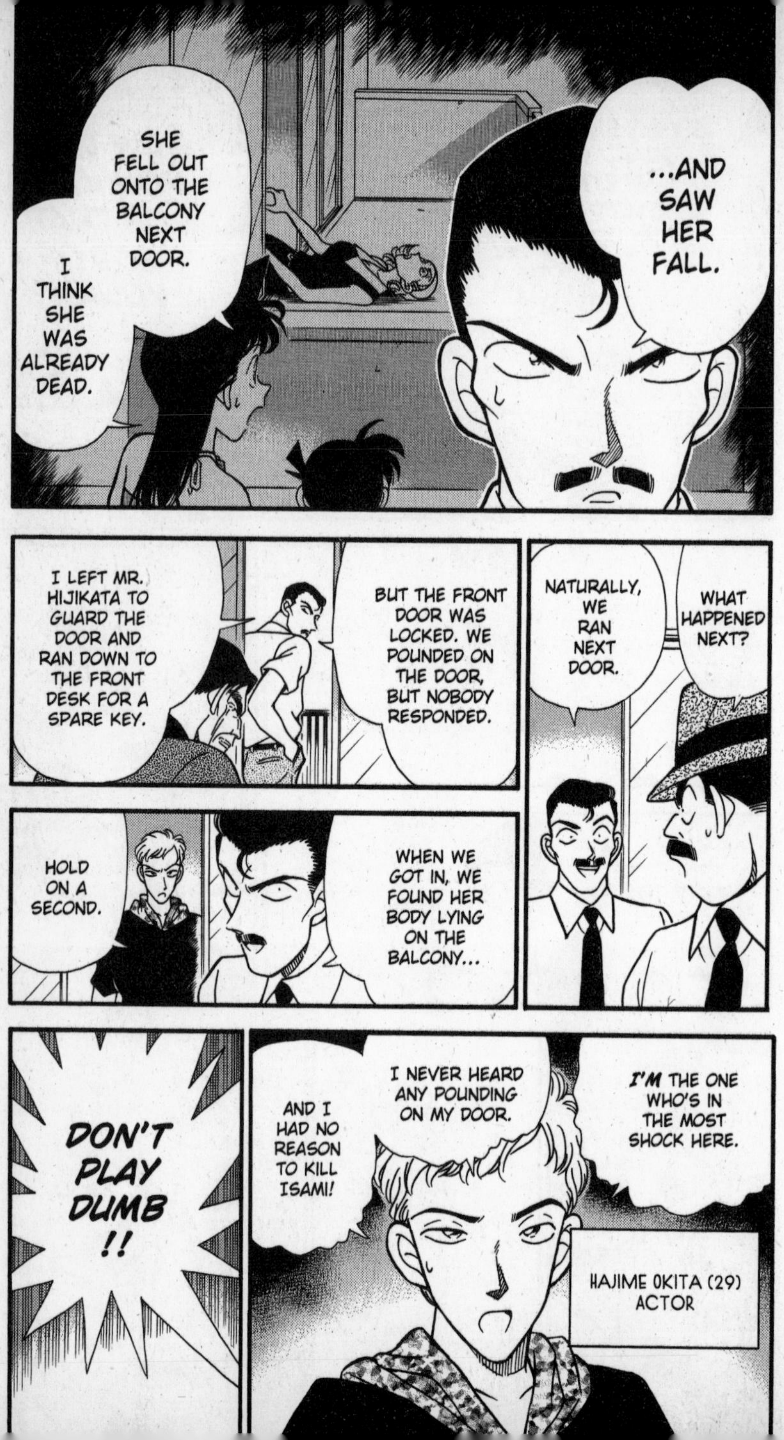

...AND SAW HER FALL.
SHE FELL OUT ONTO THE BALCONY NEXT DOOR.
I THINK SHE WAS ALREADY DEAD.
WHAT HAPPENED NEXT?
NATURALLY, WE RAN NEXT DOOR.
BUT THE FRONT DOOR WAS LOCKED. WE POUNDED ON THE DOOR, BUT NOBODY RESPONDED.
I LEFT MR. HIJIKATA TO GUARD THE DOOR AND RAN DOWN TO THE FRONT DESK FOR A SPARE KEY.
WHEN WE GOT IN, WE FOUND HER BODY LYING ON THE BALCONY...
HOLD ON A SECOND.
I'M THE ONE WHO'S IN THE MOST SHOCK HERE.
I NEVER HEARD ANY POUNDING ON MY DOOR.
AND I HAD NO REASON TO KILL ISAMI!
HAJIME OKITA (29) ACTOR
DON'T PLAY DUMB!!

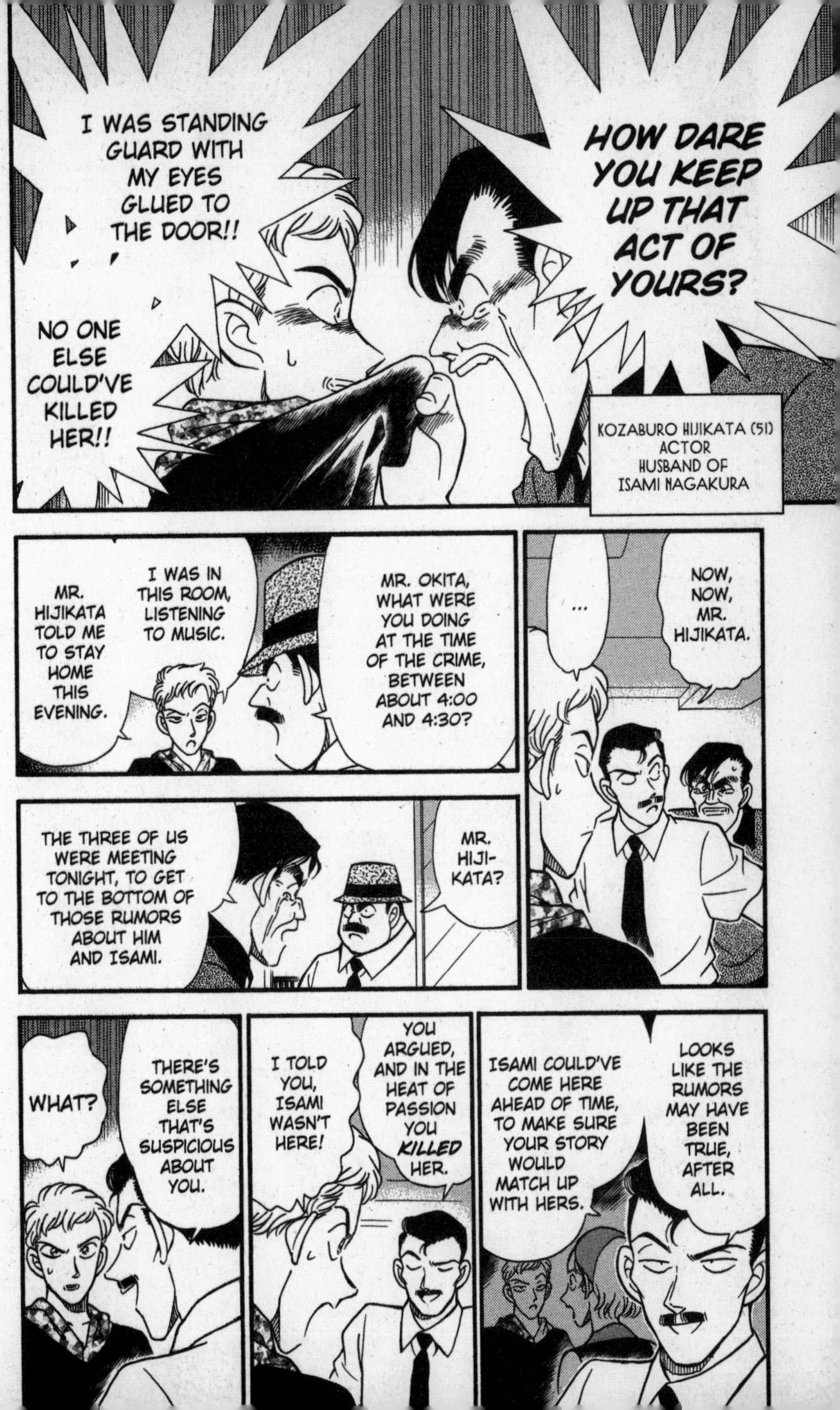
HOW DARE YOU KEEP UP THAT ACT OF YOURS?
KOZABURO HIJIKATA (51) ACTOR HUSBAND OF ISAMI NAGAKURA
I WAS STANDING GUARD WITH MY EYES GLUED TO THE DOOR!!
NO ONE ELSE COULD'VE KILLED HER!!
NOW, NOW, MR. HIJIKATA.
...
MR. OKITA, WHAT WERE YOU DOING AT THE TIME OF THE CRIME, BETWEEN ABOUT 4:00 AND 4:30?
I WAS IN THIS ROOM, LISTENING TO MUSIC.
MR. HIJIKATA TOLD ME TO STAY HOME THIS EVENING.
MR. HIJI-KATA?
THE THREE OF US WERE MEETING TONIGHT, TO GET TO THE BOTTOM OF THOSE RUMORS ABOUT HIM AND ISAMI.
LOOKS LIKE THE RUMORS MAY HAVE BEEN TRUE, AFTER ALL.
ISAMI COULD'VE COME HERE AHEAD OF TIME, TO MAKE SURE YOUR STORY WOULD MATCH UP WITH HERS.
YOU ARGUED, AND IN THE HEAT OF PASSION YOU *KILLED* HER.
I TOLD YOU, ISAMI WASN'T HERE!
THERE'S SOMETHING ELSE THAT'S SUSPICIOUS ABOUT YOU.
WHAT?

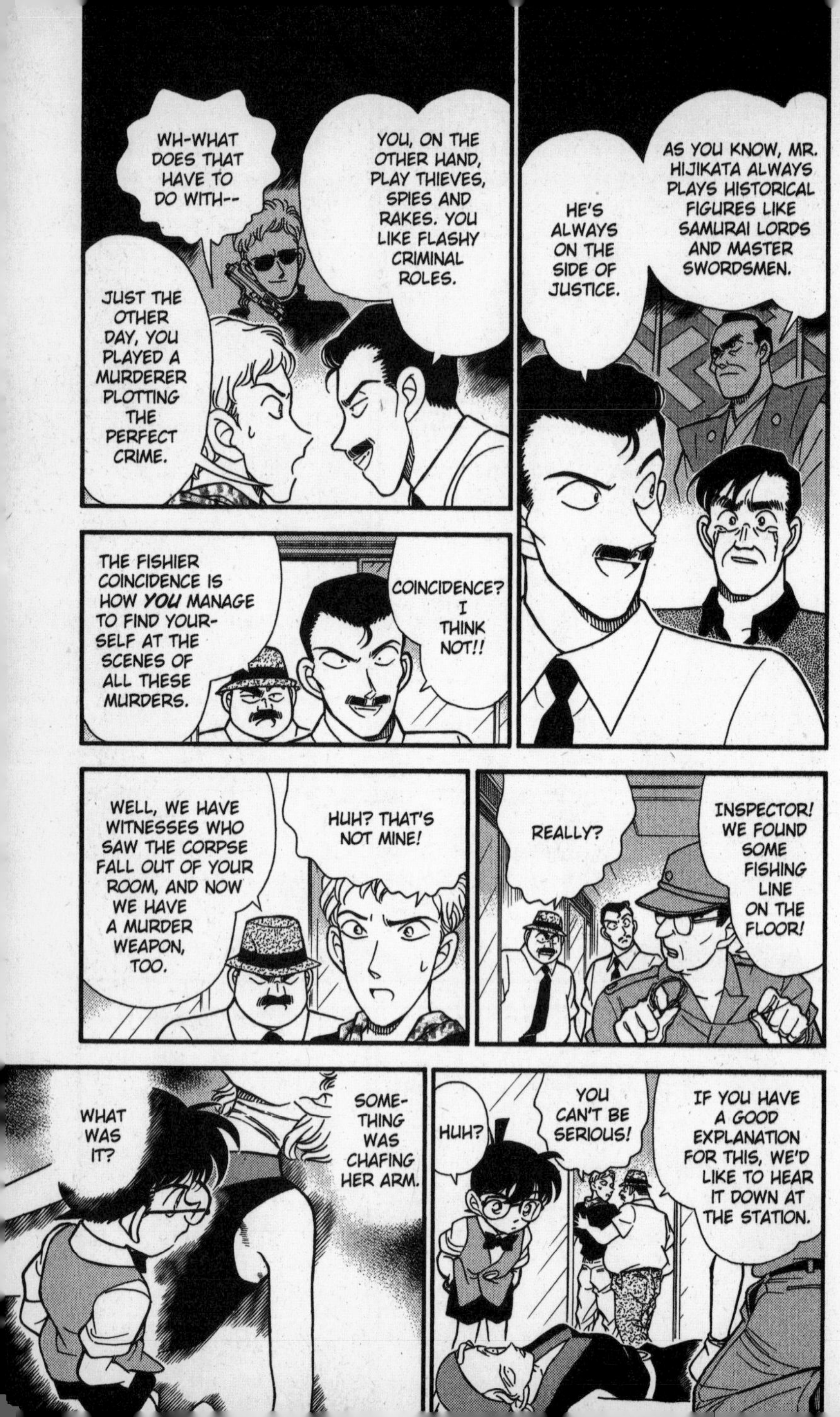
AS YOU KNOW, MR. HIJIKATA ALWAYS PLAYS HISTORICAL FIGURES LIKE SAMURAI LORDS AND MASTER SWORDSMEN.
HE'S ALWAYS ON THE SIDE OF JUSTICE.
YOU, ON THE OTHER HAND, PLAY THIEVES, SPIES AND RAKES. YOU LIKE FLASHY CRIMINAL ROLES.
WH-WHAT DOES THAT HAVE TO DO WITH--
JUST THE OTHER DAY, YOU PLAYED A MURDERER PLOTTING THE PERFECT CRIME.
COINCIDENCE? I THINK NOT!!
THE FISHIER COINCIDENCE IS HOW *YOU* MANAGE TO FIND YOURSELF AT THE SCENES OF ALL THESE MURDERS.
INSPECTOR! WE FOUND SOME FISHING LINE ON THE FLOOR!
REALLY?
HUH? THAT'S NOT MINE!
WELL, WE HAVE WITNESSES WHO SAW THE CORPSE FALL OUT OF YOUR ROOM, AND NOW WE HAVE A MURDER WEAPON, TOO.
IF YOU HAVE A GOOD EXPLANATION FOR THIS, WE'D LIKE TO HEAR IT DOWN AT THE STATION.
YOU CAN'T BE SERIOUS!
HUH?
SOMETHING WAS CHAFING HER ARM.
WHAT WAS IT?

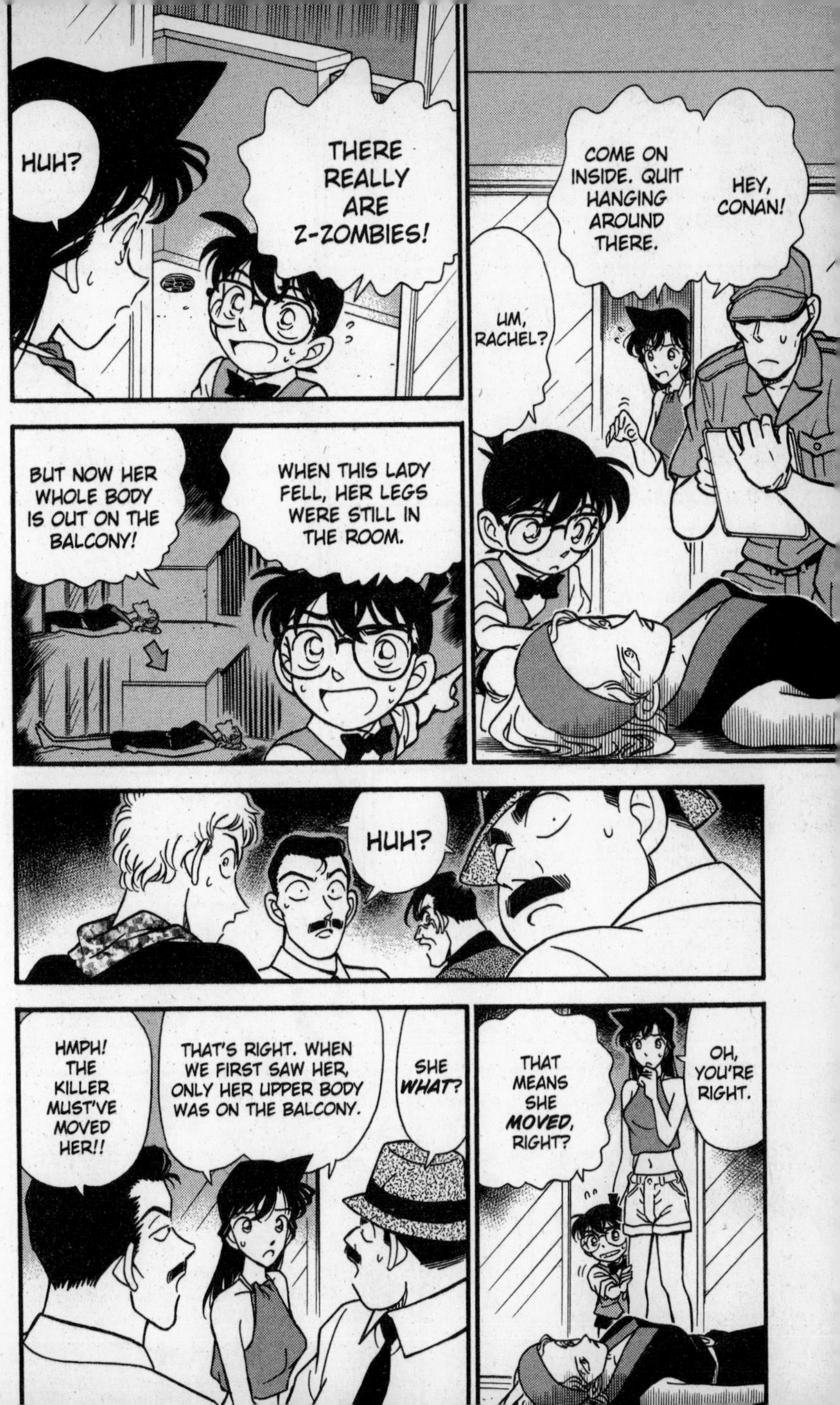
HEY, CONAN!
COME ON INSIDE. QUIT HANGING AROUND THERE.
UM, RACHEL?
THERE REALLY ARE Z-ZOMBIES!
HUH?
WHEN THIS LADY FELL, HER LEGS WERE STILL IN THE ROOM.
BUT NOW HER WHOLE BODY IS OUT ON THE BALCONY!
HUH?
OH, YOU'RE RIGHT.
THAT MEANS SHE *MOVED*, RIGHT?
SHE *WHAT*?
THAT'S RIGHT. WHEN WE FIRST SAW HER, ONLY HER UPPER BODY WAS ON THE BALCONY.
HMPH! THE KILLER MUST'VE MOVED HER!!

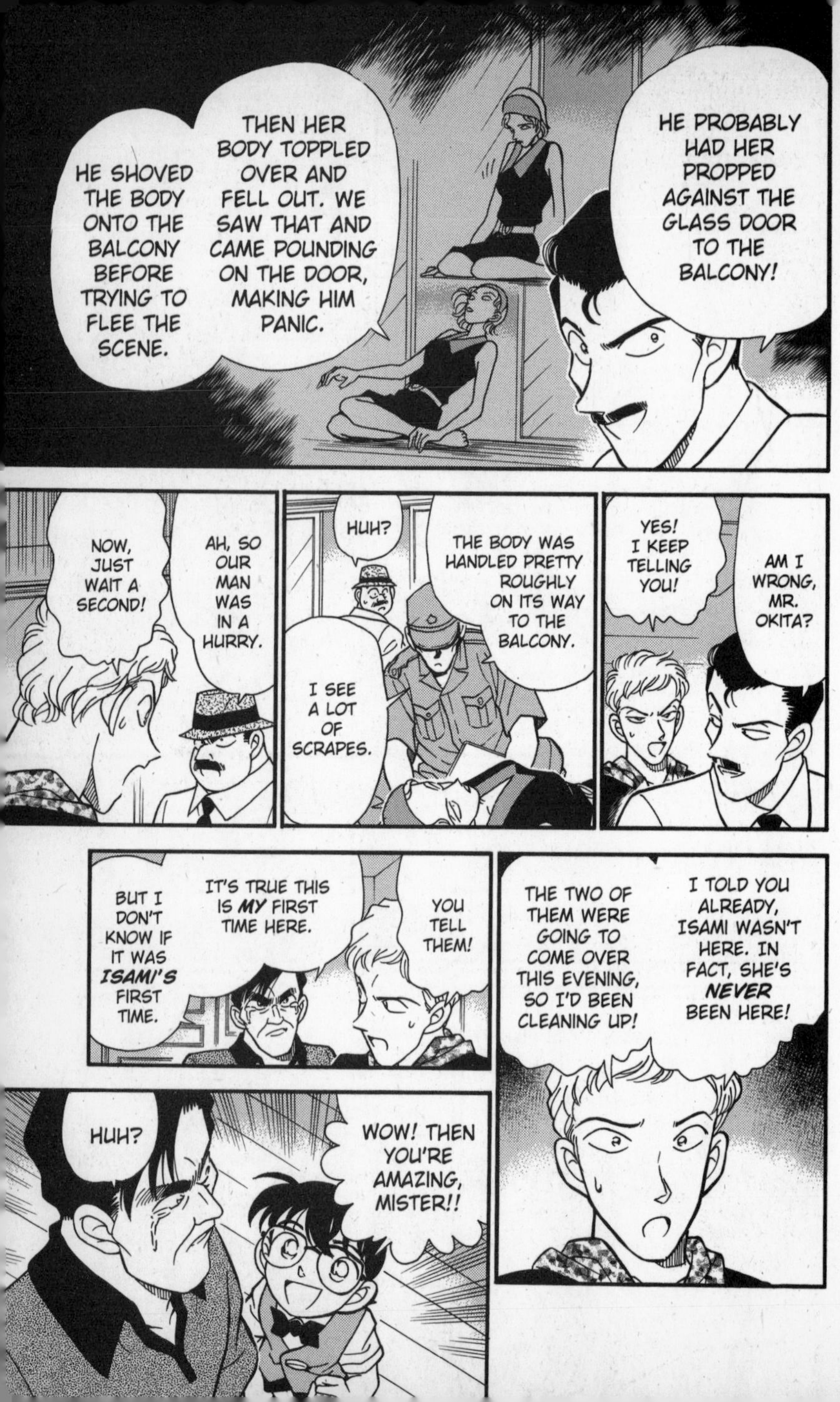
HE PROBABLY HAD HER PROPPED AGAINST THE GLASS DOOR TO THE BALCONY!
THEN HER BODY TOPPLED OVER AND FELL OUT. WE SAW THAT AND CAME POUNDING ON THE DOOR, MAKING HIM PANIC.
HE SHOVED THE BODY ONTO THE BALCONY BEFORE TRYING TO FLEE THE SCENE.
AM I WRONG, MR. OKITA?
YES! I KEEP TELLING YOU!
THE BODY WAS HANDLED PRETTY ROUGHLY ON ITS WAY TO THE BALCONY.
HUH?
I SEE A LOT OF SCRAPES.
AH, SO OUR MAN WAS IN A HURRY.
NOW, JUST WAIT A SECOND!
I TOLD YOU ALREADY, ISAMI WASN'T HERE. IN FACT, SHE'S NEVER BEEN HERE!
THE TWO OF THEM WERE GOING TO COME OVER THIS EVENING, SO I'D BEEN CLEANING UP!
YOU TELL THEM!
IT'S TRUE THIS IS MY FIRST TIME HERE.
BUT I DON'T KNOW IF IT WAS ISAMI'S FIRST TIME.
WOW! THEN YOU'RE AMAZING, MISTER!!
HUH?

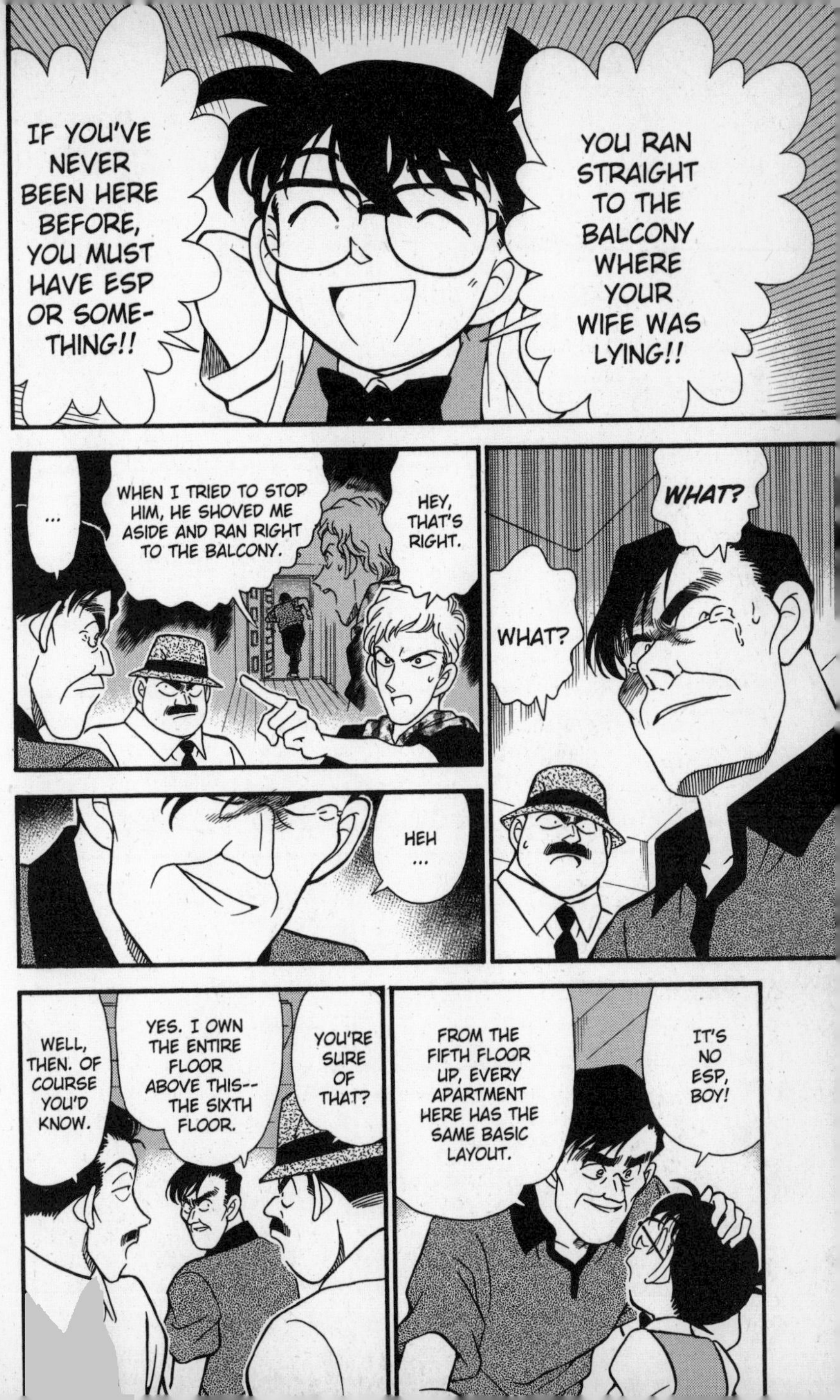
YOU RAN STRAIGHT TO THE BALCONY WHERE YOUR WIFE WAS LYING!!
IF YOU'VE NEVER BEEN HERE BEFORE, YOU MUST HAVE ESP OR SOME-THING!!
WHAT?
WHAT?
HEY, THAT'S RIGHT.
WHEN I TRIED TO STOP HIM, HE SHOVED ME ASIDE AND RAN RIGHT TO THE BALCONY.
...
HEH ...
IT'S NO ESP, BOY!
FROM THE FIFTH FLOOR UP, EVERY APARTMENT HERE HAS THE SAME BASIC LAYOUT.
YOU'RE SURE OF THAT?
YES. I OWN THE ENTIRE FLOOR ABOVE THIS-- THE SIXTH FLOOR.
WELL, THEN. OF COURSE YOU'D KNOW.

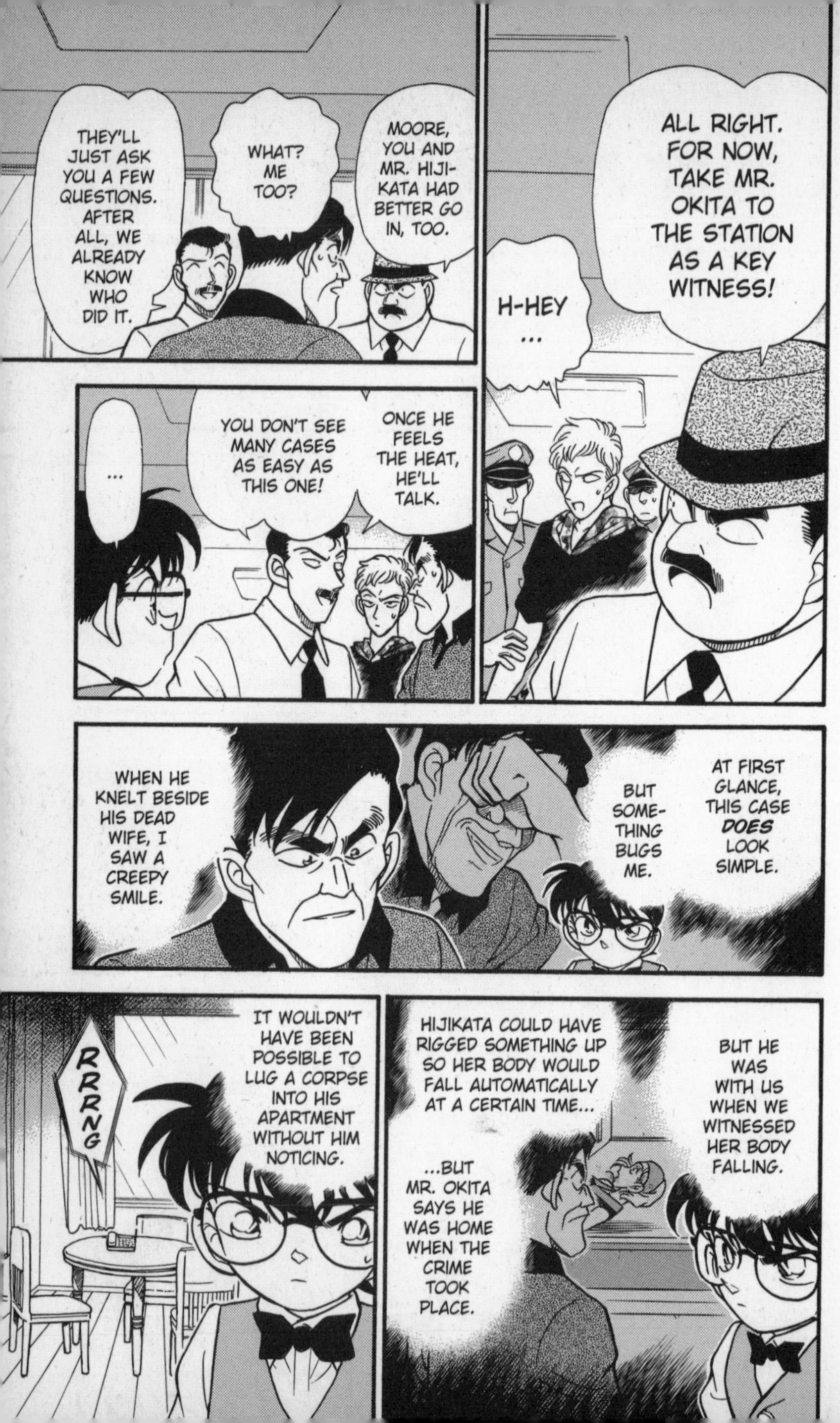
ALL RIGHT. FOR NOW, TAKE MR. OKITA TO THE STATION AS A KEY WITNESS!
H-HEY ...
MOORE, YOU AND MR. HIJIKATA HAD BETTER GO IN, TOO.
WHAT? ME TOO?
THEY'LL JUST ASK YOU A FEW QUESTIONS. AFTER ALL, WE ALREADY KNOW WHO DID IT.
ONCE HE FEELS THE HEAT, HE'LL TALK.
YOU DON'T SEE MANY CASES AS EASY AS THIS ONE!
...
AT FIRST GLANCE, THIS CASE *DOES* LOOK SIMPLE.
BUT SOMETHING BUGS ME.
WHEN HE KNELT BESIDE HIS DEAD WIFE, I SAW A CREEPY SMILE.
BUT HE WAS WITH US WHEN WE WITNESSED HER BODY FALLING.
HIJIKATA COULD HAVE RIGGED SOMETHING UP SO HER BODY WOULD FALL AUTOMATICALLY AT A CERTAIN TIME...
...BUT MR. OKITA SAYS HE WAS HOME WHEN THE CRIME TOOK PLACE.
IT WOULDN'T HAVE BEEN POSSIBLE TO LUG A CORPSE INTO HIS APARTMENT WITHOUT HIM NOTICING.
RRRNG

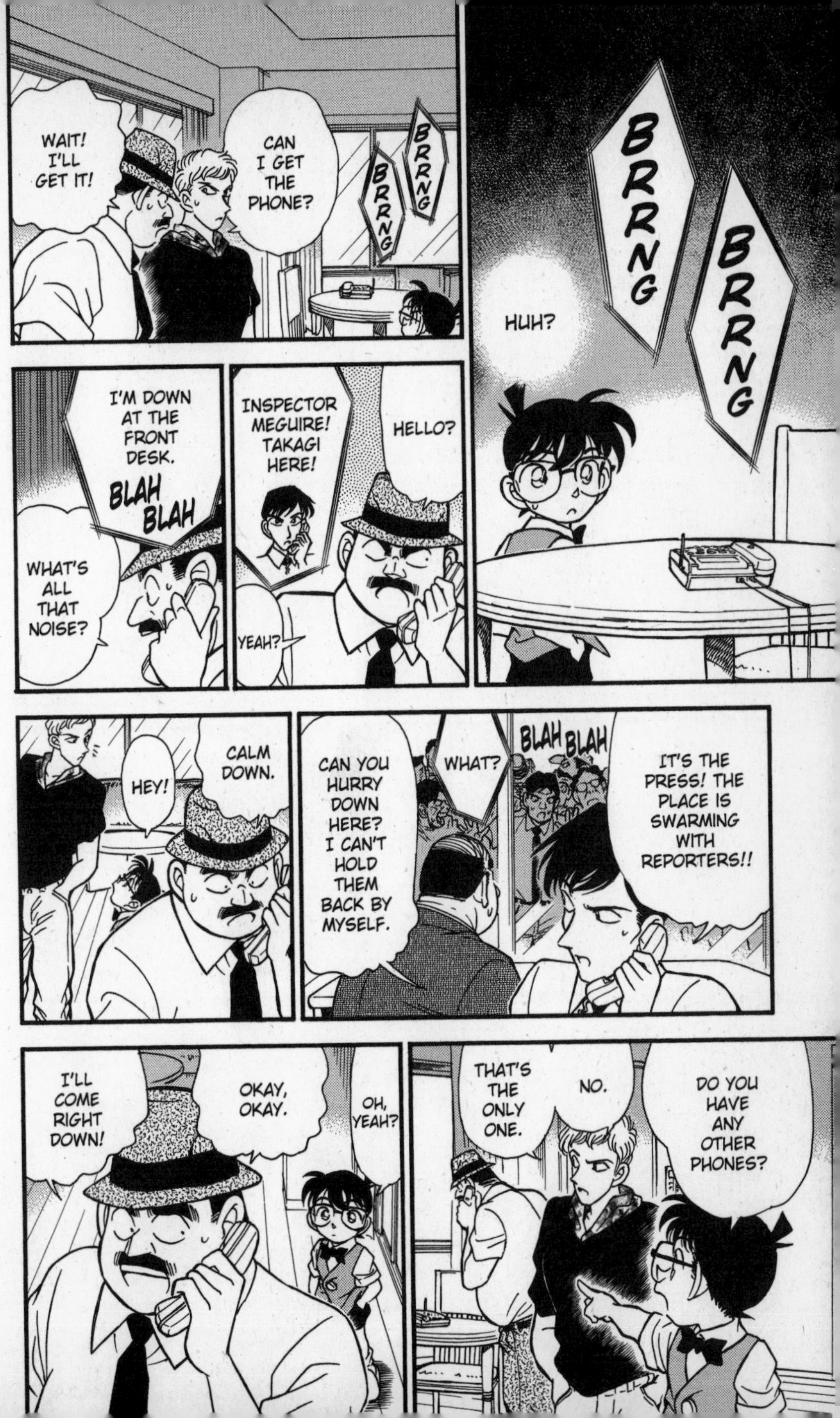

BRRNG
BRRNG
HUH?
BRRNG
BRRNG
CAN I GET THE PHONE?
WAIT! I'LL GET IT!
HELLO?
INSPECTOR MEGUIRE! TAKAGI HERE!
YEAH?
I'M DOWN AT THE FRONT DESK.
BLAH BLAH
WHAT'S ALL THAT NOISE?
IT'S THE PRESS! THE PLACE IS SWARMING WITH REPORTERS!!
BLAH BLAH
WHAT?
CAN YOU HURRY DOWN HERE? I CAN'T HOLD THEM BACK BY MYSELF.
CALM DOWN.
HEY!
DO YOU HAVE ANY OTHER PHONES?
NO.
THAT'S THE ONLY ONE.
OH, YEAH?
OKAY, OKAY.
I'LL COME RIGHT DOWN!

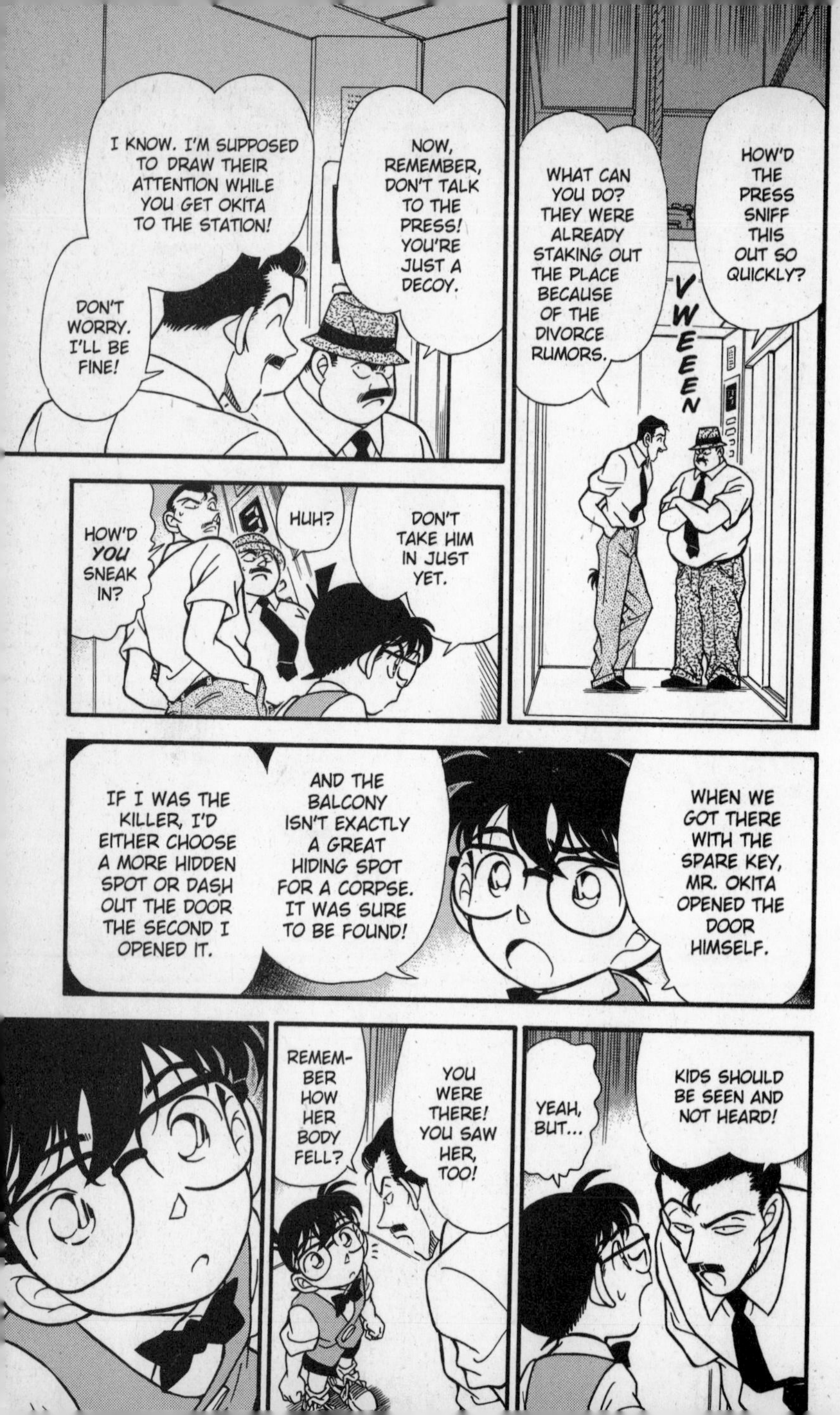
HOW'D THE PRESS SNIFF THIS OUT SO QUICKLY?
VWEEEN
WHAT CAN YOU DO? THEY WERE ALREADY STAKING OUT THE PLACE BECAUSE OF THE DIVORCE RUMORS.
NOW, REMEMBER, DON'T TALK TO THE PRESS! YOU'RE JUST A DECOY.
I KNOW. I'M SUPPOSED TO DRAW THEIR ATTENTION WHILE YOU GET OKITA TO THE STATION!
DON'T WORRY. I'LL BE FINE!
DON'T TAKE HIM IN JUST YET.
HUH?
HOW'D *YOU* SNEAK IN?
WHEN WE GOT THERE WITH THE SPARE KEY, MR. OKITA OPENED THE DOOR HIMSELF.
AND THE BALCONY ISN'T EXACTLY A GREAT HIDING SPOT FOR A CORPSE. IT WAS SURE TO BE FOUND!
IF I WAS THE KILLER, I'D EITHER CHOOSE A MORE HIDDEN SPOT OR DASH OUT THE DOOR THE SECOND I OPENED IT.
KIDS SHOULD BE SEEN AND NOT HEARD!
YEAH, BUT...
YOU WERE THERE! YOU SAW HER, TOO!
REMEM-BER HOW HER BODY FELL?

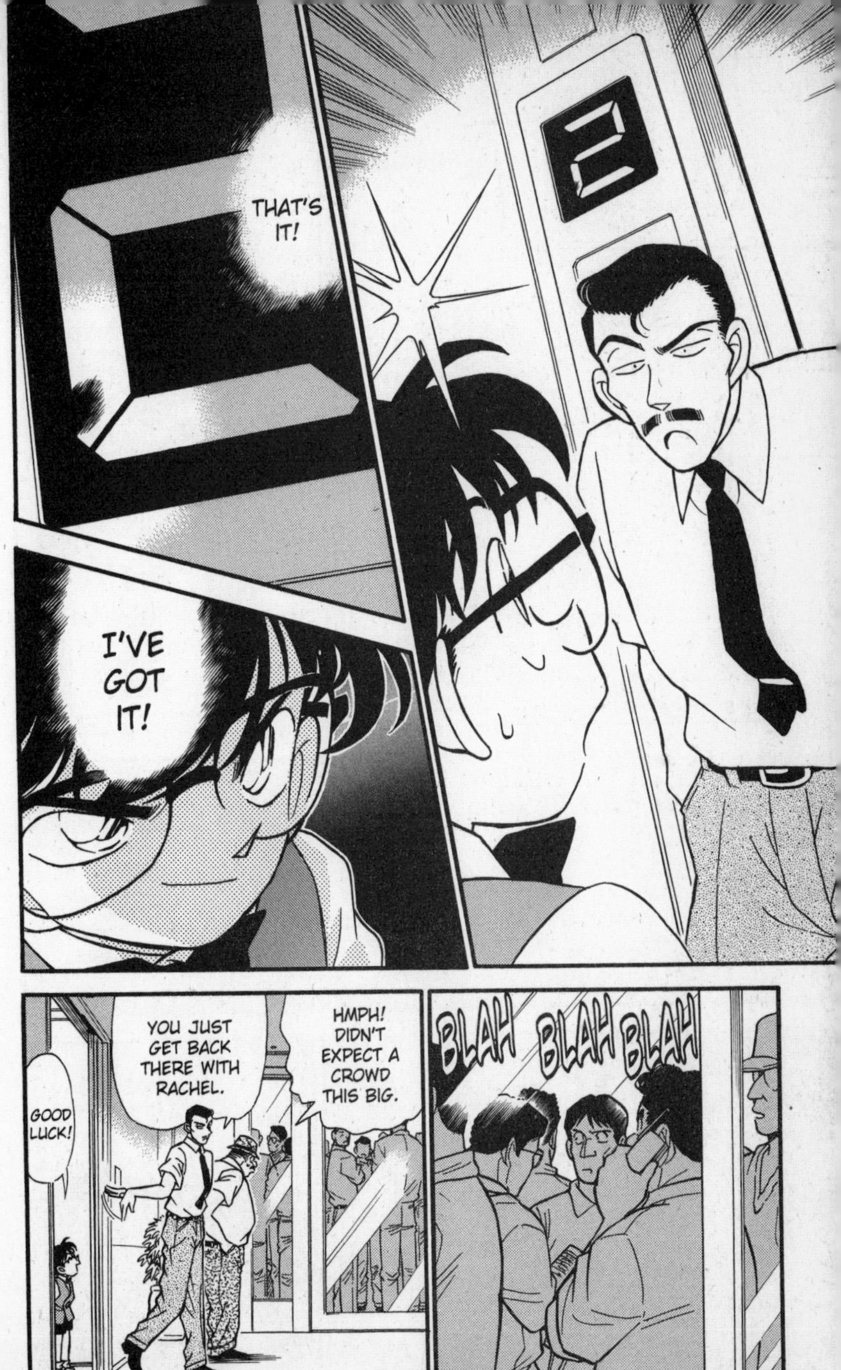
THAT'S IT!
I'VE GOT IT!
BLAH BLAH BLAH
HMPH! DIDN'T EXPECT A CROWD THIS BIG.
YOU JUST GET BACK THERE WITH RACHEL.
GOOD LUCK!

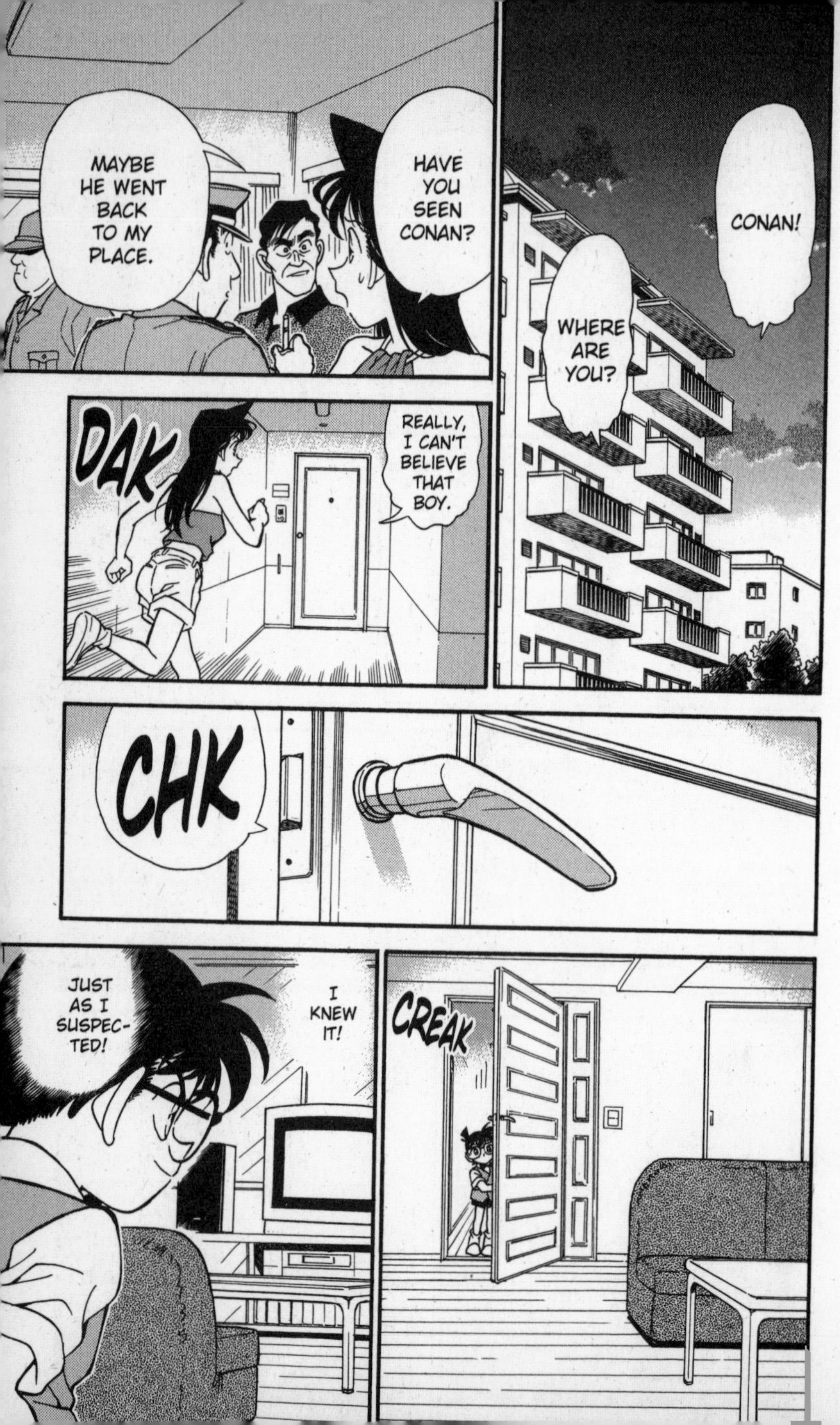

CONAN!
WHERE ARE YOU?
HAVE YOU SEEN CONAN?
MAYBE HE WENT BACK TO MY PLACE.
REALLY, I CAN'T BELIEVE THAT BOY.
DAK
CHK
CREAK
I KNEW IT!
JUST AS I SUSPEC-TED!

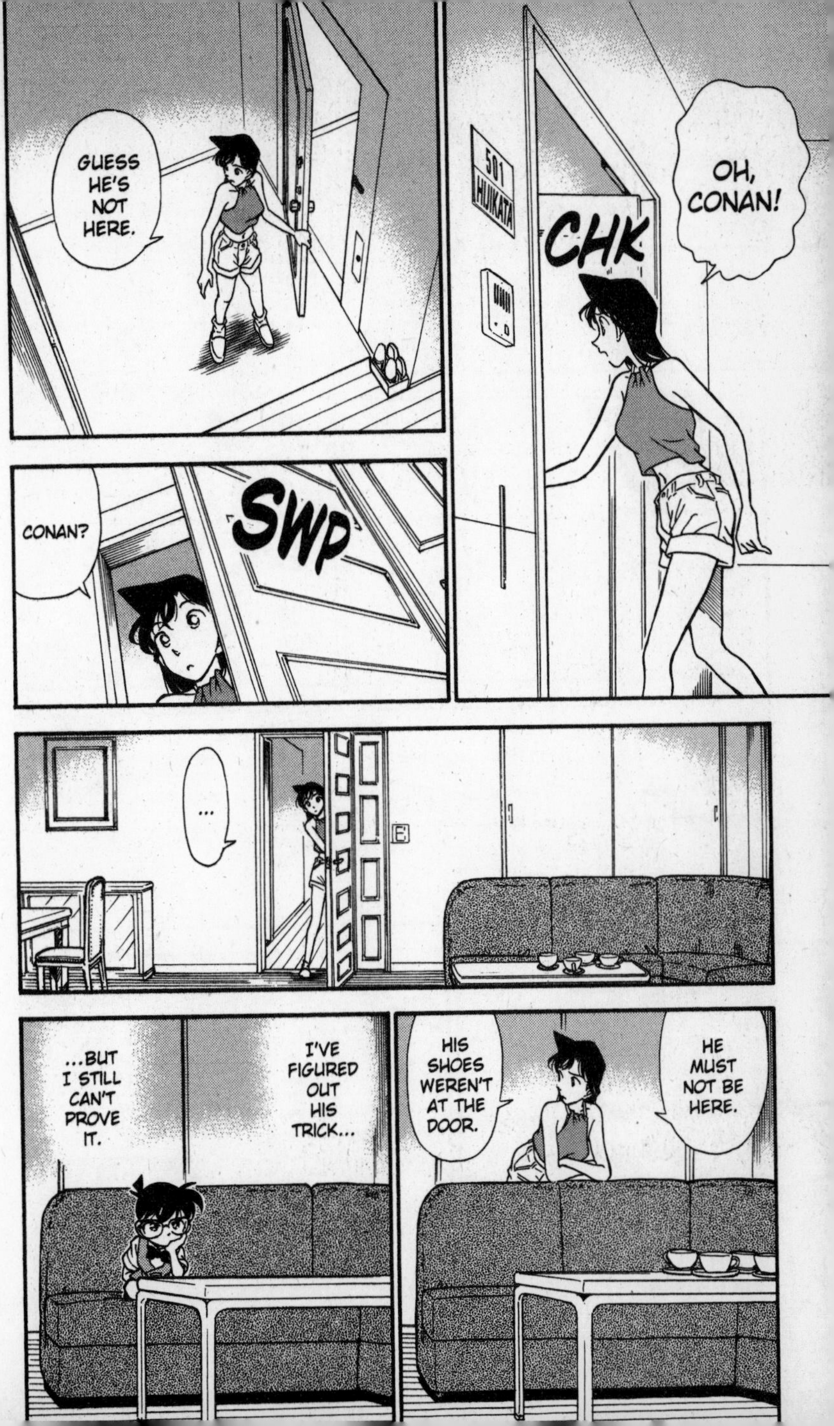
501
HIJIKATA
CHK
OH, CONAN!
GUESS HE'S NOT HERE.
SWP
CONAN?
...
HE MUST NOT BE HERE.
HIS SHOES WEREN'T AT THE DOOR.
I'VE FIGURED OUT HIS TRICK...
...BUT I STILL CAN'T PROVE IT.

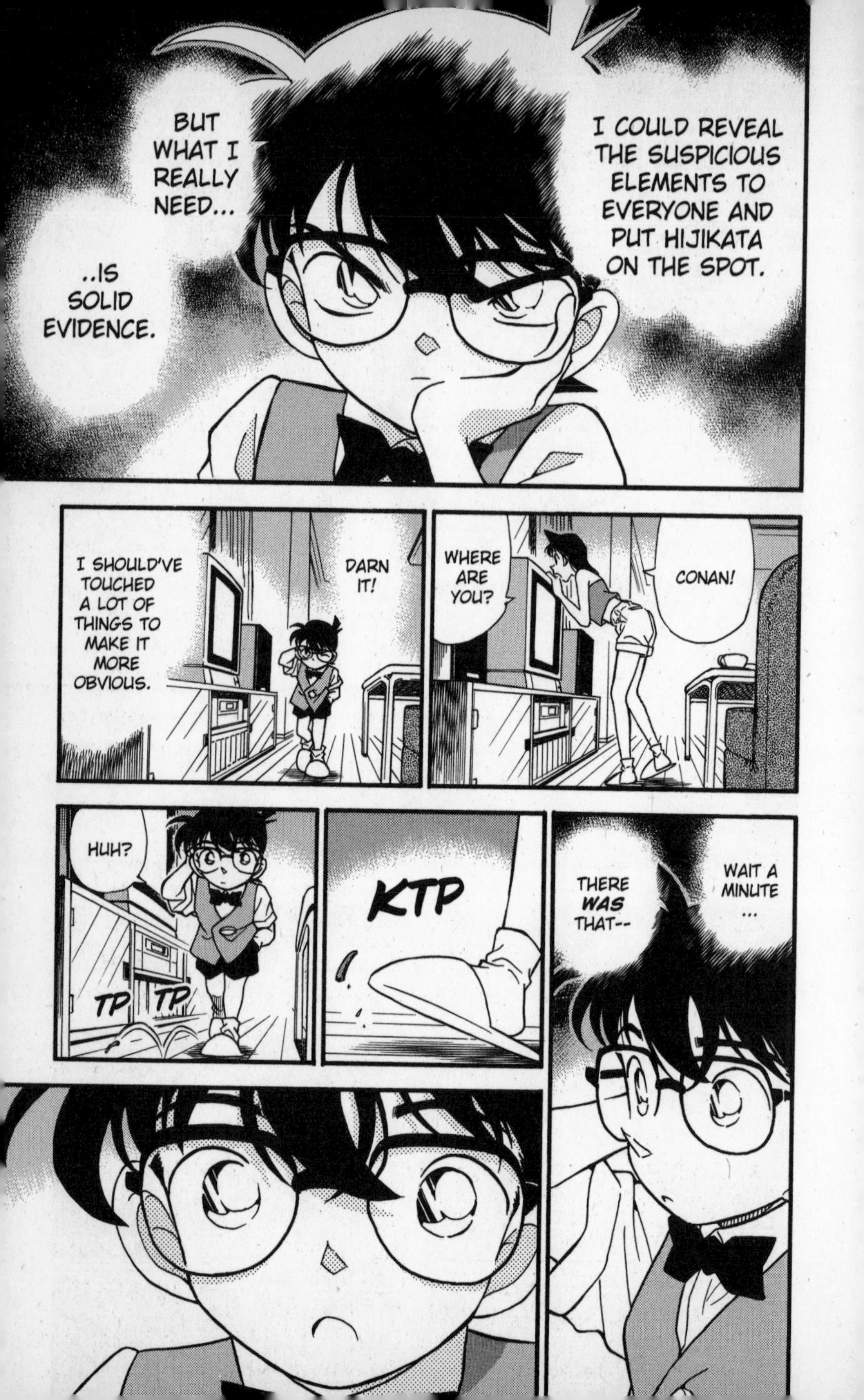
I COULD REVEAL THE SUSPICIOUS ELEMENTS TO EVERYONE AND PUT HIJIKATA ON THE SPOT.
BUT WHAT I REALLY NEED...
..IS SOLID EVIDENCE.
CONAN!
WHERE ARE YOU?
DARN IT!
I SHOULD'VE TOUCHED A LOT OF THINGS TO MAKE IT MORE OBVIOUS.
WAIT A MINUTE ...
THERE WAS THAT--
KTP
HUH?
TP TP

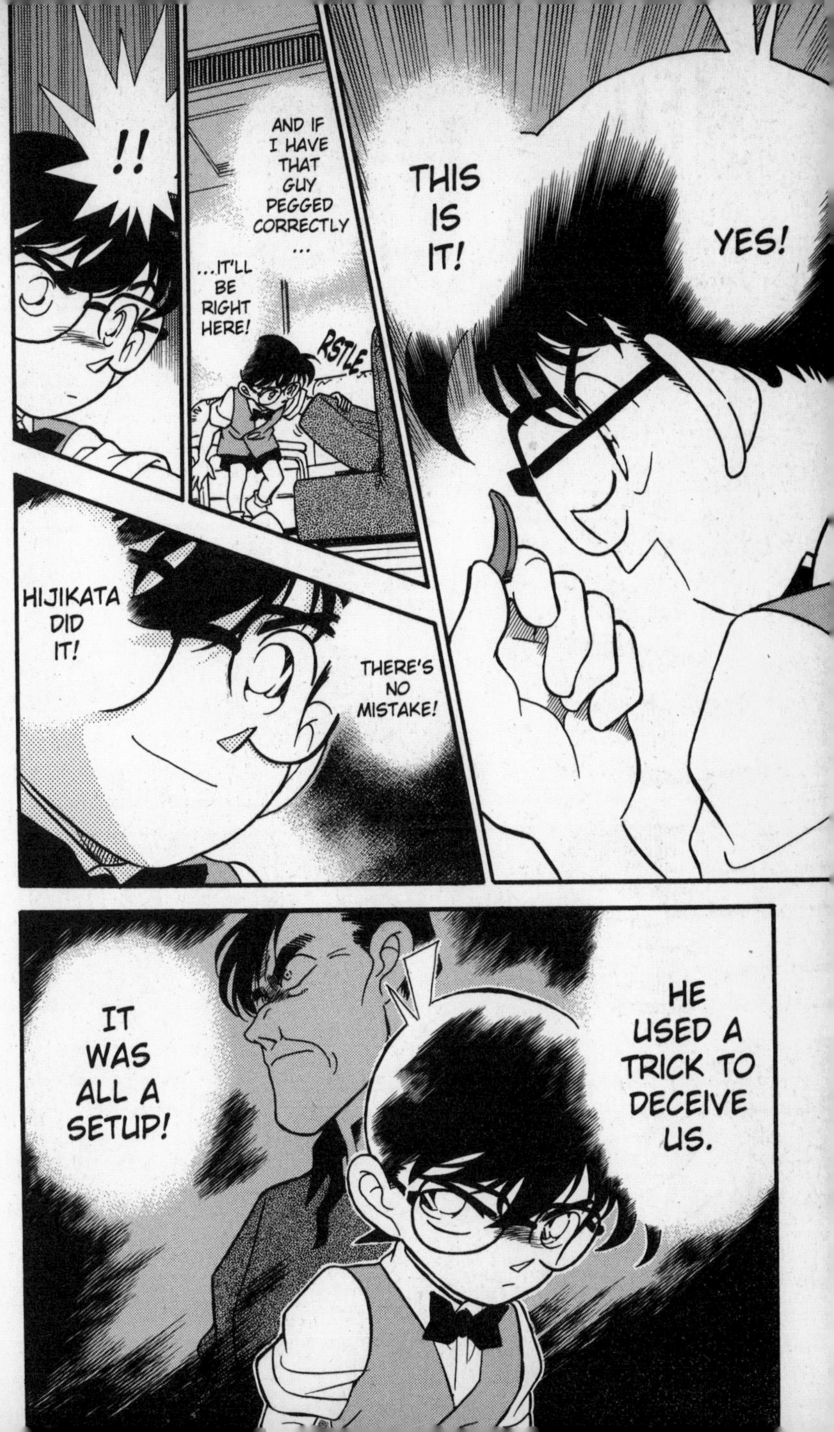
YES!
THIS IS IT!
AND IF I HAVE THAT GUY PEGGED CORRECTLY ...
...IT'LL BE RIGHT HERE!
RSTLE
!!
THERE'S NO MISTAKE!
HIJIKATA DID IT!
HE USED A TRICK TO DECEIVE US.
IT WAS ALL A SETUP!

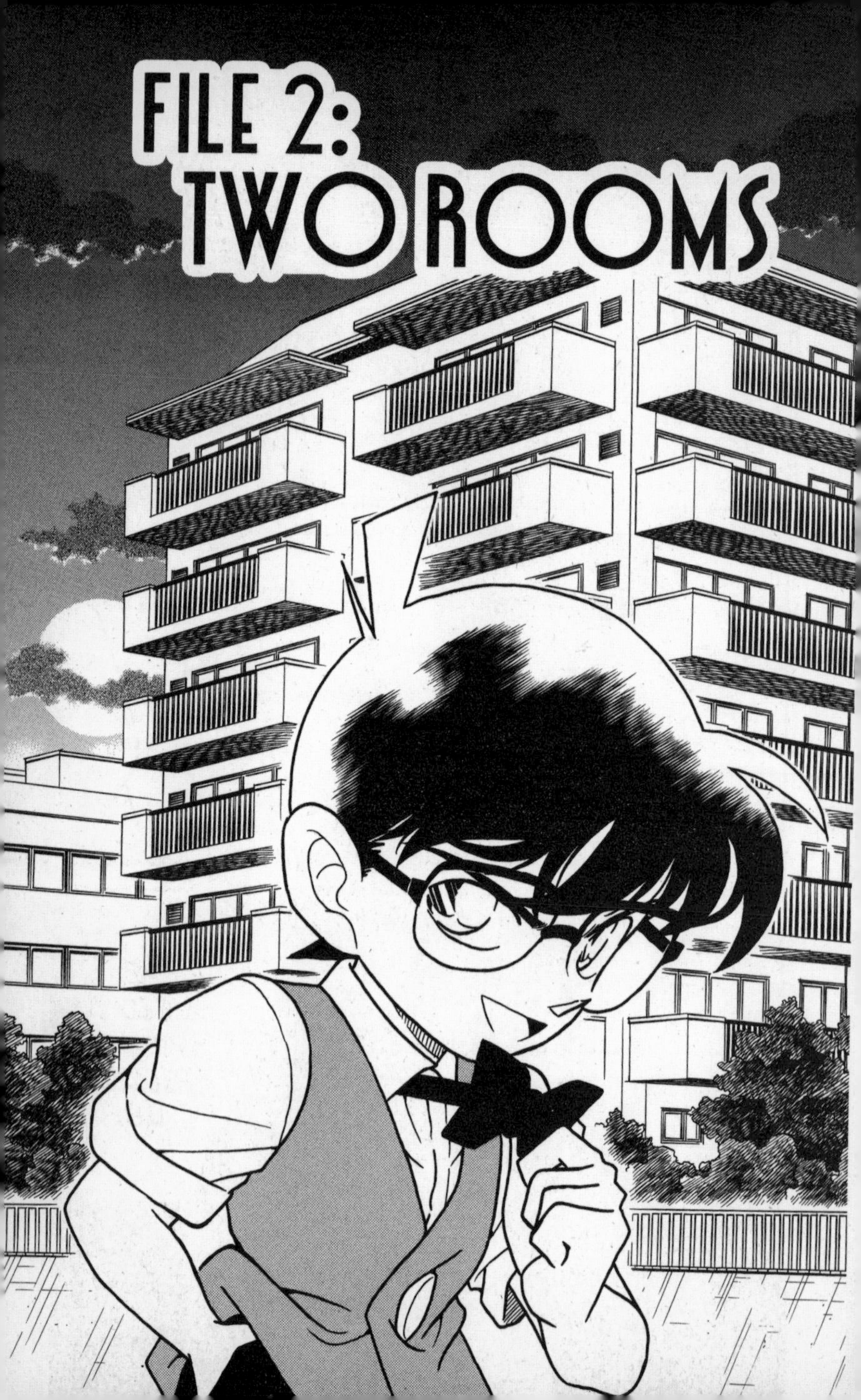
FILE 2:
TWO ROOMS

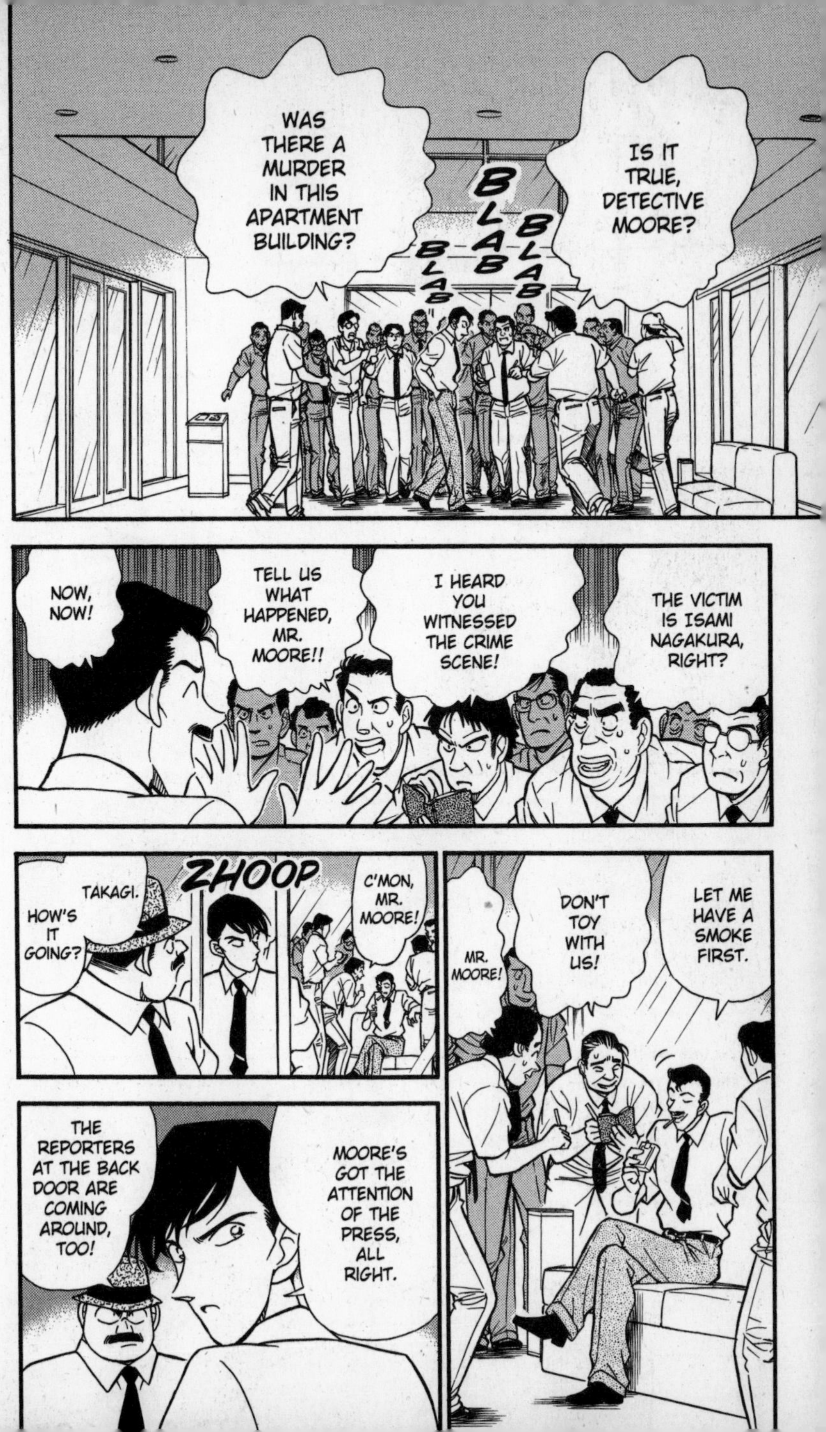

IS IT TRUE, DETECTIVE MOORE?
BLAB BLAB BLAB
WAS THERE A MURDER IN THIS APARTMENT BUILDING?
THE VICTIM IS ISAMI NAGAKURA, RIGHT?
I HEARD YOU WITNESSED THE CRIME SCENE!
TELL US WHAT HAPPENED, MR. MOORE!!
NOW, NOW!
LET ME HAVE A SMOKE FIRST.
DON'T TOY WITH US!
MR. MOORE!
C'MON, MR. MOORE!
ZHOOP
TAKAGI.
HOW'S IT GOING?
MOORE'S GOT THE ATTENTION OF THE PRESS, ALL RIGHT.
THE REPORTERS AT THE BACK DOOR ARE COMING AROUND, TOO!

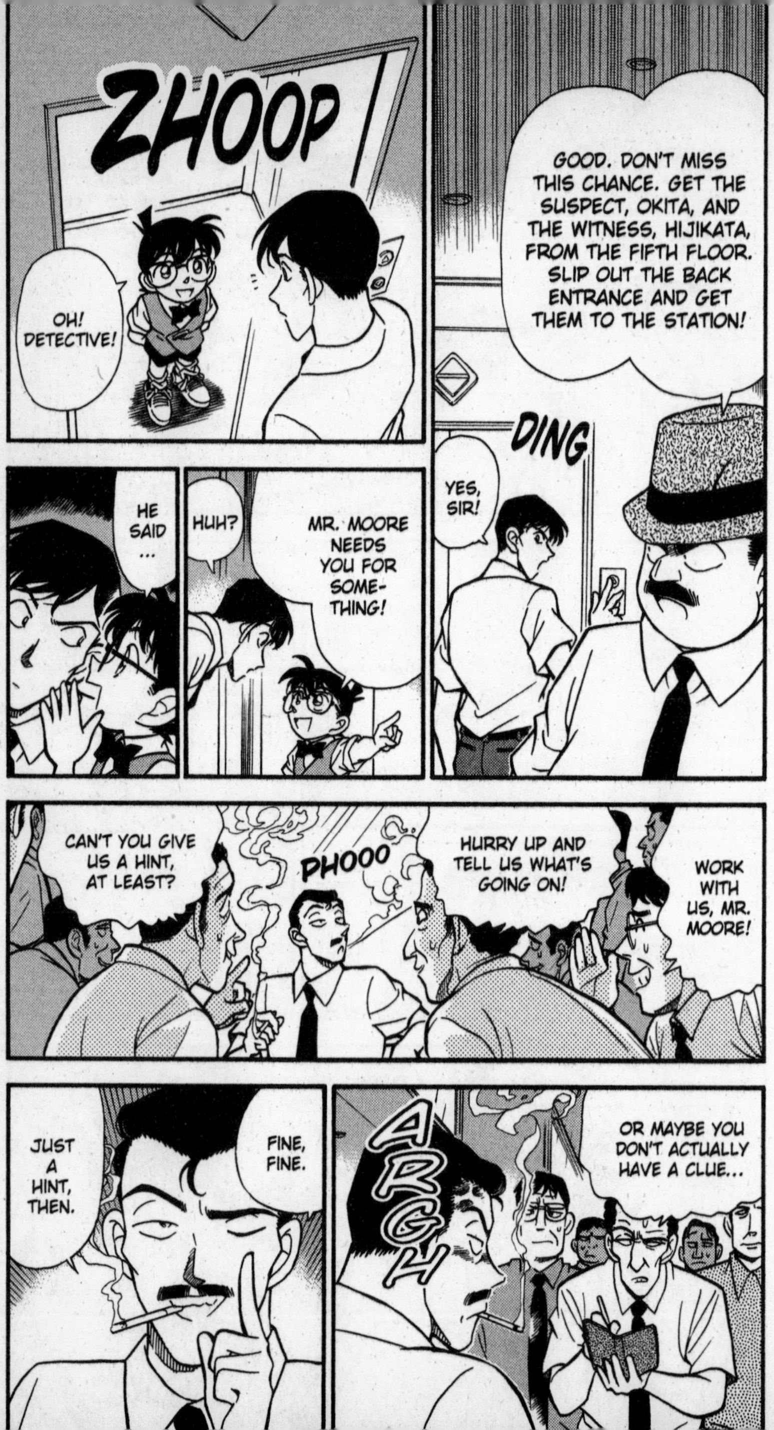
GOOD. DON'T MISS THIS CHANCE. GET THE SUSPECT, OKITA, AND THE WITNESS, HIJIKATA, FROM THE FIFTH FLOOR. SLIP OUT THE BACK ENTRANCE AND GET THEM TO THE STATION!
DING
YES, SIR!
ZHOOP
OH! DETECTIVE!
MR. MOORE NEEDS YOU FOR SOME-THING!
HUH?
HE SAID ...
WORK WITH US, MR. MOORE!
HURRY UP AND TELL US WHAT'S GOING ON!
PHOOO
CAN'T YOU GIVE US A HINT, AT LEAST?
OR MAYBE YOU DON'T ACTUALLY HAVE A CLUE...
ARGH
FINE, FINE.
JUST A HINT, THEN.

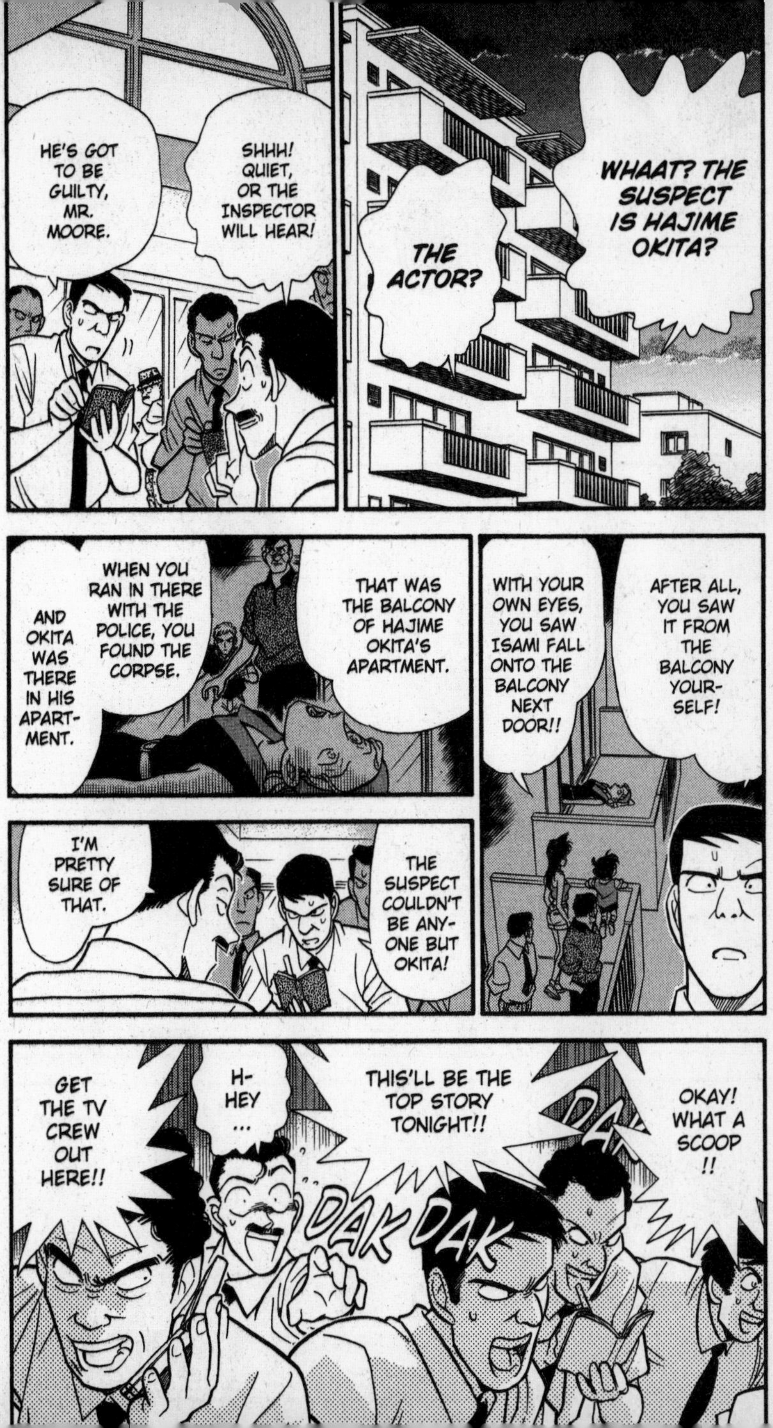
WHAAT? THE SUSPECT IS HAJIME OKITA?
THE ACTOR?
SHHH! QUIET, OR THE INSPECTOR WILL HEAR!
HE'S GOT TO BE GUILTY, MR. MOORE.
AFTER ALL, YOU SAW IT FROM THE BALCONY YOUR-SELF!
WITH YOUR OWN EYES, YOU SAW ISAMI FALL ONTO THE BALCONY NEXT DOOR!!
THAT WAS THE BALCONY OF HAJIME OKITA'S APARTMENT.
WHEN YOU RAN IN THERE WITH THE POLICE, YOU FOUND THE CORPSE.
AND OKITA WAS THERE IN HIS APART-MENT.
THE SUSPECT COULDN'T BE ANY-ONE BUT OKITA!
I'M PRETTY SURE OF THAT.
OKAY! WHAT A SCOOP!!
DAK
THIS'LL BE THE TOP STORY TONIGHT!!
H-HEY ...
GET THE TV CREW OUT HERE!!
DAK DAK

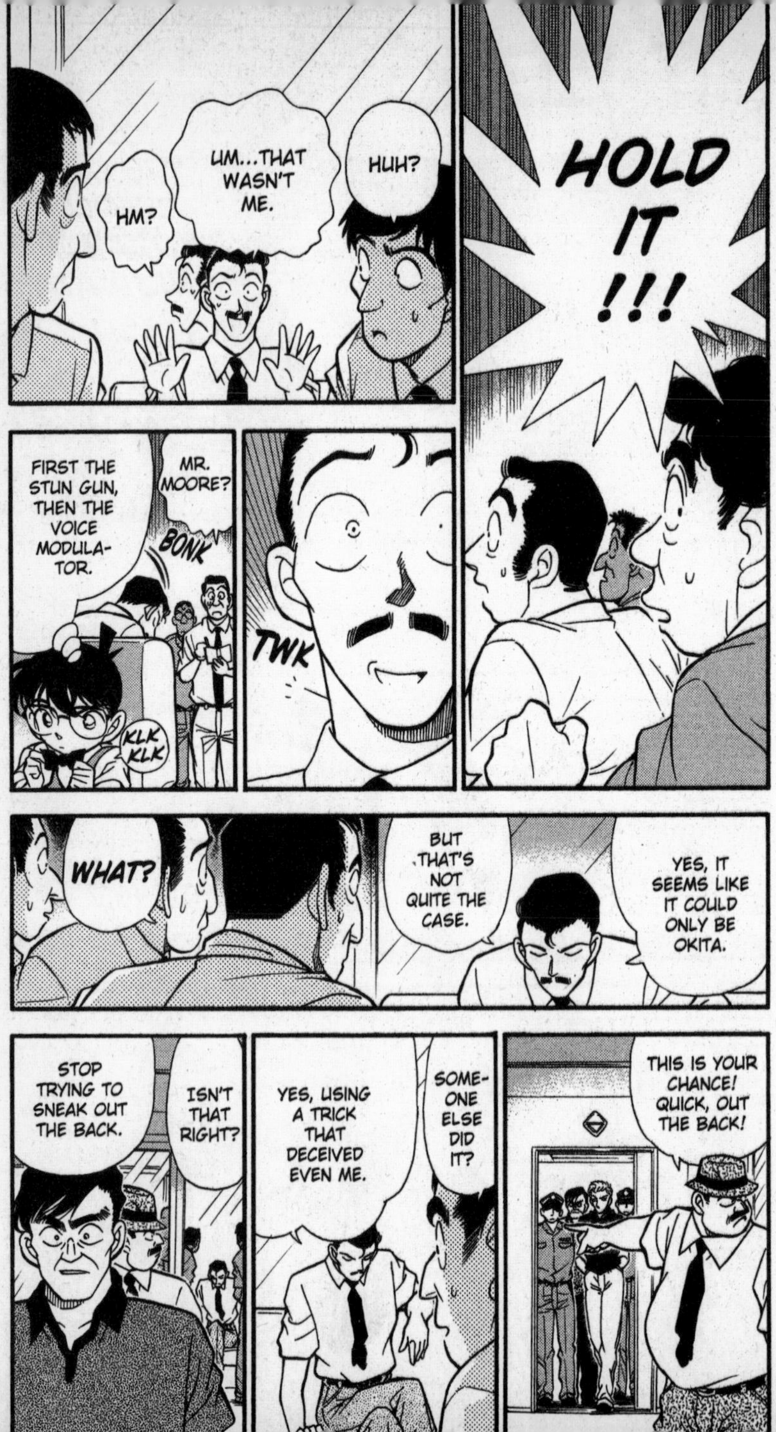
HOLD IT !!!
HUH?
UM...THAT WASN'T ME.
HM?
TWK
MR. MOORE?
BONK
FIRST THE STUN GUN, THEN THE VOICE MODULATOR.
KLK KLK
YES, IT SEEMS LIKE IT COULD ONLY BE OKITA.
BUT THAT'S NOT QUITE THE CASE.
WHAT?
THIS IS YOUR CHANCE! QUICK, OUT THE BACK!
SOME-ONE ELSE DID IT?
YES, USING A TRICK THAT DECEIVED EVEN ME.
ISN'T THAT RIGHT?
STOP TRYING TO SNEAK OUT THE BACK.

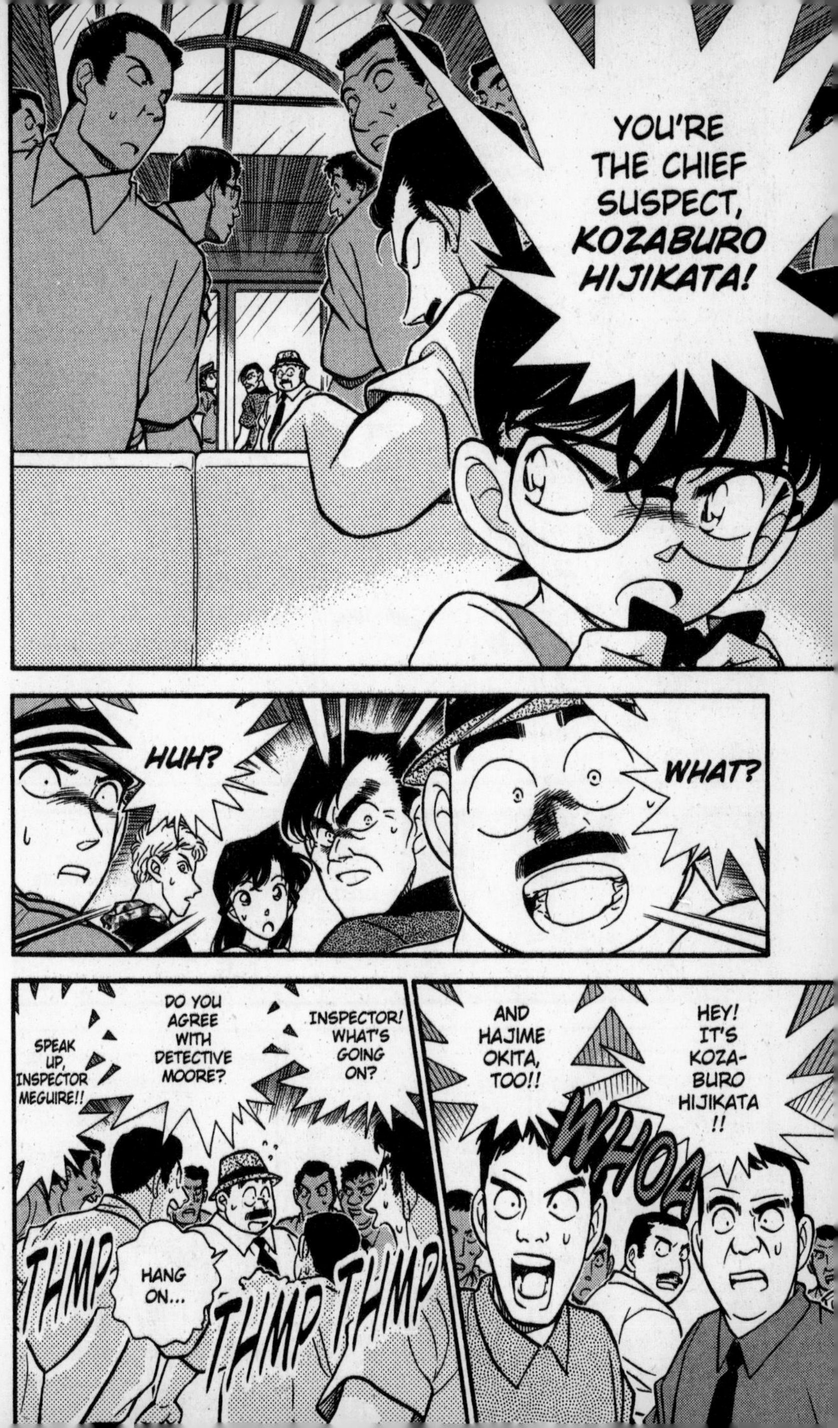
YOU'RE THE CHIEF SUSPECT, KOZABURO HIJIKATA!
WHAT?
HUH?
HEY! IT'S KOZA-BURO HIJIKATA!!
WHOA
AND HAJIME OKITA, TOO!!
INSPECTOR! WHAT'S GOING ON?
DO YOU AGREE WITH DETECTIVE MOORE?
SPEAK UP, INSPECTOR MEGUIRE!!
THMP THMP THMP
HANG ON...

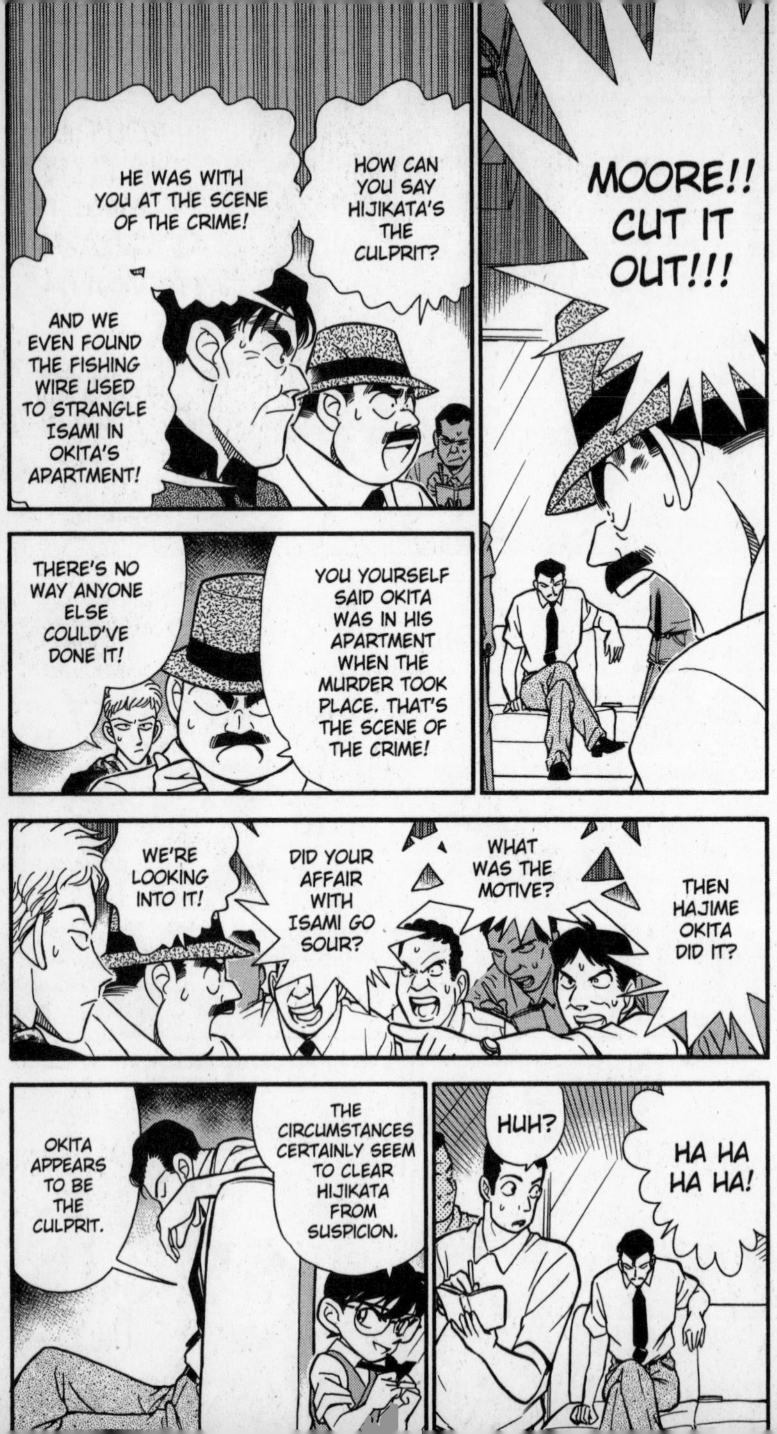
MOORE!! CUT IT OUT!!!
HOW CAN YOU SAY HIJIKATA'S THE CULPRIT?
HE WAS WITH YOU AT THE SCENE OF THE CRIME!
AND WE EVEN FOUND THE FISHING WIRE USED TO STRANGLE ISAMI IN OKITA'S APARTMENT!
YOU YOURSELF SAID OKITA WAS IN HIS APARTMENT WHEN THE MURDER TOOK PLACE. THAT'S THE SCENE OF THE CRIME!
THERE'S NO WAY ANYONE ELSE COULD'VE DONE IT!
THEN HAJIME OKITA DID IT?
WHAT WAS THE MOTIVE?
DID YOUR AFFAIR WITH ISAMI GO SOUR?
WE'RE LOOKING INTO IT!
HA HA HA HA!
HUH?
THE CIRCUMSTANCES CERTAINLY SEEM TO CLEAR HIJIKATA FROM SUSPICION.
OKITA APPEARS TO BE THE CULPRIT.

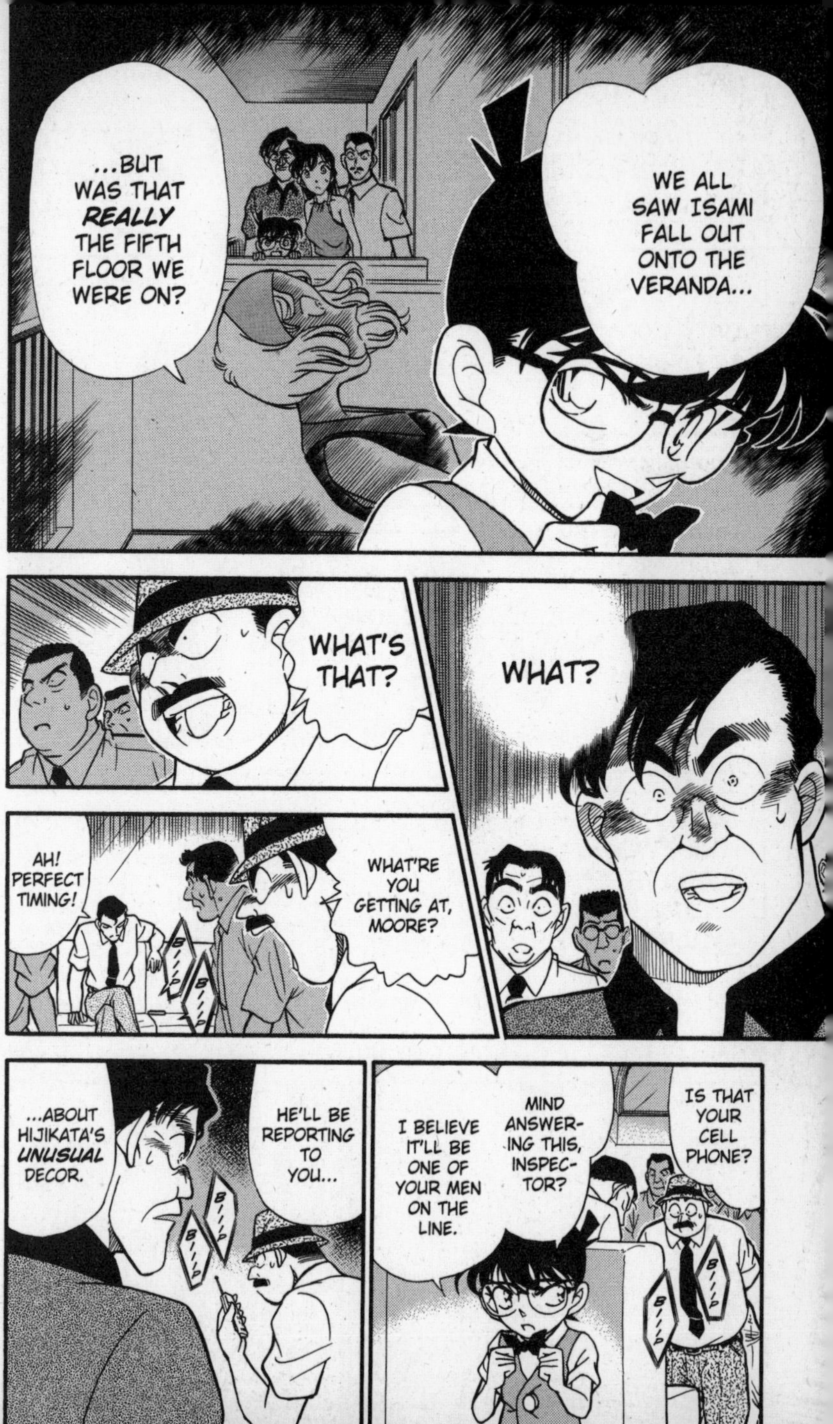
WE ALL SAW ISAMI FALL OUT ONTO THE VERANDA...
...BUT WAS THAT *REALLY* THE FIFTH FLOOR WE WERE ON?
WHAT?
WHAT'S THAT?
WHAT'RE YOU GETTING AT, MOORE?
AH! PERFECT TIMING!
BIIP
BIIP
IS THAT YOUR CELL PHONE?
BIIP
BIIP
MIND ANSWERING THIS, INSPECTOR?
I BELIEVE IT'LL BE ONE OF YOUR MEN ON THE LINE.
HE'LL BE REPORTING TO YOU...
...ABOUT HIJIKATA'S *UNUSUAL* DECOR.
BIIP
BIIP

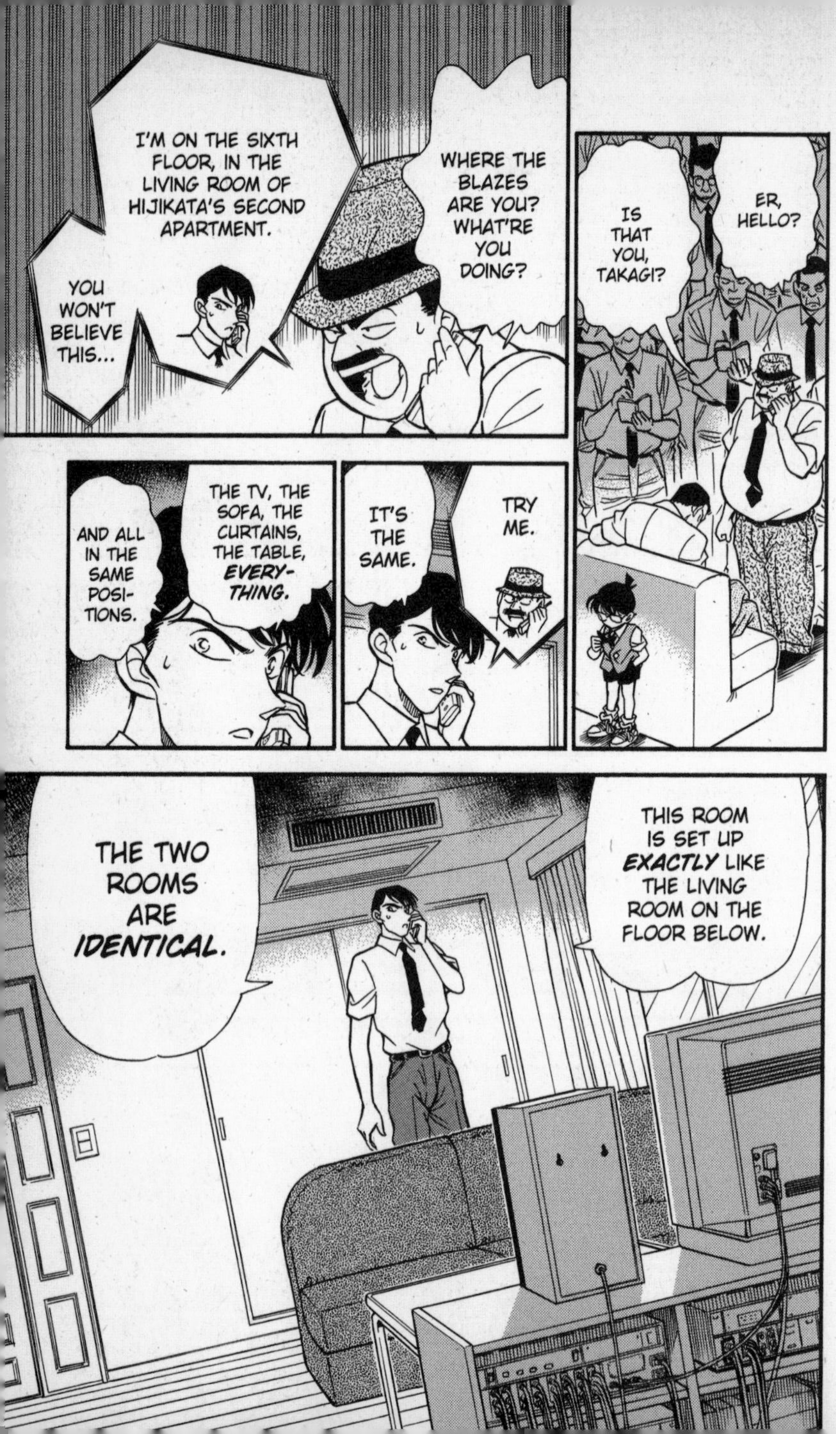
ER, HELLO?
IS THAT YOU, TAKAGI?
WHERE THE BLAZES ARE YOU? WHAT'RE YOU DOING?
I'M ON THE SIXTH FLOOR, IN THE LIVING ROOM OF HIJIKATA'S SECOND APARTMENT.
YOU WON'T BELIEVE THIS...
TRY ME.
IT'S THE SAME.
THE TV, THE SOFA, THE CURTAINS, THE TABLE, *EVERYTHING.*
AND ALL IN THE SAME POSITIONS.
THIS ROOM IS SET UP *EXACTLY* LIKE THE LIVING ROOM ON THE FLOOR BELOW.
THE TWO ROOMS ARE *IDENTICAL.*

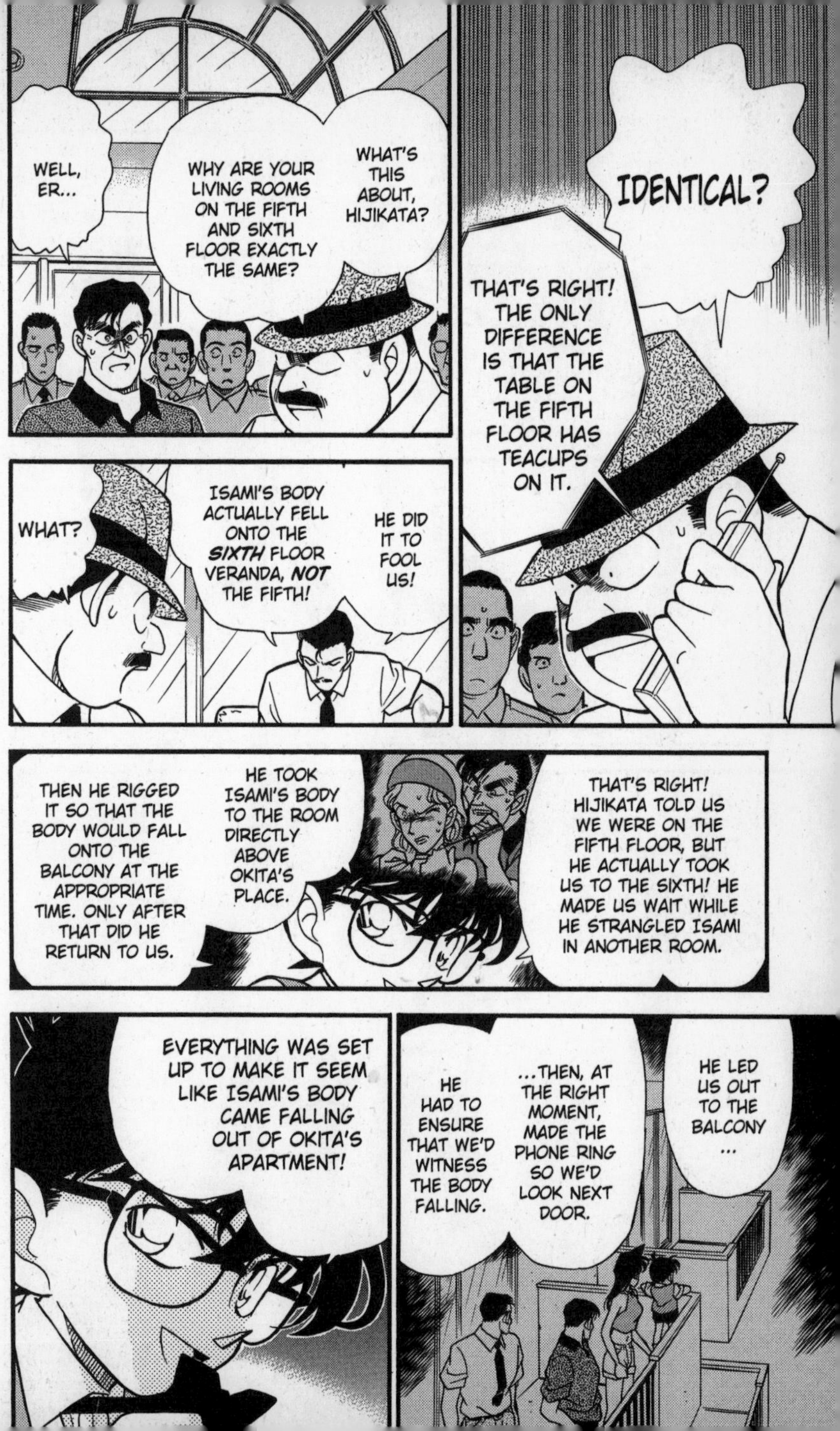
IDENTICAL?
THAT'S RIGHT! THE ONLY DIFFERENCE IS THAT THE TABLE ON THE FIFTH FLOOR HAS TEACUPS ON IT.
WHAT'S THIS ABOUT, HIJIKATA?
WHY ARE YOUR LIVING ROOMS ON THE FIFTH AND SIXTH FLOOR EXACTLY THE SAME?
WELL, ER...
HE DID IT TO FOOL US!
ISAMI'S BODY ACTUALLY FELL ONTO THE *SIXTH* FLOOR VERANDA, *NOT* THE FIFTH!
WHAT?
THAT'S RIGHT! HIJIKATA TOLD US WE WERE ON THE FIFTH FLOOR, BUT HE ACTUALLY TOOK US TO THE SIXTH! HE MADE US WAIT WHILE HE STRANGLED ISAMI IN ANOTHER ROOM.
HE TOOK ISAMI'S BODY TO THE ROOM DIRECTLY ABOVE OKITA'S PLACE.
THEN HE RIGGED IT SO THAT THE BODY WOULD FALL ONTO THE BALCONY AT THE APPROPRIATE TIME. ONLY AFTER THAT DID HE RETURN TO US.
HE LED US OUT TO THE BALCONY ...
...THEN, AT THE RIGHT MOMENT, MADE THE PHONE RING SO WE'D LOOK NEXT DOOR.
HE HAD TO ENSURE THAT WE'D WITNESS THE BODY FALLING.
EVERYTHING WAS SET UP TO MAKE IT SEEM LIKE ISAMI'S BODY CAME FALLING OUT OF OKITA'S APARTMENT!

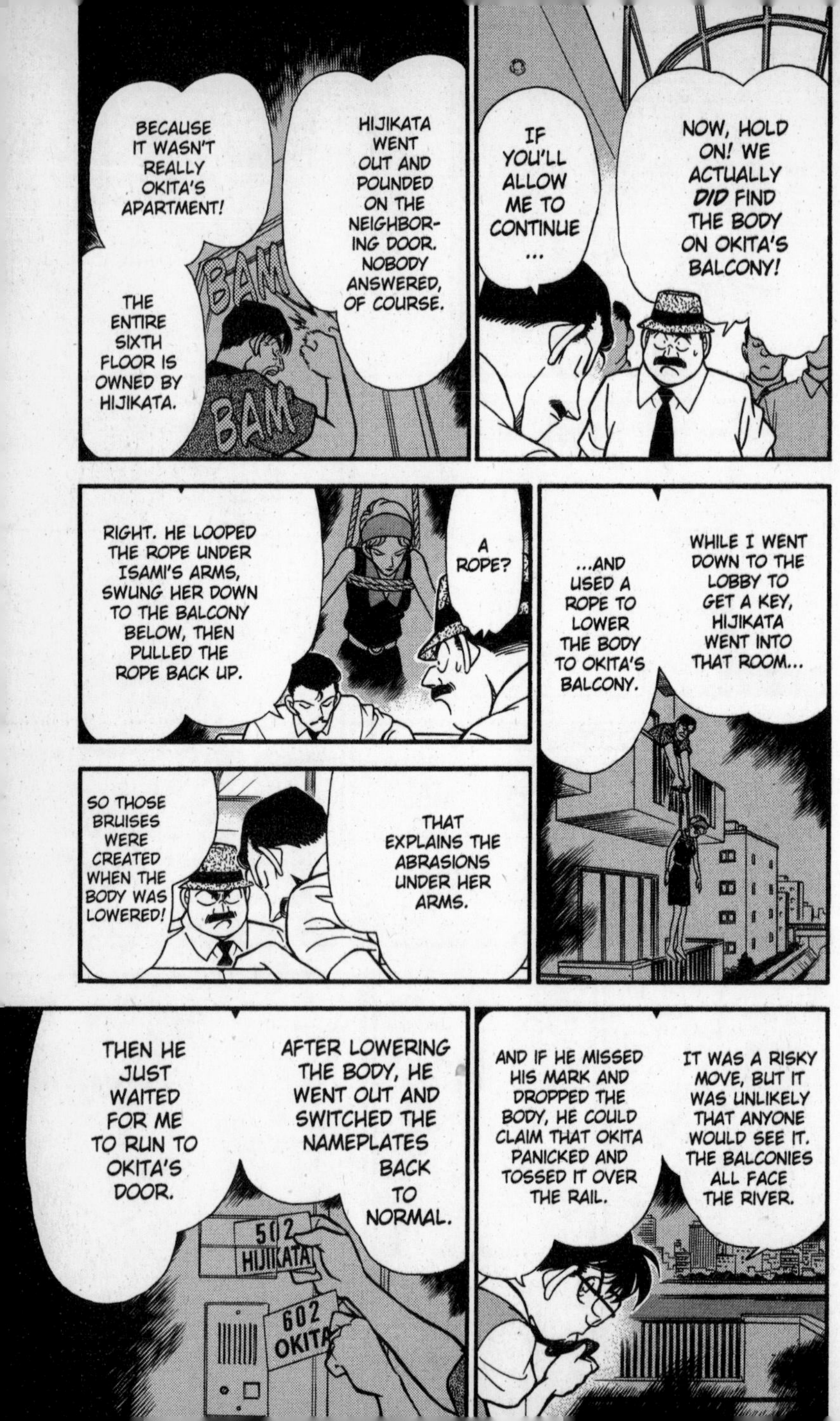
NOW, HOLD ON! WE ACTUALLY *DID* FIND THE BODY ON OKITA'S BALCONY!
IF YOU'LL ALLOW ME TO CONTINUE ...
HIJIKATA WENT OUT AND POUNDED ON THE NEIGHBOR-ING DOOR. NOBODY ANSWERED, OF COURSE.
BECAUSE IT WASN'T REALLY OKITA'S APARTMENT!
BAM
BAM
THE ENTIRE SIXTH FLOOR IS OWNED BY HIJIKATA.
WHILE I WENT DOWN TO THE LOBBY TO GET A KEY, HIJIKATA WENT INTO THAT ROOM...
...AND USED A ROPE TO LOWER THE BODY TO OKITA'S BALCONY.
A ROPE?
RIGHT. HE LOOPED THE ROPE UNDER ISAMI'S ARMS, SWUNG HER DOWN TO THE BALCONY BELOW, THEN PULLED THE ROPE BACK UP.
THAT EXPLAINS THE ABRASIONS UNDER HER ARMS.
SO THOSE BRUISES WERE CREATED WHEN THE BODY WAS LOWERED!
IT WAS A RISKY MOVE, BUT IT WAS UNLIKELY THAT ANYONE WOULD SEE IT. THE BALCONIES ALL FACE THE RIVER.
AND IF HE MISSED HIS MARK AND DROPPED THE BODY, HE COULD CLAIM THAT OKITA PANICKED AND TOSSED IT OVER THE RAIL.
AFTER LOWERING THE BODY, HE WENT OUT AND SWITCHED THE NAMEPLATES BACK TO NORMAL.
THEN HE JUST WAITED FOR ME TO RUN TO OKITA'S DOOR.
502 HIJIKATA
602 OKITA

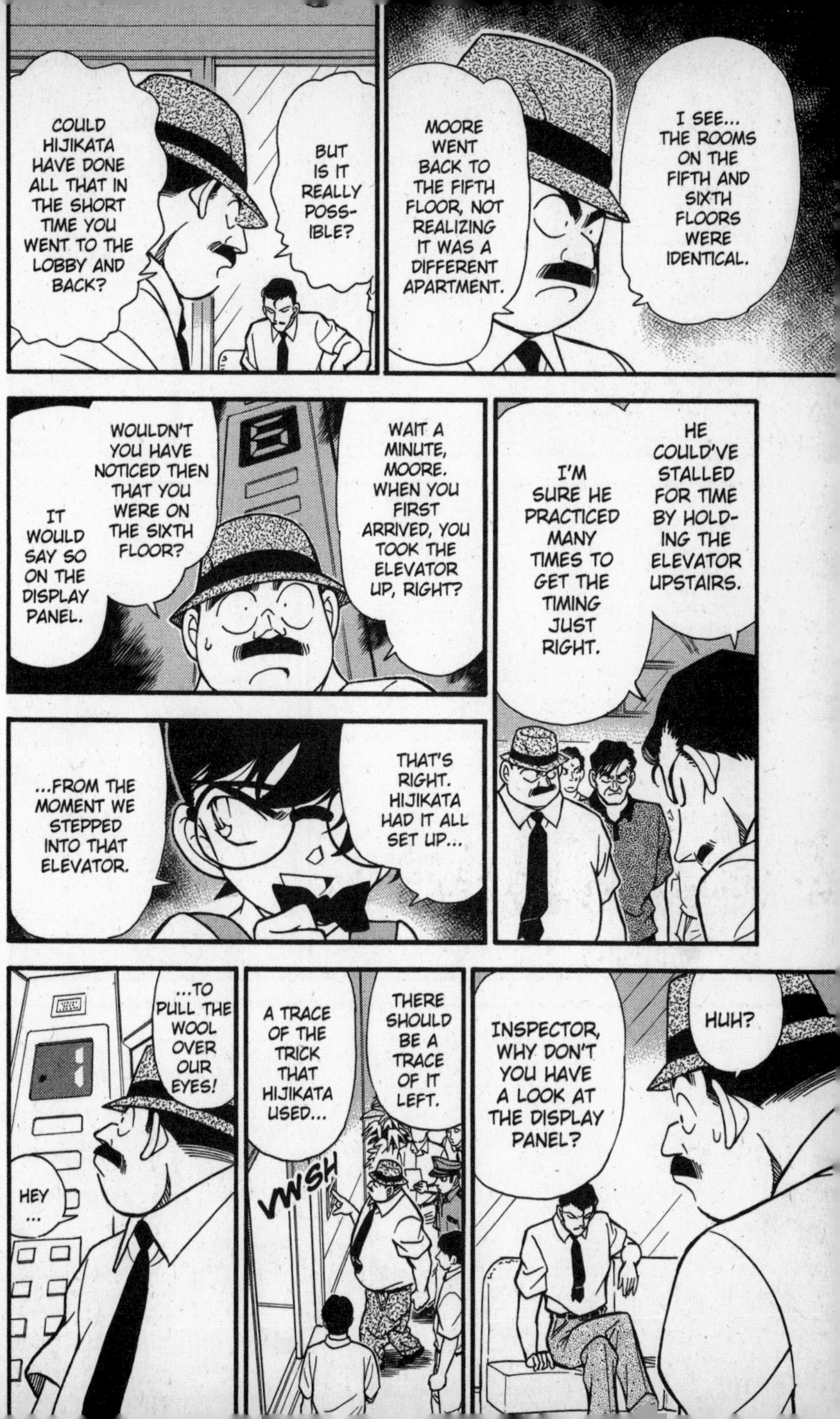
I SEE... THE ROOMS ON THE FIFTH AND SIXTH FLOORS WERE IDENTICAL.
MOORE WENT BACK TO THE FIFTH FLOOR, NOT REALIZING IT WAS A DIFFERENT APARTMENT.
BUT IS IT REALLY POSS-IBLE?
COULD HIJIKATA HAVE DONE ALL THAT IN THE SHORT TIME YOU WENT TO THE LOBBY AND BACK?
HE COULD'VE STALLED FOR TIME BY HOLD-ING THE ELEVATOR UPSTAIRS.
I'M SURE HE PRACTICED MANY TIMES TO GET THE TIMING JUST RIGHT.
WAIT A MINUTE, MOORE. WHEN YOU FIRST ARRIVED, YOU TOOK THE ELEVATOR UP, RIGHT?
WOULDN'T YOU HAVE NOTICED THEN THAT YOU WERE ON THE SIXTH FLOOR?
IT WOULD SAY SO ON THE DISPLAY PANEL.
THAT'S RIGHT. HIJIKATA HAD IT ALL SET UP...
...FROM THE MOMENT WE STEPPED INTO THAT ELEVATOR.
HUH?
INSPECTOR, WHY DON'T YOU HAVE A LOOK AT THE DISPLAY PANEL?
THERE SHOULD BE A TRACE OF IT LEFT.
A TRACE OF THE TRICK THAT HIJIKATA USED...
VWSH
...TO PULL THE WOOL OVER OUR EYES!
HEY ...

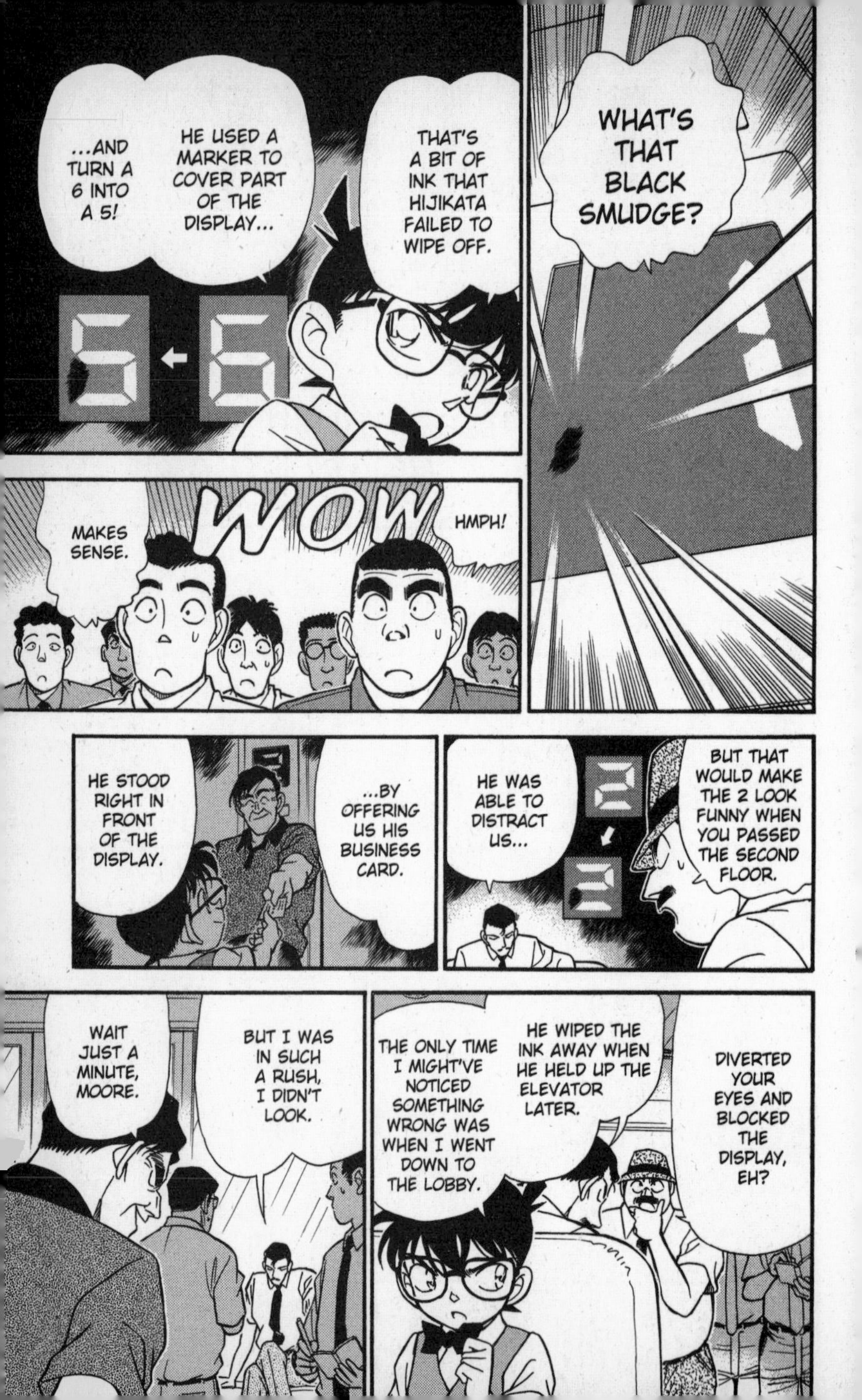
WHAT'S THAT BLACK SMUDGE?
THAT'S A BIT OF INK THAT HIJIKATA FAILED TO WIPE OFF.
HE USED A MARKER TO COVER PART OF THE DISPLAY...
...AND TURN A 6 INTO A 5!
HMPH!
WOW
MAKES SENSE.
BUT THAT WOULD MAKE THE 2 LOOK FUNNY WHEN YOU PASSED THE SECOND FLOOR.
HE WAS ABLE TO DISTRACT US...
...BY OFFERING US HIS BUSINESS CARD.
HE STOOD RIGHT IN FRONT OF THE DISPLAY.
DIVERTED YOUR EYES AND BLOCKED THE DISPLAY, EH?
HE WIPED THE INK AWAY WHEN HE HELD UP THE ELEVATOR LATER.
THE ONLY TIME I MIGHT'VE NOTICED SOMETHING WRONG WAS WHEN I WENT DOWN TO THE LOBBY.
BUT I WAS IN SUCH A RUSH, I DIDN'T LOOK.
WAIT JUST A MINUTE, MOORE.

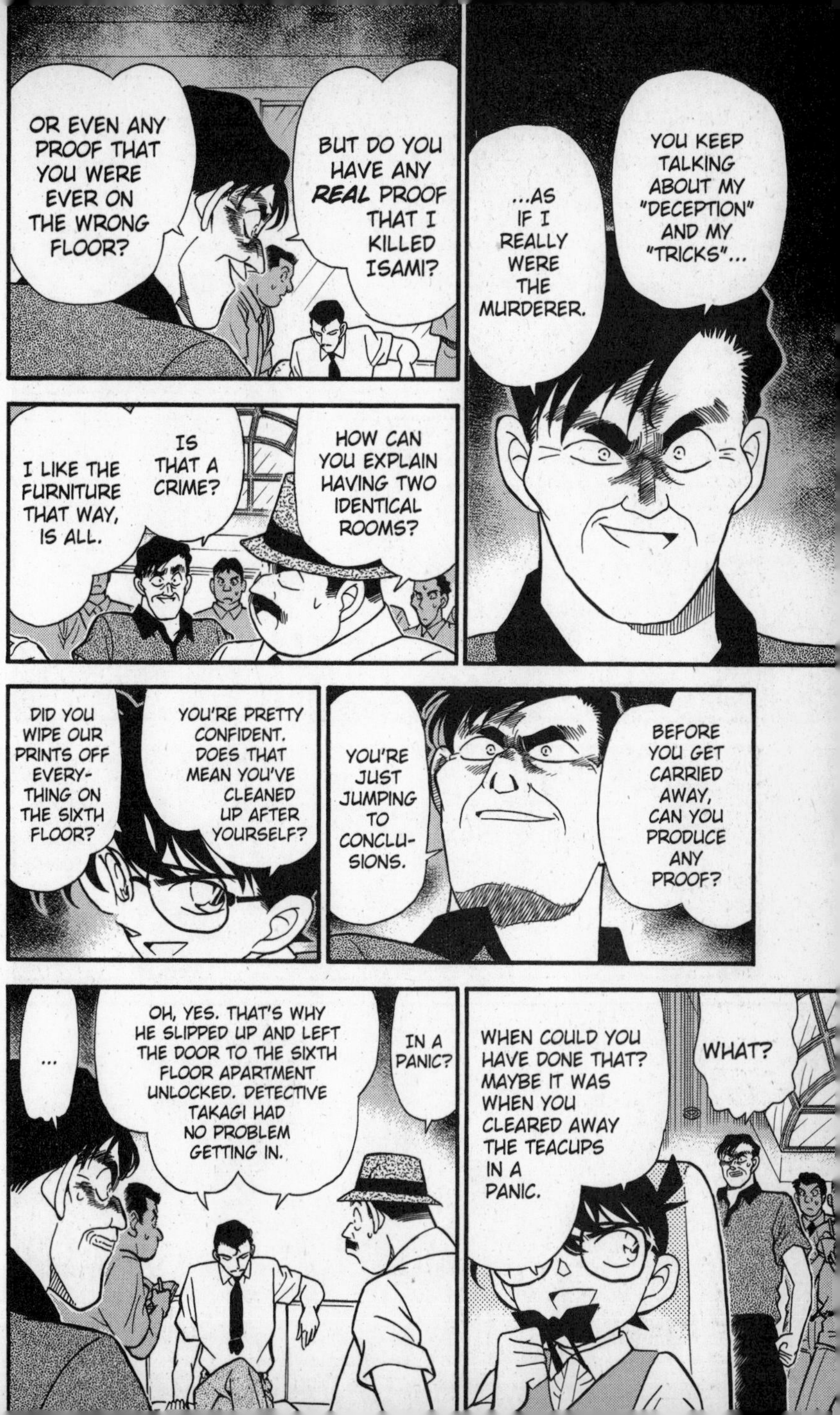

YOU KEEP TALKING ABOUT MY "DECEPTION" AND MY "TRICKS"...
...AS IF I REALLY WERE THE MURDERER.
BUT DO YOU HAVE ANY **REAL** PROOF THAT I KILLED ISAMI?
OR EVEN ANY PROOF THAT YOU WERE EVER ON THE WRONG FLOOR?
HOW CAN YOU EXPLAIN HAVING TWO IDENTICAL ROOMS?
IS THAT A CRIME?
I LIKE THE FURNITURE THAT WAY, IS ALL.
BEFORE YOU GET CARRIED AWAY, CAN YOU PRODUCE ANY PROOF?
YOU'RE JUST JUMPING TO CONCLUSIONS.
YOU'RE PRETTY CONFIDENT. DOES THAT MEAN YOU'VE CLEANED UP AFTER YOURSELF?
DID YOU WIPE OUR PRINTS OFF EVERYTHING ON THE SIXTH FLOOR?
WHAT?
WHEN COULD YOU HAVE DONE THAT? MAYBE IT WAS WHEN YOU CLEARED AWAY THE TEACUPS IN A PANIC.
IN A PANIC?
OH, YES. THAT'S WHY HE SLIPPED UP AND LEFT THE DOOR TO THE SIXTH FLOOR APARTMENT UNLOCKED. DETECTIVE TAKAGI HAD NO PROBLEM GETTING IN.
...

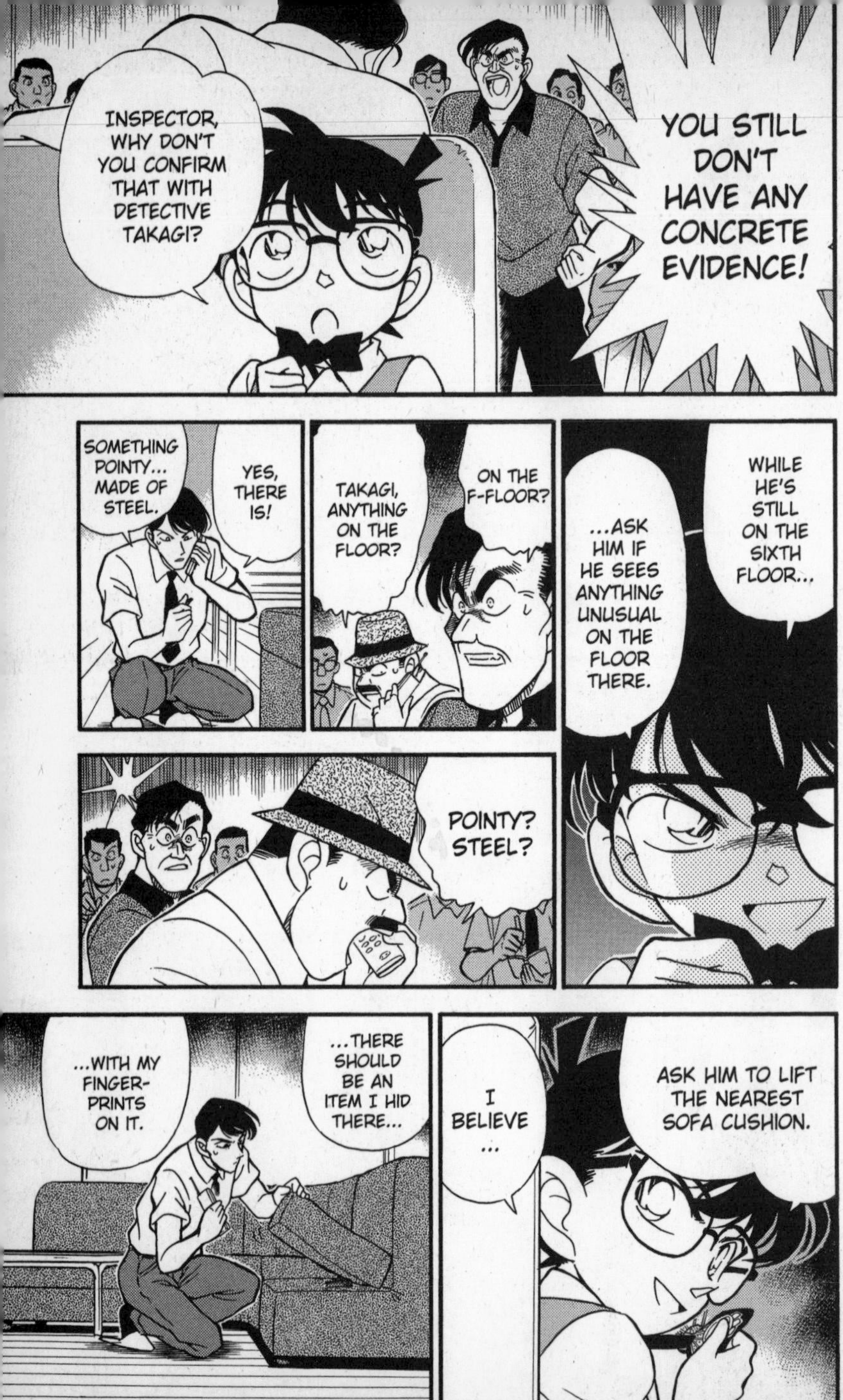
YOU STILL DON'T HAVE ANY CONCRETE EVIDENCE!
INSPECTOR, WHY DON'T YOU CONFIRM THAT WITH DETECTIVE TAKAGI?
WHILE HE'S STILL ON THE SIXTH FLOOR...
...ASK HIM IF HE SEES ANYTHING UNUSUAL ON THE FLOOR THERE.
ON THE F-FLOOR?
TAKAGI, ANYTHING ON THE FLOOR?
YES, THERE IS!
SOMETHING POINTY... MADE OF STEEL.
POINTY? STEEL?
ASK HIM TO LIFT THE NEAREST SOFA CUSHION.
I BELIEVE ...
...THERE SHOULD BE AN ITEM I HID THERE...
...WITH MY FINGER-PRINTS ON IT.

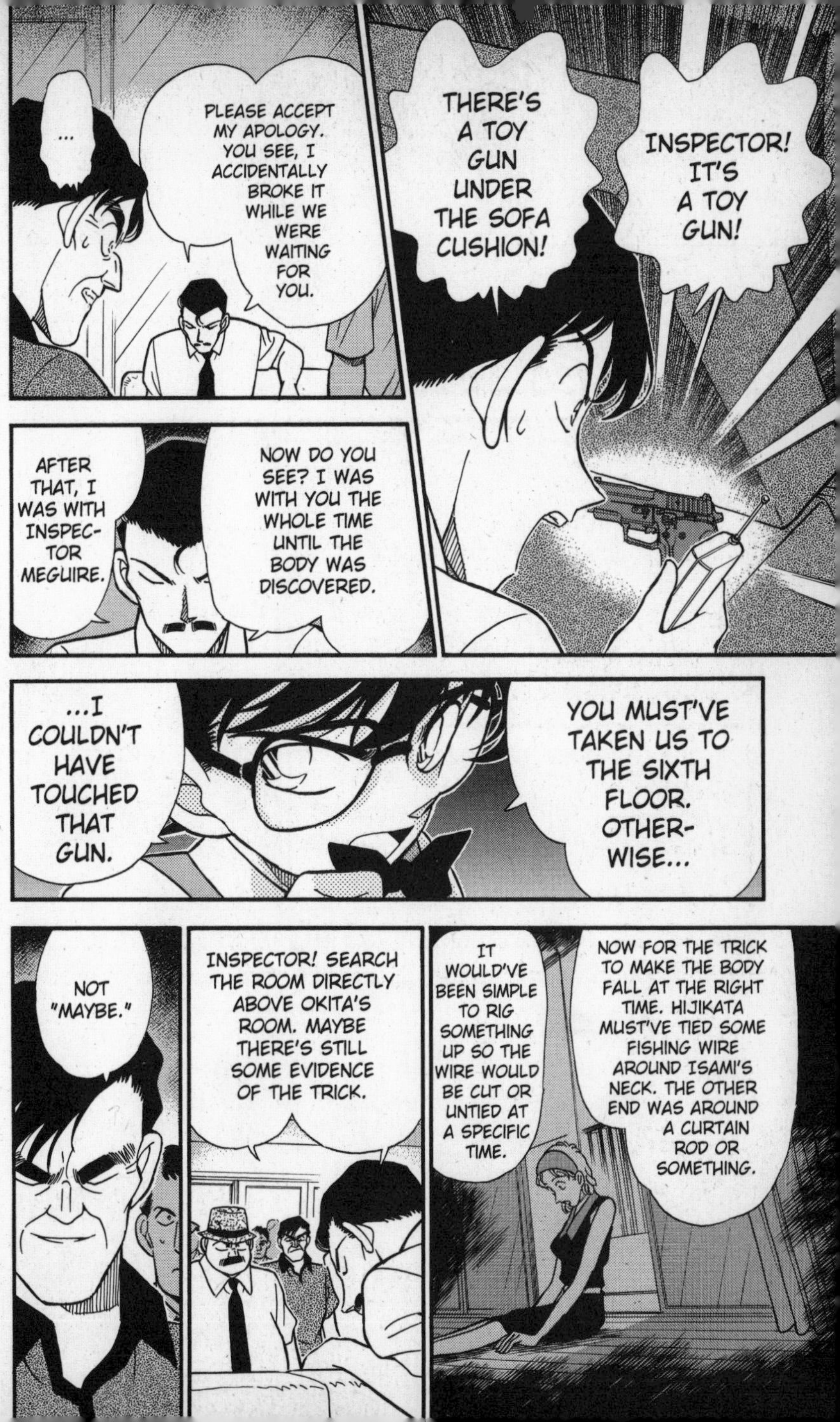
INSPECTOR! IT'S A TOY GUN!
THERE'S A TOY GUN UNDER THE SOFA CUSHION!
PLEASE ACCEPT MY APOLOGY. YOU SEE, I ACCIDENTALLY BROKE IT WHILE WE WERE WAITING FOR YOU.
...
NOW DO YOU SEE? I WAS WITH YOU THE WHOLE TIME UNTIL THE BODY WAS DISCOVERED.
AFTER THAT, I WAS WITH INSPECTOR MEGUIRE.
YOU MUST'VE TAKEN US TO THE SIXTH FLOOR. OTHERWISE...
...I COULDN'T HAVE TOUCHED THAT GUN.
NOW FOR THE TRICK TO MAKE THE BODY FALL AT THE RIGHT TIME. HIJIKATA MUST'VE TIED SOME FISHING WIRE AROUND ISAMI'S NECK. THE OTHER END WAS AROUND A CURTAIN ROD OR SOMETHING.
IT WOULD'VE BEEN SIMPLE TO RIG SOMETHING UP SO THE WIRE WOULD BE CUT OR UNTIED AT A SPECIFIC TIME.
INSPECTOR! SEARCH THE ROOM DIRECTLY ABOVE OKITA'S ROOM. MAYBE THERE'S STILL SOME EVIDENCE OF THE TRICK.
NOT "MAYBE."

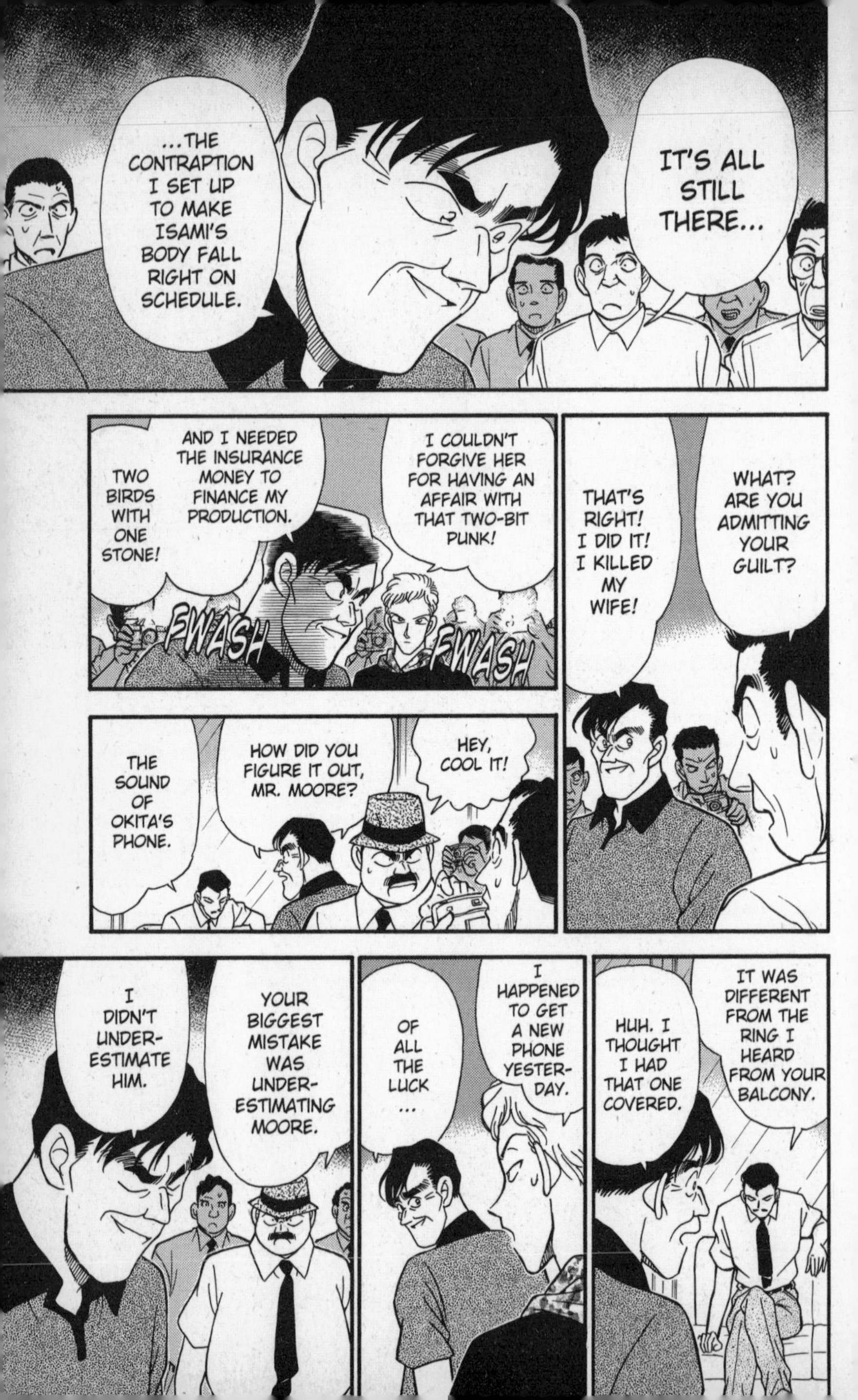
IT'S ALL STILL THERE...
...THE CONTRAPTION I SET UP TO MAKE ISAMI'S BODY FALL RIGHT ON SCHEDULE.
WHAT? ARE YOU ADMITTING YOUR GUILT?
THAT'S RIGHT! I DID IT! I KILLED MY WIFE!
I COULDN'T FORGIVE HER FOR HAVING AN AFFAIR WITH THAT TWO-BIT PUNK!
AND I NEEDED THE INSURANCE MONEY TO FINANCE MY PRODUCTION.
TWO BIRDS WITH ONE STONE!
FWASH
FWASH
HEY, COOL IT!
HOW DID YOU FIGURE IT OUT, MR. MOORE?
THE SOUND OF OKITA'S PHONE.
IT WAS DIFFERENT FROM THE RING I HEARD FROM YOUR BALCONY.
HUH. I THOUGHT I HAD THAT ONE COVERED.
I HAPPENED TO GET A NEW PHONE YESTER-DAY.
OF ALL THE LUCK...
YOUR BIGGEST MISTAKE WAS UNDER-ESTIMATING MOORE.
I DIDN'T UNDER-ESTIMATE HIM.

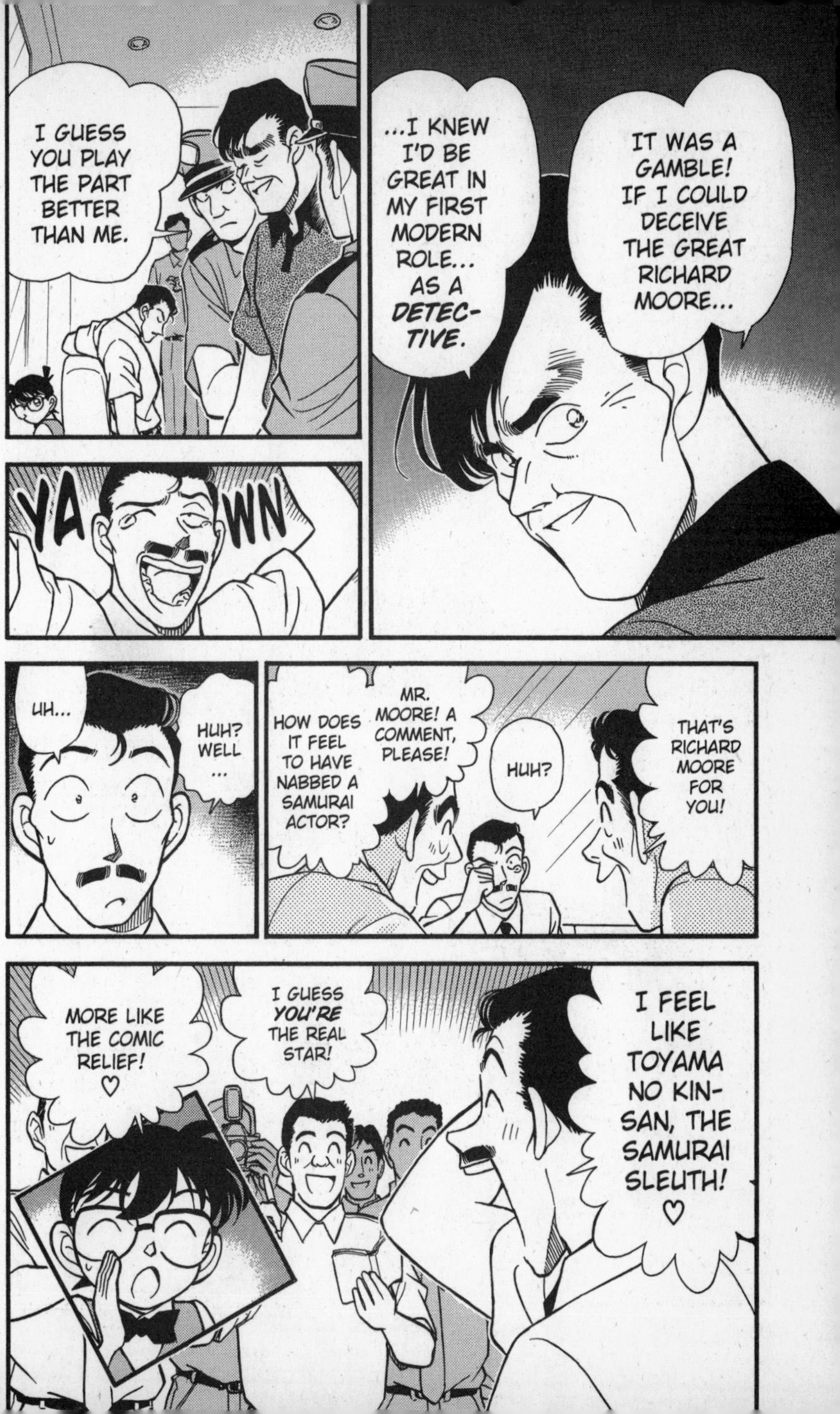
IT WAS A GAMBLE! IF I COULD DECEIVE THE GREAT RICHARD MOORE...
...I KNEW I'D BE GREAT IN MY FIRST MODERN ROLE... AS A *DETECTIVE*.
I GUESS YOU PLAY THE PART BETTER THAN ME.
YAWN
THAT'S RICHARD MOORE FOR YOU!
HUH?
MR. MOORE! A COMMENT, PLEASE!
HOW DOES IT FEEL TO HAVE NABBED A SAMURAI ACTOR?
HUH? WELL ...
UH...
I FEEL LIKE TOYAMA NO KIN-SAN, THE SAMURAI SLEUTH! ♡
I GUESS *YOU'RE* THE REAL STAR!
MORE LIKE THE COMIC RELIEF! ♡

FILE 3: FIRST LOVE

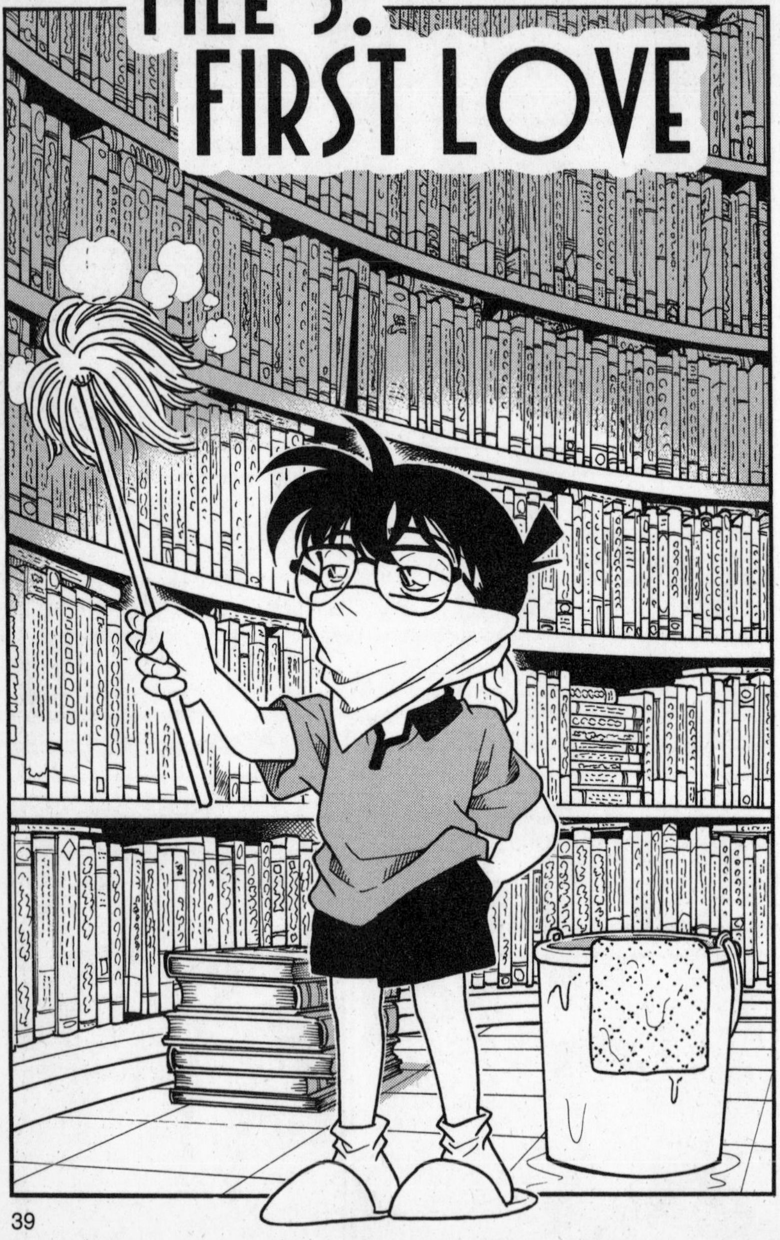

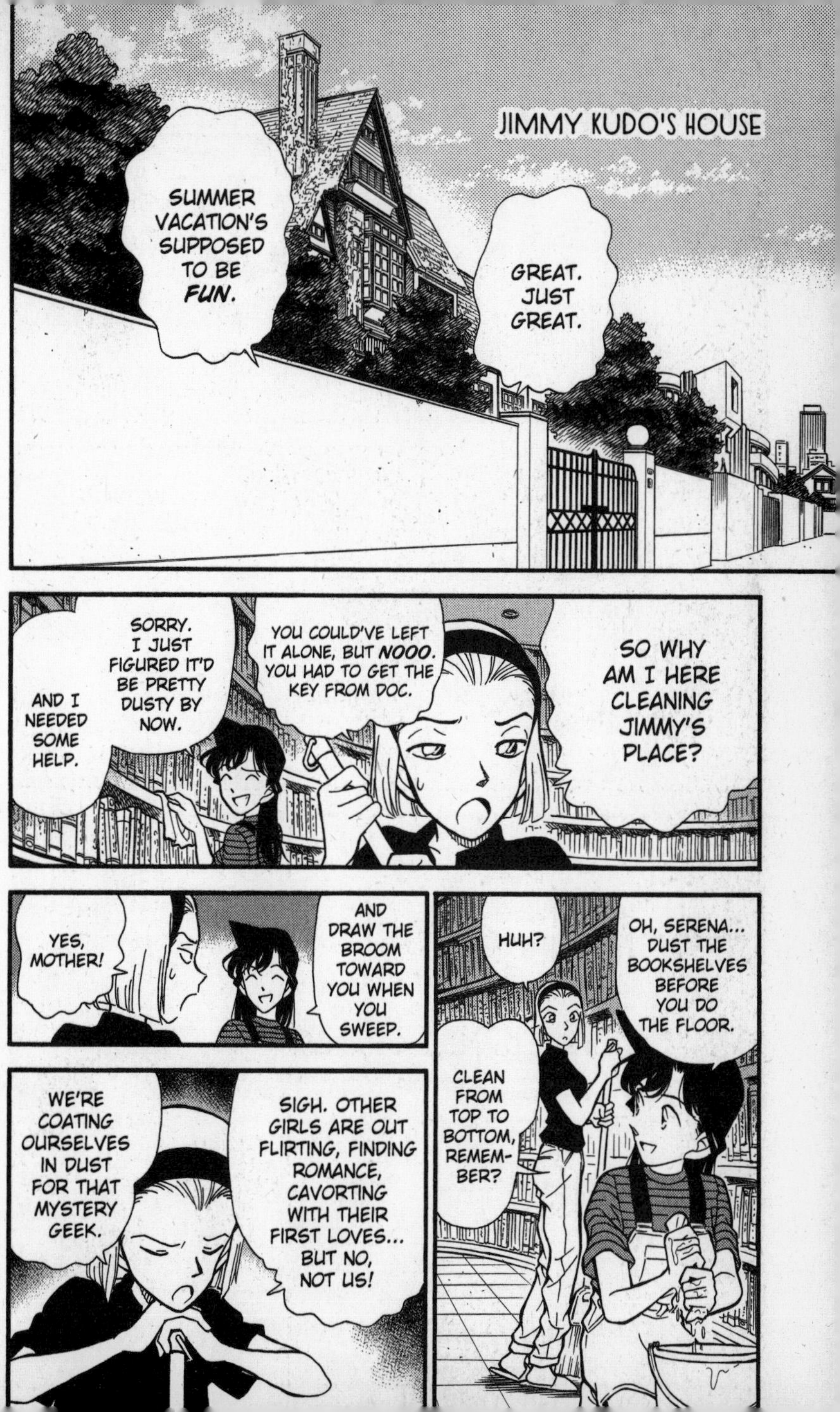
JIMMY KUDO'S HOUSE
GREAT. JUST GREAT.
SUMMER VACATION'S SUPPOSED TO BE FUN.
SO WHY AM I HERE CLEANING JIMMY'S PLACE?
YOU COULD'VE LEFT IT ALONE, BUT NOOO. YOU HAD TO GET THE KEY FROM DOC.
SORRY. I JUST FIGURED IT'D BE PRETTY DUSTY BY NOW.
AND I NEEDED SOME HELP.
OH, SERENA... DUST THE BOOKSHELVES BEFORE YOU DO THE FLOOR.
HUH?
CLEAN FROM TOP TO BOTTOM, REMEMBER?
AND DRAW THE BROOM TOWARD YOU WHEN YOU SWEEP.
YES, MOTHER!
SIGH. OTHER GIRLS ARE OUT FLIRTING, FINDING ROMANCE, CAVORTING WITH THEIR FIRST LOVES... BUT NO, NOT US!
WE'RE COATING OURSELVES IN DUST FOR THAT MYSTERY GEEK.

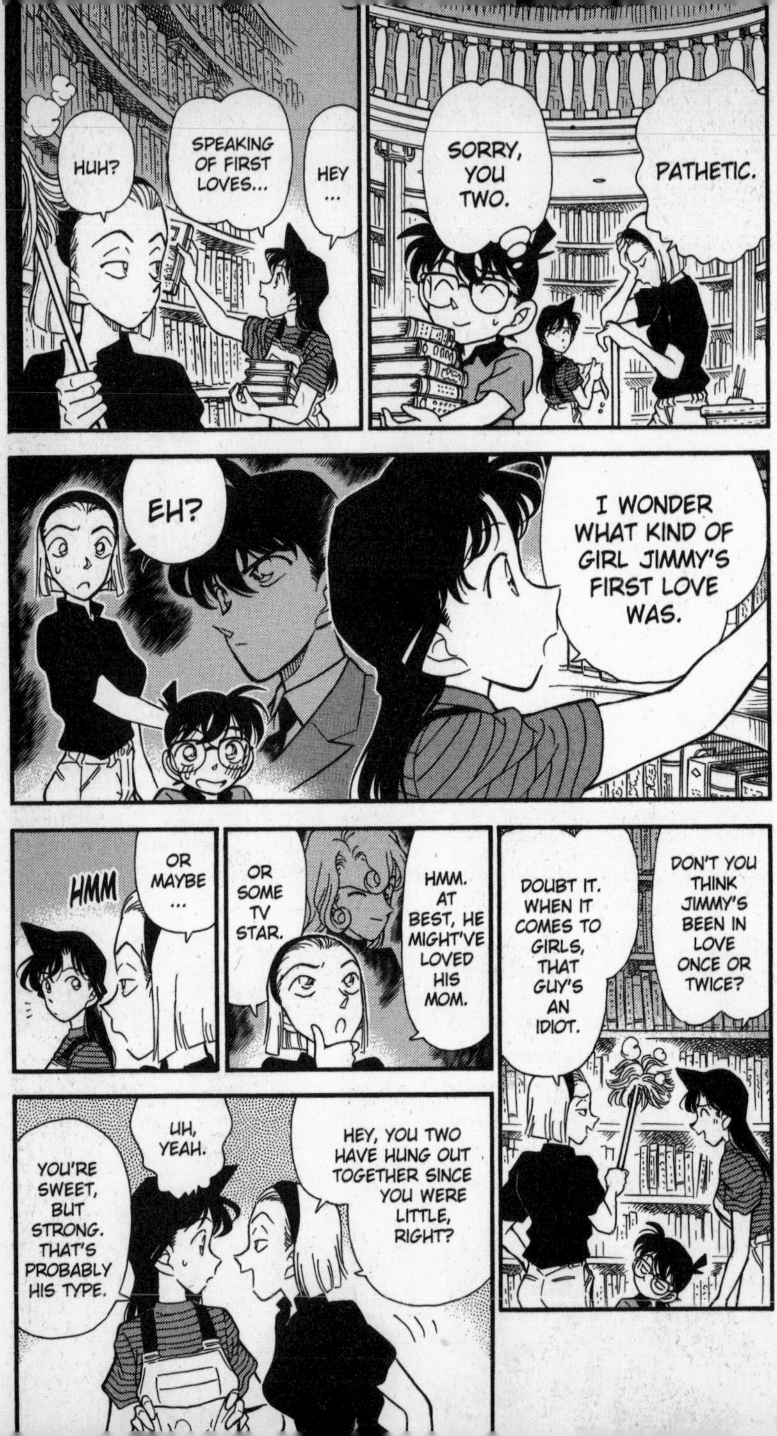
PATHETIC.
SORRY, YOU TWO.
HEY ...
SPEAKING OF FIRST LOVES...
HUH?
I WONDER WHAT KIND OF GIRL JIMMY'S FIRST LOVE WAS.
EH?
DON'T YOU THINK JIMMY'S BEEN IN LOVE ONCE OR TWICE?
DOUBT IT. WHEN IT COMES TO GIRLS, THAT GUY'S AN IDIOT.
HMM. AT BEST, HE MIGHT'VE LOVED HIS MOM.
OR SOME TV STAR.
OR MAYBE ...
HMM
HEY, YOU TWO HAVE HUNG OUT TOGETHER SINCE YOU WERE LITTLE, RIGHT?
UH, YEAH.
YOU'RE SWEET, BUT STRONG. THAT'S PROBABLY HIS TYPE.

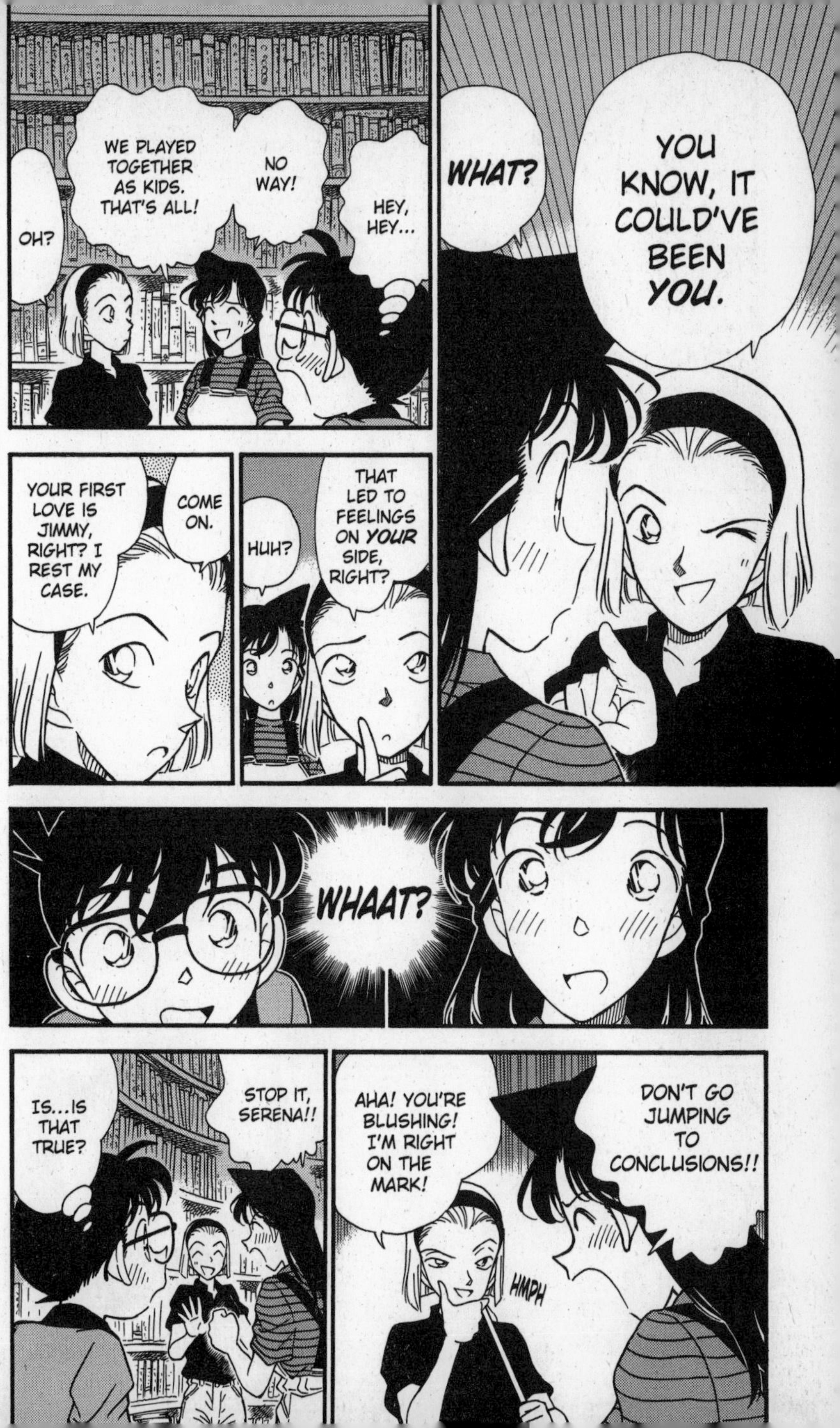
YOU KNOW, IT COULD'VE BEEN *YOU.*
WHAT?
HEY, HEY...
NO WAY!
WE PLAYED TOGETHER AS KIDS. THAT'S ALL!
OH?
THAT LED TO FEELINGS ON ***YOUR*** SIDE, RIGHT?
HUH?
COME ON.
YOUR FIRST LOVE IS JIMMY, RIGHT? I REST MY CASE.
WHAAT?
DON'T GO JUMPING TO CONCLUSIONS!!
HMPH
AHA! YOU'RE BLUSHING! I'M RIGHT ON THE MARK!
STOP IT, SERENA!!
IS...IS THAT TRUE?

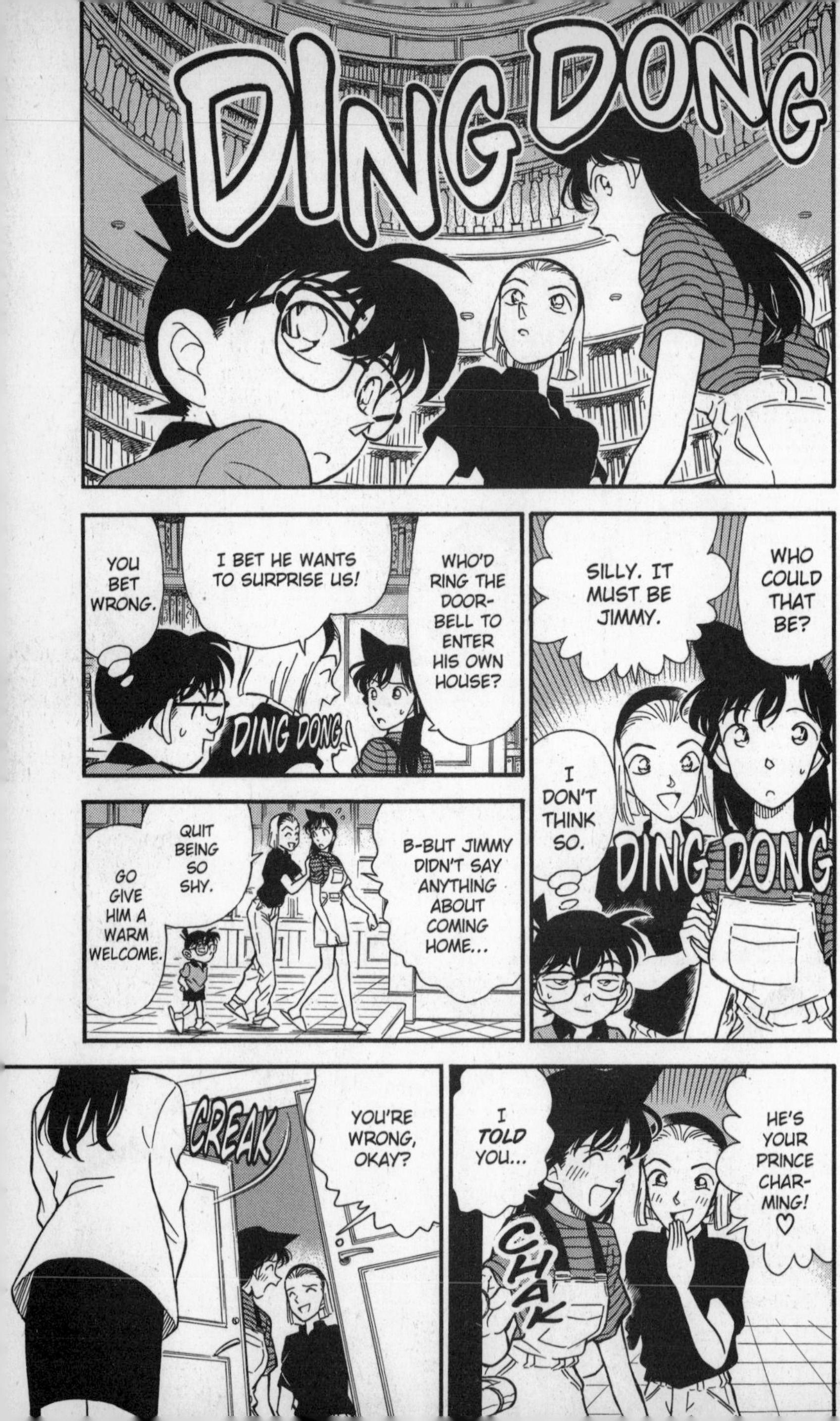
DING DONG
WHO COULD THAT BE?
SILLY. IT MUST BE JIMMY.
I DON'T THINK SO.
DING DONG
WHO'D RING THE DOOR-BELL TO ENTER HIS OWN HOUSE?
I BET HE WANTS TO SURPRISE US!
YOU BET WRONG.
DING DONG
B-BUT JIMMY DIDN'T SAY ANYTHING ABOUT COMING HOME...
QUIT BEING SO SHY.
GO GIVE HIM A WARM WELCOME.
HE'S YOUR PRINCE CHAR-MING! ♡
I *TOLD* YOU...
CHAK
YOU'RE WRONG, OKAY?
CREAK

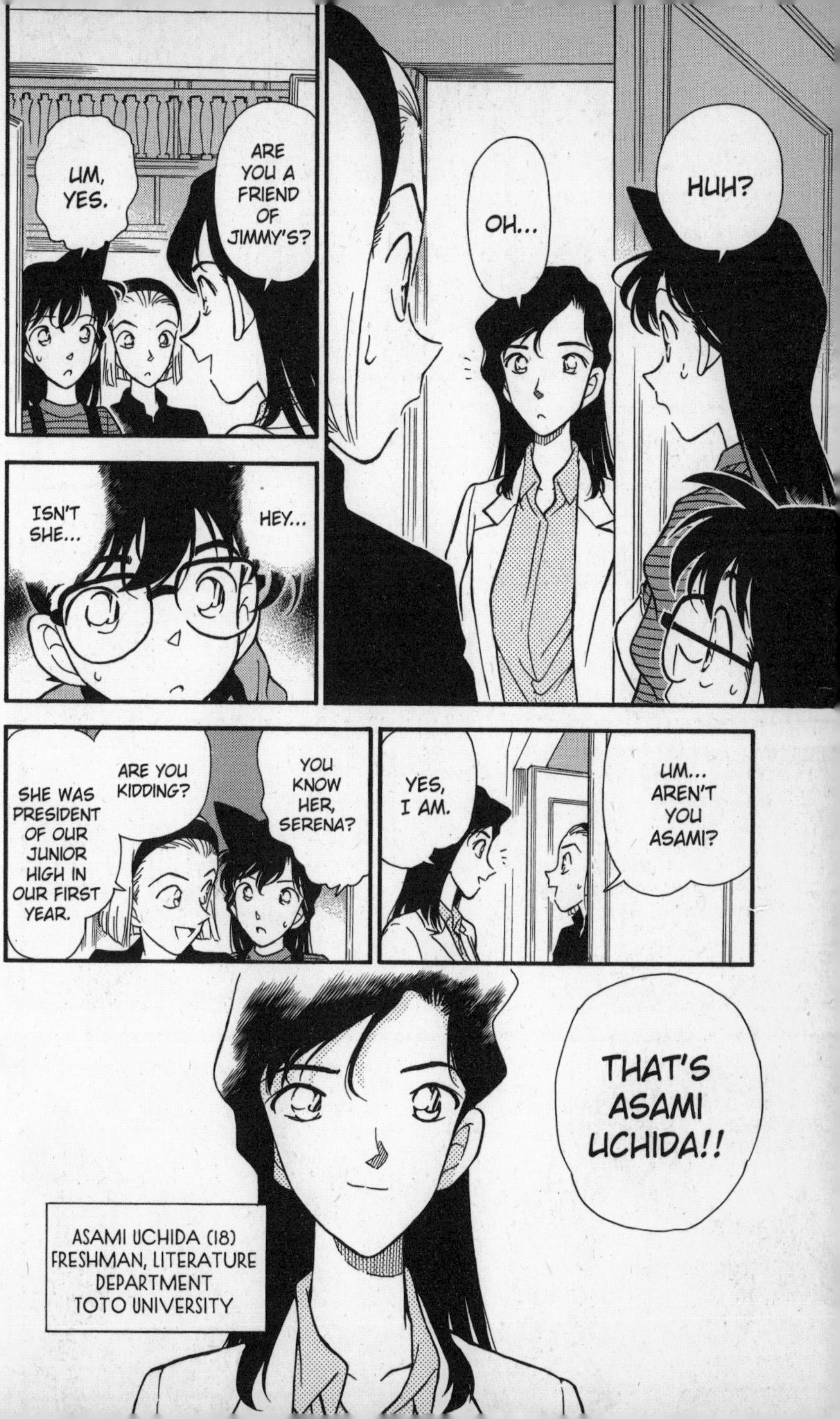
HUH?
OH...
ARE YOU A FRIEND OF JIMMY'S?
UM, YES.
HEY...
ISN'T SHE...
UM... AREN'T YOU ASAMI?
YES, I AM.
YOU KNOW HER, SERENA?
ARE YOU KIDDING?
SHE WAS PRESIDENT OF OUR JUNIOR HIGH IN OUR FIRST YEAR.
THAT'S ASAMI UCHIDA!!
ASAMI UCHIDA (18)
FRESHMAN, LITERATURE DEPARTMENT
TOTO UNIVERSITY

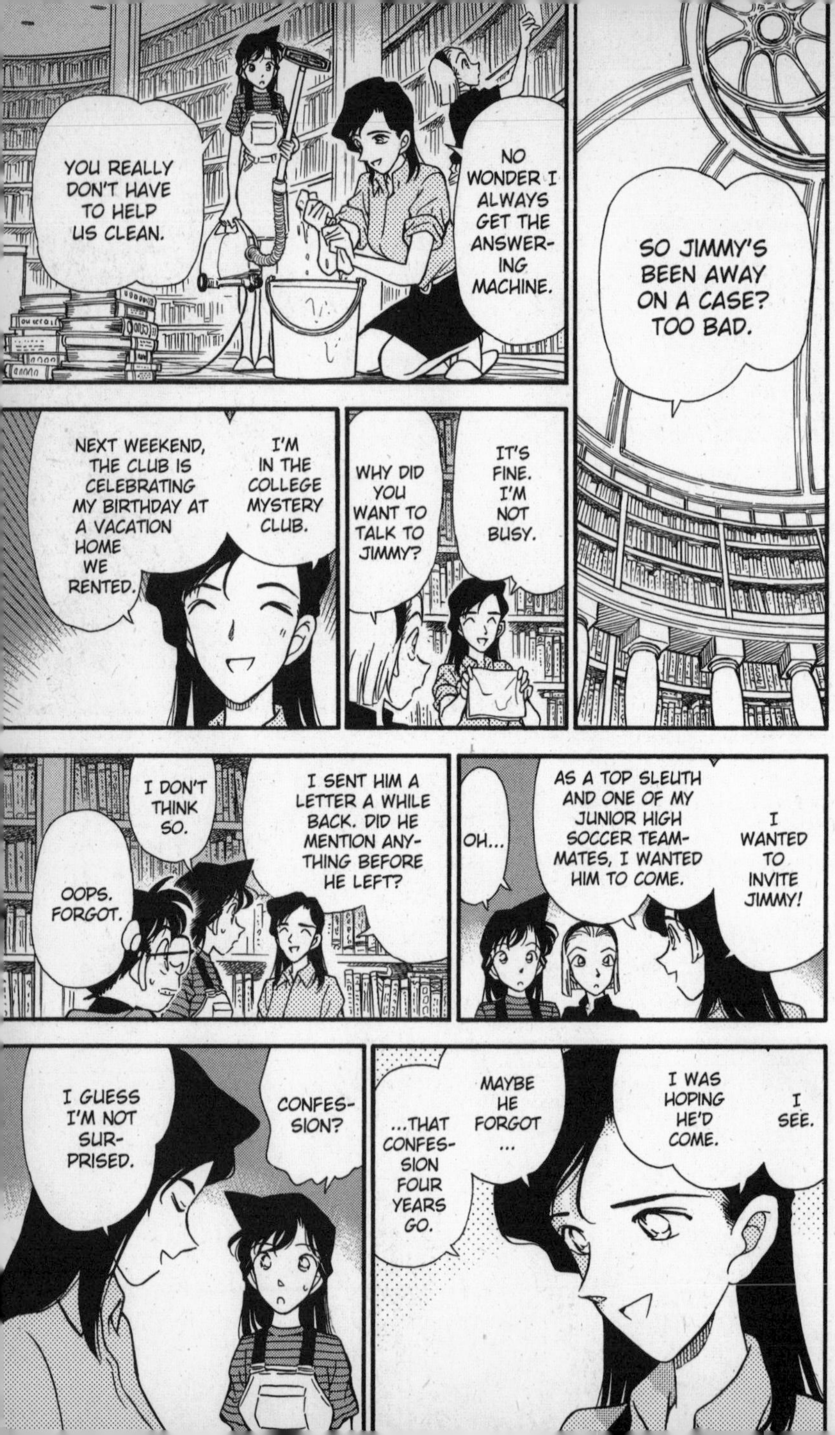
SO JIMMY'S BEEN AWAY ON A CASE? TOO BAD.
NO WONDER I ALWAYS GET THE ANSWERING MACHINE.
YOU REALLY DON'T HAVE TO HELP US CLEAN.
IT'S FINE. I'M NOT BUSY.
WHY DID YOU WANT TO TALK TO JIMMY?
I'M IN THE COLLEGE MYSTERY CLUB.
NEXT WEEKEND, THE CLUB IS CELEBRATING MY BIRTHDAY AT A VACATION HOME WE RENTED.
I WANTED TO INVITE JIMMY!
AS A TOP SLEUTH AND ONE OF MY JUNIOR HIGH SOCCER TEAMMATES, I WANTED HIM TO COME.
OH...
I SENT HIM A LETTER A WHILE BACK. DID HE MENTION ANYTHING BEFORE HE LEFT?
I DON'T THINK SO.
OOPS. FORGOT.
I SEE.
I WAS HOPING HE'D COME.
MAYBE HE FORGOT...
...THAT CONFESSION FOUR YEARS GO.
CONFESSION?
I GUESS I'M NOT SURPRISED.

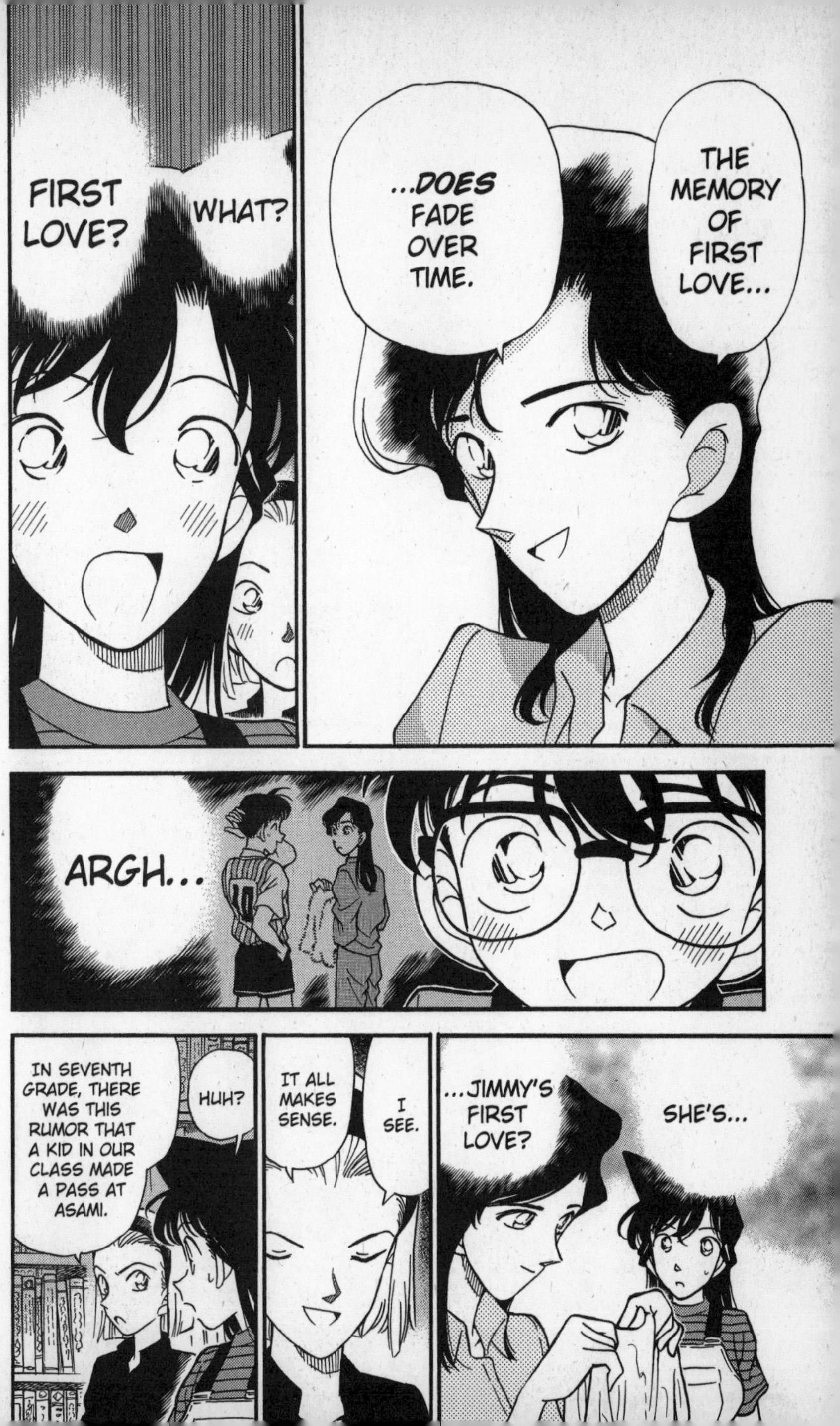
THE MEMORY OF FIRST LOVE...
...DOES FADE OVER TIME.
WHAT?
FIRST LOVE?
ARGH...
SHE'S...
...JIMMY'S FIRST LOVE?
I SEE.
IT ALL MAKES SENSE.
HUH?
IN SEVENTH GRADE, THERE WAS THIS RUMOR THAT A KID IN OUR CLASS MADE A PASS AT ASAMI.

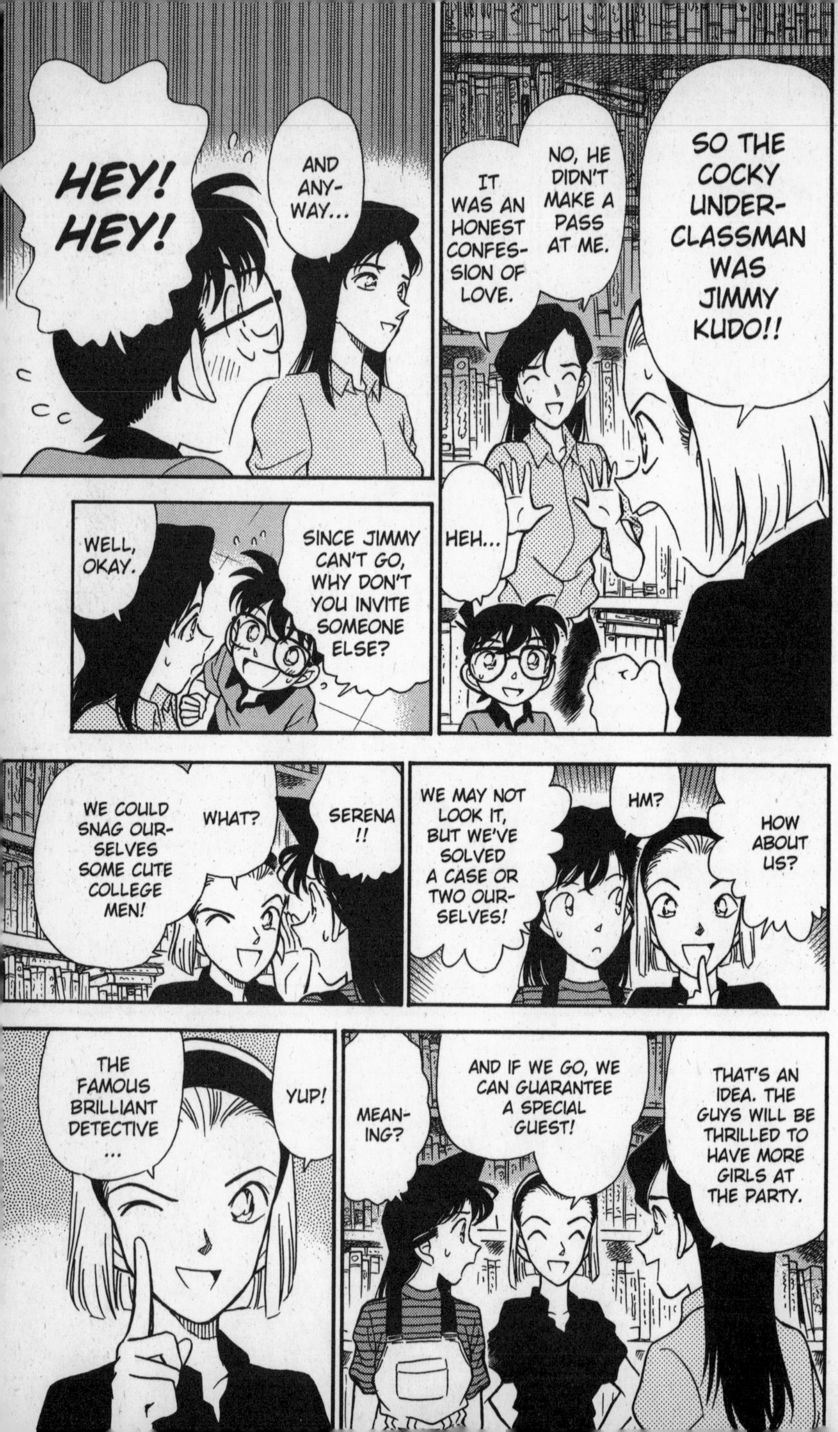
SO THE COCKY UNDERCLASSMAN WAS JIMMY KUDO!!
NO, HE DIDN'T MAKE A PASS AT ME.
IT WAS AN HONEST CONFESSION OF LOVE.
HEH...
AND ANYWAY...
HEY! HEY!
SINCE JIMMY CAN'T GO, WHY DON'T YOU INVITE SOMEONE ELSE?
WELL, OKAY.
HOW ABOUT US?
HM?
WE MAY NOT LOOK IT, BUT WE'VE SOLVED A CASE OR TWO OURSELVES!
SERENA !!
WHAT?
WE COULD SNAG OURSELVES SOME CUTE COLLEGE MEN!
THAT'S AN IDEA. THE GUYS WILL BE THRILLED TO HAVE MORE GIRLS AT THE PARTY.
AND IF WE GO, WE CAN GUARANTEE A SPECIAL GUEST!
MEANING?
YUP!
THE FAMOUS BRILLIANT DETECTIVE ...

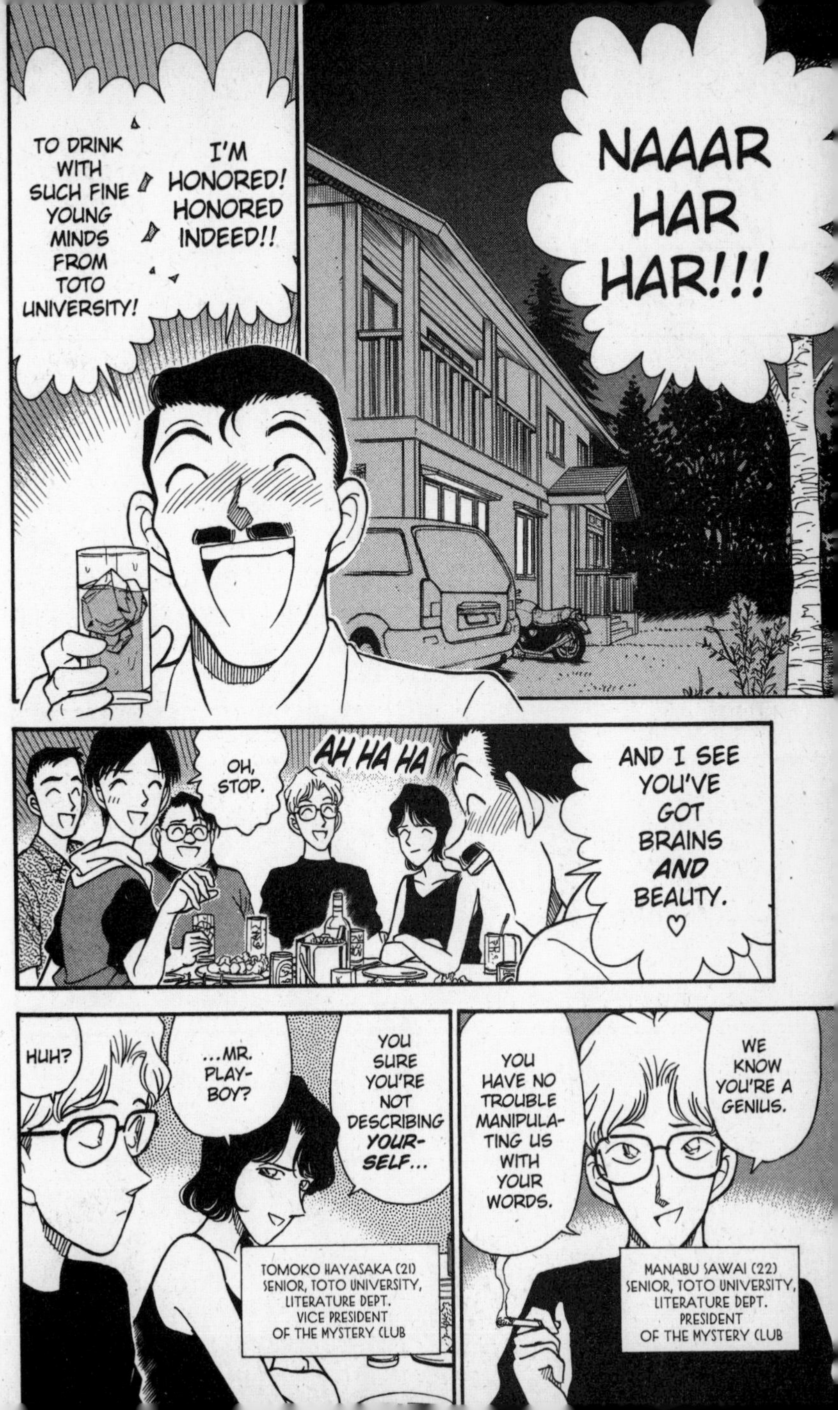
NAAAR HAR HAR!!!
I'M HONORED! HONORED INDEED!!
TO DRINK WITH SUCH FINE YOUNG MINDS FROM TOTO UNIVERSITY!
AND I SEE YOU'VE GOT BRAINS AND BEAUTY. ♡
AH HA HA
OH, STOP.
WE KNOW YOU'RE A GENIUS.
YOU HAVE NO TROUBLE MANIPULATING US WITH YOUR WORDS.
MANABU SAWAI (22) SENIOR, TOTO UNIVERSITY, LITERATURE DEPT. PRESIDENT OF THE MYSTERY CLUB
YOU SURE YOU'RE NOT DESCRIBING YOURSELF...
...MR. PLAYBOY?
HUH?
TOMOKO HAYASAKA (21) SENIOR, TOTO UNIVERSITY, LITERATURE DEPT. VICE PRESIDENT OF THE MYSTERY CLUB

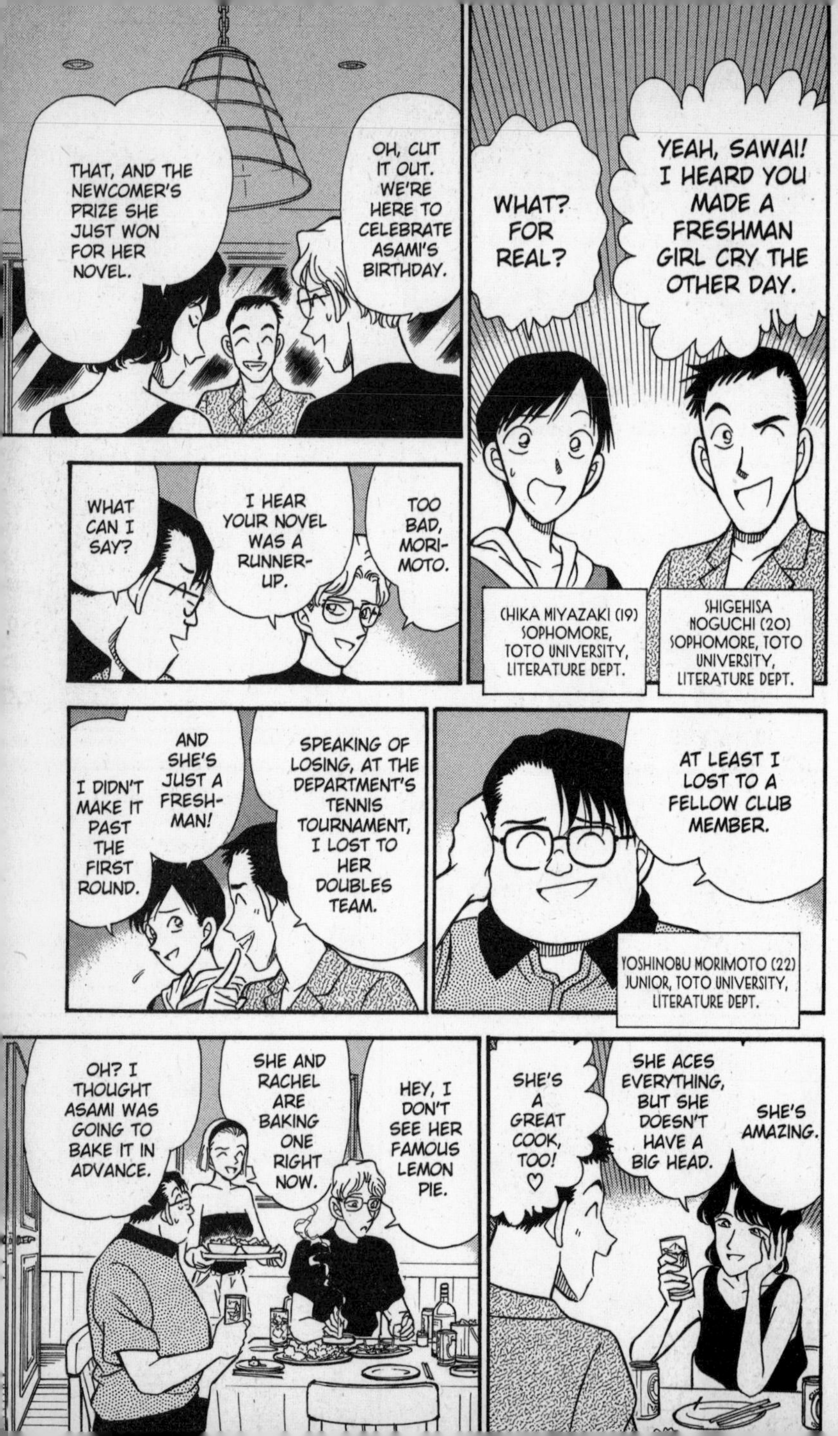
YEAH, SAWAI! I HEARD YOU MADE A FRESHMAN GIRL CRY THE OTHER DAY.
WHAT? FOR REAL?
SHIGEHISA NOGUCHI (20) SOPHOMORE, TOTO UNIVERSITY, LITERATURE DEPT.
CHIKA MIYAZAKI (19) SOPHOMORE, TOTO UNIVERSITY, LITERATURE DEPT.
OH, CUT IT OUT. WE'RE HERE TO CELEBRATE ASAMI'S BIRTHDAY.
THAT, AND THE NEWCOMER'S PRIZE SHE JUST WON FOR HER NOVEL.
TOO BAD, MORIMOTO.
I HEAR YOUR NOVEL WAS A RUNNER-UP.
WHAT CAN I SAY?
AT LEAST I LOST TO A FELLOW CLUB MEMBER.
YOSHINOBU MORIMOTO (22) JUNIOR, TOTO UNIVERSITY, LITERATURE DEPT.
SPEAKING OF LOSING, AT THE DEPARTMENT'S TENNIS TOURNAMENT, I LOST TO HER DOUBLES TEAM.
AND SHE'S JUST A FRESHMAN!
I DIDN'T MAKE IT PAST THE FIRST ROUND.
SHE'S AMAZING.
SHE ACES EVERYTHING, BUT SHE DOESN'T HAVE A BIG HEAD.
SHE'S A GREAT COOK, TOO! ♡
HEY, I DON'T SEE HER FAMOUS LEMON PIE.
SHE AND RACHEL ARE BAKING ONE RIGHT NOW.
OH? I THOUGHT ASAMI WAS GOING TO BAKE IT IN ADVANCE.

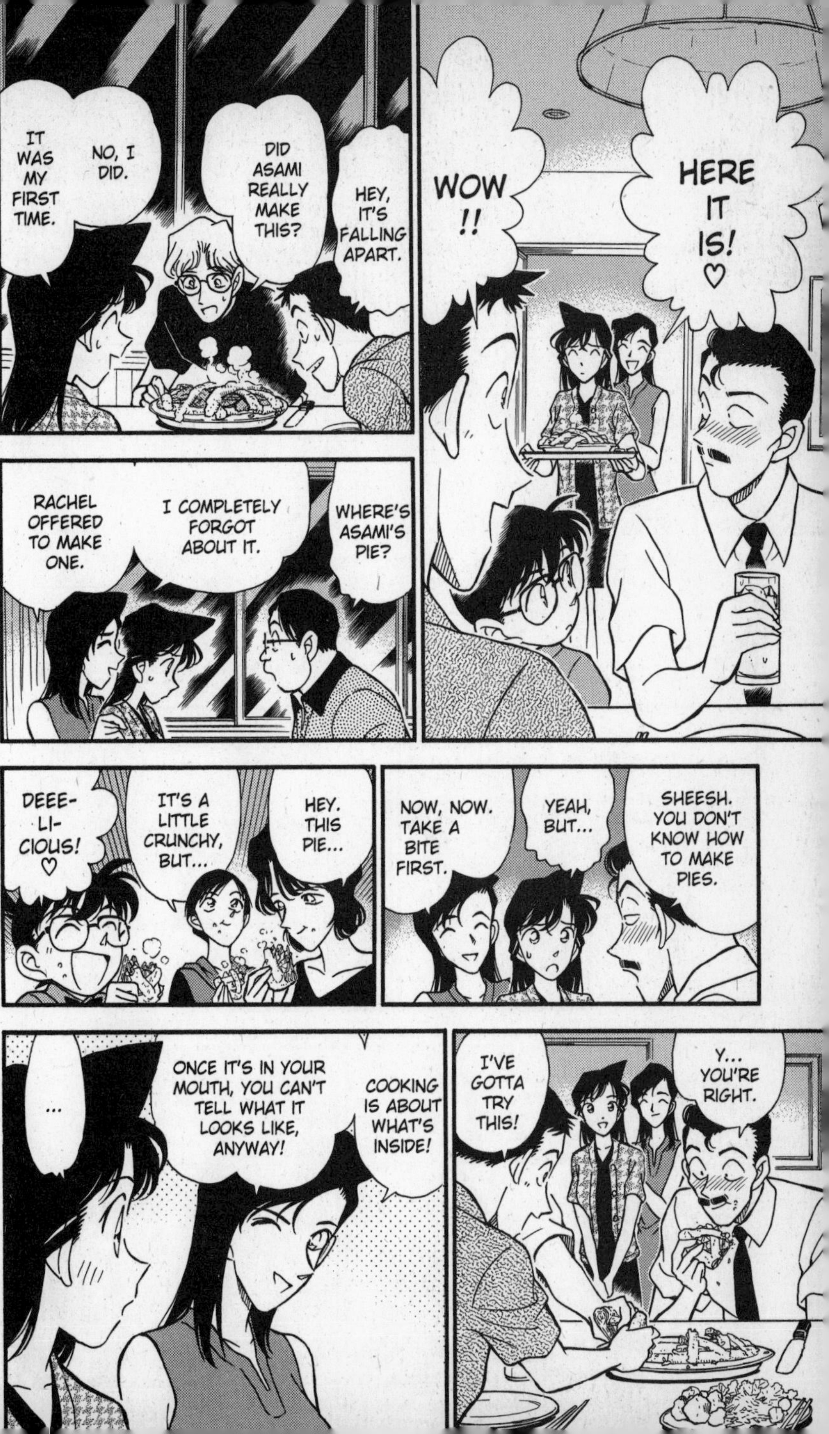
HERE IT IS! ♡
WOW!!
HEY, IT'S FALLING APART.
DID ASAMI REALLY MAKE THIS?
NO, I DID.
IT WAS MY FIRST TIME.
WHERE'S ASAMI'S PIE?
I COMPLETELY FORGOT ABOUT IT.
RACHEL OFFERED TO MAKE ONE.
SHEESH. YOU DON'T KNOW HOW TO MAKE PIES.
YEAH, BUT...
NOW, NOW. TAKE A BITE FIRST.
HEY. THIS PIE...
IT'S A LITTLE CRUNCHY, BUT...
DEEE-LI-CIOUS! ♡
Y... YOU'RE RIGHT.
I'VE GOTTA TRY THIS!
COOKING IS ABOUT WHAT'S INSIDE!
ONCE IT'S IN YOUR MOUTH, YOU CAN'T TELL WHAT IT LOOKS LIKE, ANYWAY!
...

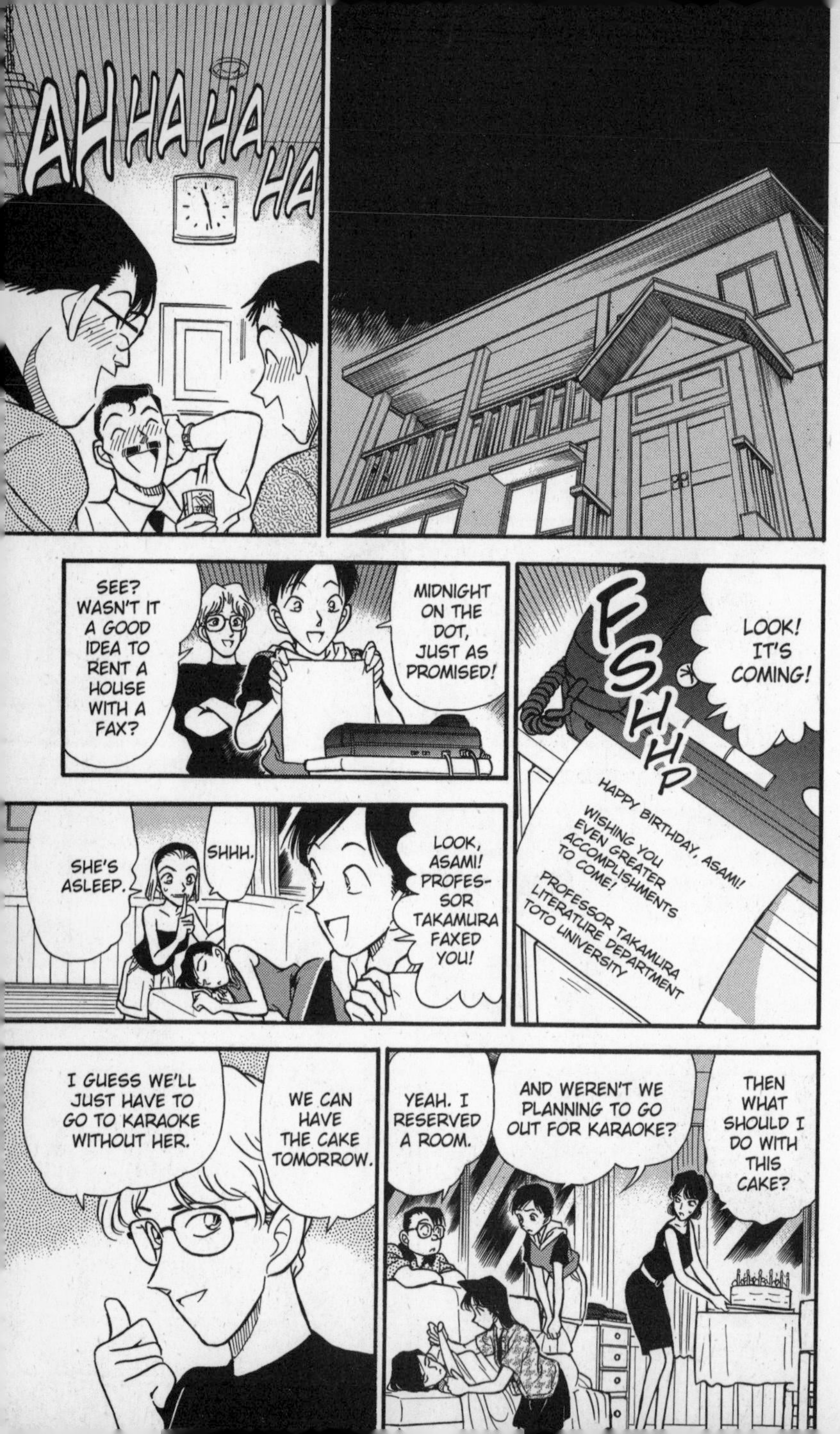
AHHAHAHA
HA
LOOK! IT'S COMING!
FSHHP
HAPPY BIRTHDAY, ASAMI!
WISHING YOU EVEN GREATER ACCOMPLISHMENTS TO COME!
PROFESSOR TAKAMURA
LITERATURE DEPARTMENT
TOTO UNIVERSITY
MIDNIGHT ON THE DOT, JUST AS PROMISED!
SEE? WASN'T IT A GOOD IDEA TO RENT A HOUSE WITH A FAX?
LOOK, ASAMI! PROFESSOR TAKAMURA FAXED YOU!
SHHH.
SHE'S ASLEEP.
THEN WHAT SHOULD I DO WITH THIS CAKE?
AND WEREN'T WE PLANNING TO GO OUT FOR KARAOKE?
YEAH. I RESERVED A ROOM.
WE CAN HAVE THE CAKE TOMORROW.
I GUESS WE'LL JUST HAVE TO GO TO KARAOKE WITHOUT HER.

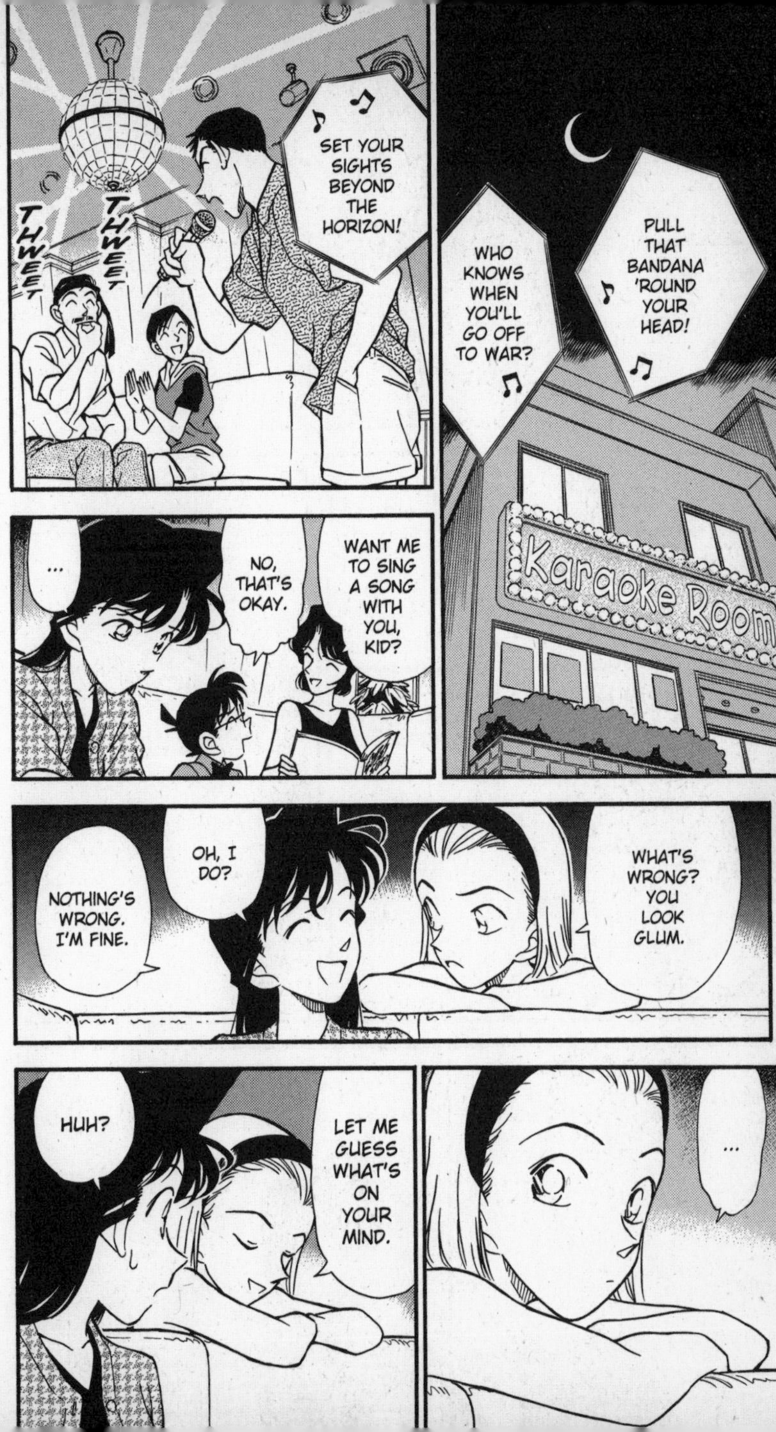
PULL THAT BANDANA 'ROUND YOUR HEAD!
WHO KNOWS WHEN YOU'LL GO OFF TO WAR?
Karaoke Room
SET YOUR SIGHTS BEYOND THE HORIZON!
THWEET
THWEET
WANT ME TO SING A SONG WITH YOU, KID?
NO, THAT'S OKAY.
...
WHAT'S WRONG? YOU LOOK GLUM.
OH, I DO?
NOTHING'S WRONG. I'M FINE.
...
LET ME GUESS WHAT'S ON YOUR MIND.
HUH?

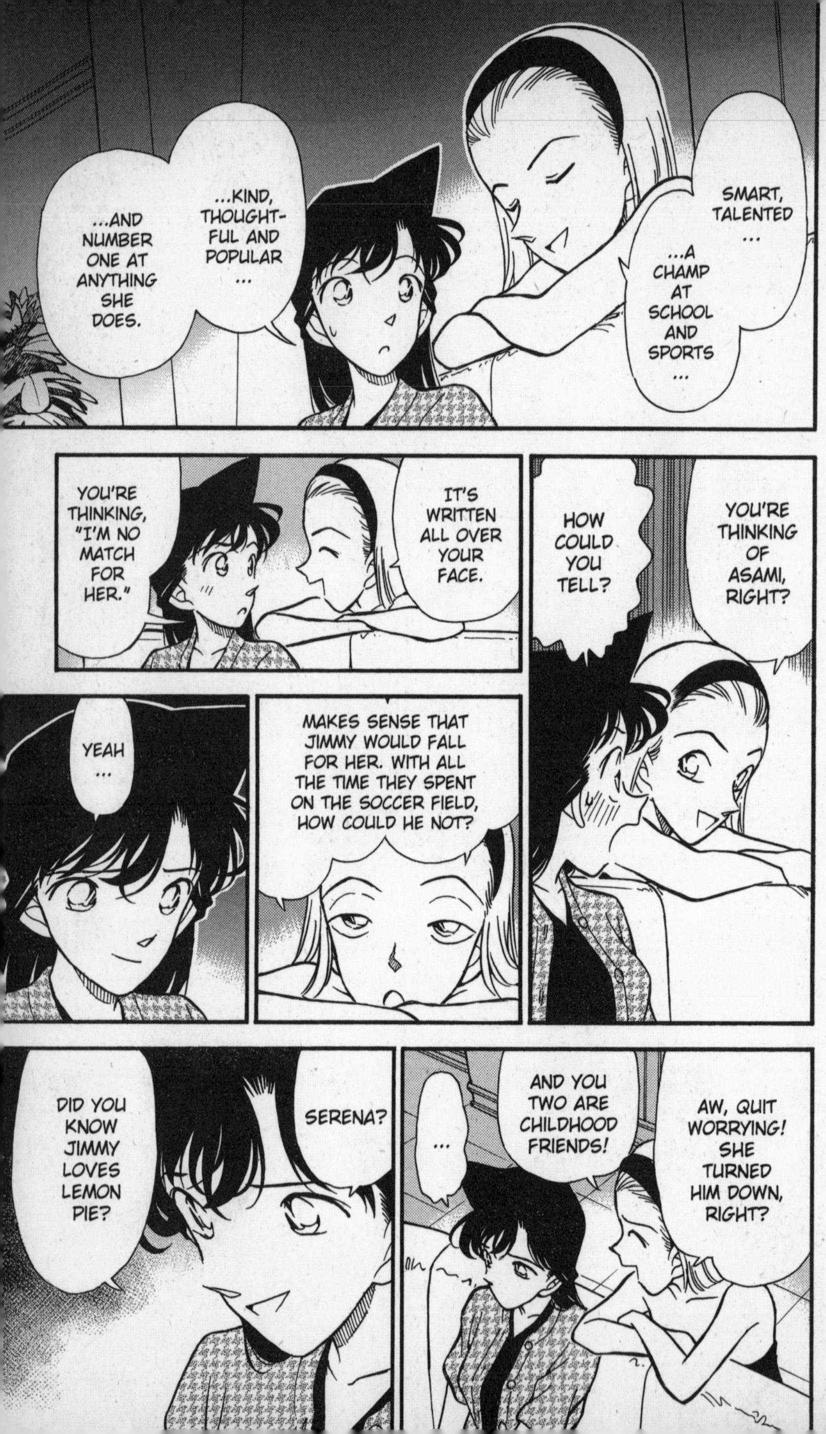
SMART, TALENTED ...
...A CHAMP AT SCHOOL AND SPORTS ...
...KIND, THOUGHT-FUL AND POPULAR ...
...AND NUMBER ONE AT ANYTHING SHE DOES.
YOU'RE THINKING OF ASAMI, RIGHT?
HOW COULD YOU TELL?
IT'S WRITTEN ALL OVER YOUR FACE.
YOU'RE THINKING, "I'M NO MATCH FOR HER."
MAKES SENSE THAT JIMMY WOULD FALL FOR HER. WITH ALL THE TIME THEY SPENT ON THE SOCCER FIELD, HOW COULD HE NOT?
YEAH ...
AW, QUIT WORRYING! SHE TURNED HIM DOWN, RIGHT?
AND YOU TWO ARE CHILDHOOD FRIENDS!
...
SERENA?
DID YOU KNOW JIMMY LOVES LEMON PIE?

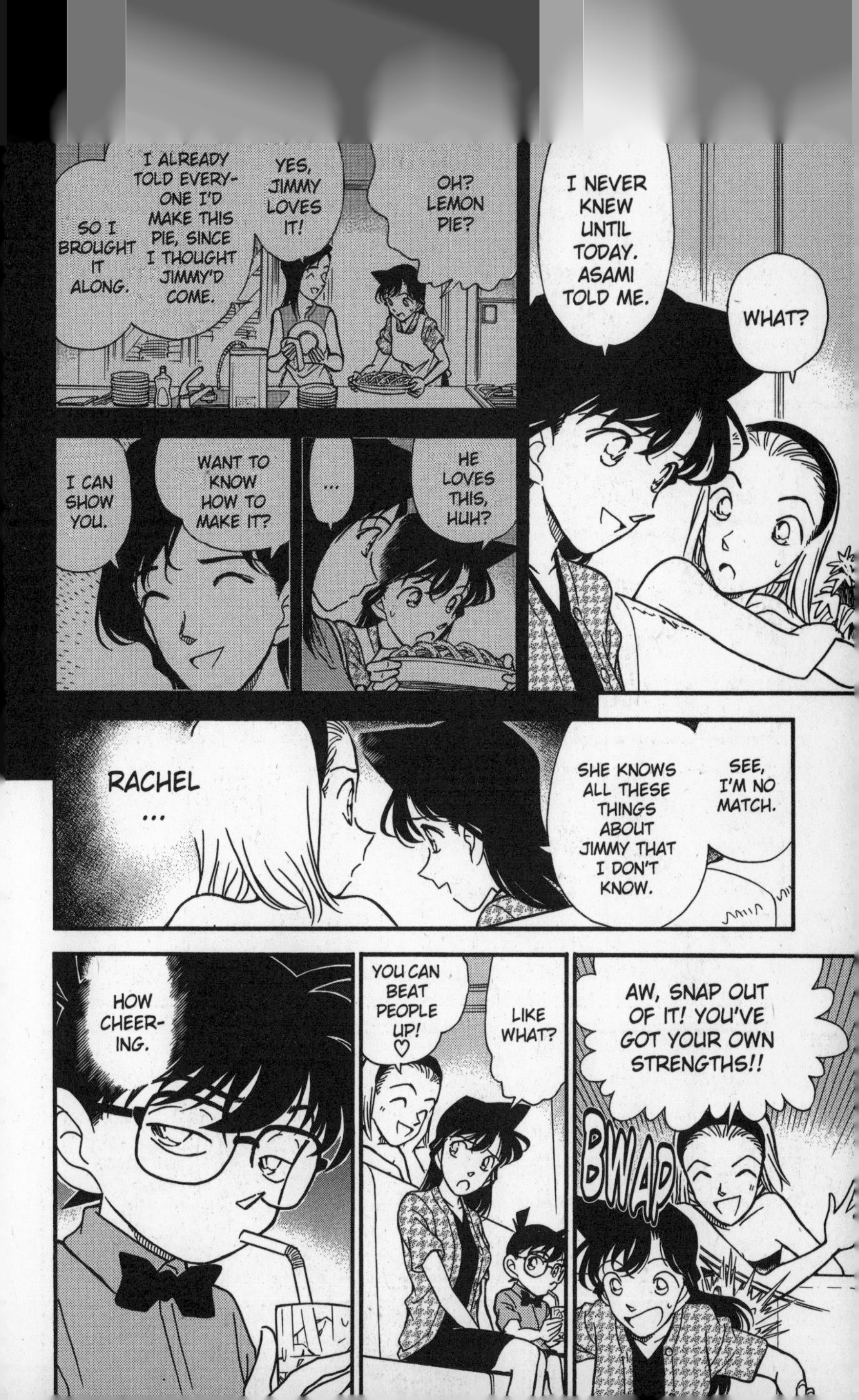
I NEVER KNEW UNTIL TODAY. ASAMI TOLD ME.
WHAT?
OH? LEMON PIE?
YES, JIMMY LOVES IT!
I ALREADY TOLD EVERY-ONE I'D MAKE THIS PIE, SINCE I THOUGHT JIMMY'D COME.
SO I BROUGHT IT ALONG.
HE LOVES THIS, HUH?
...
WANT TO KNOW HOW TO MAKE IT?
I CAN SHOW YOU.
SEE, I'M NO MATCH.
SHE KNOWS ALL THESE THINGS ABOUT JIMMY THAT I DON'T KNOW.
RACHEL ...
AW, SNAP OUT OF IT! YOU'VE GOT YOUR OWN STRENGTHS!!
BWAP
LIKE WHAT?
YOU CAN BEAT PEOPLE UP! ♡
HOW CHEER-ING.

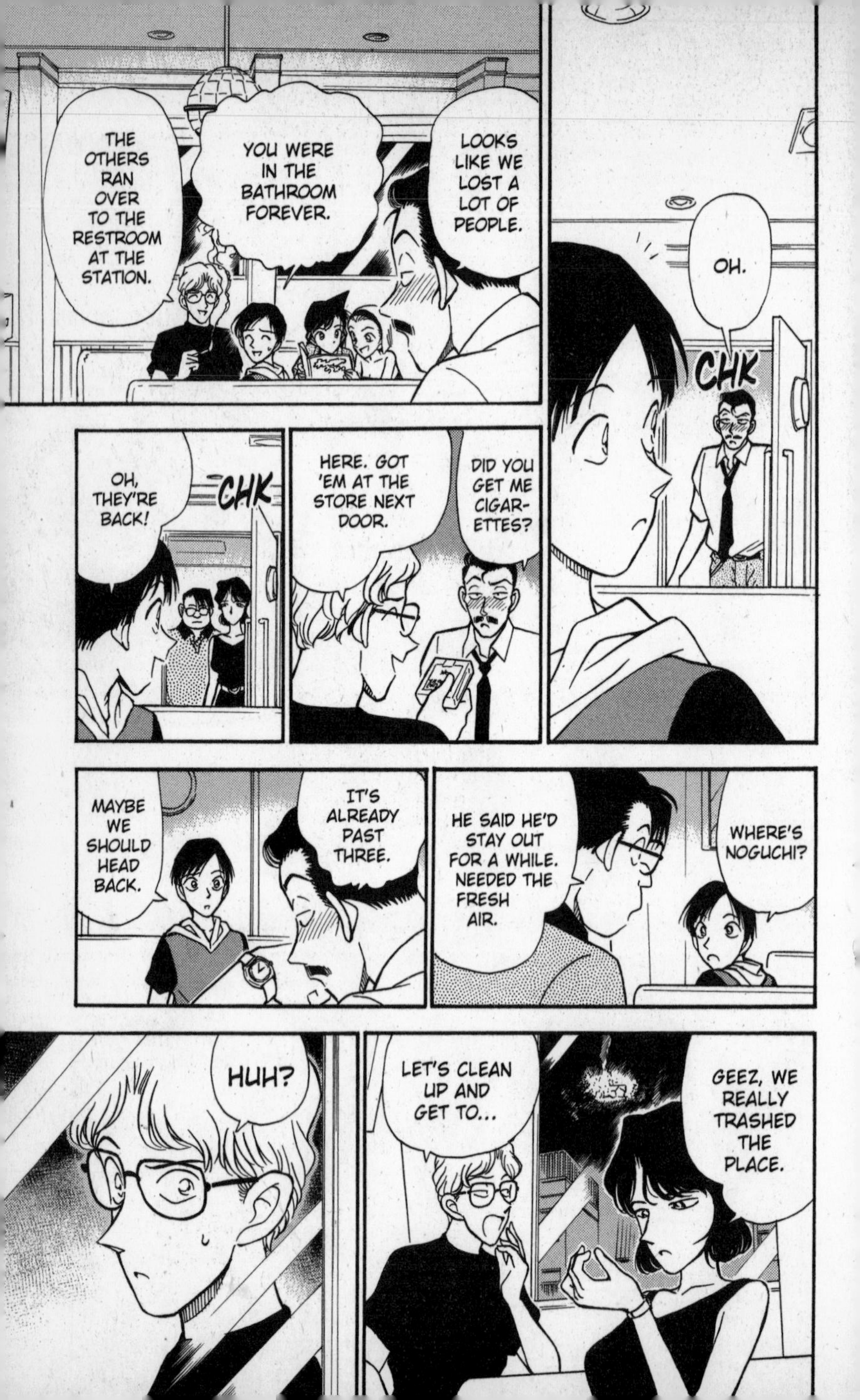
OH.
CHK
LOOKS LIKE WE LOST A LOT OF PEOPLE.
YOU WERE IN THE BATHROOM FOREVER.
THE OTHERS RAN OVER TO THE RESTROOM AT THE STATION.
DID YOU GET ME CIGARETTES?
HERE. GOT 'EM AT THE STORE NEXT DOOR.
CHK
OH, THEY'RE BACK!
WHERE'S NOGUCHI?
HE SAID HE'D STAY OUT FOR A WHILE. NEEDED THE FRESH AIR.
IT'S ALREADY PAST THREE.
MAYBE WE SHOULD HEAD BACK.
GEEZ, WE REALLY TRASHED THE PLACE.
LET'S CLEAN UP AND GET TO...
HUH?

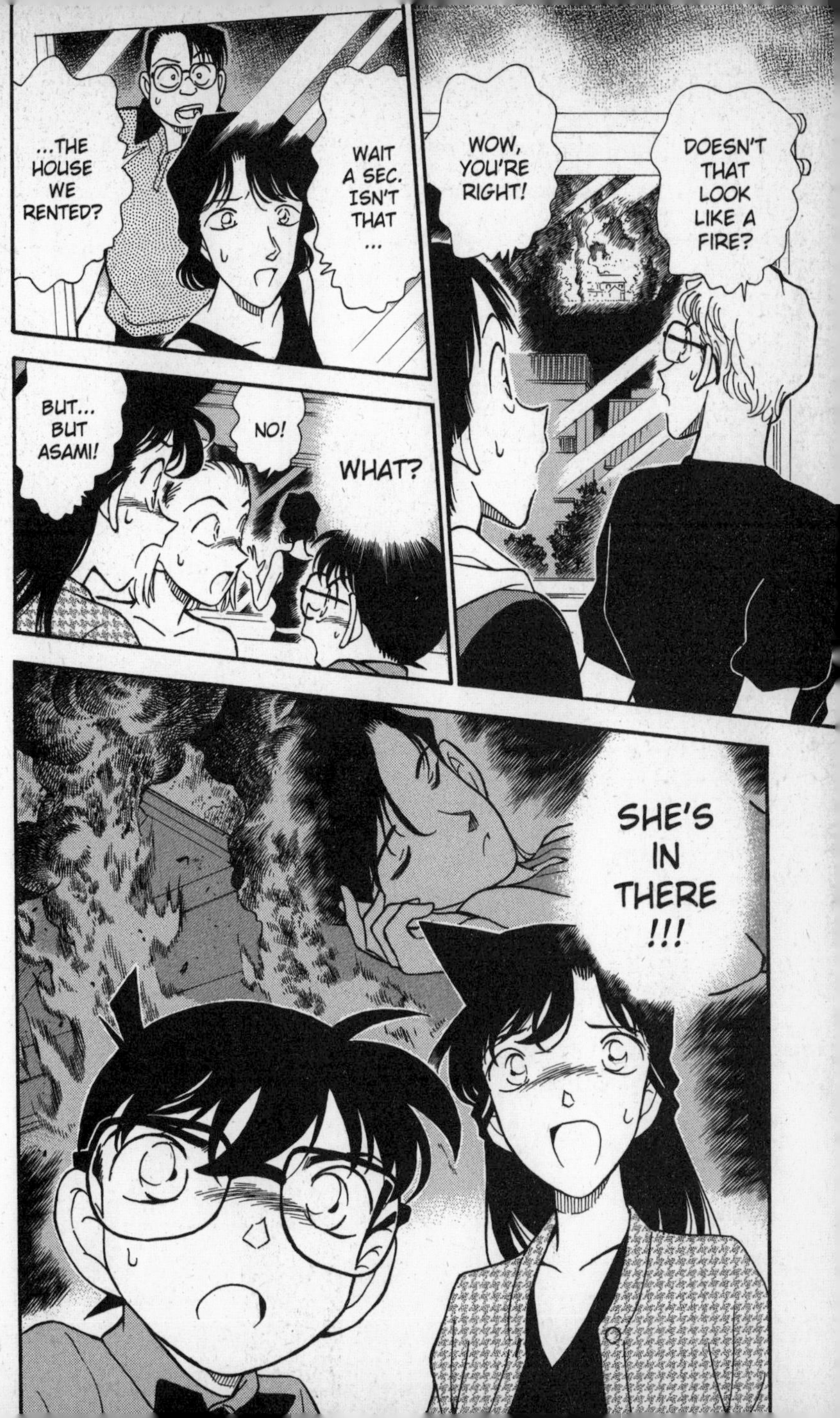
DOESN'T THAT LOOK LIKE A FIRE?
WOW, YOU'RE RIGHT!
WAIT A SEC. ISN'T THAT ...
...THE HOUSE WE RENTED?
WHAT?
NO!
BUT... BUT ASAMI!
SHE'S IN THERE !!!

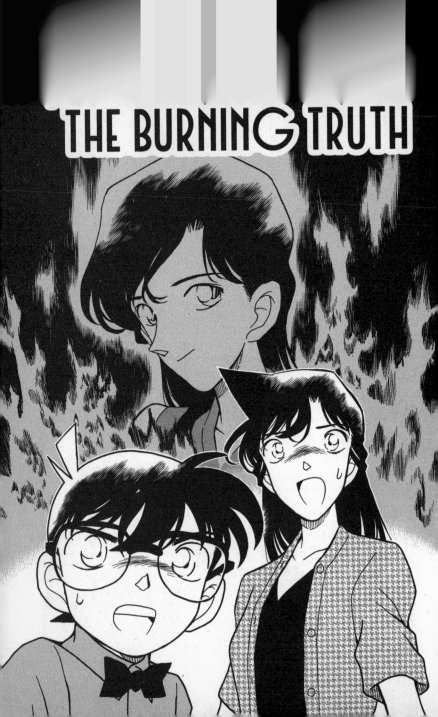

THE BURNING TRUTH

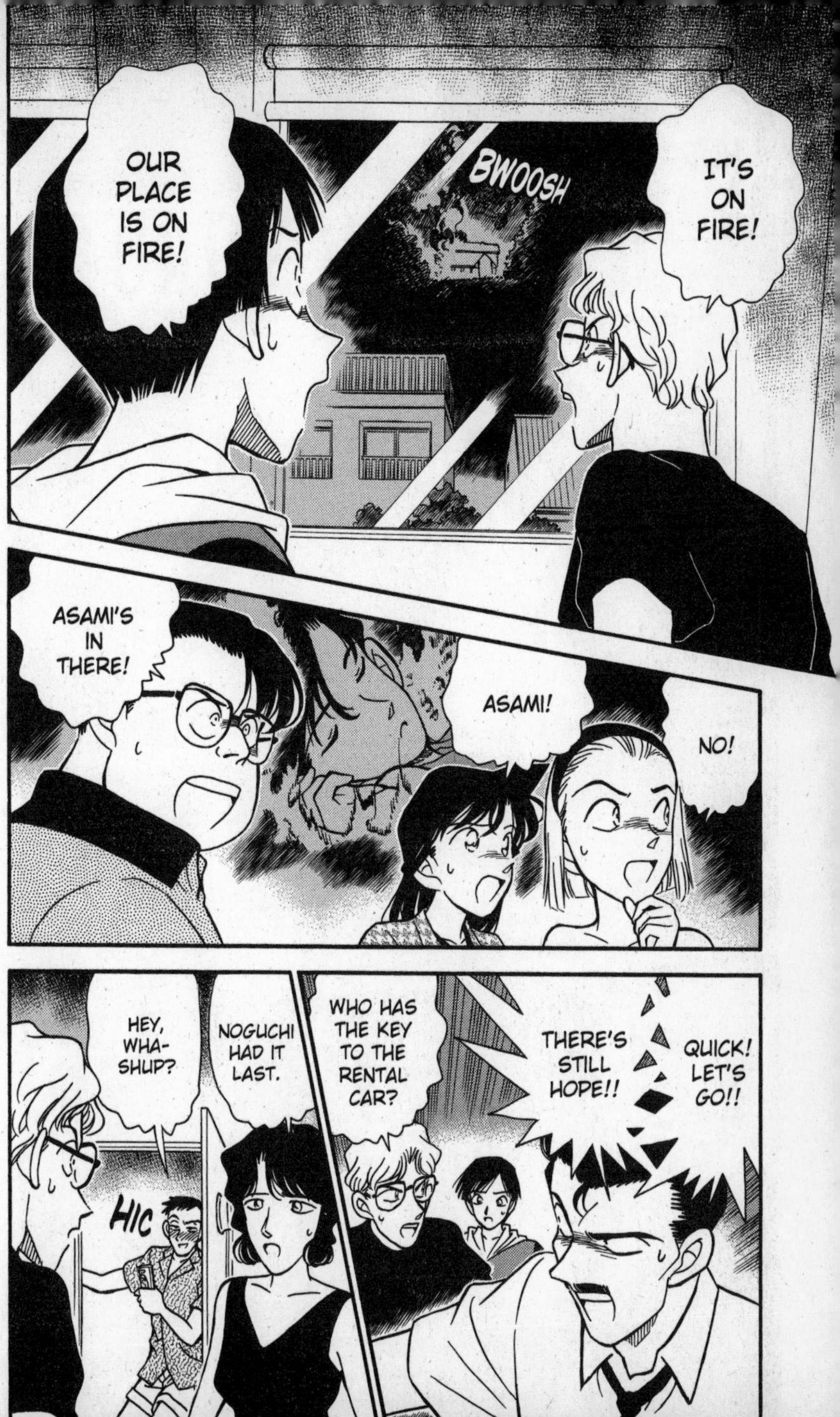
IT'S ON FIRE!
BWOOSH
OUR PLACE IS ON FIRE!
NO!
ASAMI!
ASAMI'S IN THERE!
QUICK! LET'S GO!!
THERE'S STILL HOPE!!
WHO HAS THE KEY TO THE RENTAL CAR?
NOGUCHI HAD IT LAST.
HEY, WHA-SHUP?
HIC

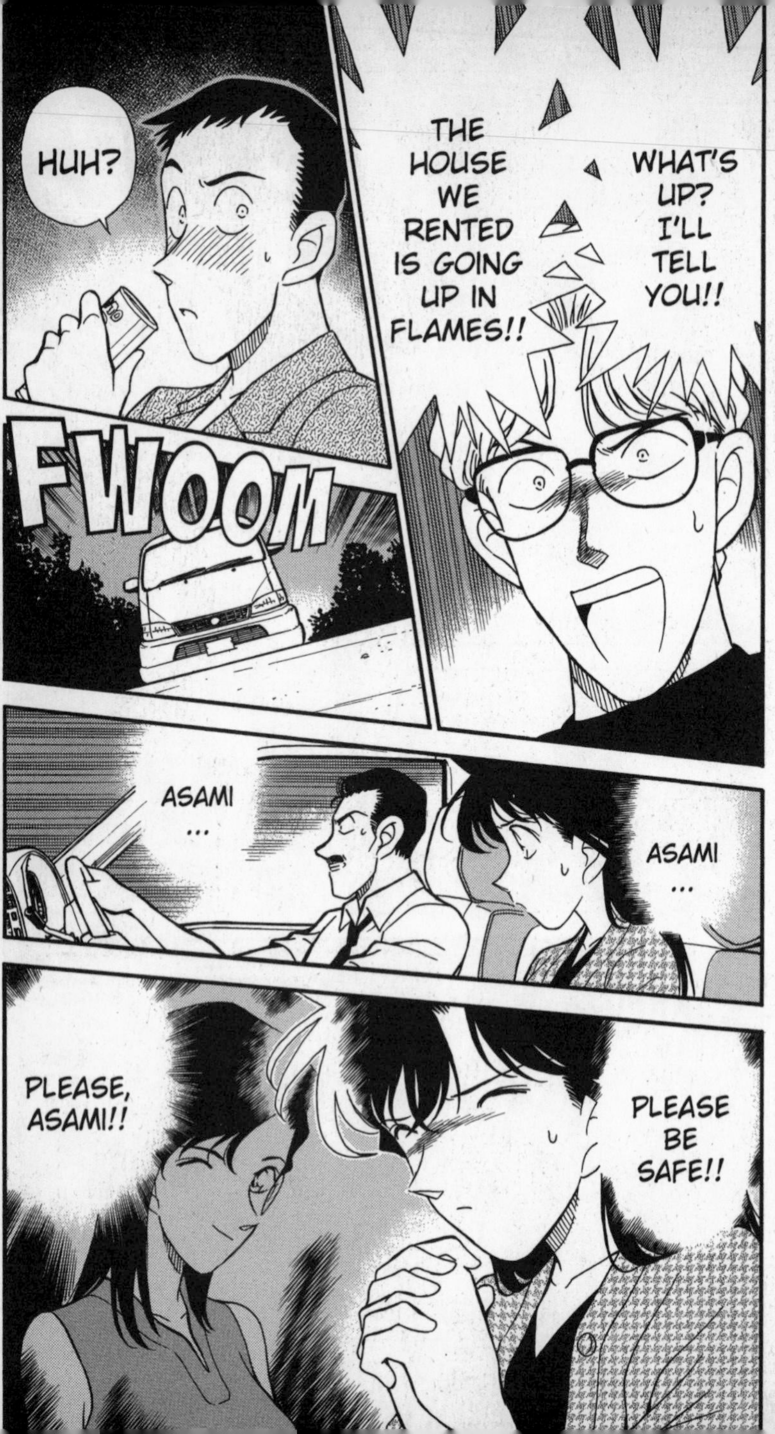
WHAT'S UP? I'LL TELL YOU!!
THE HOUSE WE RENTED IS GOING UP IN FLAMES!!
HUH?
FWOOM
ASAMI ...
ASAMI ...
PLEASE BE SAFE!!
PLEASE, ASAMI!!

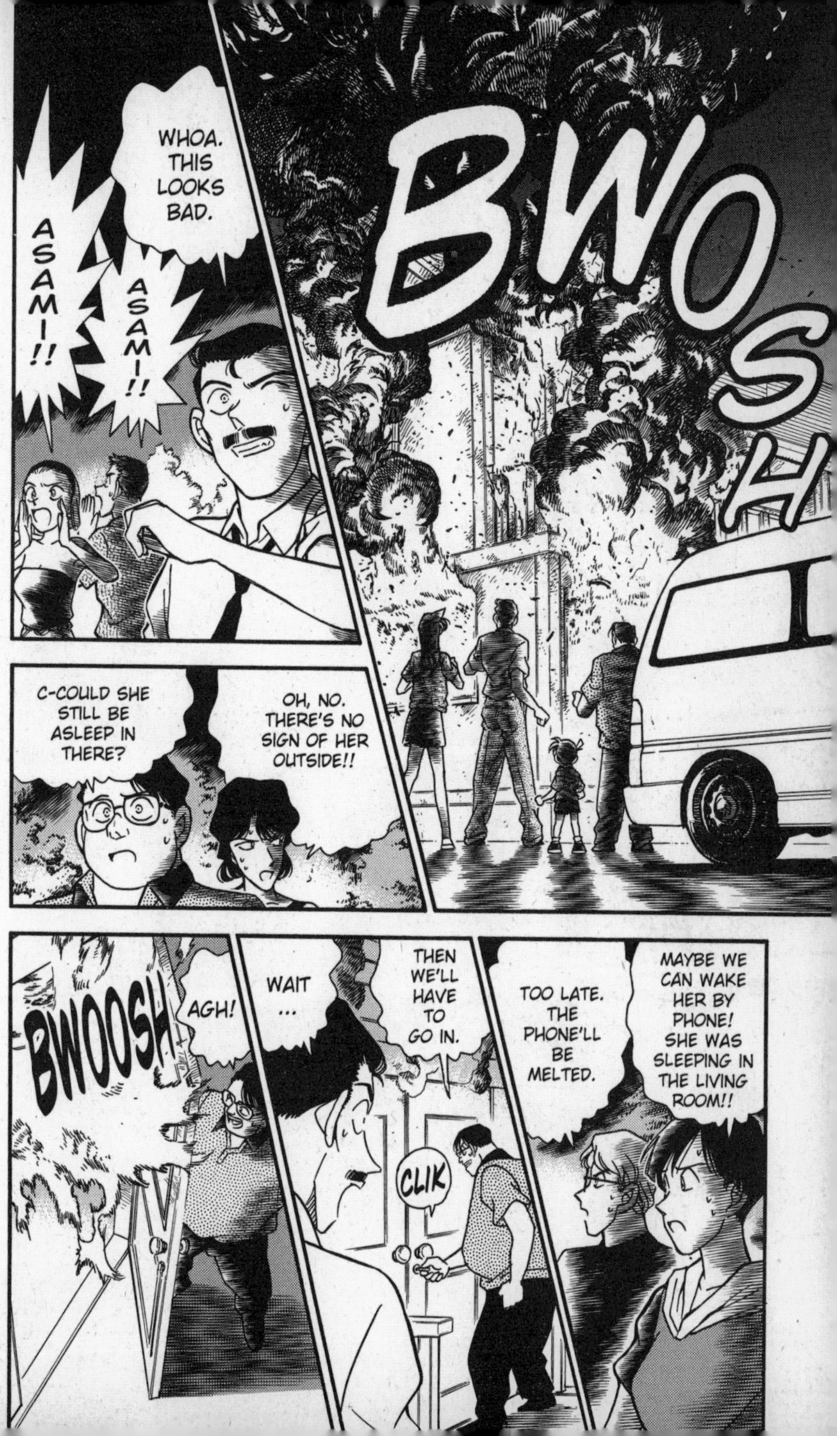
BWOSH
WHOA. THIS LOOKS BAD.
ASAMI!!
ASAMI!!
OH, NO. THERE'S NO SIGN OF HER OUTSIDE!!
C-COULD SHE STILL BE ASLEEP IN THERE?
MAYBE WE CAN WAKE HER BY PHONE! SHE WAS SLEEPING IN THE LIVING ROOM!!
TOO LATE. THE PHONE'LL BE MELTED.
THEN WE'LL HAVE TO GO IN.
WAIT ...
CLIK
AGH!
BWOOSH

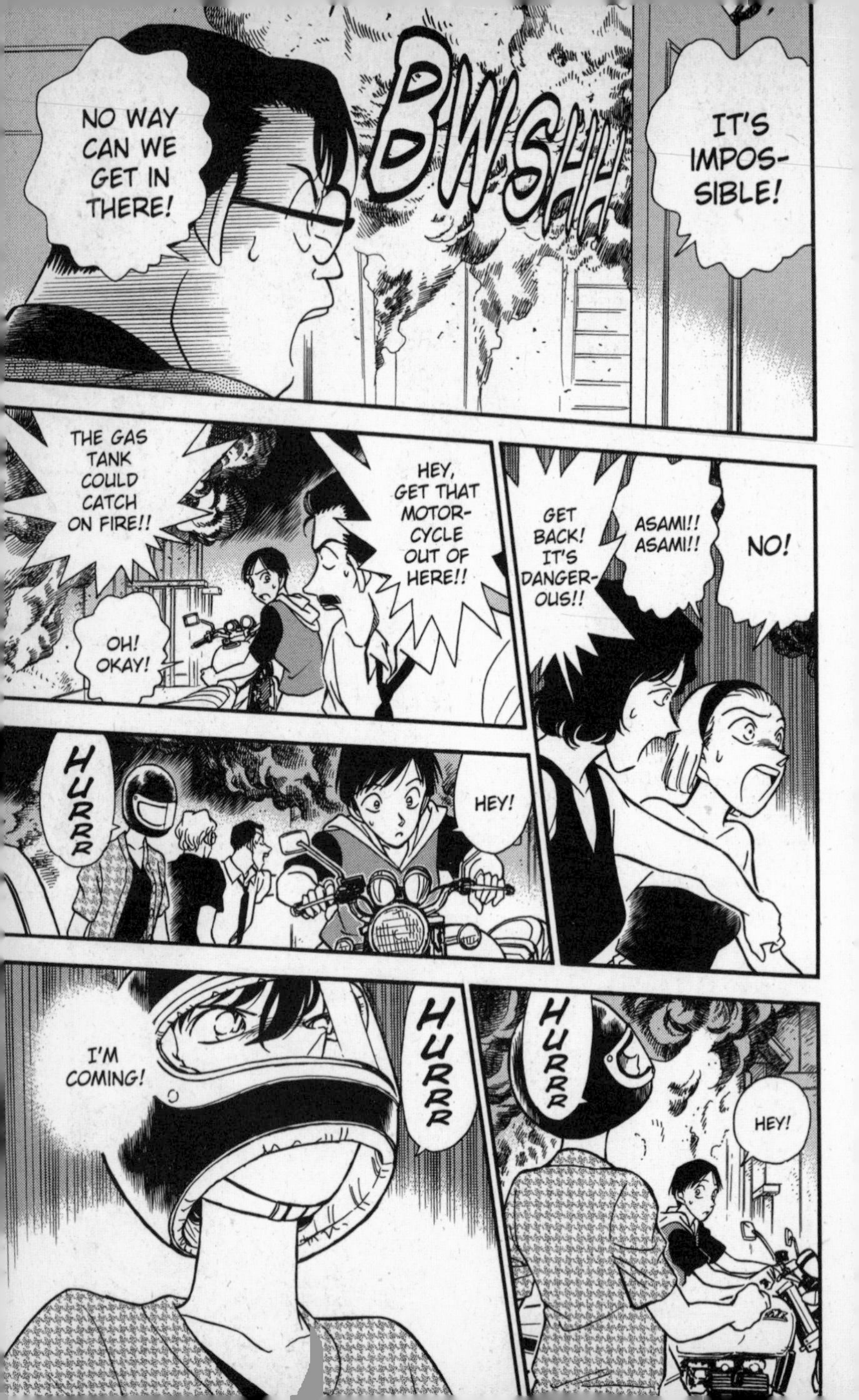
IT'S IMPOSSIBLE!
BWSHH
NO WAY CAN WE GET IN THERE!
NO!
ASAMI!! ASAMI!!
GET BACK! IT'S DANGEROUS!!
HEY, GET THAT MOTORCYCLE OUT OF HERE!!
THE GAS TANK COULD CATCH ON FIRE!!
OH! OKAY!
HEY!
HURRR
HURRR
HEY!
HURRR
I'M COMING!

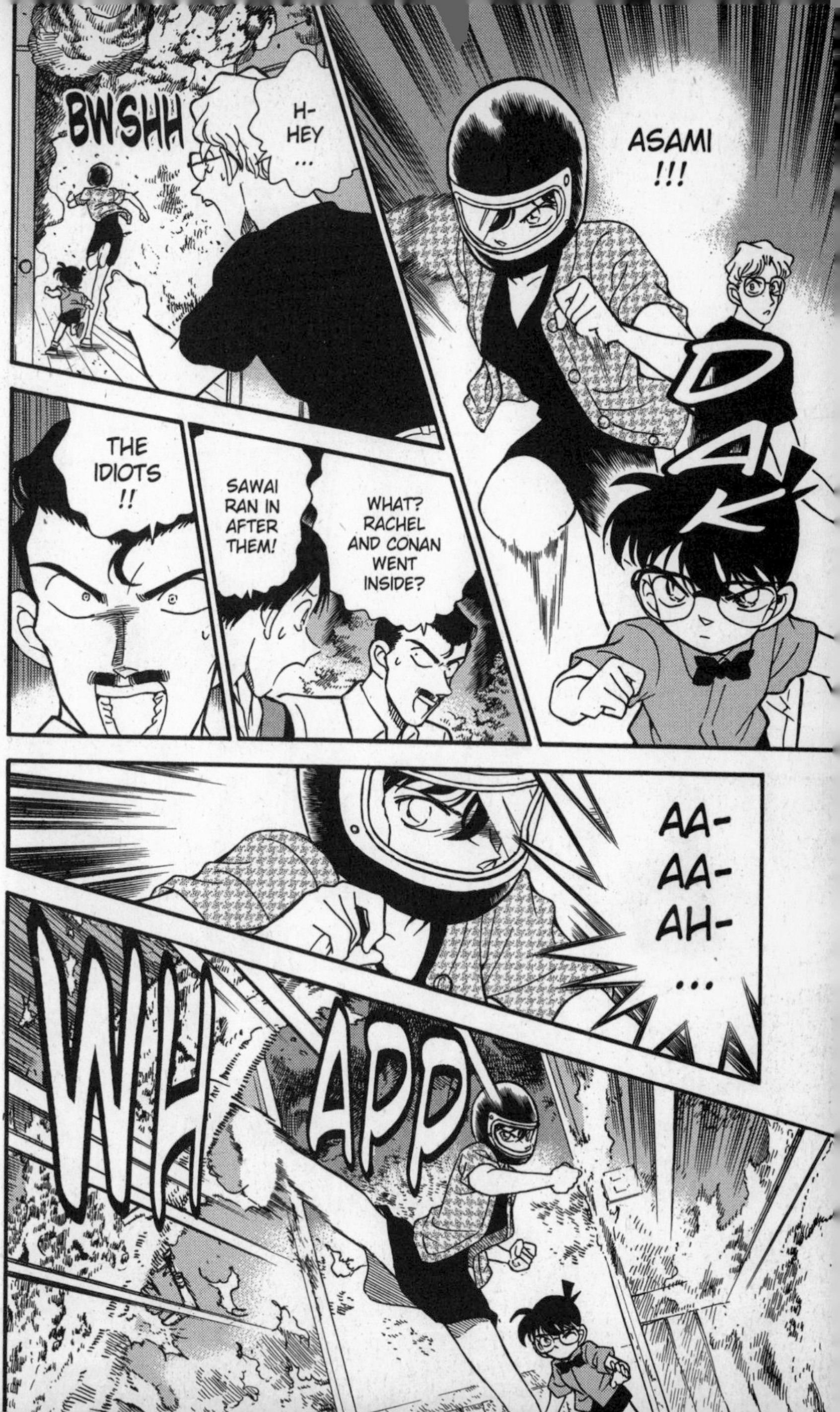
ASAMI !!!
DAK
H-HEY ...
BWSHH
WHAT? RACHEL AND CONAN WENT INSIDE?
SAWAI RAN IN AFTER THEM!
THE IDIOTS !!
AA-AA-AH- ...
WHAPP

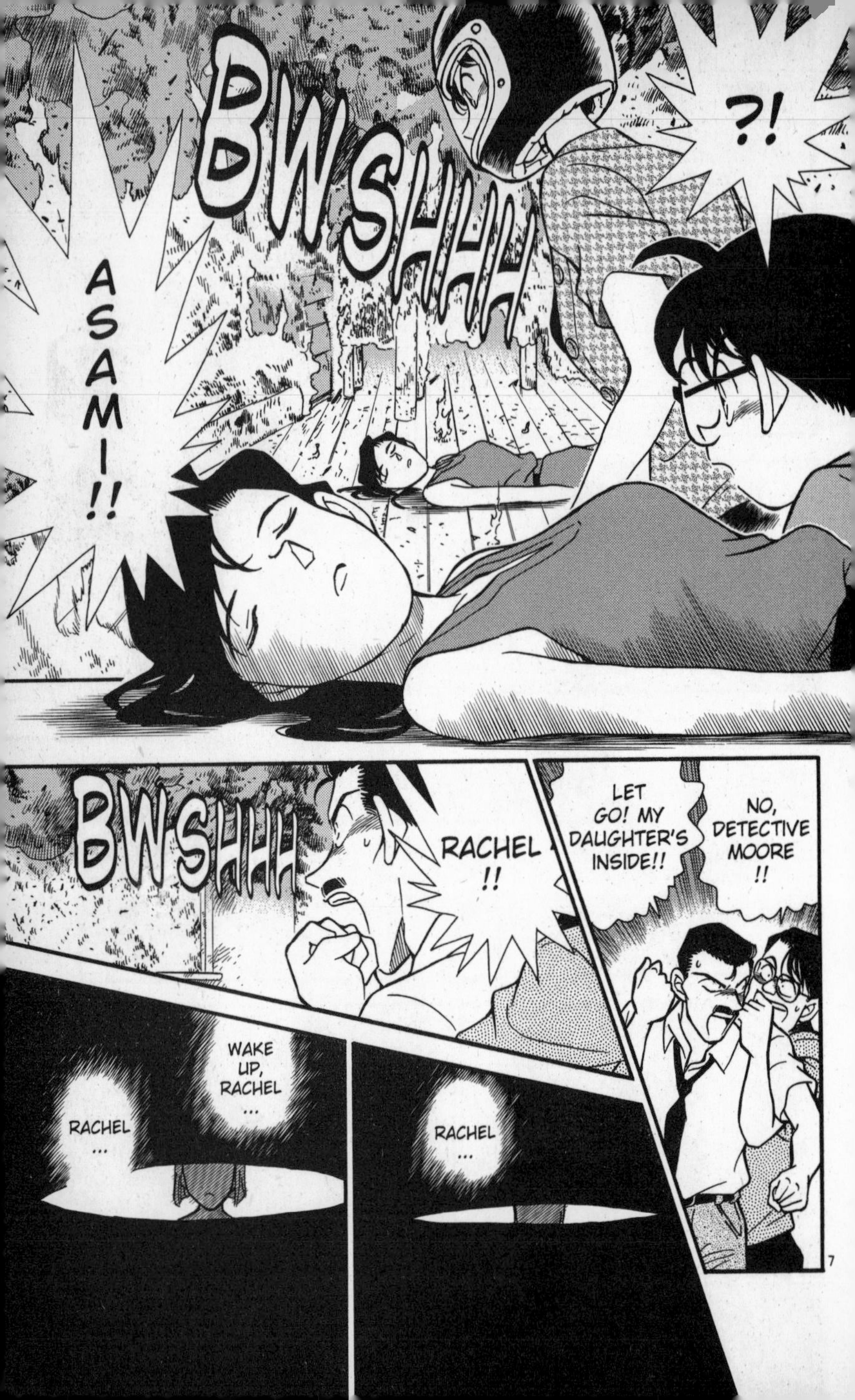

BWSHHH
?!
ASAMI!!
BWSHHH
RACHEL!!
NO, DETECTIVE MOORE!!
LET GO! MY DAUGHTER'S INSIDE!!
WAKE UP, RACHEL...
RACHEL...
RACHEL...

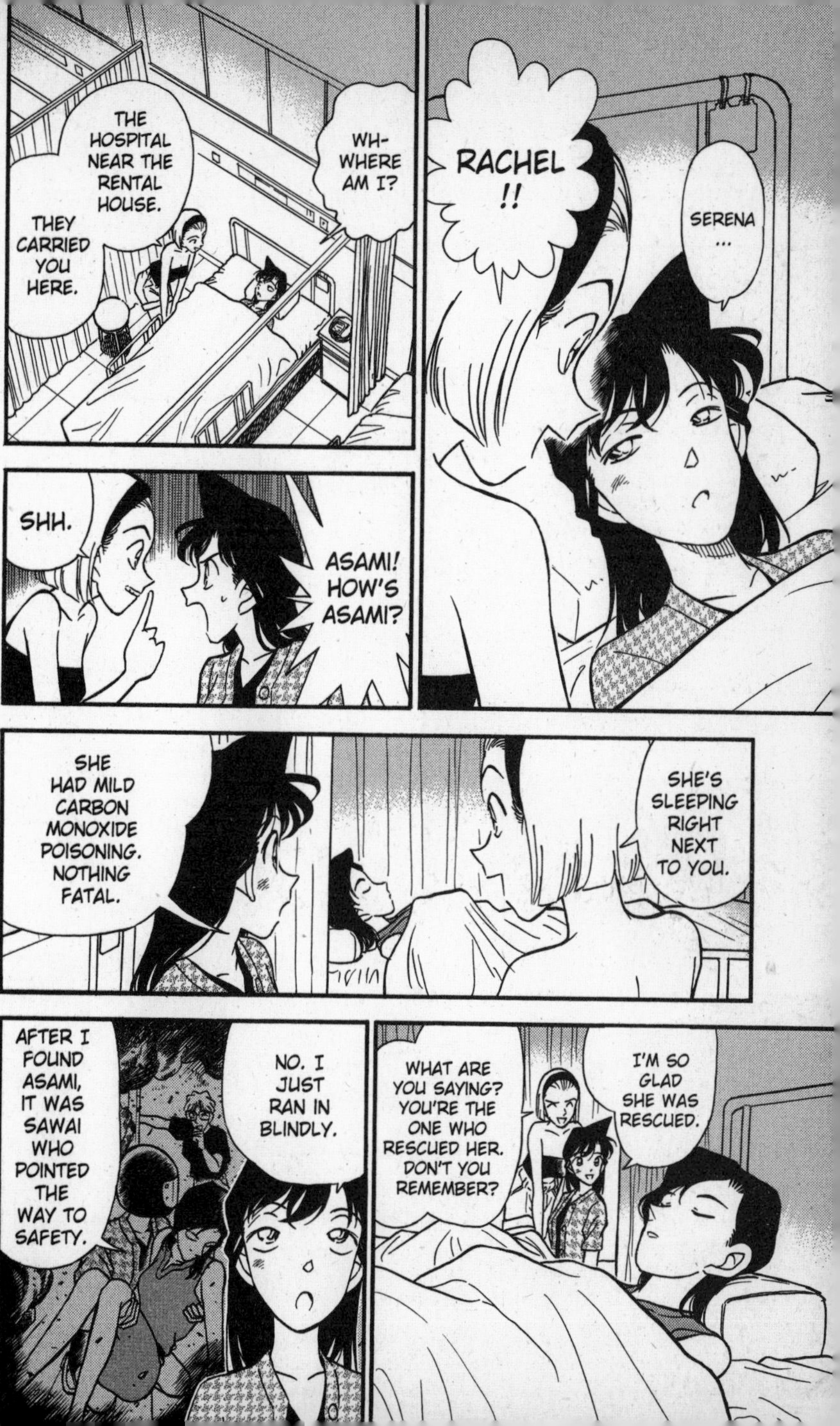
RACHEL !!
SERENA ...
WH- WHERE AM I?
THE HOSPITAL NEAR THE RENTAL HOUSE.
THEY CARRIED YOU HERE.
ASAMI! HOW'S ASAMI?
SHH.
SHE'S SLEEPING RIGHT NEXT TO YOU.
SHE HAD MILD CARBON MONOXIDE POISONING. NOTHING FATAL.
I'M SO GLAD SHE WAS RESCUED.
WHAT ARE YOU SAYING? YOU'RE THE ONE WHO RESCUED HER. DON'T YOU REMEMBER?
NO. I JUST RAN IN BLINDLY.
AFTER I FOUND ASAMI, IT WAS SAWAI WHO POINTED THE WAY TO SAFETY.

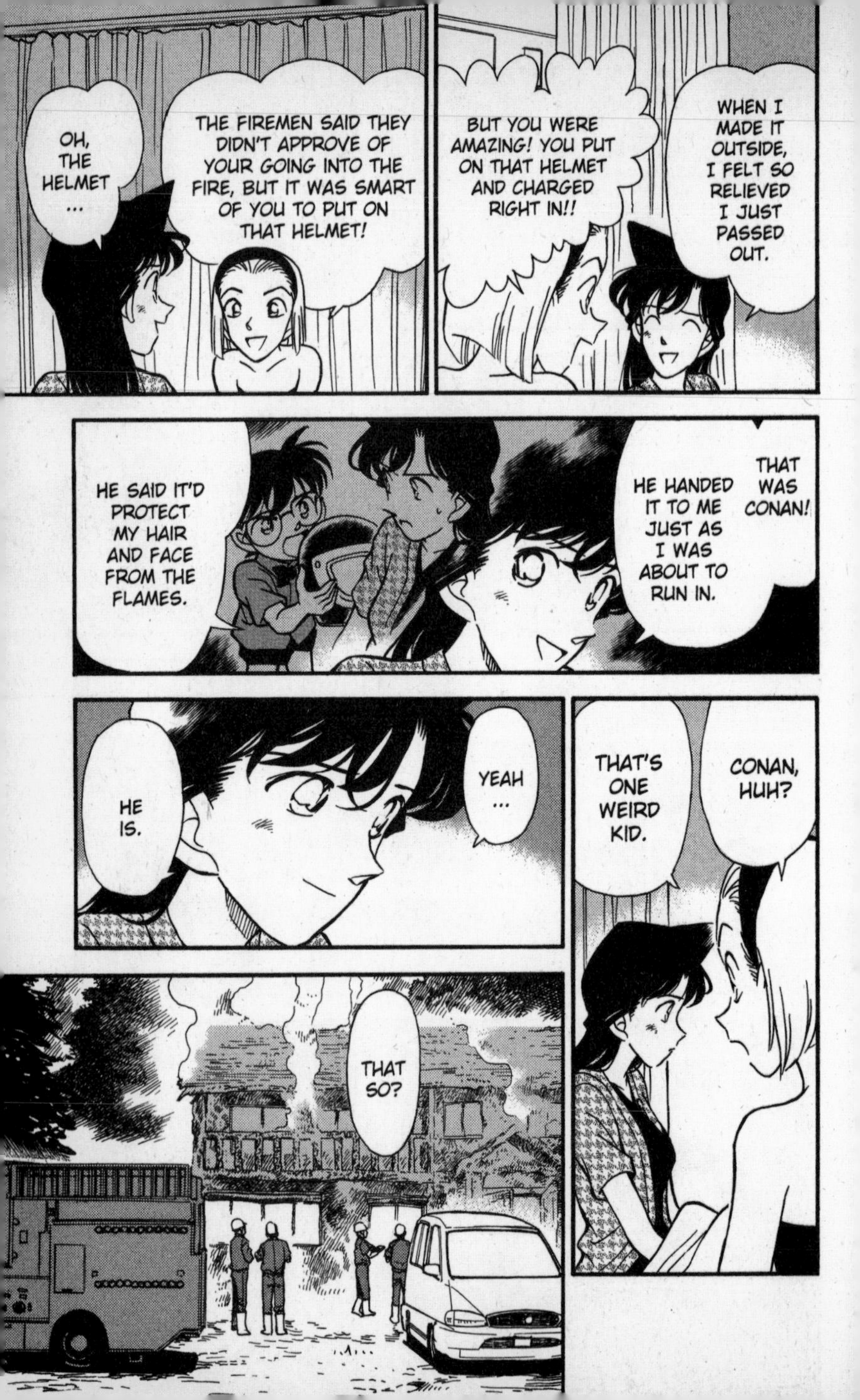
WHEN I MADE IT OUTSIDE, I FELT SO RELIEVED I JUST PASSED OUT.
BUT YOU WERE AMAZING! YOU PUT ON THAT HELMET AND CHARGED RIGHT IN!!
THE FIREMEN SAID THEY DIDN'T APPROVE OF YOUR GOING INTO THE FIRE, BUT IT WAS SMART OF YOU TO PUT ON THAT HELMET!
OH, THE HELMET ...
THAT WAS CONAN!
HE HANDED IT TO ME JUST AS I WAS ABOUT TO RUN IN.
HE SAID IT'D PROTECT MY HAIR AND FACE FROM THE FLAMES.
CONAN, HUH?
THAT'S ONE WEIRD KID.
YEAH ...
HE IS.
THAT SO?

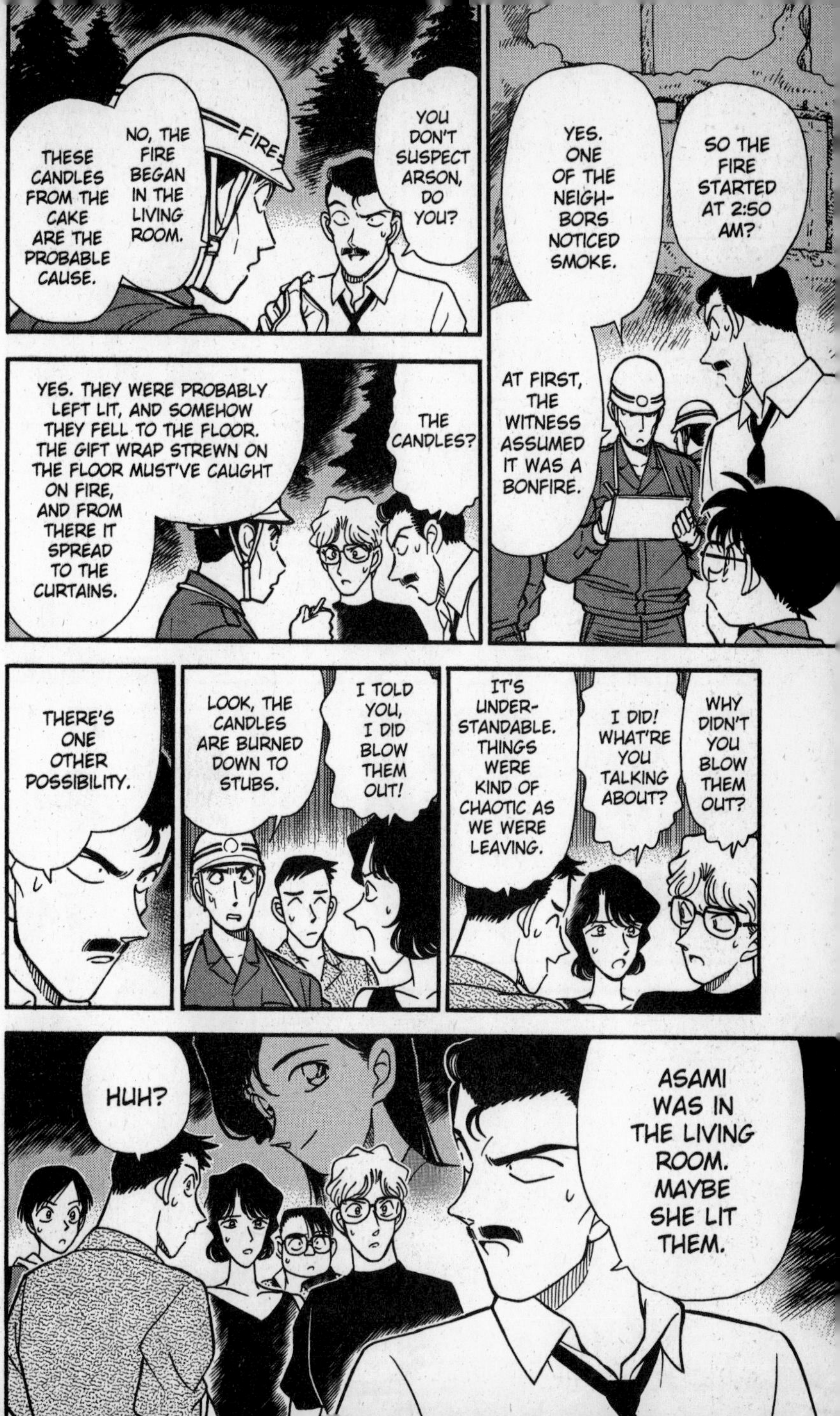
SO THE FIRE STARTED AT 2:50 AM?
YES. ONE OF THE NEIGHBORS NOTICED SMOKE.
AT FIRST, THE WITNESS ASSUMED IT WAS A BONFIRE.
YOU DON'T SUSPECT ARSON, DO YOU?
NO, THE FIRE BEGAN IN THE LIVING ROOM.
THESE CANDLES FROM THE CAKE ARE THE PROBABLE CAUSE.
THE CANDLES?
YES. THEY WERE PROBABLY LEFT LIT, AND SOMEHOW THEY FELL TO THE FLOOR. THE GIFT WRAP STREWN ON THE FLOOR MUST'VE CAUGHT ON FIRE, AND FROM THERE IT SPREAD TO THE CURTAINS.
WHY DIDN'T YOU BLOW THEM OUT?
I DID! WHAT'RE YOU TALKING ABOUT?
IT'S UNDERSTANDABLE. THINGS WERE KIND OF CHAOTIC AS WE WERE LEAVING.
I TOLD YOU, I DID BLOW THEM OUT!
LOOK, THE CANDLES ARE BURNED DOWN TO STUBS.
THERE'S ONE OTHER POSSIBILITY.
ASAMI WAS IN THE LIVING ROOM. MAYBE SHE LIT THEM.
HUH?

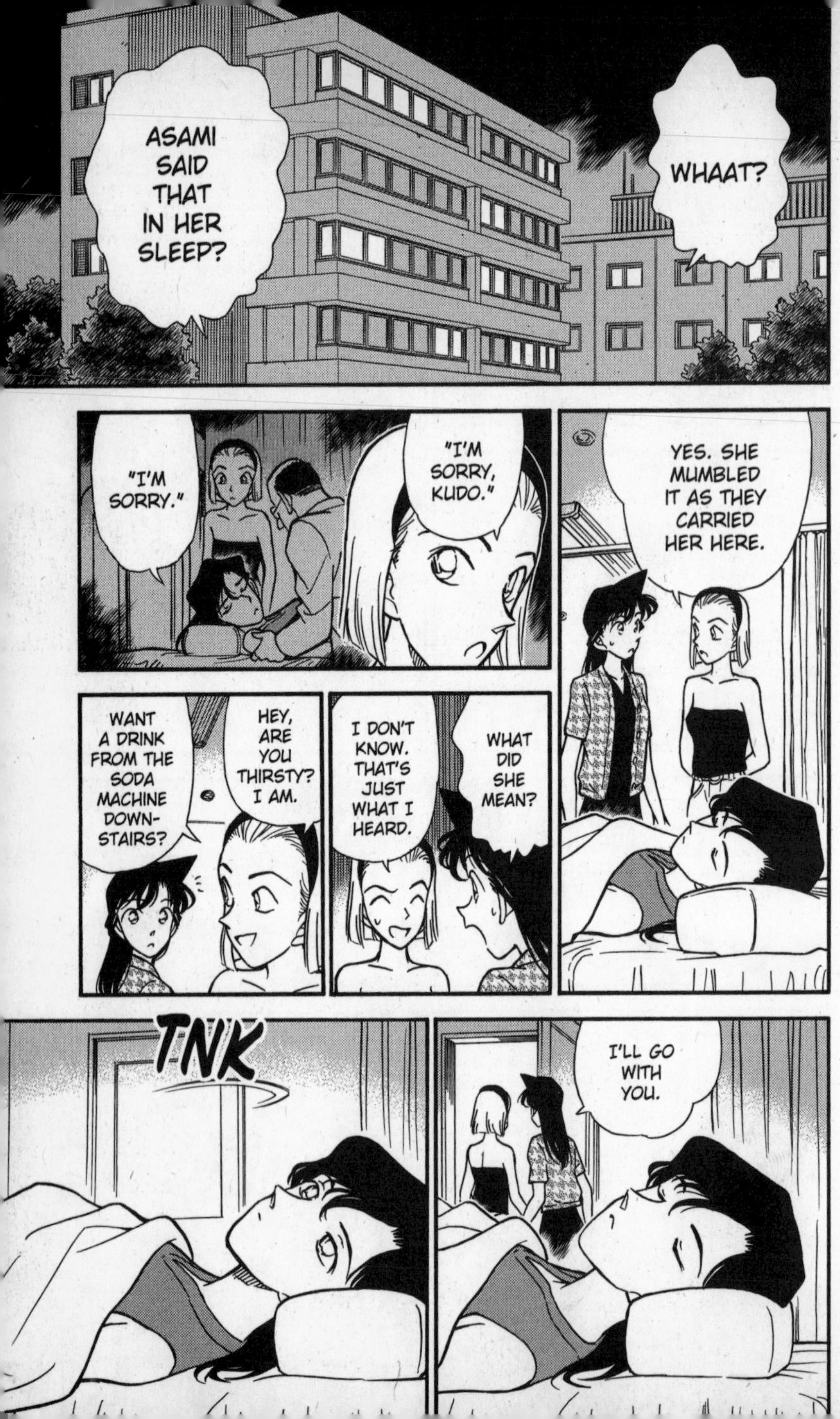
WHAAT?
ASAMI SAID THAT IN HER SLEEP?
YES. SHE MUMBLED IT AS THEY CARRIED HER HERE.
"I'M SORRY, KUDO."
"I'M SORRY."
WHAT DID SHE MEAN?
I DON'T KNOW. THAT'S JUST WHAT I HEARD.
HEY, ARE YOU THIRSTY? I AM.
WANT A DRINK FROM THE SODA MACHINE DOWN-STAIRS?
I'LL GO WITH YOU.
TNK

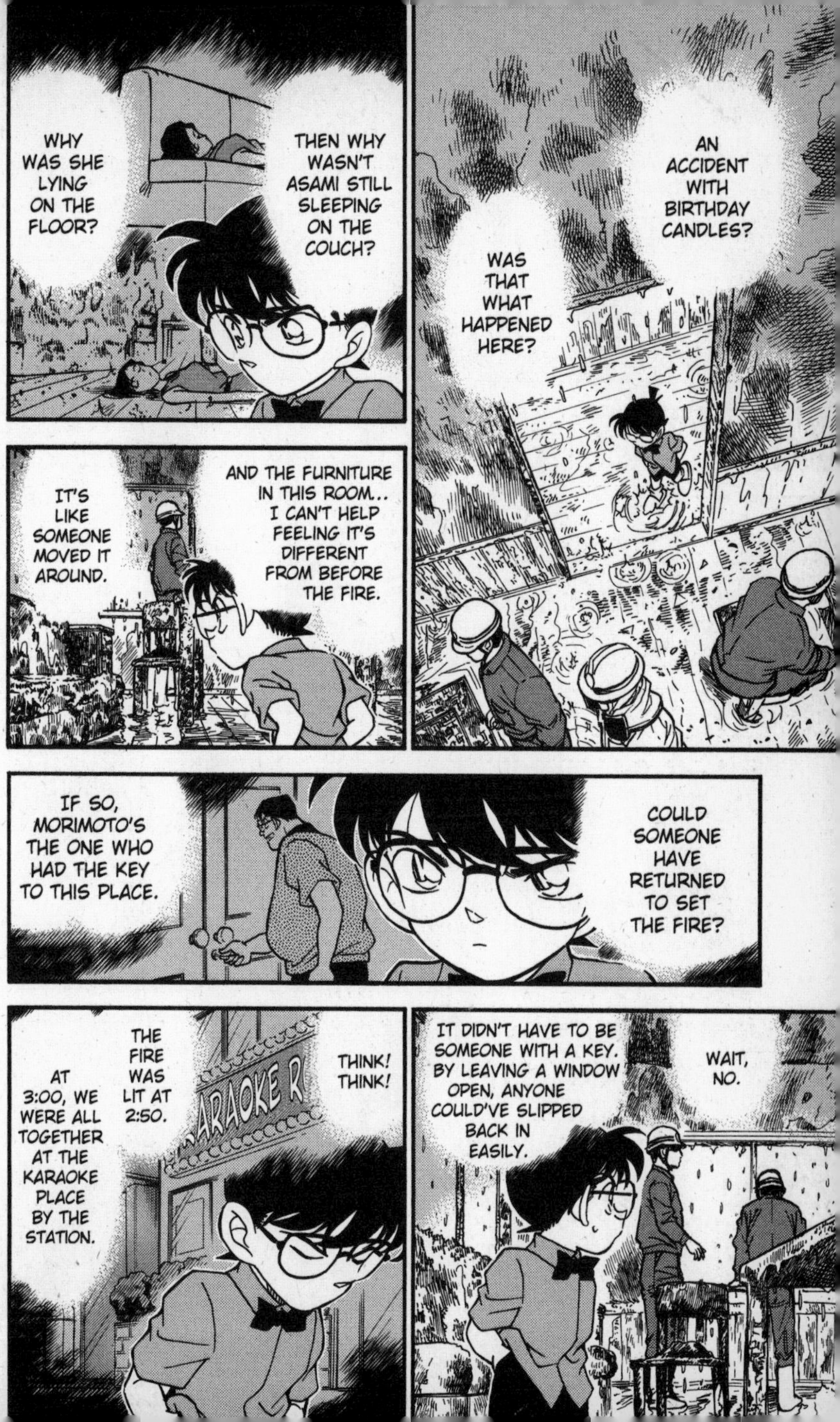
AN ACCIDENT WITH BIRTHDAY CANDLES?
WAS THAT WHAT HAPPENED HERE?
THEN WHY WASN'T ASAMI STILL SLEEPING ON THE COUCH?
WHY WAS SHE LYING ON THE FLOOR?
AND THE FURNITURE IN THIS ROOM... I CAN'T HELP FEELING IT'S DIFFERENT FROM BEFORE THE FIRE.
IT'S LIKE SOMEONE MOVED IT AROUND.
COULD SOMEONE HAVE RETURNED TO SET THE FIRE?
IF SO, MORIMOTO'S THE ONE WHO HAD THE KEY TO THIS PLACE.
WAIT, NO.
IT DIDN'T HAVE TO BE SOMEONE WITH A KEY. BY LEAVING A WINDOW OPEN, ANYONE COULD'VE SLIPPED BACK IN EASILY.
THINK! THINK!
THE FIRE WAS LIT AT 2:50.
AT 3:00, WE WERE ALL TOGETHER AT THE KARAOKE PLACE BY THE STATION.

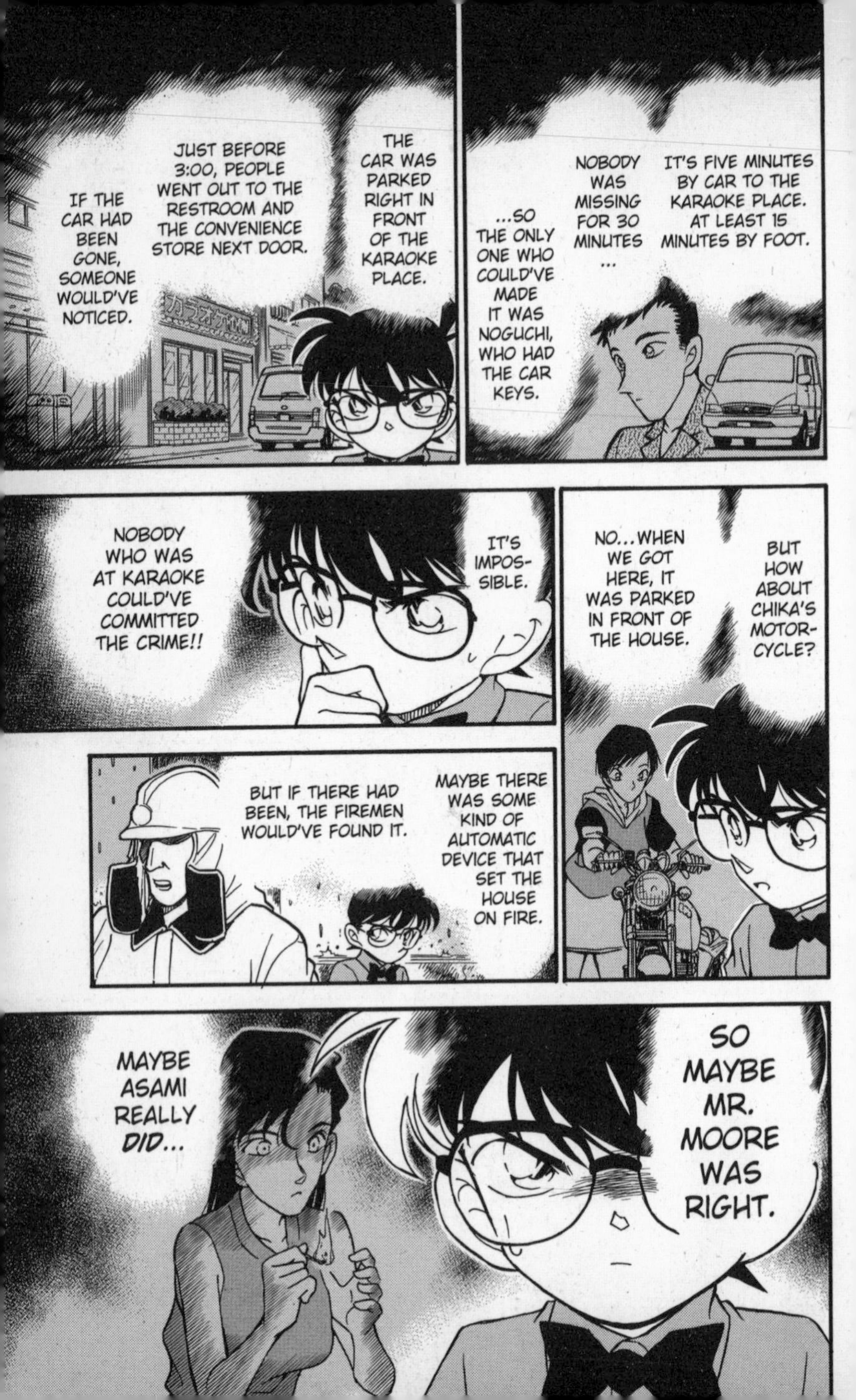
IT'S FIVE MINUTES BY CAR TO THE KARAOKE PLACE. AT LEAST 15 MINUTES BY FOOT.
NOBODY WAS MISSING FOR 30 MINUTES...
...SO THE ONLY ONE WHO COULD'VE MADE IT WAS NOGUCHI, WHO HAD THE CAR KEYS.
THE CAR WAS PARKED RIGHT IN FRONT OF THE KARAOKE PLACE.
JUST BEFORE 3:00, PEOPLE WENT OUT TO THE RESTROOM AND THE CONVENIENCE STORE NEXT DOOR.
IF THE CAR HAD BEEN GONE, SOMEONE WOULD'VE NOTICED.
BUT HOW ABOUT CHIKA'S MOTOR-CYCLE?
NO...WHEN WE GOT HERE, IT WAS PARKED IN FRONT OF THE HOUSE.
IT'S IMPOS-SIBLE.
NOBODY WHO WAS AT KARAOKE COULD'VE COMMITTED THE CRIME!!
MAYBE THERE WAS SOME KIND OF AUTOMATIC DEVICE THAT SET THE HOUSE ON FIRE.
BUT IF THERE HAD BEEN, THE FIREMEN WOULD'VE FOUND IT.
SO MAYBE MR. MOORE WAS RIGHT.
MAYBE ASAMI REALLY *DID*...

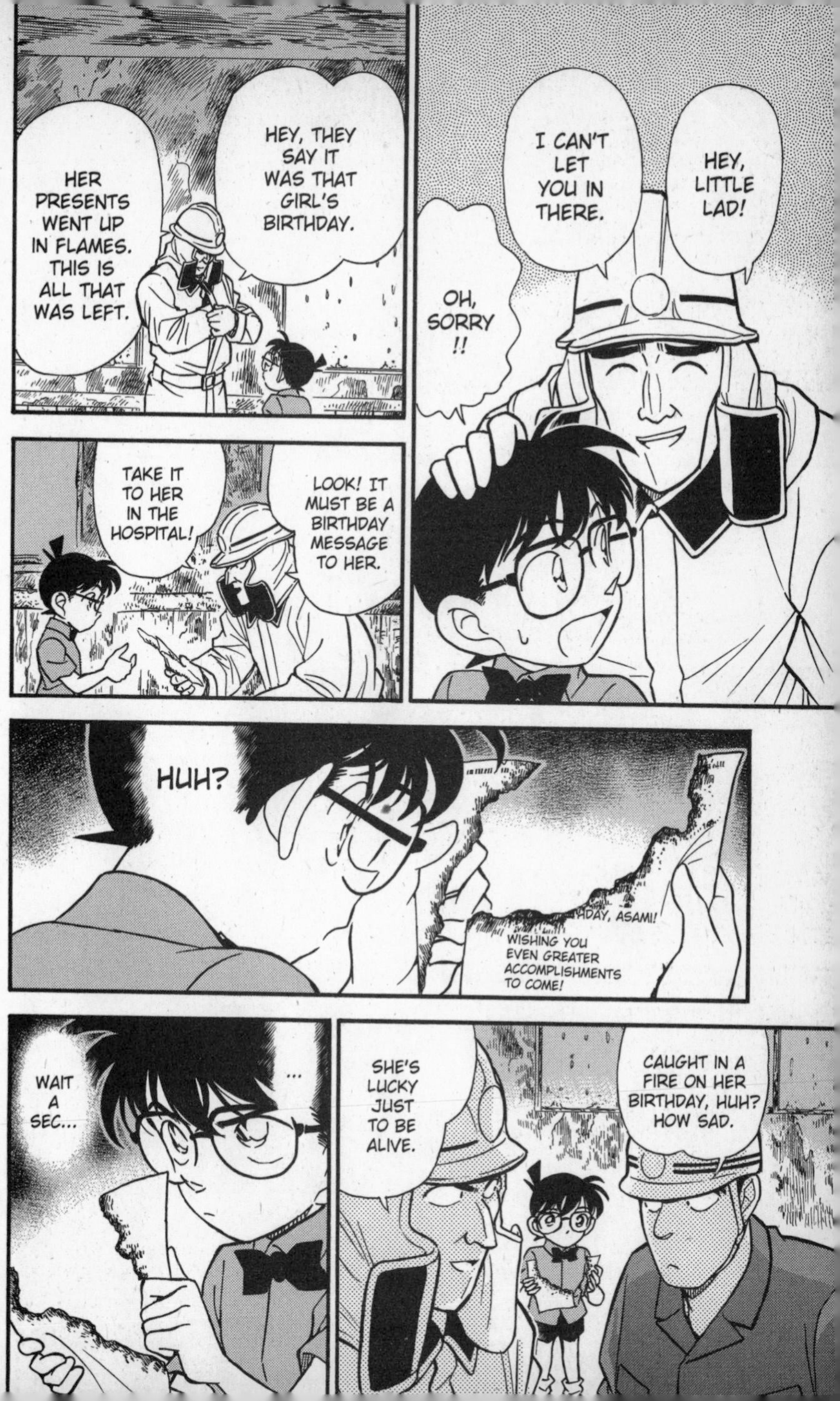
HEY, LITTLE LAD!
I CAN'T LET YOU IN THERE.
OH, SORRY !!
HEY, THEY SAY IT WAS THAT GIRL'S BIRTHDAY.
HER PRESENTS WENT UP IN FLAMES. THIS IS ALL THAT WAS LEFT.
LOOK! IT MUST BE A BIRTHDAY MESSAGE TO HER.
TAKE IT TO HER IN THE HOSPITAL!
HUH?
HDAY, ASAMI!
WISHING YOU EVEN GREATER ACCOMPLISHMENTS TO COME!
CAUGHT IN A FIRE ON HER BIRTHDAY, HUH? HOW SAD.
SHE'S LUCKY JUST TO BE ALIVE.
...
WAIT A SEC...

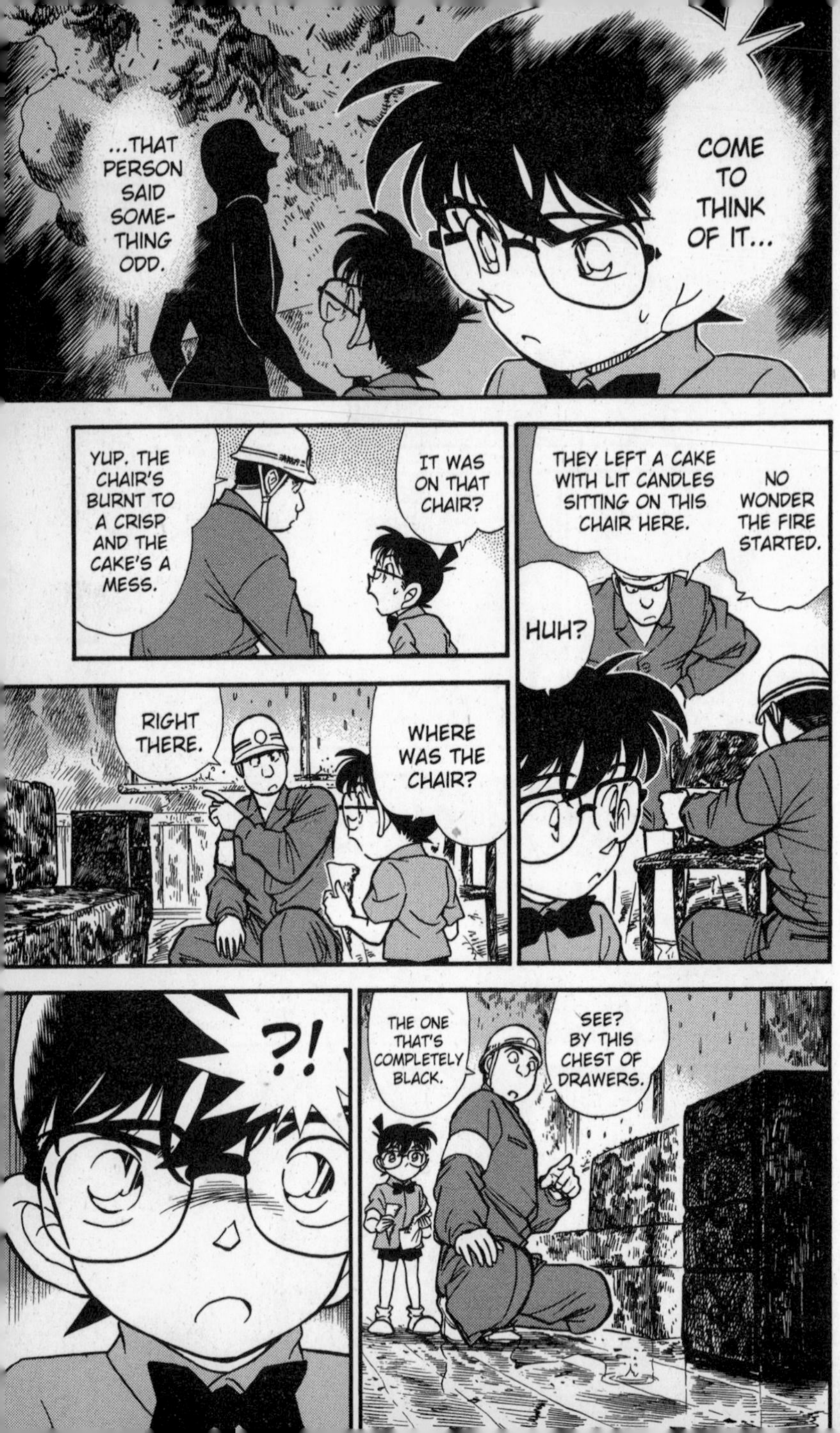
COME TO THINK OF IT...
...THAT PERSON SAID SOME-THING ODD.
THEY LEFT A CAKE WITH LIT CANDLES SITTING ON THIS CHAIR HERE.
NO WONDER THE FIRE STARTED.
HUH?
IT WAS ON THAT CHAIR?
YUP. THE CHAIR'S BURNT TO A CRISP AND THE CAKE'S A MESS.
WHERE WAS THE CHAIR?
RIGHT THERE.
SEE? BY THIS CHEST OF DRAWERS.
THE ONE THAT'S COMPLETELY BLACK.
?!

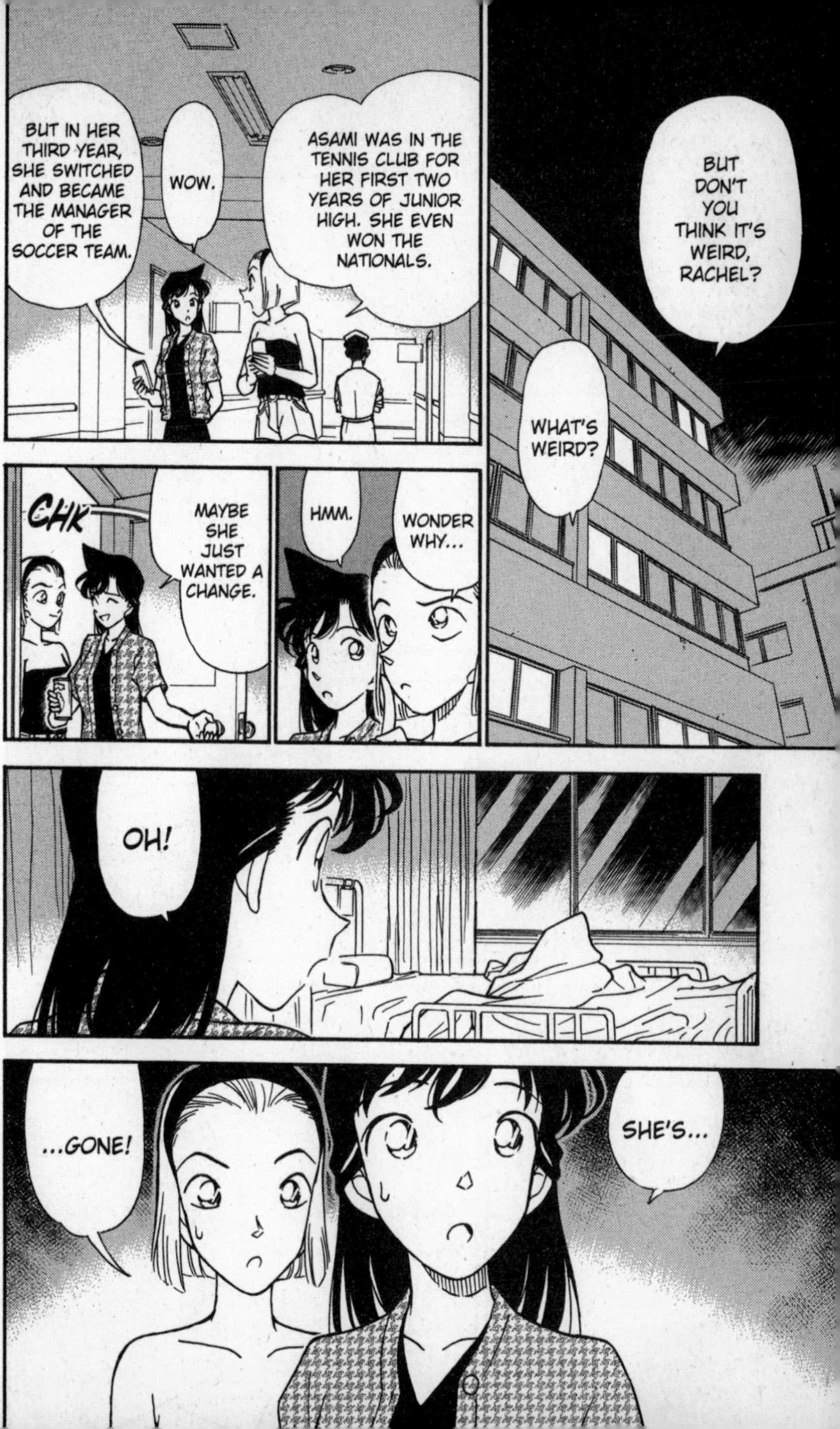
BUT DON'T YOU THINK IT'S WEIRD, RACHEL?
WHAT'S WEIRD?
ASAMI WAS IN THE TENNIS CLUB FOR HER FIRST TWO YEARS OF JUNIOR HIGH. SHE EVEN WON THE NATIONALS.
WOW.
BUT IN HER THIRD YEAR, SHE SWITCHED AND BECAME THE MANAGER OF THE SOCCER TEAM.
WONDER WHY...
HMM.
MAYBE SHE JUST WANTED A CHANGE.
CHK
OH!
SHE'S...
...GONE!

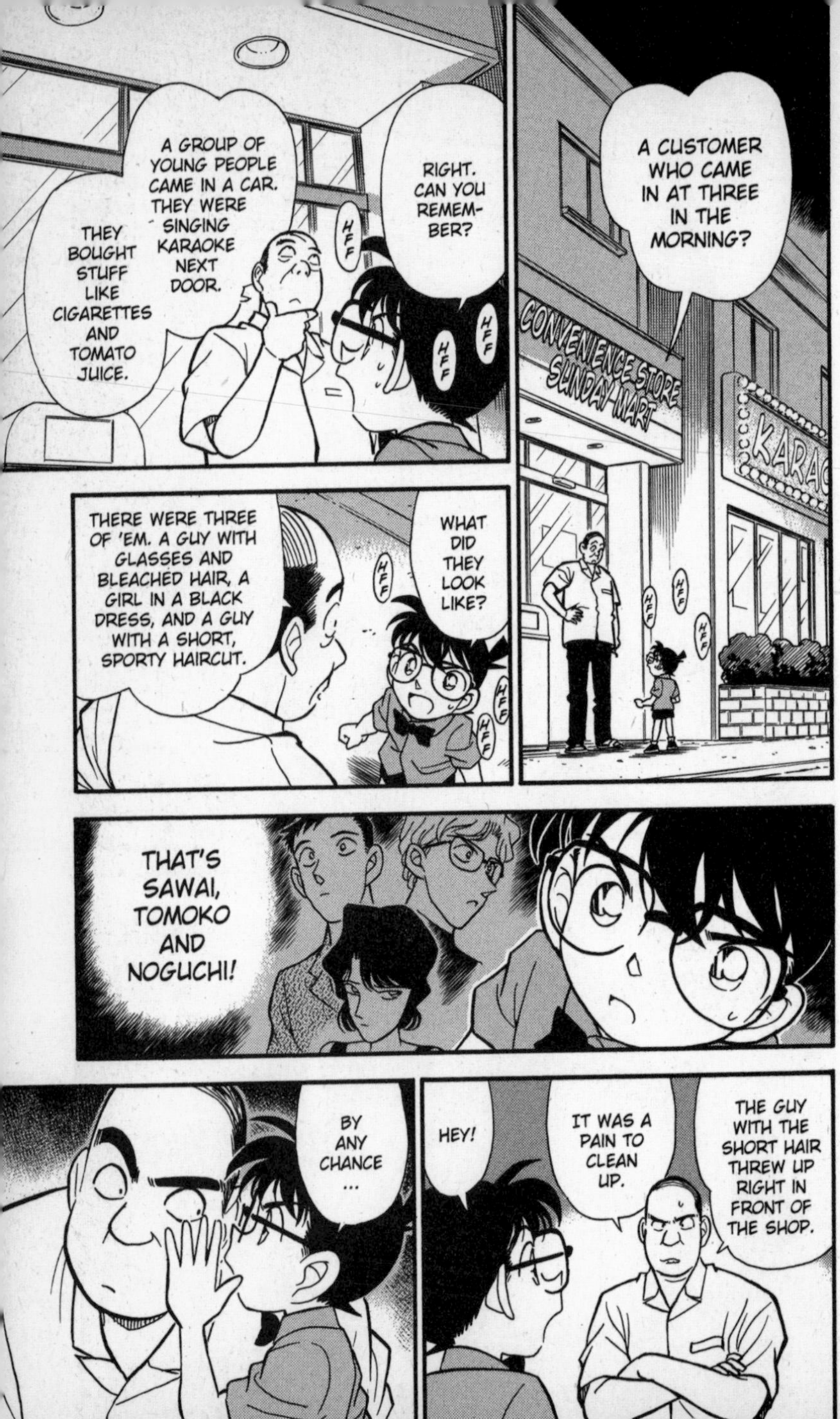
A CUSTOMER WHO CAME IN AT THREE IN THE MORNING?
CONVENIENCE STORE SUNDAY MART
HFF
HFF
HFF
HFF
RIGHT. CAN YOU REMEMBER?
HFF
HFF
HFF
A GROUP OF YOUNG PEOPLE CAME IN A CAR. THEY WERE SINGING KARAOKE NEXT DOOR.
THEY BOUGHT STUFF LIKE CIGARETTES AND TOMATO JUICE.
WHAT DID THEY LOOK LIKE?
HFF
HFF
HFF
THERE WERE THREE OF 'EM. A GUY WITH GLASSES AND BLEACHED HAIR, A GIRL IN A BLACK DRESS, AND A GUY WITH A SHORT, SPORTY HAIRCUT.
THAT'S SAWAI, TOMOKO AND NOGUCHI!
THE GUY WITH THE SHORT HAIR THREW UP RIGHT IN FRONT OF THE SHOP.
IT WAS A PAIN TO CLEAN UP.
HEY!
BY ANY CHANCE ...

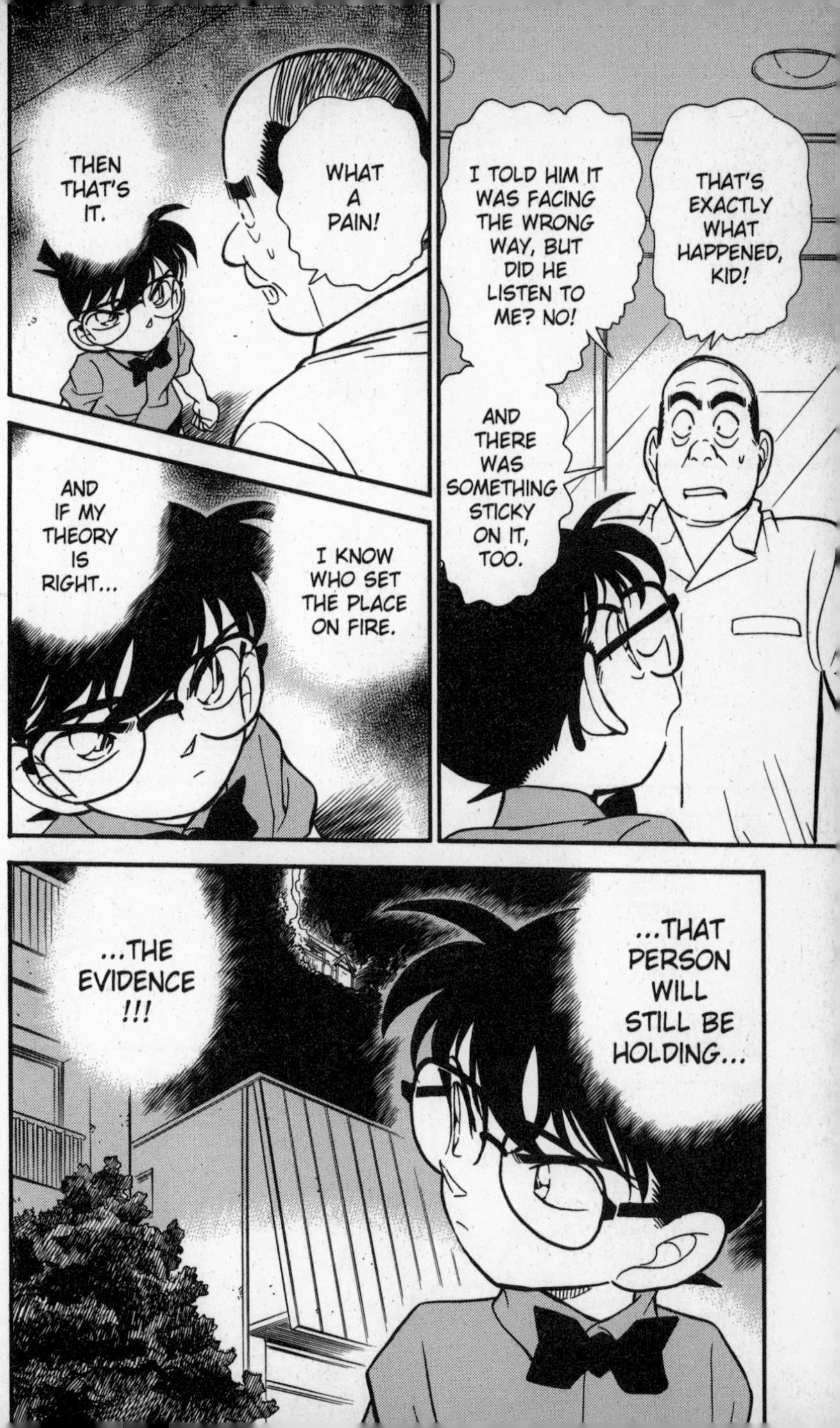
THAT'S EXACTLY WHAT HAPPENED, KID!
I TOLD HIM IT WAS FACING THE WRONG WAY, BUT DID HE LISTEN TO ME? NO!
AND THERE WAS SOMETHING STICKY ON IT, TOO.
WHAT A PAIN!
THEN THAT'S IT.
I KNOW WHO SET THE PLACE ON FIRE.
AND IF MY THEORY IS RIGHT...
...THAT PERSON WILL STILL BE HOLDING...
...THE EVIDENCE!!!

FILE 5: TO WIN A HEART

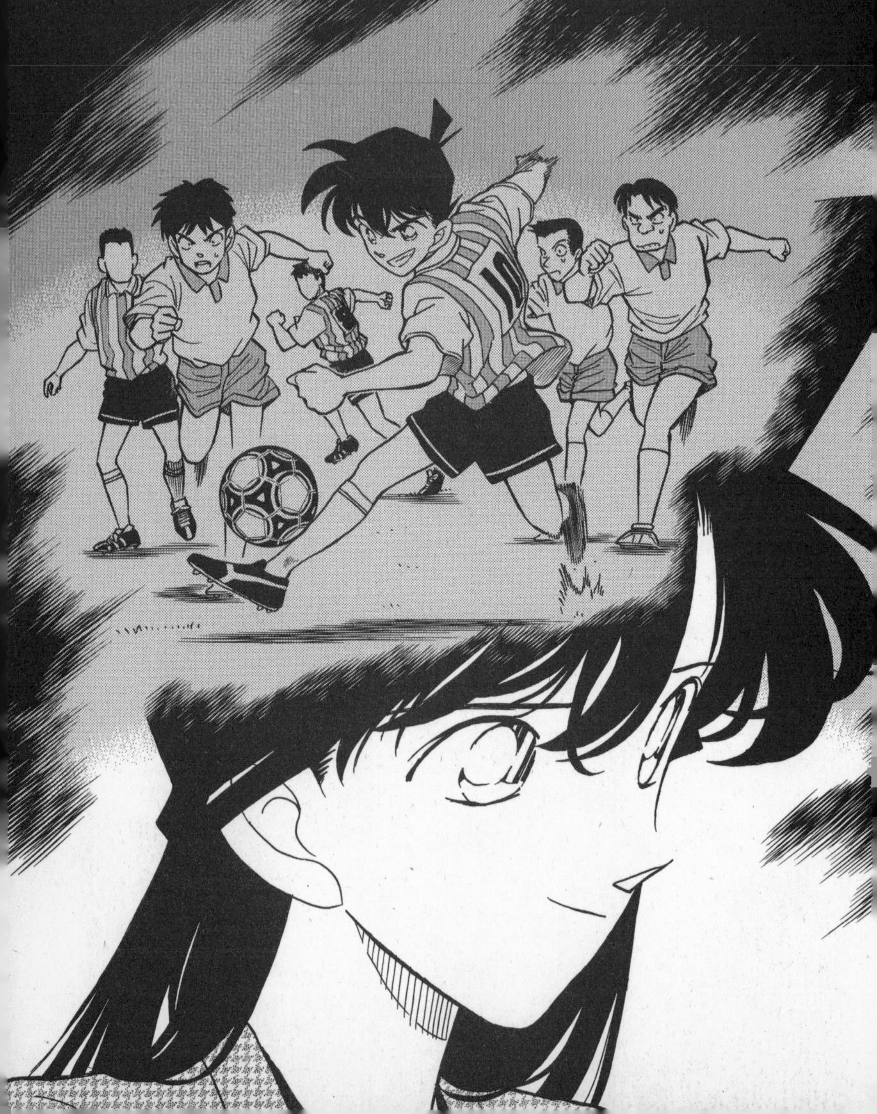

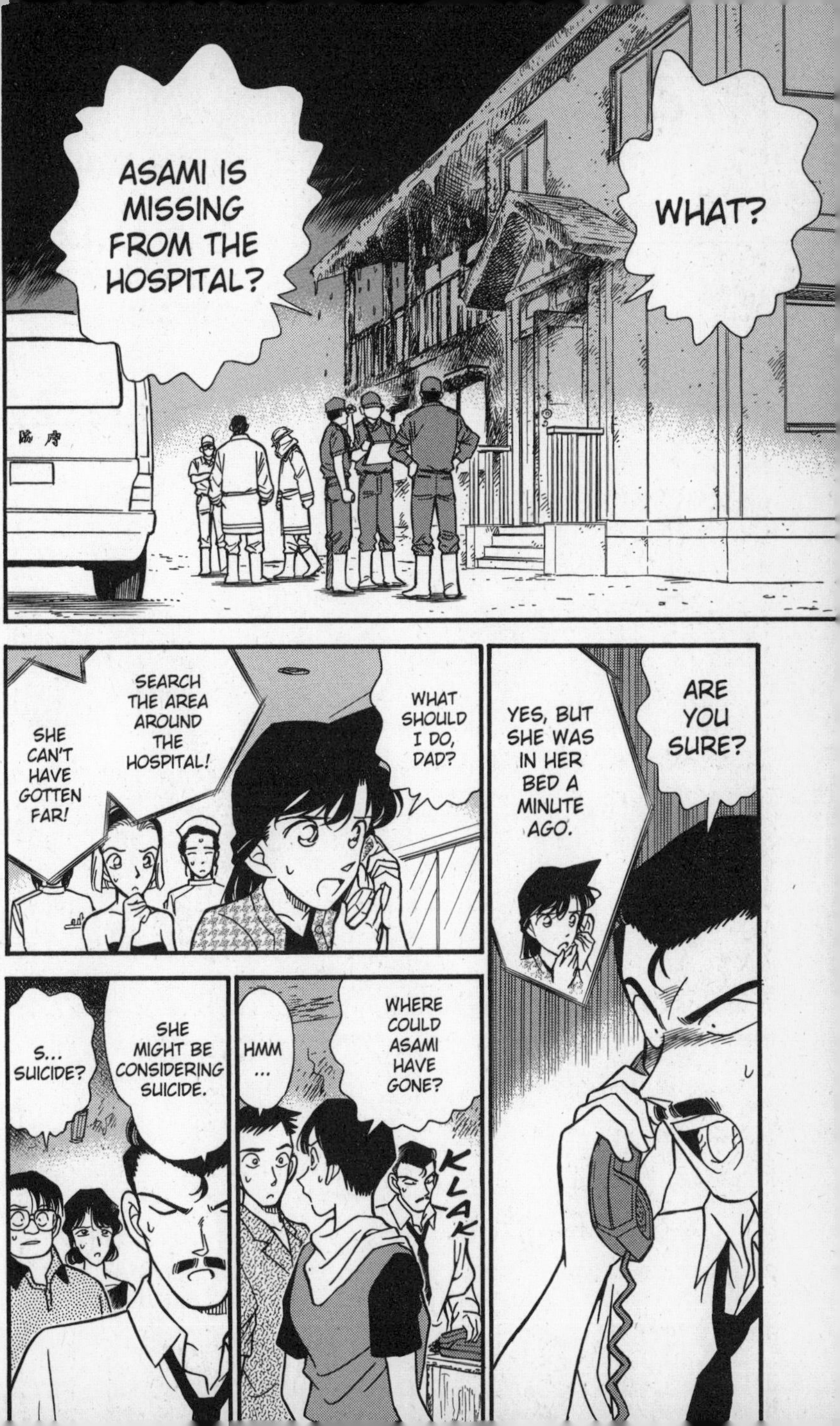
WHAT?
ASAMI IS MISSING FROM THE HOSPITAL?
ARE YOU SURE?
YES, BUT SHE WAS IN HER BED A MINUTE AGO.
WHAT SHOULD I DO, DAD?
SEARCH THE AREA AROUND THE HOSPITAL!
SHE CAN'T HAVE GOTTEN FAR!
WHERE COULD ASAMI HAVE GONE?
KLAK
HMM...
SHE MIGHT BE CONSIDERING SUICIDE.
S... SUICIDE?

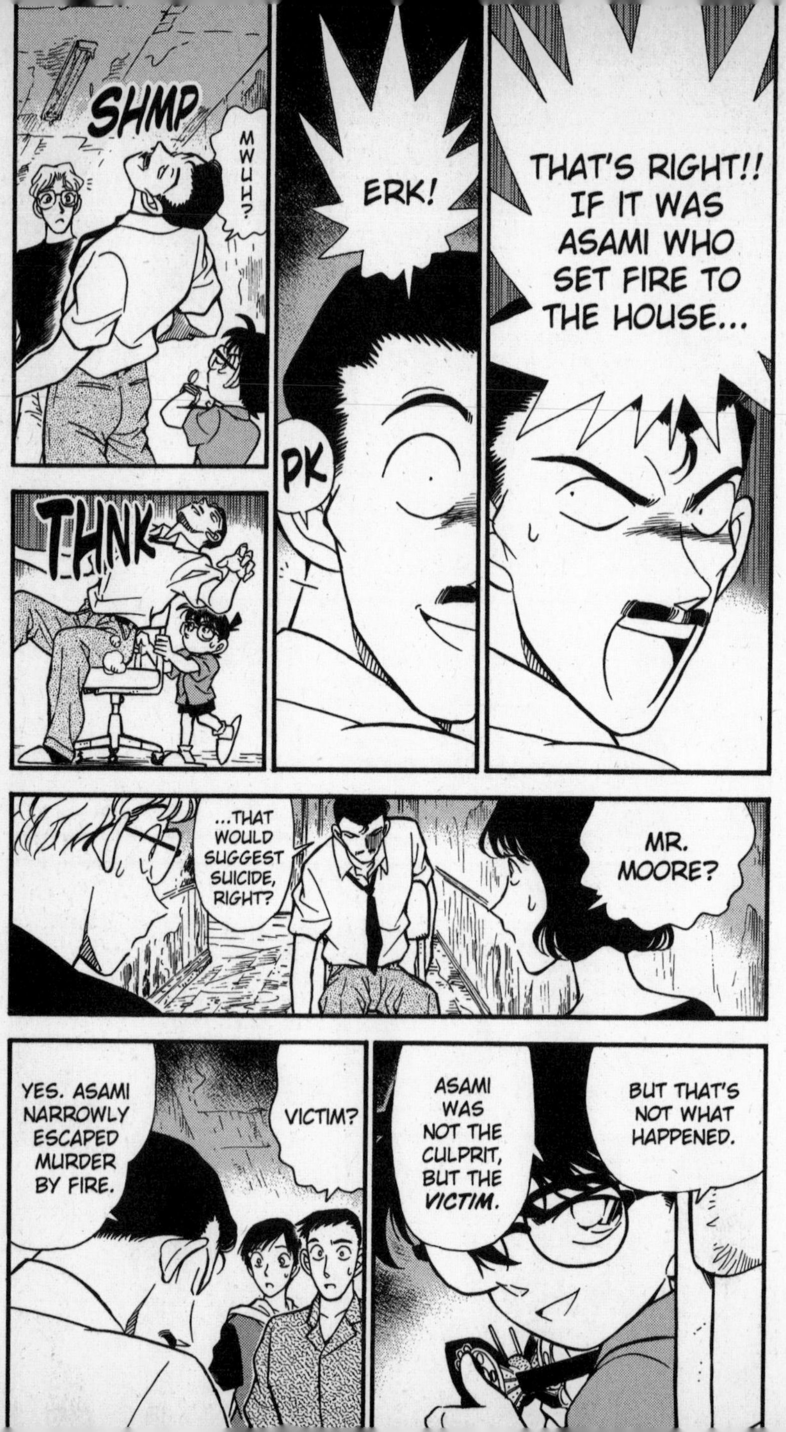
THAT'S RIGHT!! IF IT WAS ASAMI WHO SET FIRE TO THE HOUSE...
ERK!
PK
SHMP
MWUH?
THNK
MR. MOORE?
...THAT WOULD SUGGEST SUICIDE, RIGHT?
BUT THAT'S NOT WHAT HAPPENED.
ASAMI WAS NOT THE CULPRIT, BUT THE *VICTIM*.
VICTIM?
YES. ASAMI NARROWLY ESCAPED MURDER BY FIRE.

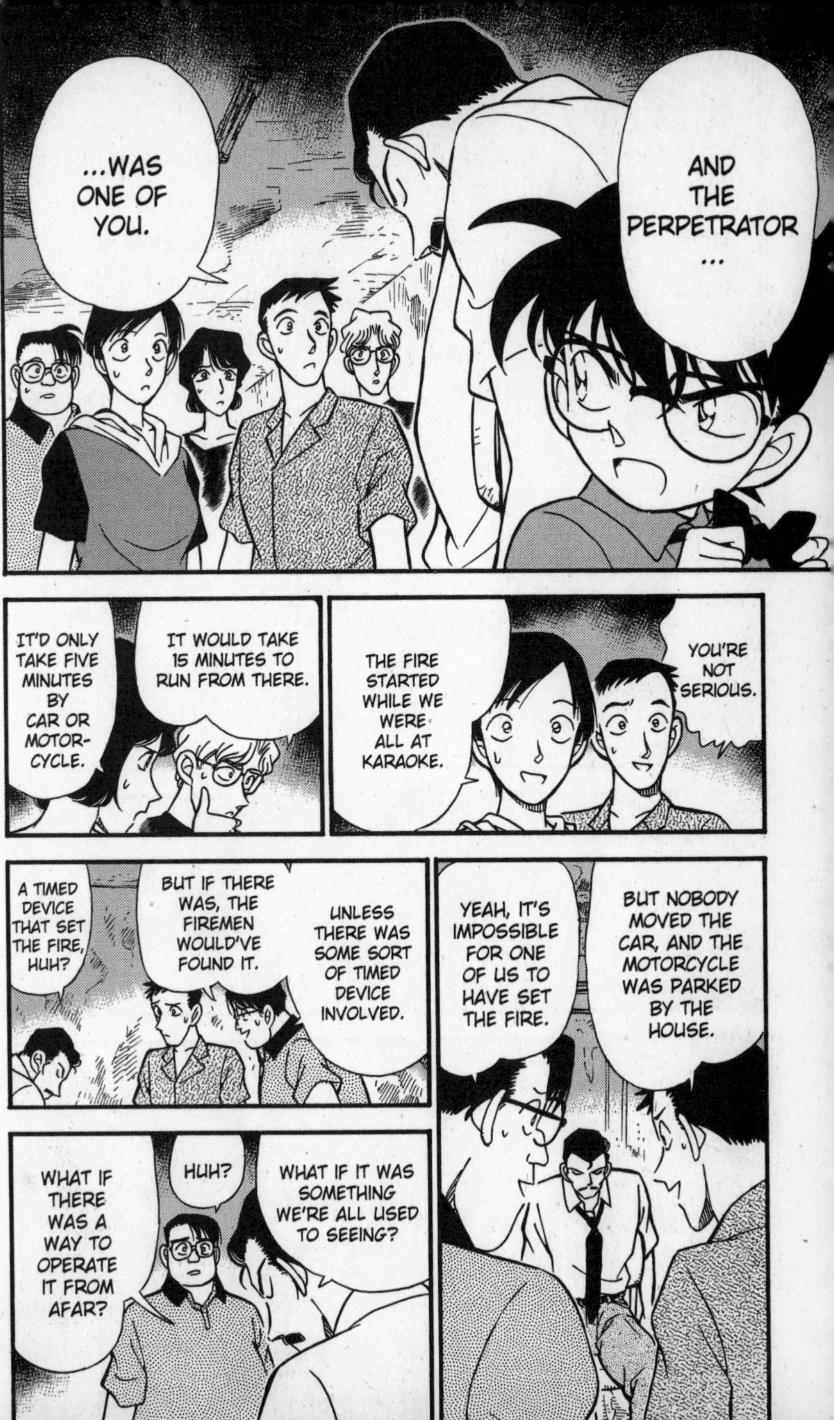
AND THE PERPETRATOR ...
...WAS ONE OF YOU.
YOU'RE NOT SERIOUS.
THE FIRE STARTED WHILE WE WERE ALL AT KARAOKE.
IT WOULD TAKE 15 MINUTES TO RUN FROM THERE.
IT'D ONLY TAKE FIVE MINUTES BY CAR OR MOTOR-CYCLE.
BUT NOBODY MOVED THE CAR, AND THE MOTORCYCLE WAS PARKED BY THE HOUSE.
YEAH, IT'S IMPOSSIBLE FOR ONE OF US TO HAVE SET THE FIRE.
UNLESS THERE WAS SOME SORT OF TIMED DEVICE INVOLVED.
BUT IF THERE WAS, THE FIREMEN WOULD'VE FOUND IT.
A TIMED DEVICE THAT SET THE FIRE, HUH?
WHAT IF IT WAS SOMETHING WE'RE ALL USED TO SEEING?
HUH?
WHAT IF THERE WAS A WAY TO OPERATE IT FROM AFAR?

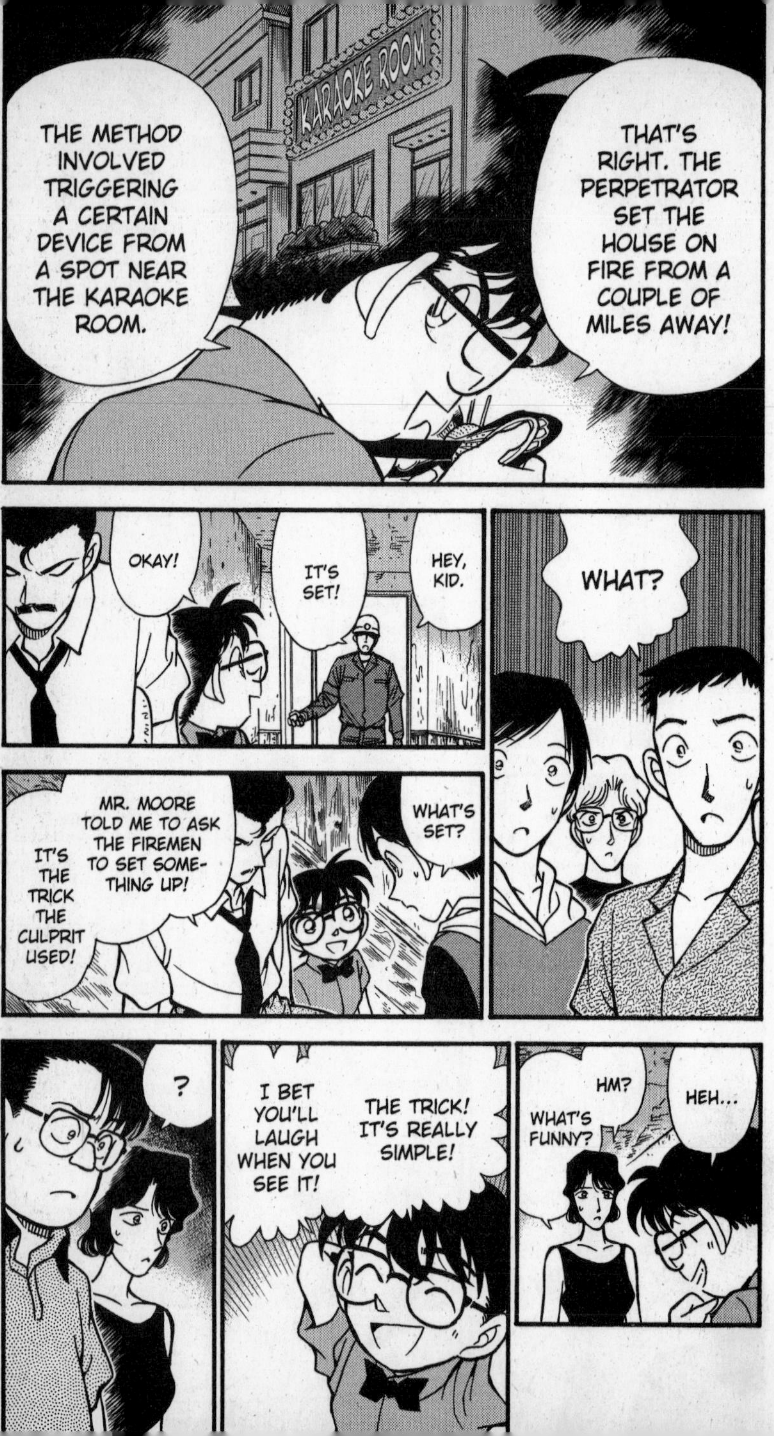
THAT'S RIGHT. THE PERPETRATOR SET THE HOUSE ON FIRE FROM A COUPLE OF MILES AWAY!
THE METHOD INVOLVED TRIGGERING A CERTAIN DEVICE FROM A SPOT NEAR THE KARAOKE ROOM.
KARAOKE ROOM
WHAT?
HEY, KID.
IT'S SET!
OKAY!
WHAT'S SET?
MR. MOORE TOLD ME TO ASK THE FIREMEN TO SET SOME-THING UP!
IT'S THE TRICK THE CULPRIT USED!
HEH...
HM? WHAT'S FUNNY?
THE TRICK! IT'S REALLY SIMPLE!
I BET YOU'LL LAUGH WHEN YOU SEE IT!
?

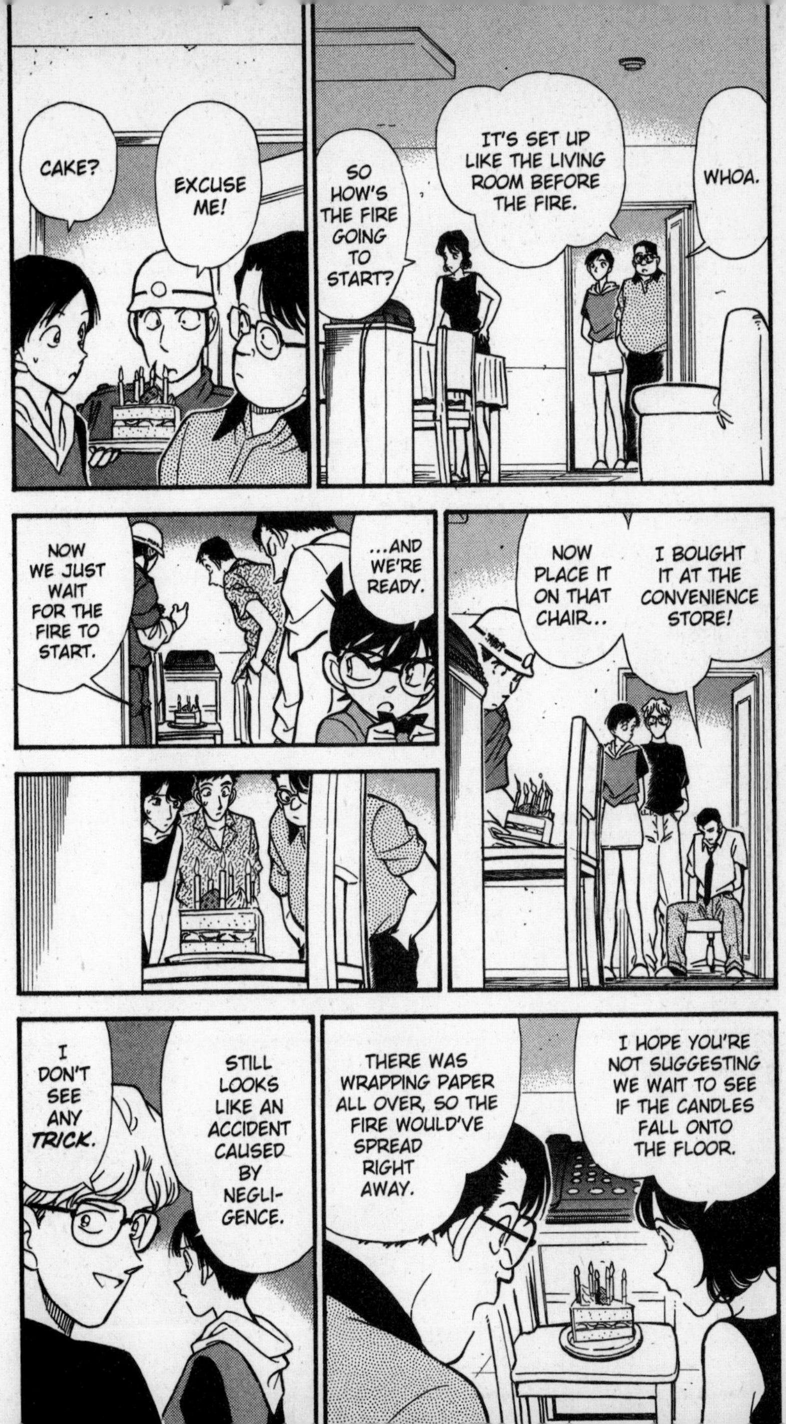
WHOA.
IT'S SET UP LIKE THE LIVING ROOM BEFORE THE FIRE.
SO HOW'S THE FIRE GOING TO START?
EXCUSE ME!
CAKE?
I BOUGHT IT AT THE CONVENIENCE STORE!
NOW PLACE IT ON THAT CHAIR..
...AND WE'RE READY.
NOW WE JUST WAIT FOR THE FIRE TO START.
I HOPE YOU'RE NOT SUGGESTING WE WAIT TO SEE IF THE CANDLES FALL ONTO THE FLOOR.
THERE WAS WRAPPING PAPER ALL OVER, SO THE FIRE WOULD'VE SPREAD RIGHT AWAY.
STILL LOOKS LIKE AN ACCIDENT CAUSED BY NEGLI-GENCE.
I DON'T SEE ANY *TRICK*.

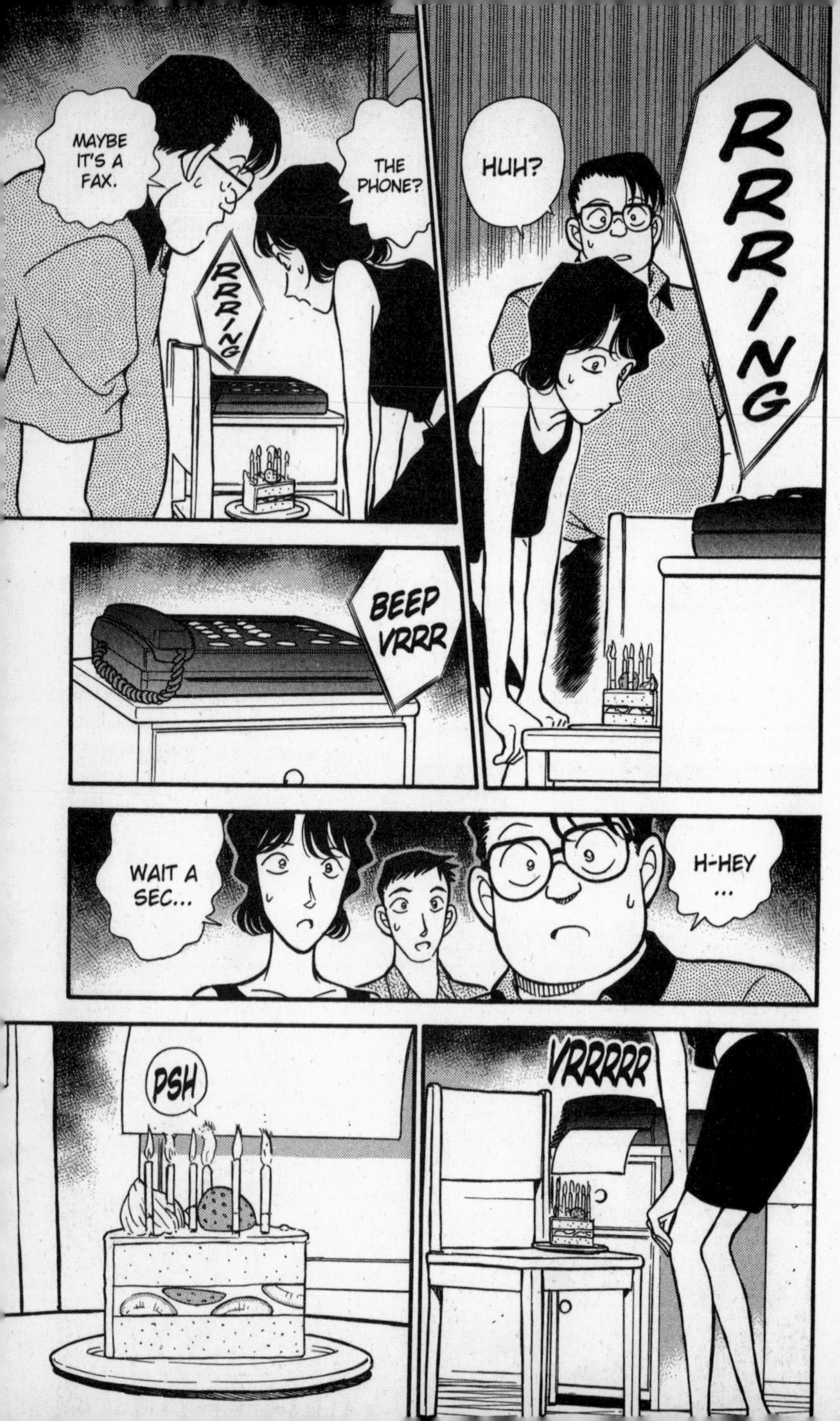
RRRRING
HUH?
THE PHONE?
MAYBE IT'S A FAX.
RRRING
BEEP VRRR
H-HEY ...
WAIT A SEC...
VRRRRR
PSH

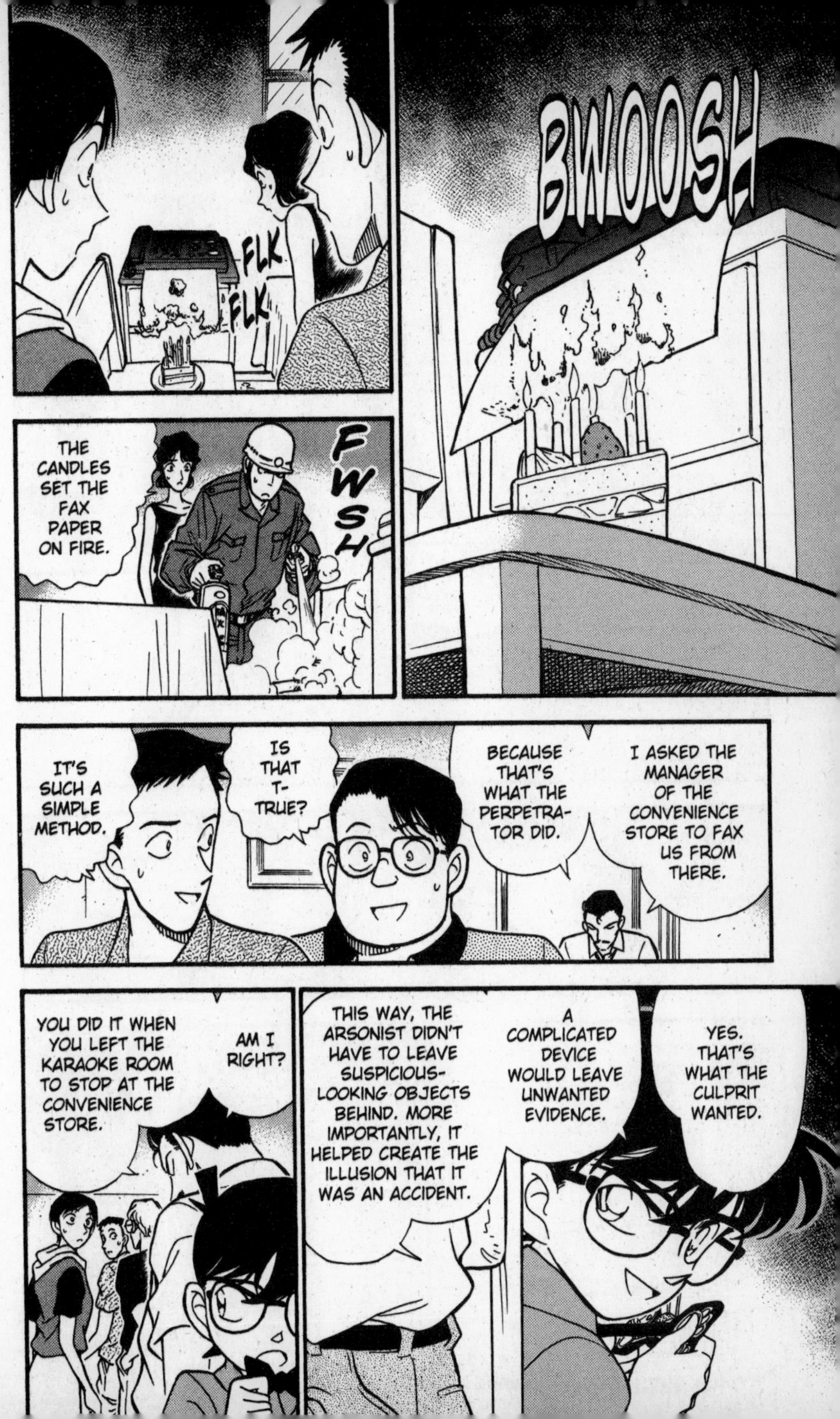
BWOOSH
FLK
FLK
FWSH
THE CANDLES SET THE FAX PAPER ON FIRE.
I ASKED THE MANAGER OF THE CONVENIENCE STORE TO FAX US FROM THERE.
BECAUSE THAT'S WHAT THE PERPETRA-TOR DID.
IS THAT T-TRUE?
IT'S SUCH A SIMPLE METHOD.
YES. THAT'S WHAT THE CULPRIT WANTED.
A COMPLICATED DEVICE WOULD LEAVE UNWANTED EVIDENCE.
THIS WAY, THE ARSONIST DIDN'T HAVE TO LEAVE SUSPICIOUS-LOOKING OBJECTS BEHIND. MORE IMPORTANTLY, IT HELPED CREATE THE ILLUSION THAT IT WAS AN ACCIDENT.
YOU DID IT WHEN YOU LEFT THE KARAOKE ROOM TO STOP AT THE CONVENIENCE STORE.
AM I RIGHT?

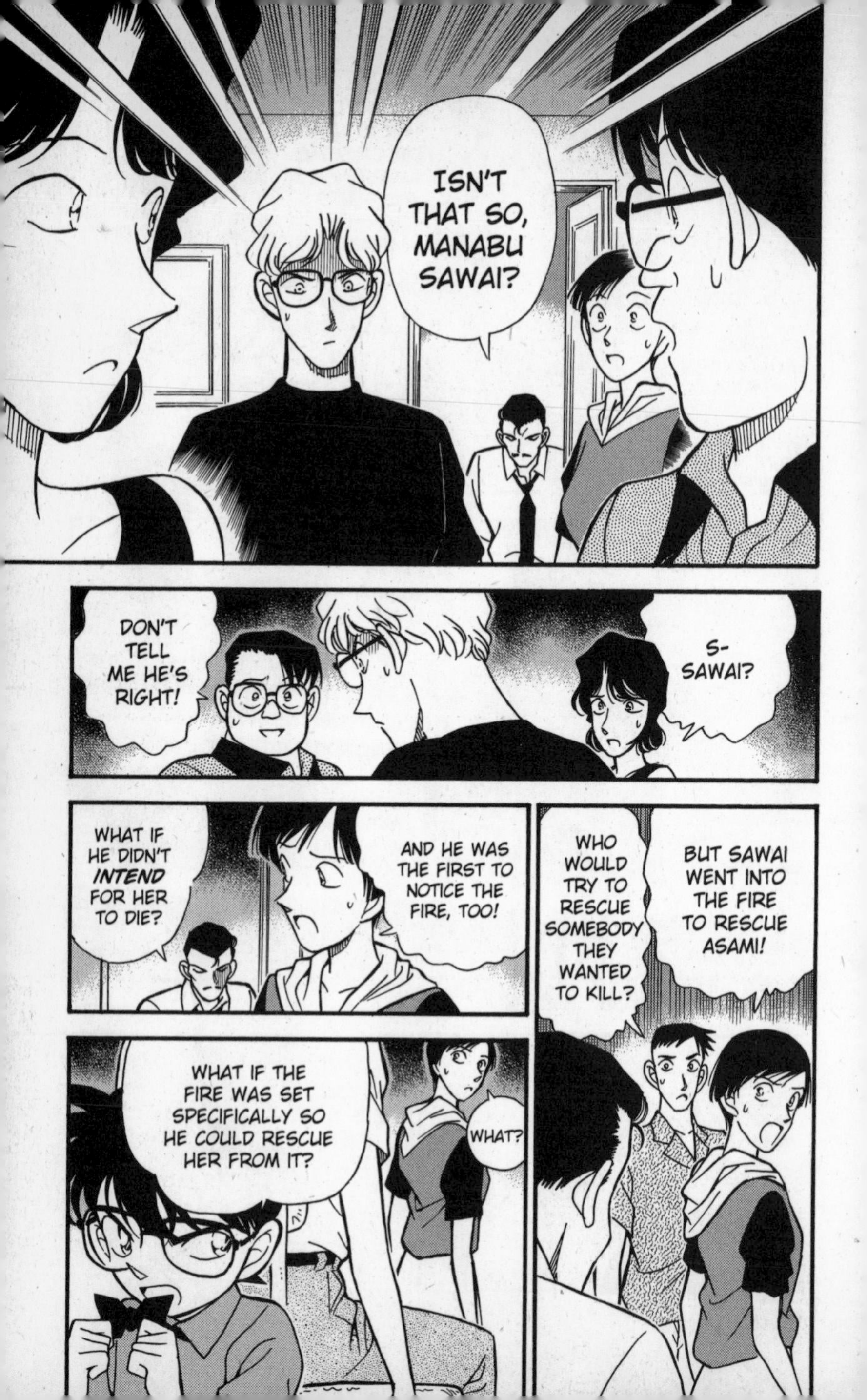
ISN'T THAT SO, MANABU SAWAI?
S- SAWAI?
DON'T TELL ME HE'S RIGHT!
BUT SAWAI WENT INTO THE FIRE TO RESCUE ASAMI!
WHO WOULD TRY TO RESCUE SOMEBODY THEY WANTED TO KILL?
AND HE WAS THE FIRST TO NOTICE THE FIRE, TOO!
WHAT IF HE DIDN'T *INTEND* FOR HER TO DIE?
WHAT?
WHAT IF THE FIRE WAS SET SPECIFICALLY SO HE COULD RESCUE HER FROM IT?

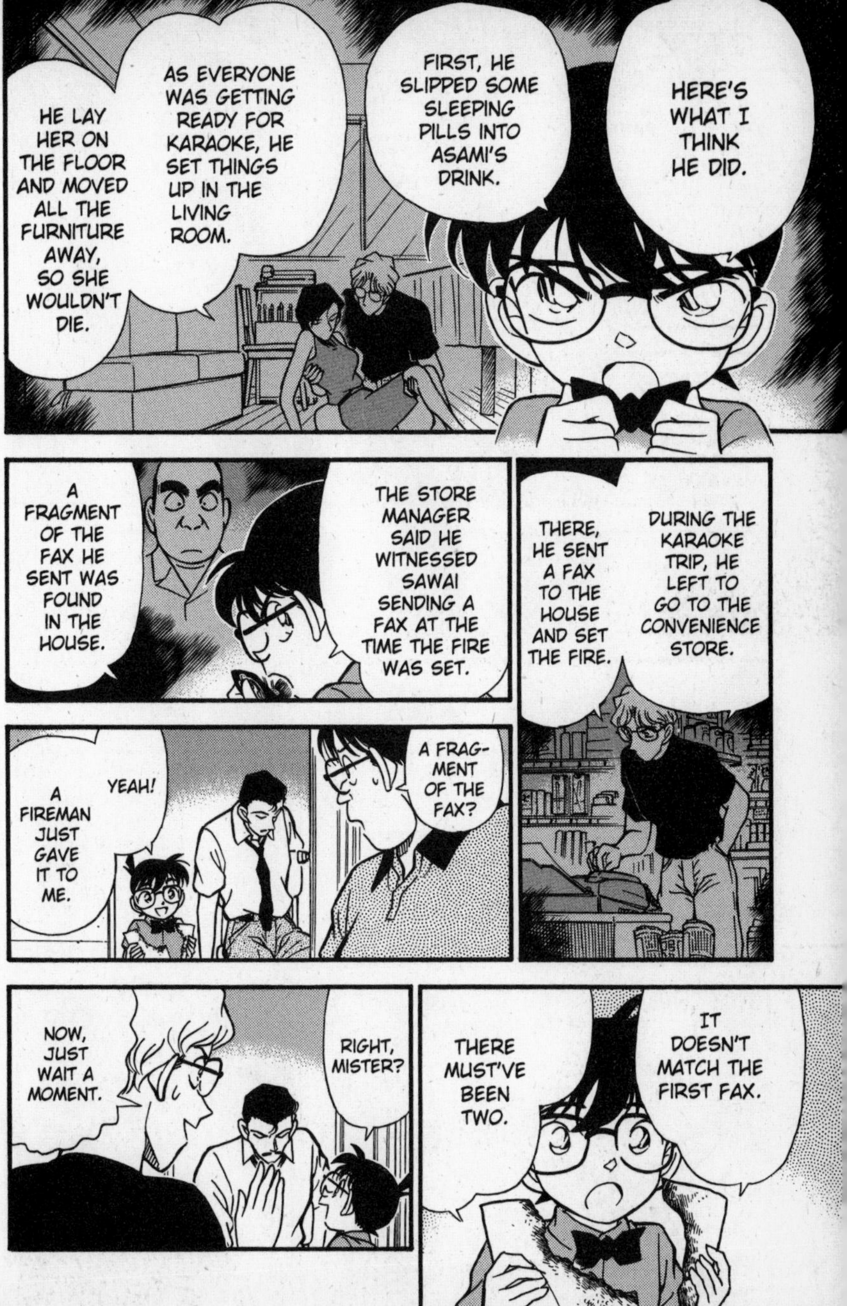
HERE'S WHAT I THINK HE DID.
FIRST, HE SLIPPED SOME SLEEPING PILLS INTO ASAMI'S DRINK.
AS EVERYONE WAS GETTING READY FOR KARAOKE, HE SET THINGS UP IN THE LIVING ROOM.
HE LAY HER ON THE FLOOR AND MOVED ALL THE FURNITURE AWAY, SO SHE WOULDN'T DIE.
DURING THE KARAOKE TRIP, HE LEFT TO GO TO THE CONVENIENCE STORE.
THERE, HE SENT A FAX TO THE HOUSE AND SET THE FIRE.
THE STORE MANAGER SAID HE WITNESSED SAWAI SENDING A FAX AT THE TIME THE FIRE WAS SET.
A FRAGMENT OF THE FAX HE SENT WAS FOUND IN THE HOUSE.
A FRAG-MENT OF THE FAX?
YEAH!
A FIREMAN JUST GAVE IT TO ME.
IT DOESN'T MATCH THE FIRST FAX.
THERE MUST'VE BEEN TWO.
RIGHT, MISTER?
NOW, JUST WAIT A MOMENT.

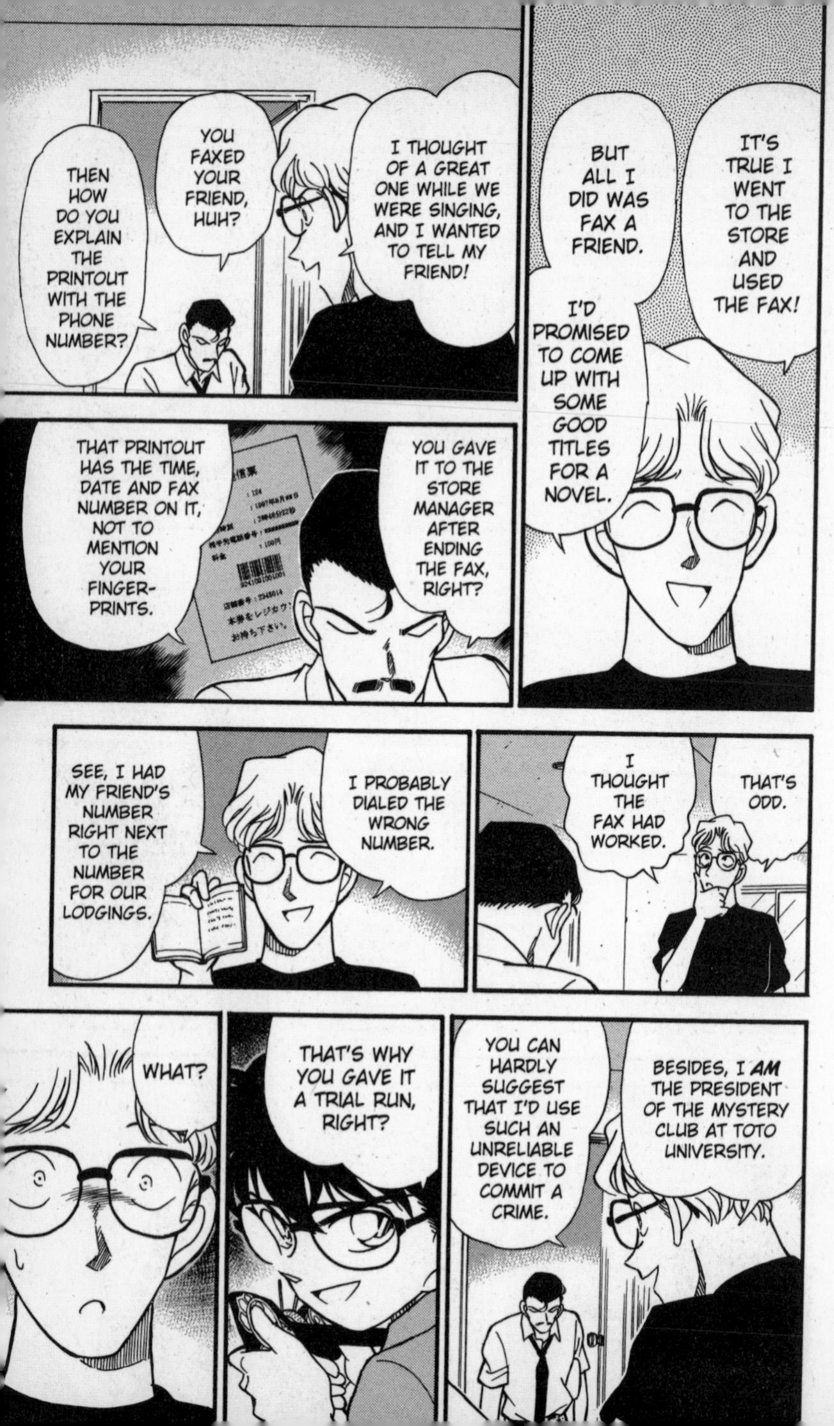
IT'S TRUE I WENT TO THE STORE AND USED THE FAX!
BUT ALL I DID WAS FAX A FRIEND.
I'D PROMISED TO COME UP WITH SOME GOOD TITLES FOR A NOVEL.
I THOUGHT OF A GREAT ONE WHILE WE WERE SINGING, AND I WANTED TO TELL MY FRIEND!
YOU FAXED YOUR FRIEND, HUH?
THEN HOW DO YOU EXPLAIN THE PRINTOUT WITH THE PHONE NUMBER?
YOU GAVE IT TO THE STORE MANAGER AFTER ENDING THE FAX, RIGHT?
THAT PRINTOUT HAS THE TIME, DATE AND FAX NUMBER ON IT, NOT TO MENTION YOUR FINGER-PRINTS.
THAT'S ODD.
I THOUGHT THE FAX HAD WORKED.
I PROBABLY DIALED THE WRONG NUMBER.
SEE, I HAD MY FRIEND'S NUMBER RIGHT NEXT TO THE NUMBER FOR OUR LODGINGS.
BESIDES, I *AM* THE PRESIDENT OF THE MYSTERY CLUB AT TOTO UNIVERSITY.
YOU CAN HARDLY SUGGEST THAT I'D USE SUCH AN UNRELIABLE DEVICE TO COMMIT A CRIME.
THAT'S WHY YOU GAVE IT A TRIAL RUN, RIGHT?
WHAT?

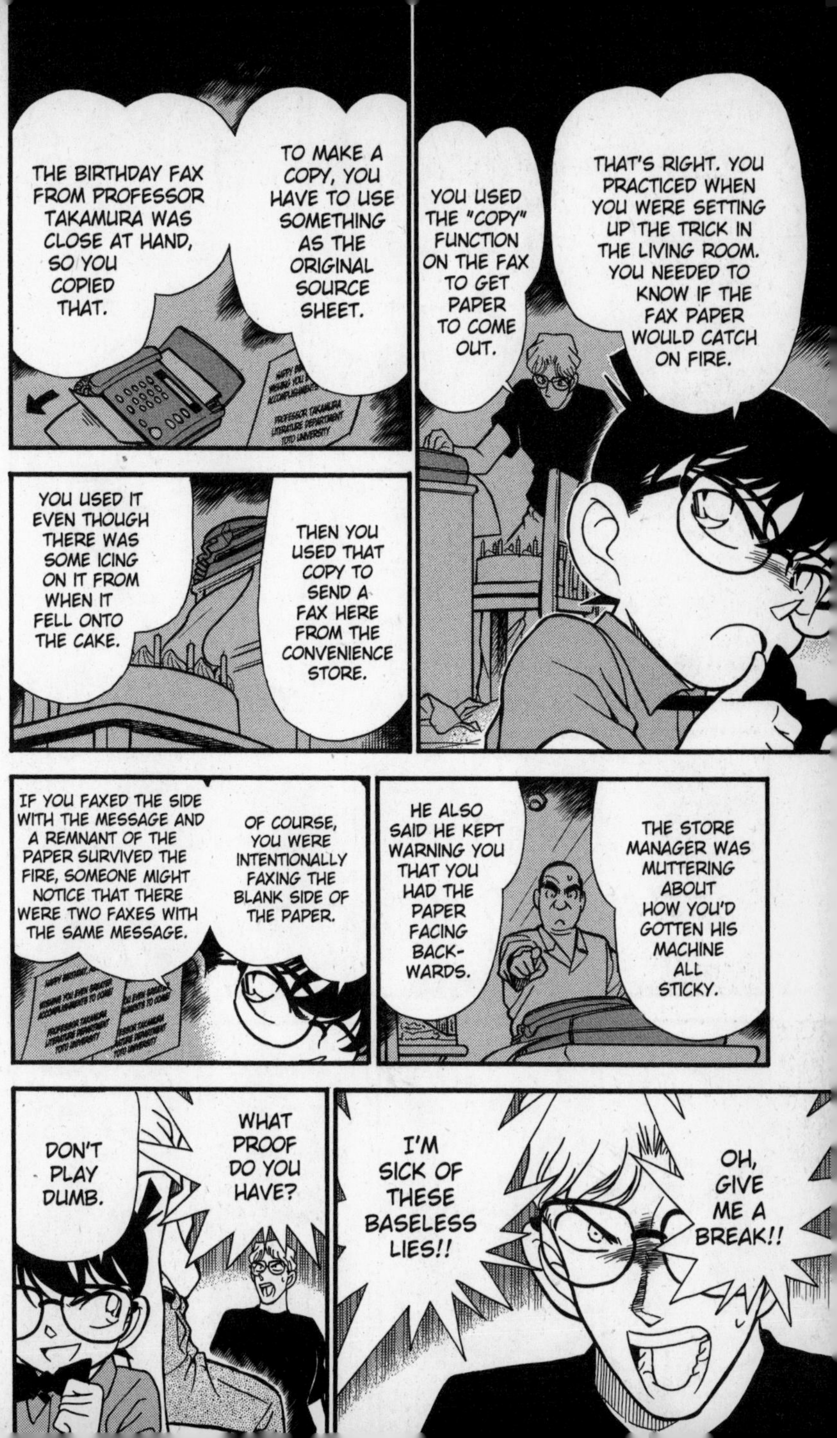
THAT'S RIGHT. YOU PRACTICED WHEN YOU WERE SETTING UP THE TRICK IN THE LIVING ROOM. YOU NEEDED TO KNOW IF THE FAX PAPER WOULD CATCH ON FIRE.
YOU USED THE "COPY" FUNCTION ON THE FAX TO GET PAPER TO COME OUT.
TO MAKE A COPY, YOU HAVE TO USE SOMETHING AS THE ORIGINAL SOURCE SHEET.
THE BIRTHDAY FAX FROM PROFESSOR TAKAMURA WAS CLOSE AT HAND, SO YOU COPIED THAT.
THEN YOU USED THAT COPY TO SEND A FAX HERE FROM THE CONVENIENCE STORE.
YOU USED IT EVEN THOUGH THERE WAS SOME ICING ON IT FROM WHEN IT FELL ONTO THE CAKE.
THE STORE MANAGER WAS MUTTERING ABOUT HOW YOU'D GOTTEN HIS MACHINE ALL STICKY.
HE ALSO SAID HE KEPT WARNING YOU THAT YOU HAD THE PAPER FACING BACK-WARDS.
OF COURSE, YOU WERE INTENTIONALLY FAXING THE BLANK SIDE OF THE PAPER.
IF YOU FAXED THE SIDE WITH THE MESSAGE AND A REMNANT OF THE PAPER SURVIVED THE FIRE, SOMEONE MIGHT NOTICE THAT THERE WERE TWO FAXES WITH THE SAME MESSAGE.
OH, GIVE ME A BREAK!!
I'M SICK OF THESE BASELESS LIES!!
WHAT PROOF DO YOU HAVE?
DON'T PLAY DUMB.

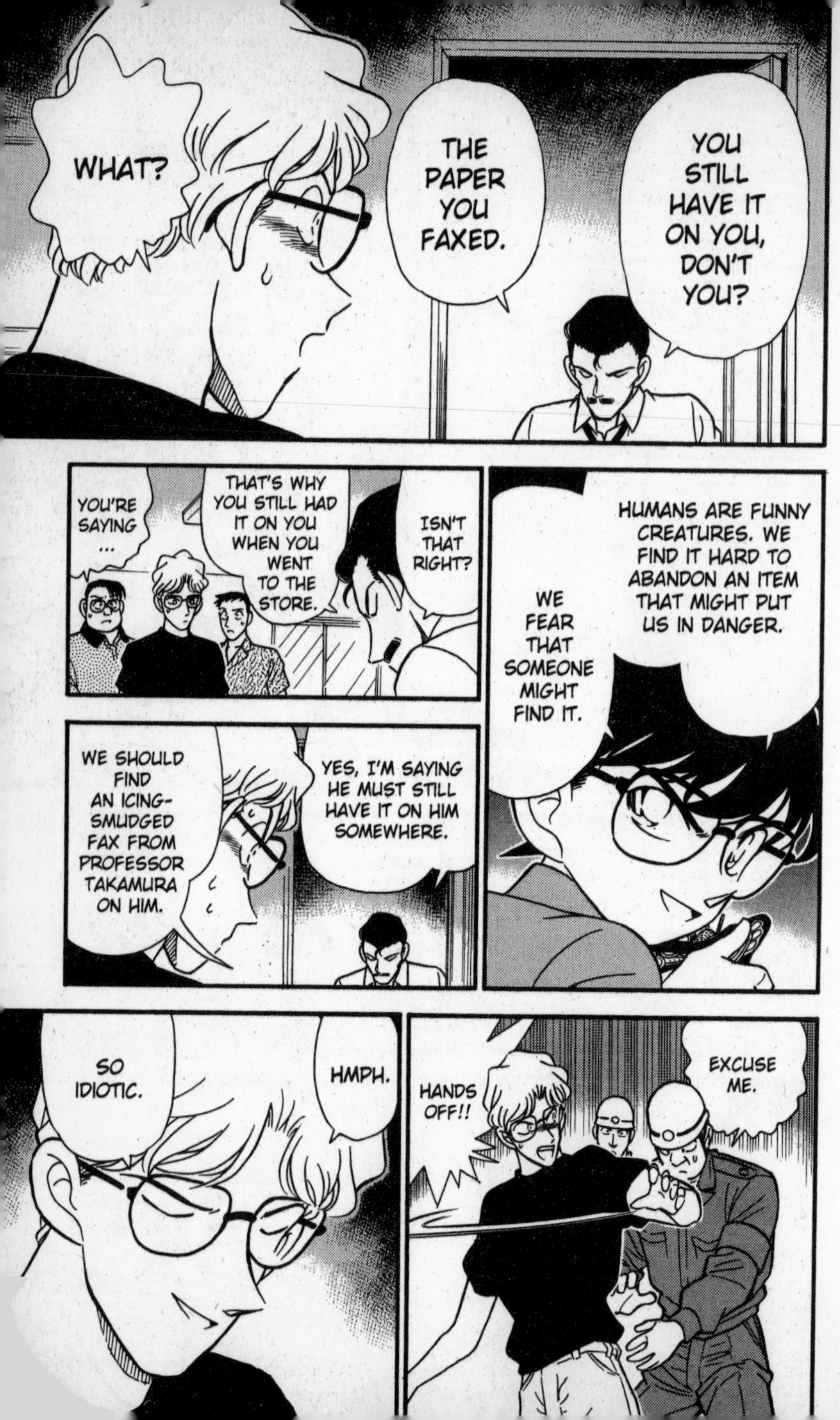
YOU STILL HAVE IT ON YOU, DON'T YOU?
THE PAPER YOU FAXED.
WHAT?
HUMANS ARE FUNNY CREATURES. WE FIND IT HARD TO ABANDON AN ITEM THAT MIGHT PUT US IN DANGER.
WE FEAR THAT SOMEONE MIGHT FIND IT.
ISN'T THAT RIGHT?
THAT'S WHY YOU STILL HAD IT ON YOU WHEN YOU WENT TO THE STORE.
YOU'RE SAYING ...
WE SHOULD FIND AN ICING-SMUDGED FAX FROM PROFESSOR TAKAMURA ON HIM.
YES, I'M SAYING HE MUST STILL HAVE IT ON HIM SOMEWHERE.
EXCUSE ME.
HANDS OFF!!
HMPH.
SO IDIOTIC.

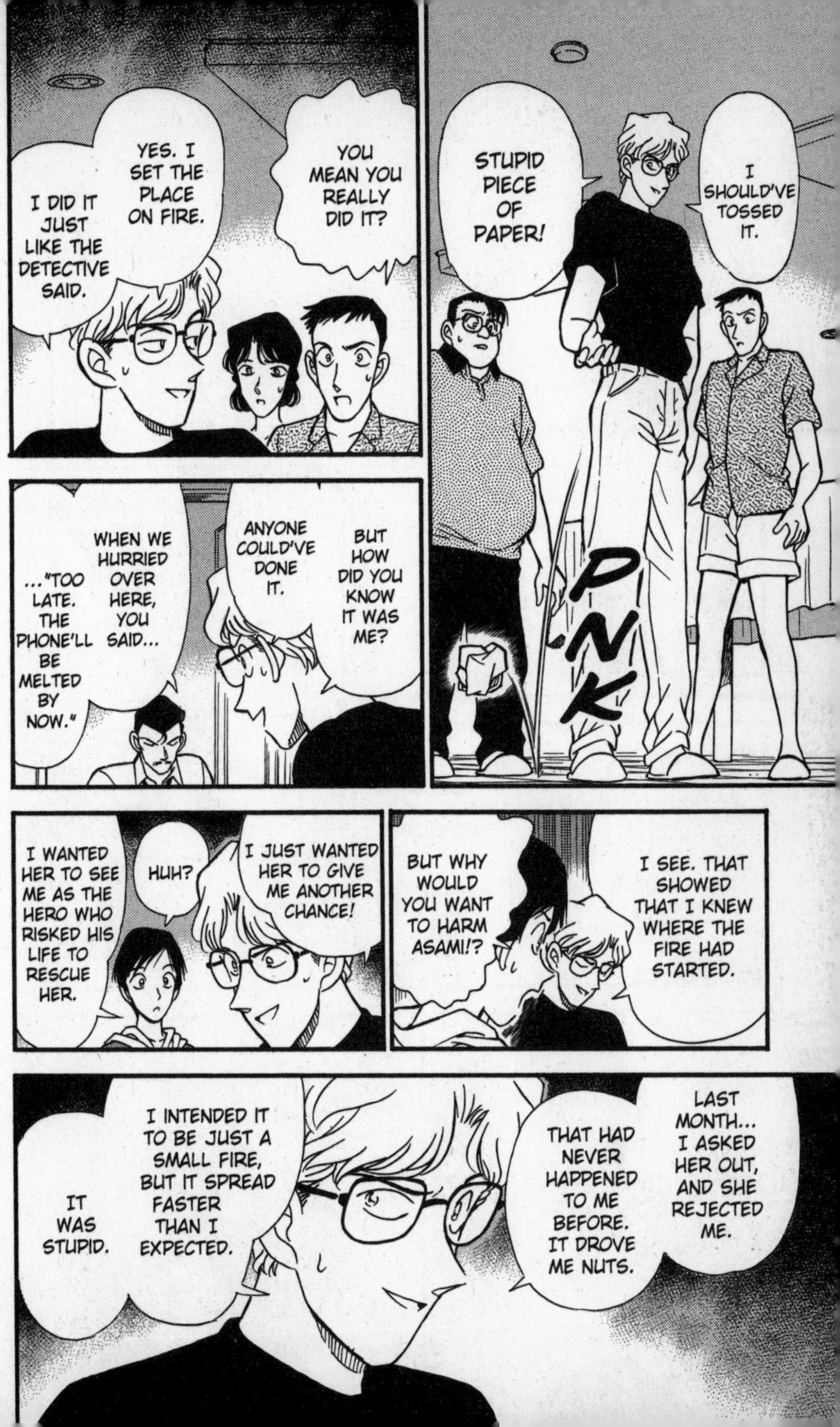
I SHOULD'VE TOSSED IT.
STUPID PIECE OF PAPER!
PNK
YOU MEAN YOU REALLY DID IT?
YES. I SET THE PLACE ON FIRE.
I DID IT JUST LIKE THE DETECTIVE SAID.
BUT HOW DID YOU KNOW IT WAS ME?
ANYONE COULD'VE DONE IT.
WHEN WE HURRIED OVER HERE, YOU SAID...
..."TOO LATE. THE PHONE'LL BE MELTED BY NOW."
I SEE. THAT SHOWED THAT I KNEW WHERE THE FIRE HAD STARTED.
BUT WHY WOULD YOU WANT TO HARM ASAMI!?
I JUST WANTED HER TO GIVE ME ANOTHER CHANCE!
HUH?
I WANTED HER TO SEE ME AS THE HERO WHO RISKED HIS LIFE TO RESCUE HER.
LAST MONTH... I ASKED HER OUT, AND SHE REJECTED ME.
THAT HAD NEVER HAPPENED TO ME BEFORE. IT DROVE ME NUTS.
I INTENDED IT TO BE JUST A SMALL FIRE, BUT IT SPREAD FASTER THAN I EXPECTED.
IT WAS STUPID.

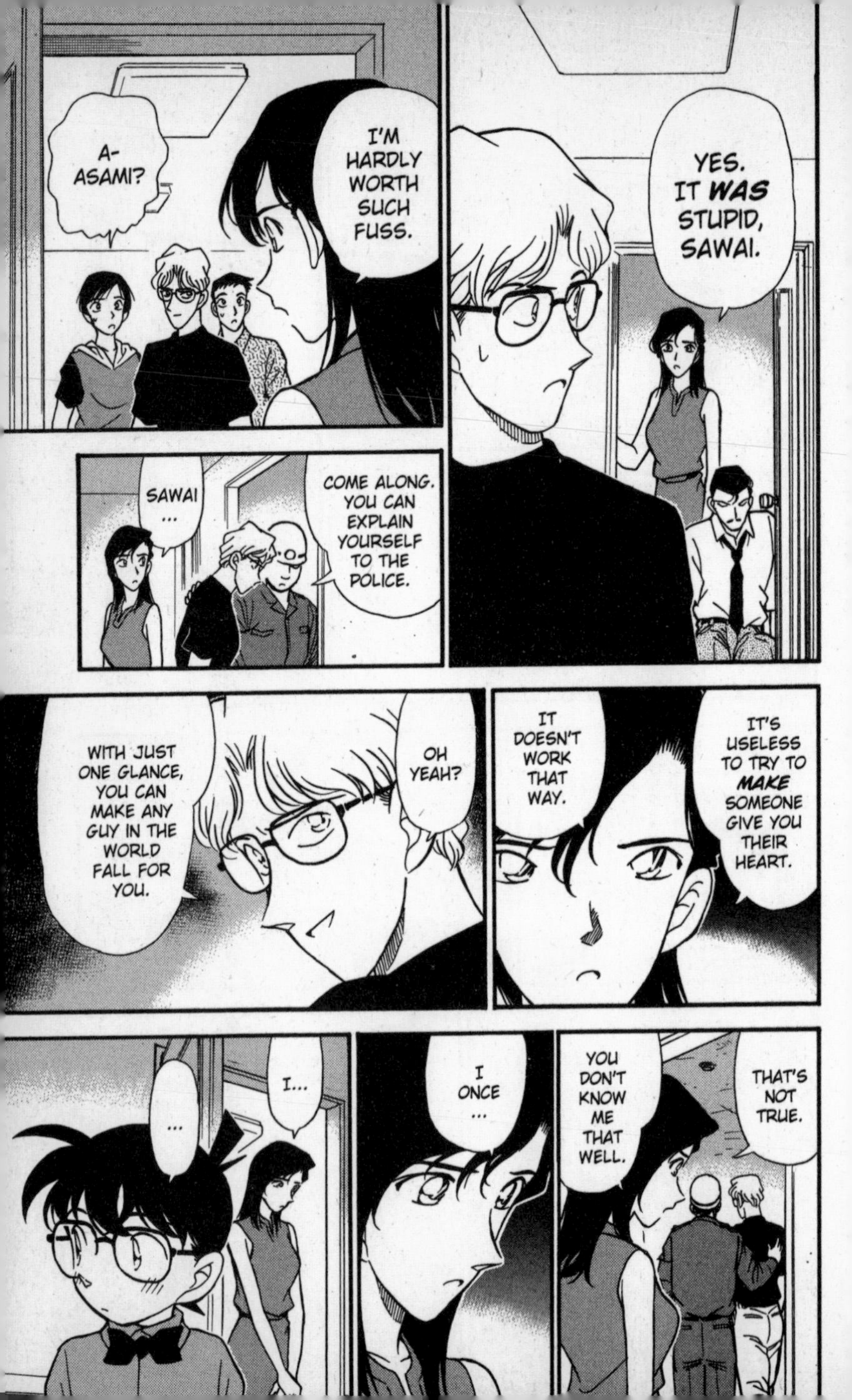
YES. IT **WAS** STUPID, SAWAI.
I'M HARDLY WORTH SUCH FUSS.
A-ASAMI?
COME ALONG. YOU CAN EXPLAIN YOURSELF TO THE POLICE.
SAWAI ...
IT'S USELESS TO TRY TO ***MAKE*** SOMEONE GIVE YOU THEIR HEART.
IT DOESN'T WORK THAT WAY.
OH YEAH?
WITH JUST ONE GLANCE, YOU CAN MAKE ANY GUY IN THE WORLD FALL FOR YOU.
THAT'S NOT TRUE.
YOU DON'T KNOW ME THAT WELL.
I ONCE ...
I...
...

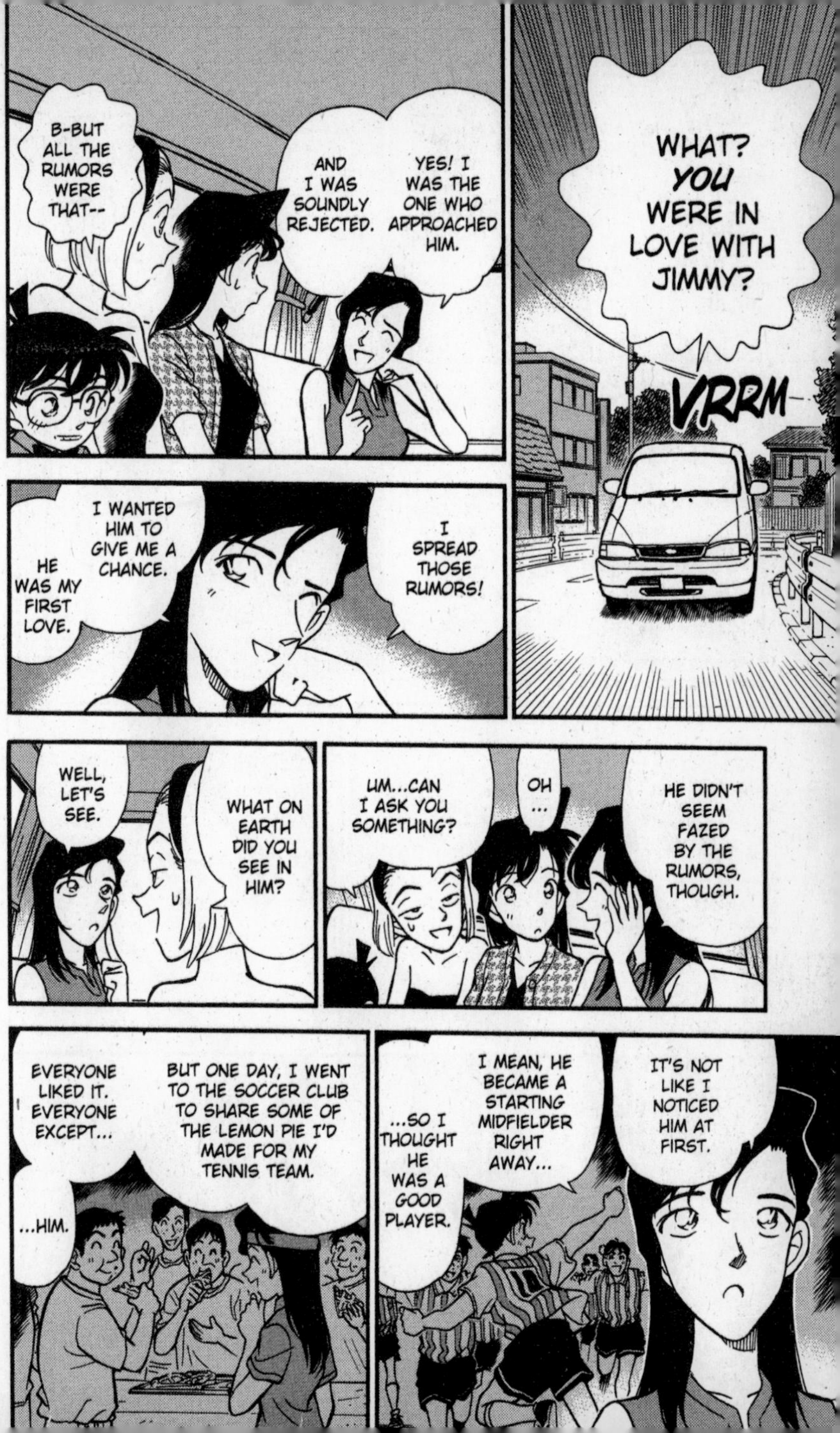
WHAT? *YOU* WERE IN LOVE WITH JIMMY?
VRRM
YES! I WAS THE ONE WHO APPROACHED HIM.
AND I WAS SOUNDLY REJECTED.
B-BUT ALL THE RUMORS WERE THAT--
I SPREAD THOSE RUMORS!
I WANTED HIM TO GIVE ME A CHANCE.
HE WAS MY FIRST LOVE.
HE DIDN'T SEEM FAZED BY THE RUMORS, THOUGH.
OH ...
UM...CAN I ASK YOU SOMETHING?
WHAT ON EARTH DID YOU SEE IN HIM?
WELL, LET'S SEE.
IT'S NOT LIKE I NOTICED HIM AT FIRST.
I MEAN, HE BECAME A STARTING MIDFIELDER RIGHT AWAY...
...SO I THOUGHT HE WAS A GOOD PLAYER.
BUT ONE DAY, I WENT TO THE SOCCER CLUB TO SHARE SOME OF THE LEMON PIE I'D MADE FOR MY TENNIS TEAM.
EVERYONE LIKED IT. EVERYONE EXCEPT...
...HIM.

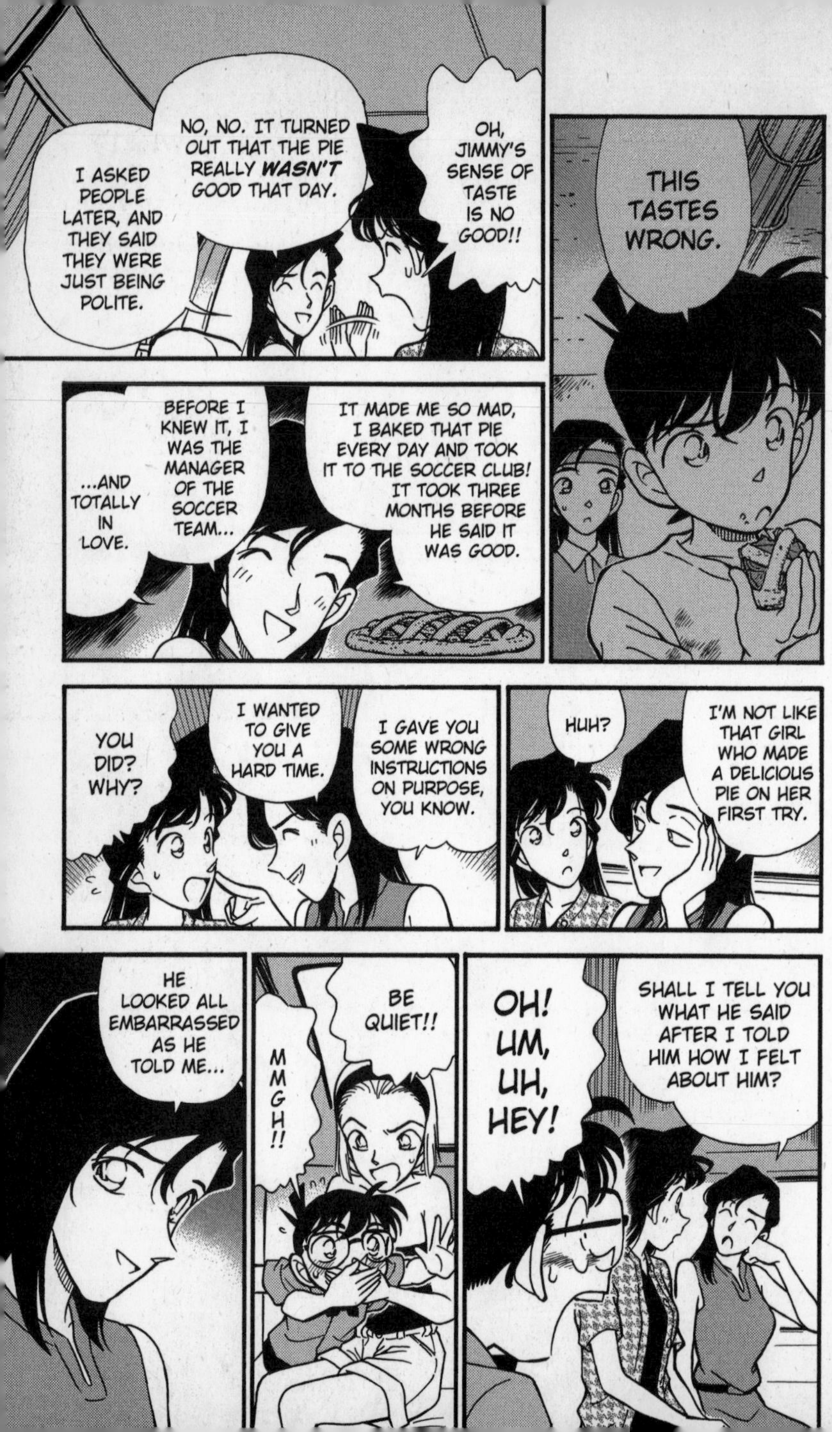
THIS TASTES WRONG.
OH, JIMMY'S SENSE OF TASTE IS NO GOOD!!
NO, NO. IT TURNED OUT THAT THE PIE REALLY ***WASN'T*** GOOD THAT DAY.
I ASKED PEOPLE LATER, AND THEY SAID THEY WERE JUST BEING POLITE.
IT MADE ME SO MAD, I BAKED THAT PIE EVERY DAY AND TOOK IT TO THE SOCCER CLUB! IT TOOK THREE MONTHS BEFORE HE SAID IT WAS GOOD.
BEFORE I KNEW IT, I WAS THE MANAGER OF THE SOCCER TEAM...
...AND TOTALLY IN LOVE.
I'M NOT LIKE THAT GIRL WHO MADE A DELICIOUS PIE ON HER FIRST TRY.
HUH?
I GAVE YOU SOME WRONG INSTRUCTIONS ON PURPOSE, YOU KNOW.
I WANTED TO GIVE YOU A HARD TIME.
YOU DID? WHY?
SHALL I TELL YOU WHAT HE SAID AFTER I TOLD HIM HOW I FELT ABOUT HIM?
OH! UM, UH, HEY!
BE QUIET!!
MMGH!!
HE LOOKED ALL EMBARRASSED AS HE TOLD ME...

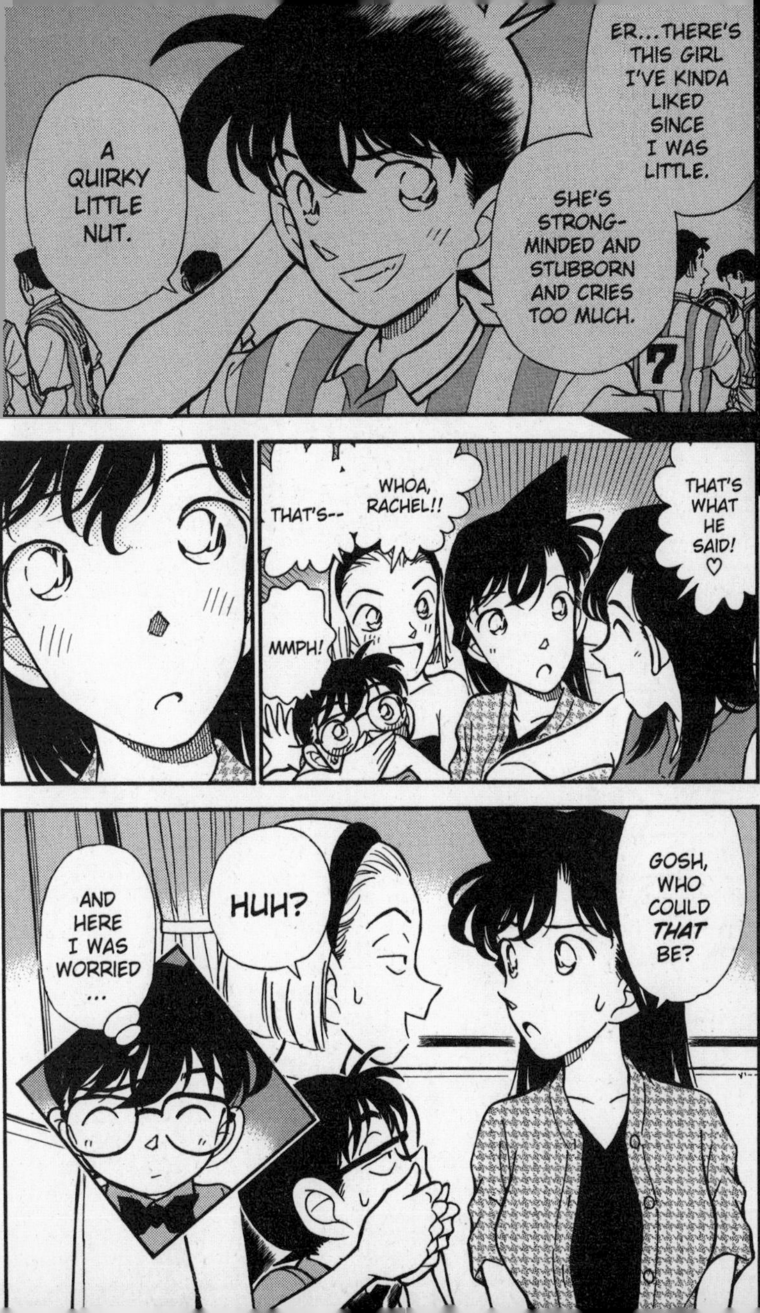
ER...THERE'S THIS GIRL I'VE KINDA LIKED SINCE I WAS LITTLE.
SHE'S STRONG-MINDED AND STUBBORN AND CRIES TOO MUCH.
A QUIRKY LITTLE NUT.
7
THAT'S WHAT HE SAID! ♡
WHOA, RACHEL!!
THAT'S--
MMPH!
GOSH, WHO COULD *THAT* BE?
HUH?
AND HERE I WAS WORRIED ...

FILE 6: THE TRANSFER STUDENT

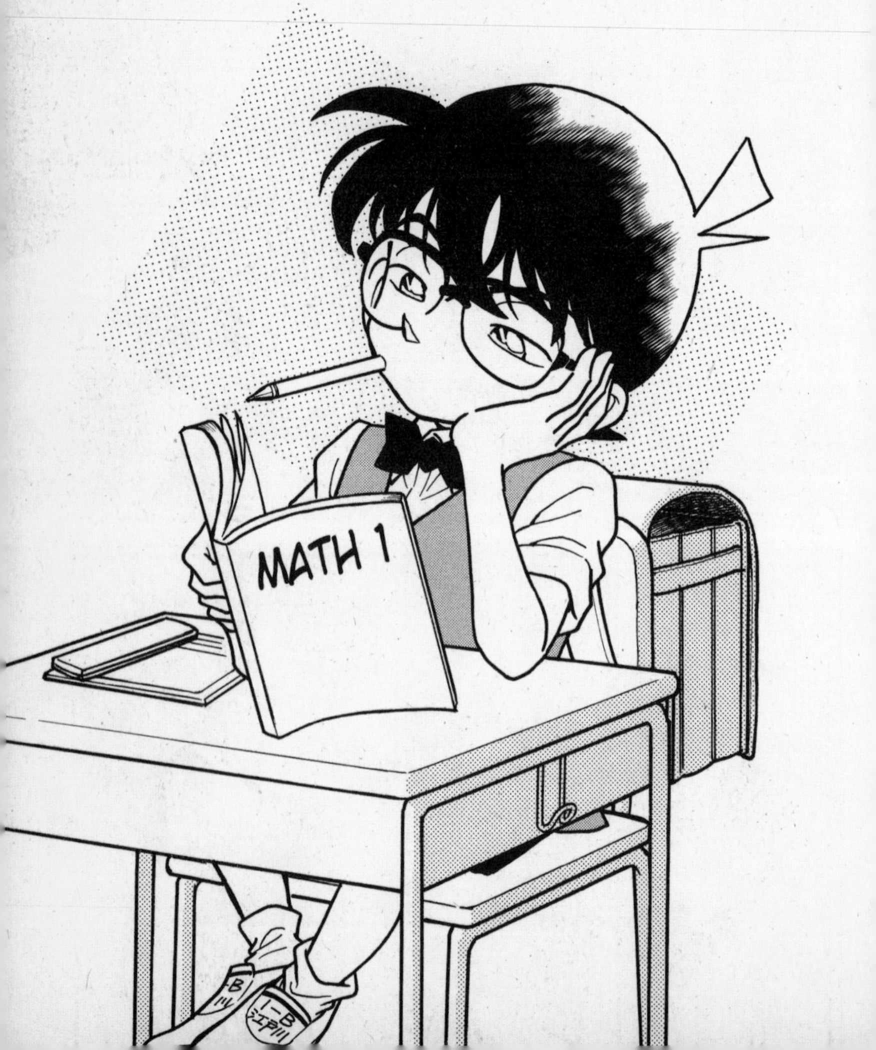
MATH 1

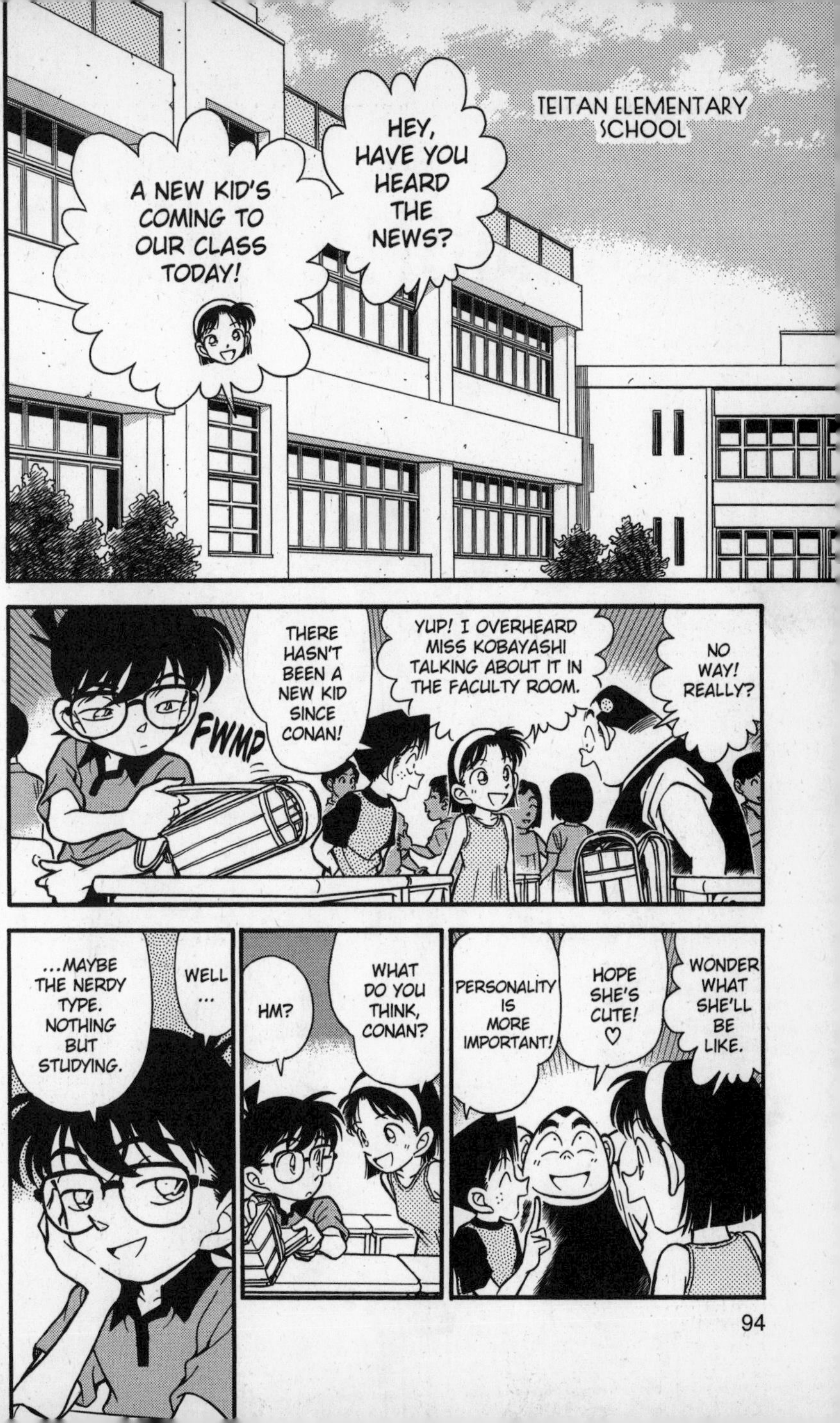
TEITAN ELEMENTARY SCHOOL
HEY, HAVE YOU HEARD THE NEWS?
A NEW KID'S COMING TO OUR CLASS TODAY!
NO WAY! REALLY?
YUP! I OVERHEARD MISS KOBAYASHI TALKING ABOUT IT IN THE FACULTY ROOM.
THERE HASN'T BEEN A NEW KID SINCE CONAN!
FWMP
WONDER WHAT SHE'LL BE LIKE.
HOPE SHE'S CUTE! ♡
PERSONALITY IS MORE IMPORTANT!
WHAT DO YOU THINK, CONAN?
HM?
WELL ...
...MAYBE THE NERDY TYPE. NOTHING BUT STUDYING.

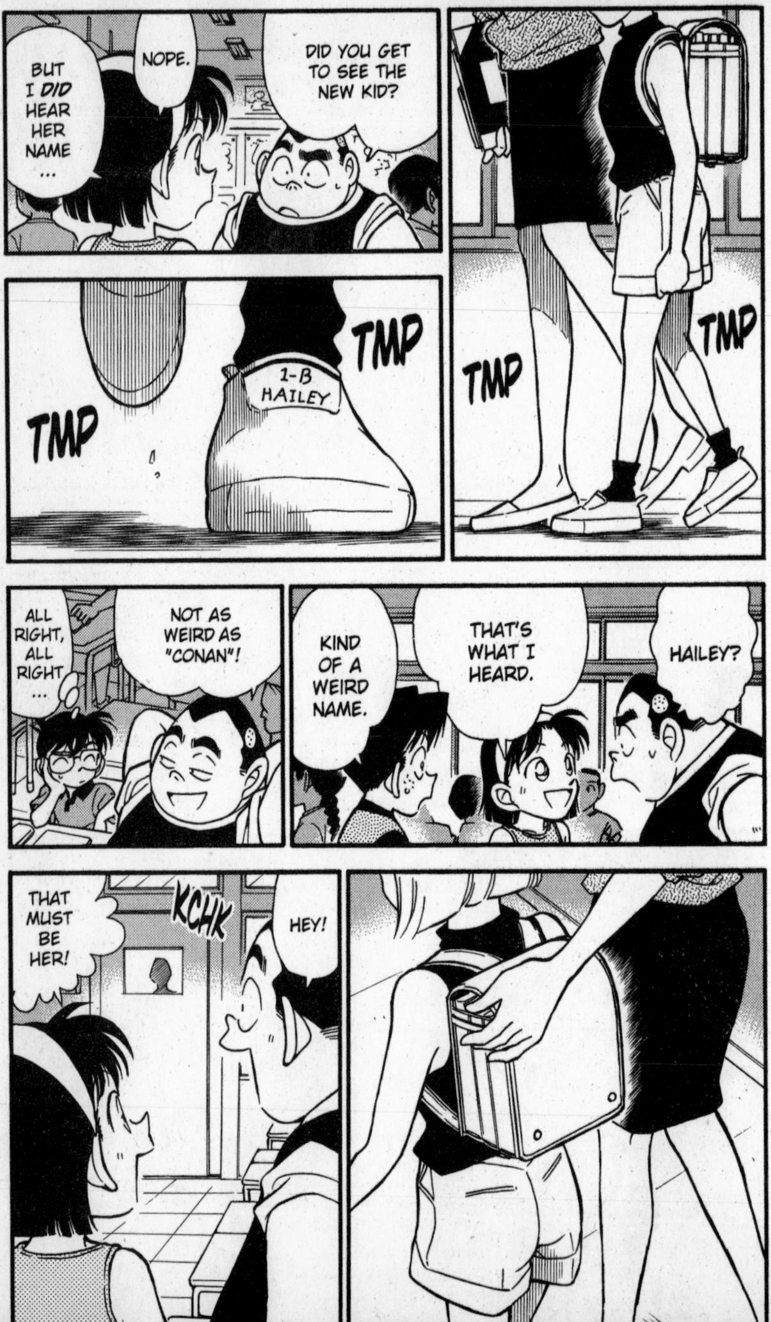
TMP
TMP
DID YOU GET TO SEE THE NEW KID?
NOPE.
BUT I DID HEAR HER NAME...
TMP
1-B HAILEY
TMP
HAILEY?
THAT'S WHAT I HEARD.
KIND OF A WEIRD NAME.
NOT AS WEIRD AS "CONAN"!
ALL RIGHT, ALL RIGHT...
HEY!
KCHK
THAT MUST BE HER!

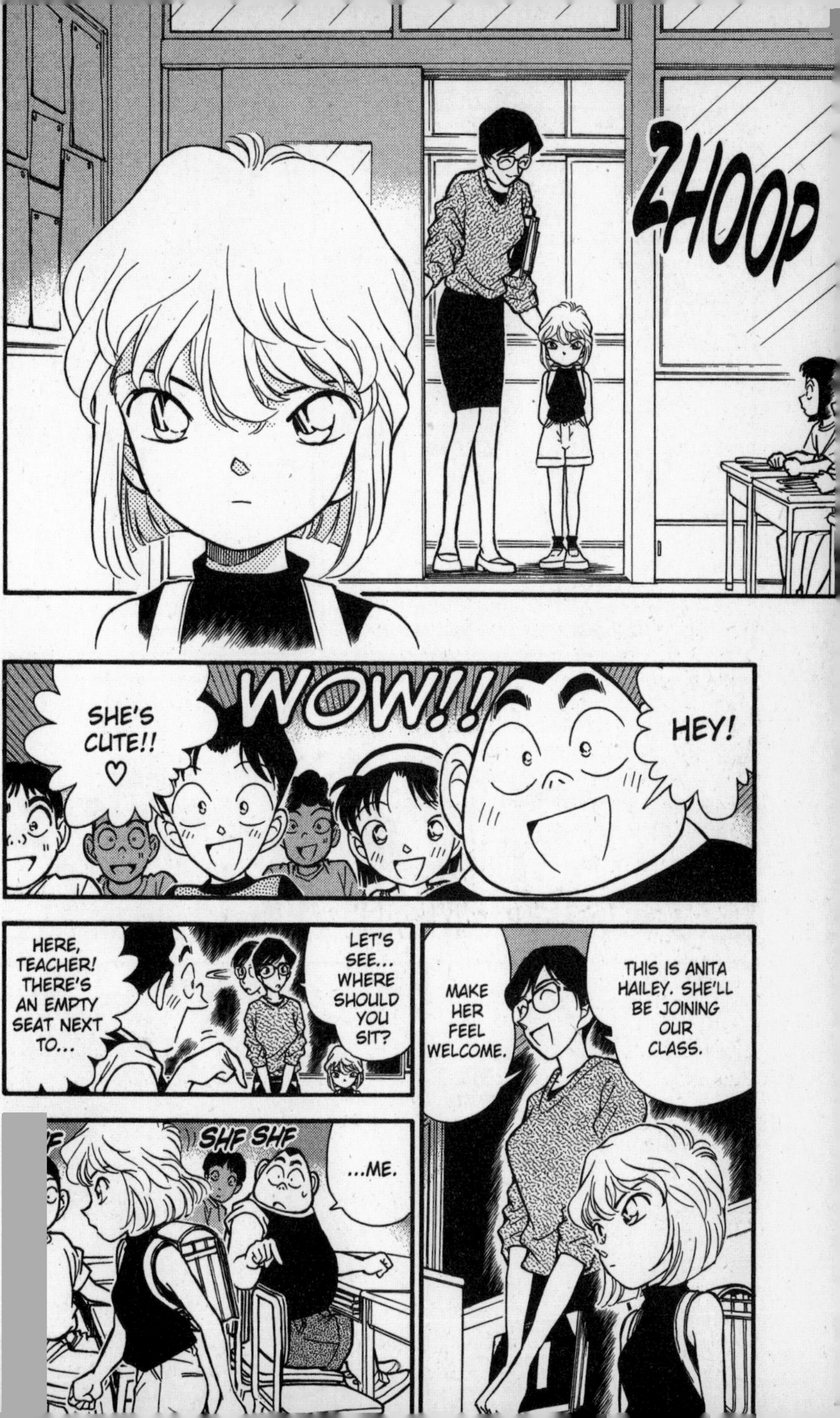
ZHOOP
HEY!
WOW!!
SHE'S CUTE!! ♡
THIS IS ANITA HAILEY. SHE'LL BE JOINING OUR CLASS.
MAKE HER FEEL WELCOME.
LET'S SEE... WHERE SHOULD YOU SIT?
HERE, TEACHER! THERE'S AN EMPTY SEAT NEXT TO...
...ME.
SHF SHF

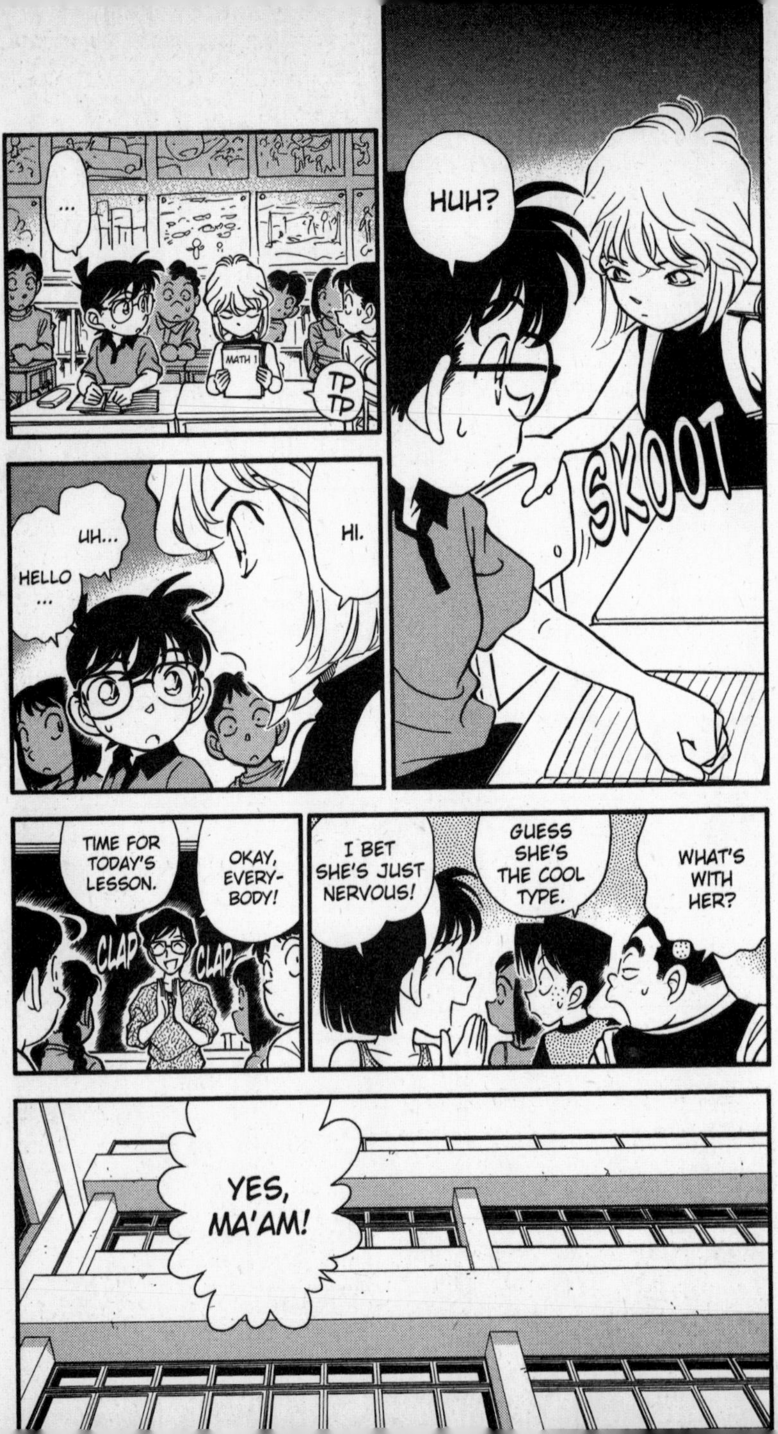
HUH?
SKOOT
...
MATH 1
TP TP
HI.
UH...
HELLO...
WHAT'S WITH HER?
GUESS SHE'S THE COOL TYPE.
I BET SHE'S JUST NERVOUS!
OKAY, EVERY-BODY!
TIME FOR TODAY'S LESSON.
CLAP
CLAP
YES, MA'AM!

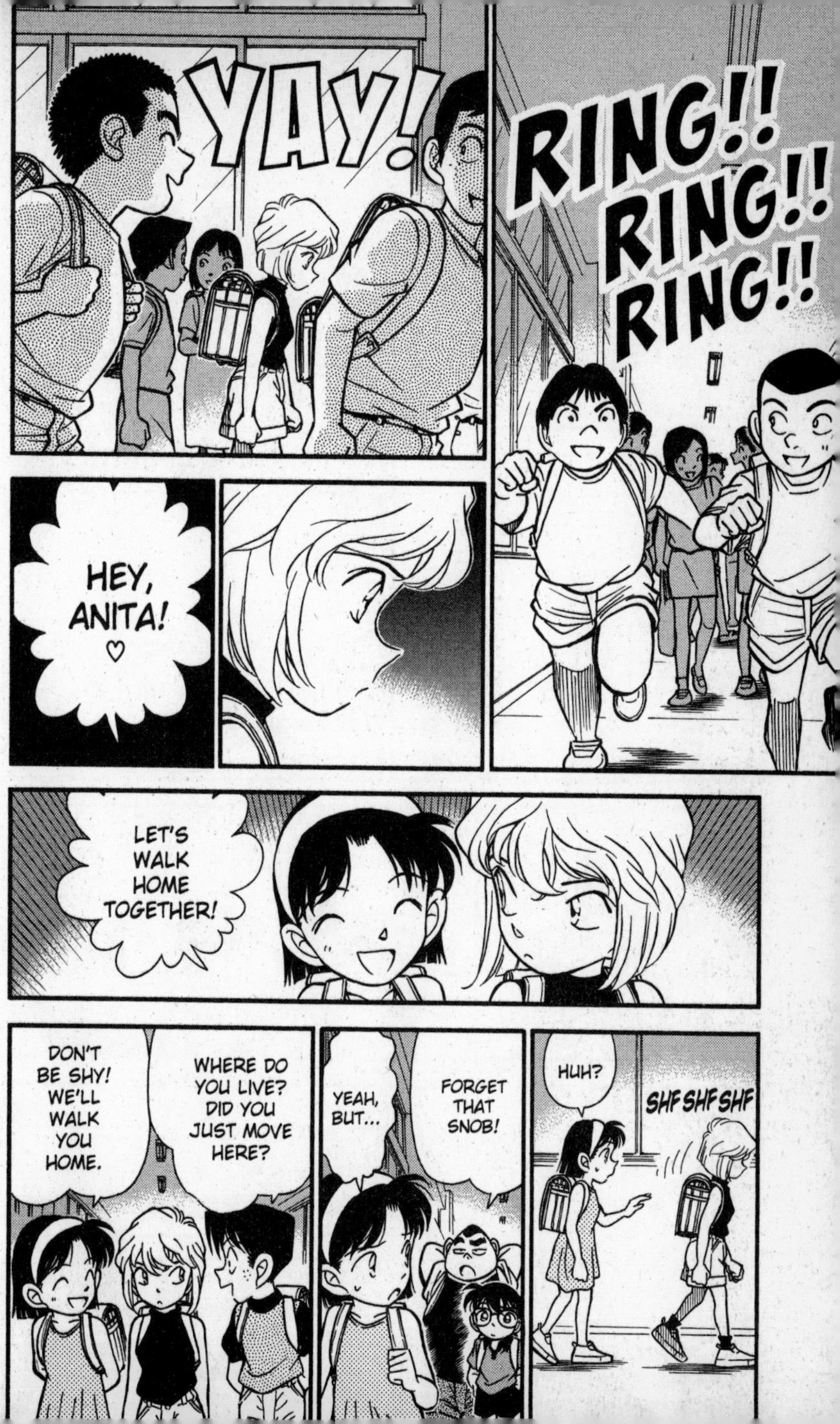
RING!! RING!! RING!!
YAY!
HEY, ANITA! ♡
LET'S WALK HOME TOGETHER!
HUH?
SHF SHF SHF
FORGET THAT SNOB!
YEAH, BUT...
WHERE DO YOU LIVE? DID YOU JUST MOVE HERE?
DON'T BE SHY! WE'LL WALK YOU HOME.

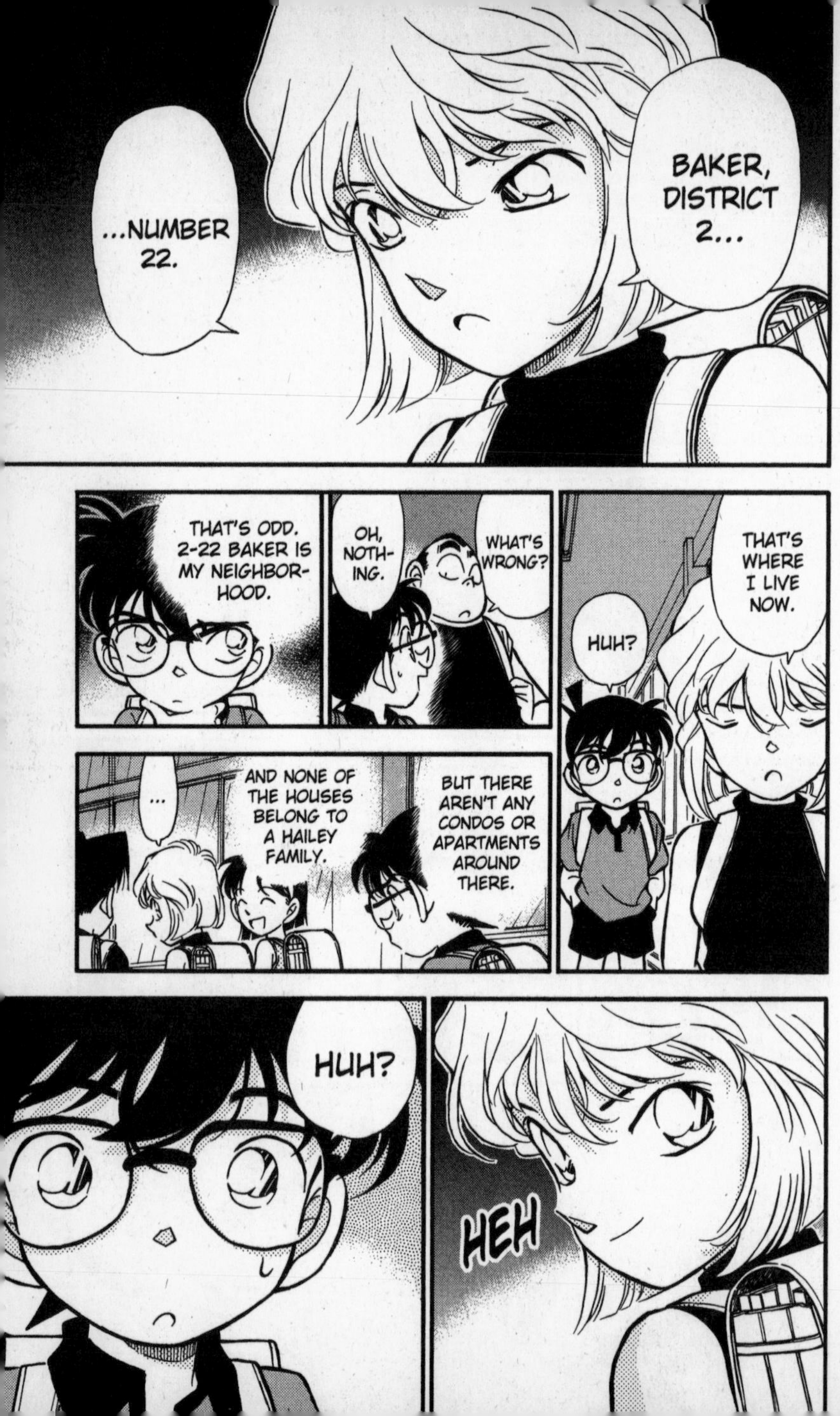
BAKER, DISTRICT 2...
...NUMBER 22.
THAT'S WHERE I LIVE NOW.
HUH?
WHAT'S WRONG?
OH, NOTH-ING.
THAT'S ODD. 2-22 BAKER IS MY NEIGHBOR-HOOD.
BUT THERE AREN'T ANY CONDOS OR APARTMENTS AROUND THERE.
AND NONE OF THE HOUSES BELONG TO A HAILEY FAMILY.
...
HEH
HUH?

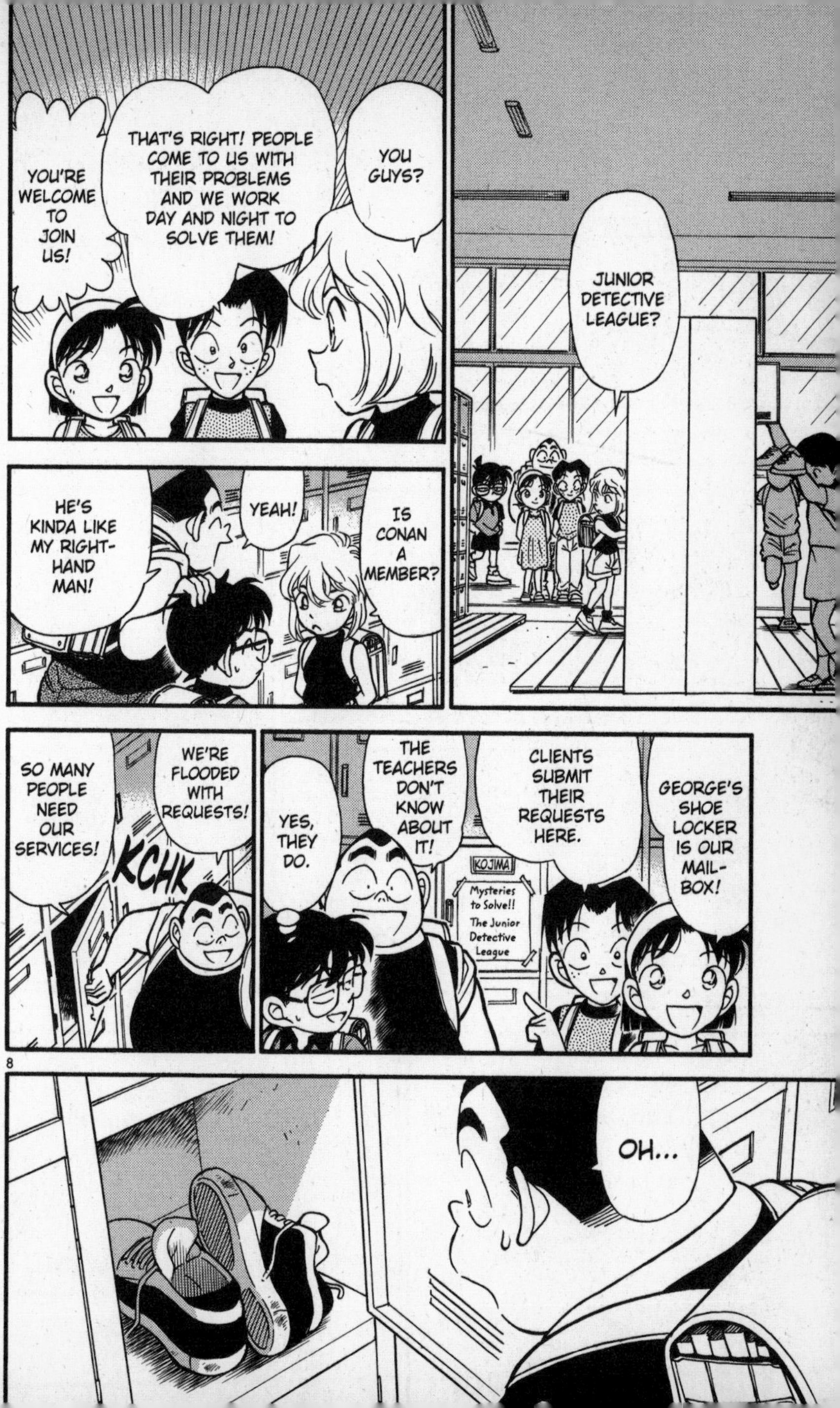
JUNIOR DETECTIVE LEAGUE?
YOU GUYS?
THAT'S RIGHT! PEOPLE COME TO US WITH THEIR PROBLEMS AND WE WORK DAY AND NIGHT TO SOLVE THEM!
YOU'RE WELCOME TO JOIN US!
IS CONAN A MEMBER?
YEAH!
HE'S KINDA LIKE MY RIGHT-HAND MAN!
GEORGE'S SHOE LOCKER IS OUR MAIL-BOX!
CLIENTS SUBMIT THEIR REQUESTS HERE.
THE TEACHERS DON'T KNOW ABOUT IT!
YES, THEY DO.
KOJIMA
Mysteries to Solve!! The Junior Detective League
WE'RE FLOODED WITH REQUESTS!
SO MANY PEOPLE NEED OUR SERVICES!
KCHK
OH...

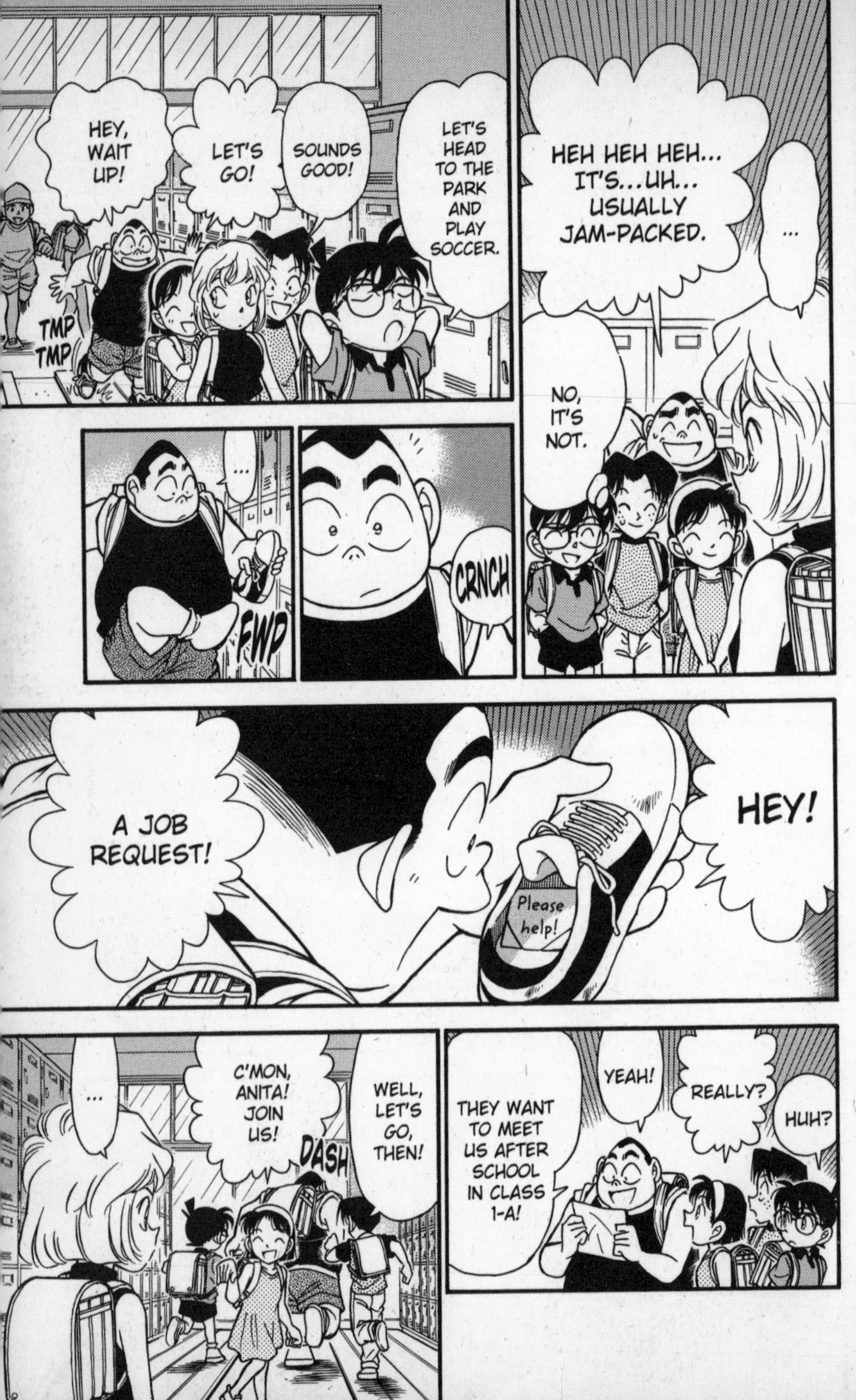
...
HEH HEH HEH... IT'S...UH... USUALLY JAM-PACKED.
NO, IT'S NOT.
LET'S HEAD TO THE PARK AND PLAY SOCCER.
SOUNDS GOOD!
LET'S GO!
HEY, WAIT UP!
TMP TMP
CRNCH
...
FWP
HEY!
Please help!
A JOB REQUEST!
HUH?
REALLY?
YEAH!
THEY WANT TO MEET US AFTER SCHOOL IN CLASS 1-A!
WELL, LET'S GO, THEN!
DASH
C'MON, ANITA! JOIN US!
...

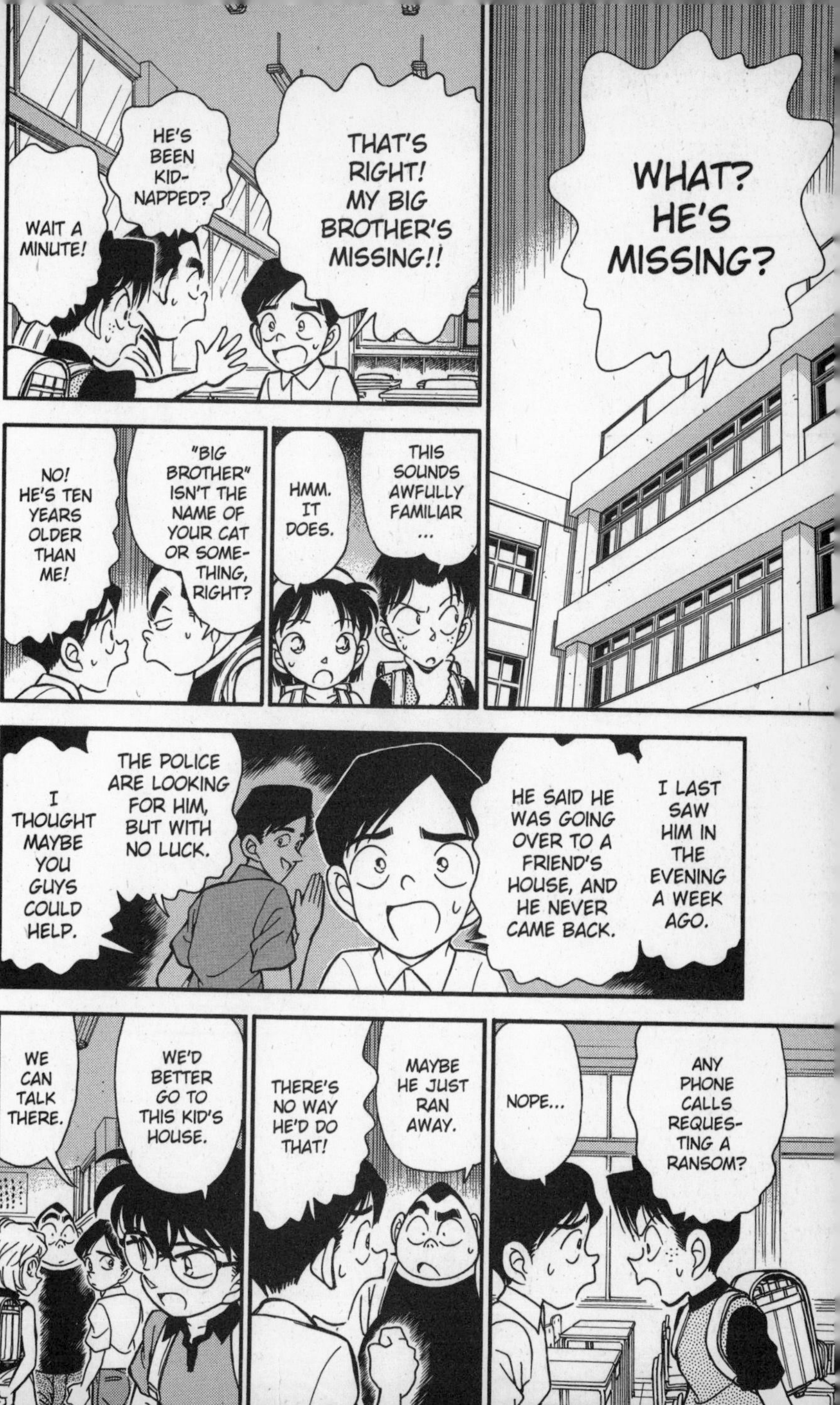
WHAT? HE'S MISSING?
THAT'S RIGHT! MY BIG BROTHER'S MISSING!!
HE'S BEEN KID-NAPPED?
WAIT A MINUTE!
THIS SOUNDS AWFULLY FAMILIAR ...
HMM. IT DOES.
"BIG BROTHER" ISN'T THE NAME OF YOUR CAT OR SOME-THING, RIGHT?
NO! HE'S TEN YEARS OLDER THAN ME!
I LAST SAW HIM IN THE EVENING A WEEK AGO.
HE SAID HE WAS GOING OVER TO A FRIEND'S HOUSE, AND HE NEVER CAME BACK.
THE POLICE ARE LOOKING FOR HIM, BUT WITH NO LUCK.
I THOUGHT MAYBE YOU GUYS COULD HELP.
ANY PHONE CALLS REQUES-TING A RANSOM?
NOPE...
MAYBE HE JUST RAN AWAY.
THERE'S NO WAY HE'D DO THAT!
WE'D BETTER GO TO THIS KID'S HOUSE.
WE CAN TALK THERE.

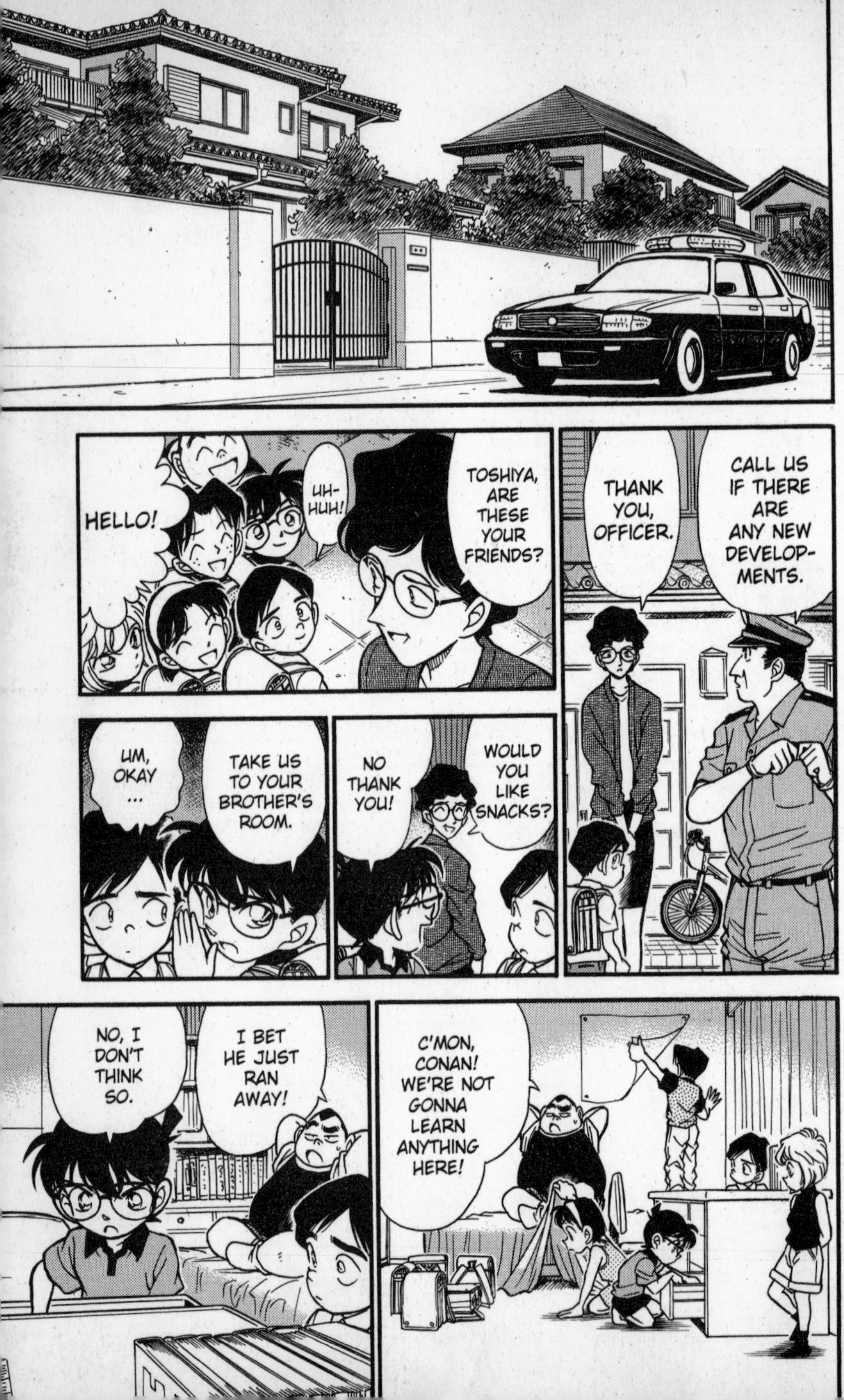
CALL US IF THERE ARE ANY NEW DEVELOPMENTS.
THANK YOU, OFFICER.
TOSHIYA, ARE THESE YOUR FRIENDS?
UH-HUH!
HELLO!
WOULD YOU LIKE SNACKS?
NO THANK YOU!
TAKE US TO YOUR BROTHER'S ROOM.
UM, OKAY ...
C'MON, CONAN! WE'RE NOT GONNA LEARN ANYTHING HERE!
I BET HE JUST RAN AWAY!
NO, I DON'T THINK SO.

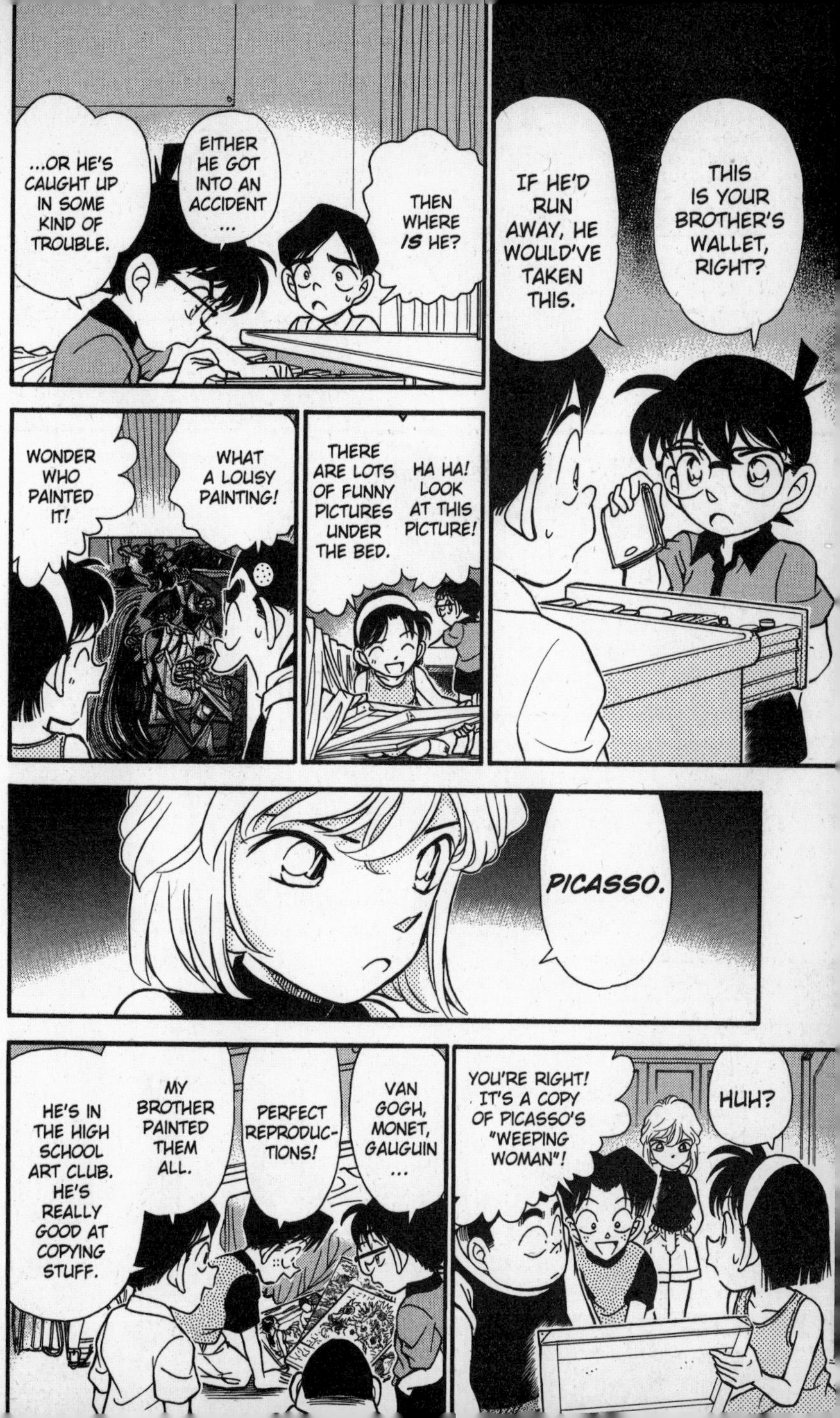
THIS IS YOUR BROTHER'S WALLET, RIGHT?
IF HE'D RUN AWAY, HE WOULD'VE TAKEN THIS.
THEN WHERE *IS* HE?
EITHER HE GOT INTO AN ACCIDENT ...
...OR HE'S CAUGHT UP IN SOME KIND OF TROUBLE.
HA HA! LOOK AT THIS PICTURE!
THERE ARE LOTS OF FUNNY PICTURES UNDER THE BED.
WHAT A LOUSY PAINTING!
WONDER WHO PAINTED IT!
PICASSO.
HUH?
YOU'RE RIGHT! IT'S A COPY OF PICASSO'S "WEEPING WOMAN"!
...
VAN GOGH, MONET, GAUGUIN ...
PERFECT REPRODUCTIONS!
MY BROTHER PAINTED THEM ALL.
HE'S IN THE HIGH SCHOOL ART CLUB. HE'S REALLY GOOD AT COPYING STUFF.

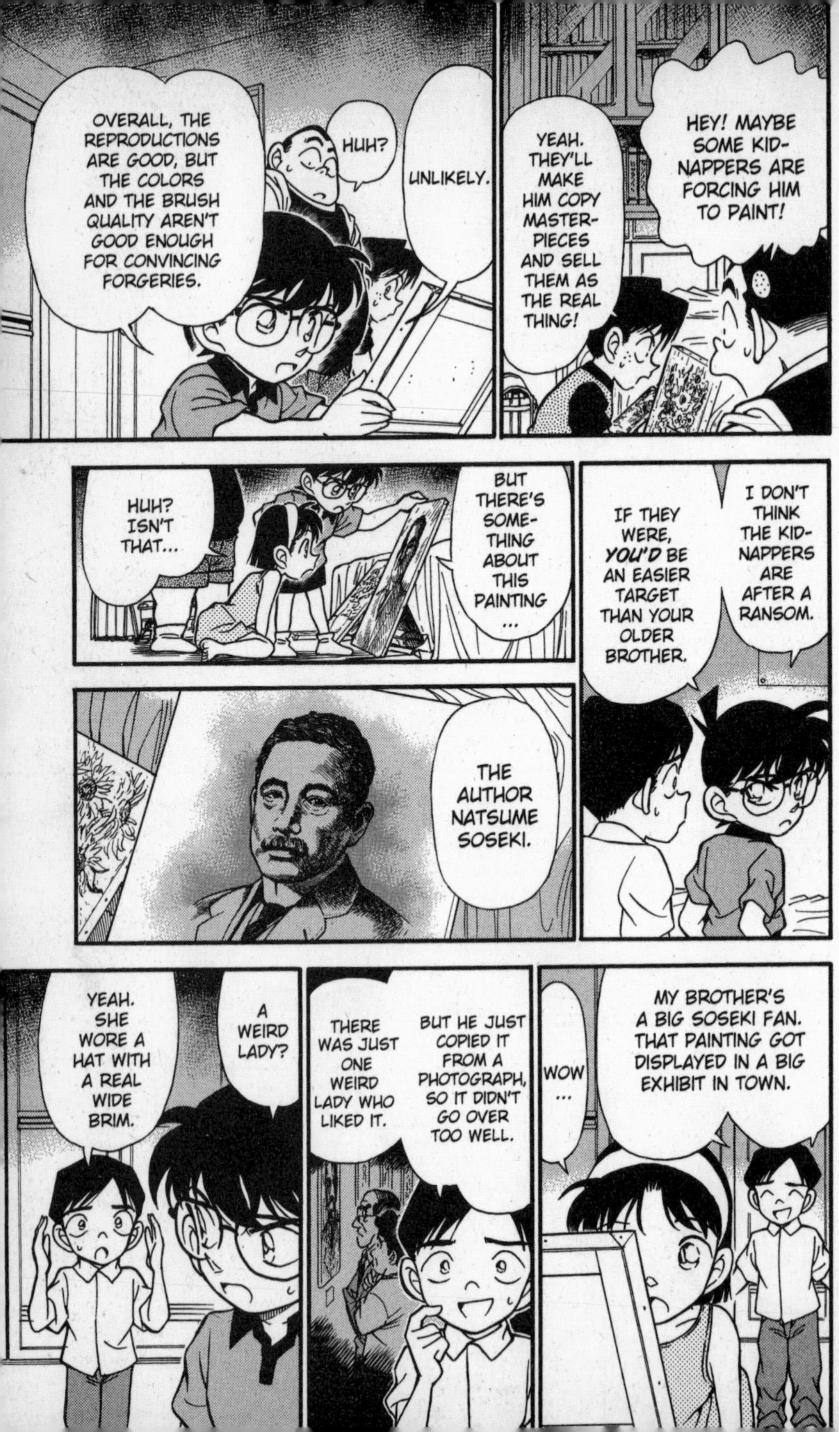
HEY! MAYBE SOME KID-NAPPERS ARE FORCING HIM TO PAINT!
YEAH. THEY'LL MAKE HIM COPY MASTER-PIECES AND SELL THEM AS THE REAL THING!
UNLIKELY.
HUH?
OVERALL, THE REPRODUCTIONS ARE GOOD, BUT THE COLORS AND THE BRUSH QUALITY AREN'T GOOD ENOUGH FOR CONVINCING FORGERIES.
I DON'T THINK THE KID-NAPPERS ARE AFTER A RANSOM.
IF THEY WERE, *YOU'D* BE AN EASIER TARGET THAN YOUR OLDER BROTHER.
BUT THERE'S SOME-THING ABOUT THIS PAINTING ...
HUH? ISN'T THAT...
THE AUTHOR NATSUME SOSEKI.
MY BROTHER'S A BIG SOSEKI FAN. THAT PAINTING GOT DISPLAYED IN A BIG EXHIBIT IN TOWN.
WOW ...
BUT HE JUST COPIED IT FROM A PHOTOGRAPH, SO IT DIDN'T GO OVER TOO WELL.
THERE WAS JUST ONE WEIRD LADY WHO LIKED IT.
A WEIRD LADY?
YEAH. SHE WORE A HAT WITH A REAL WIDE BRIM.

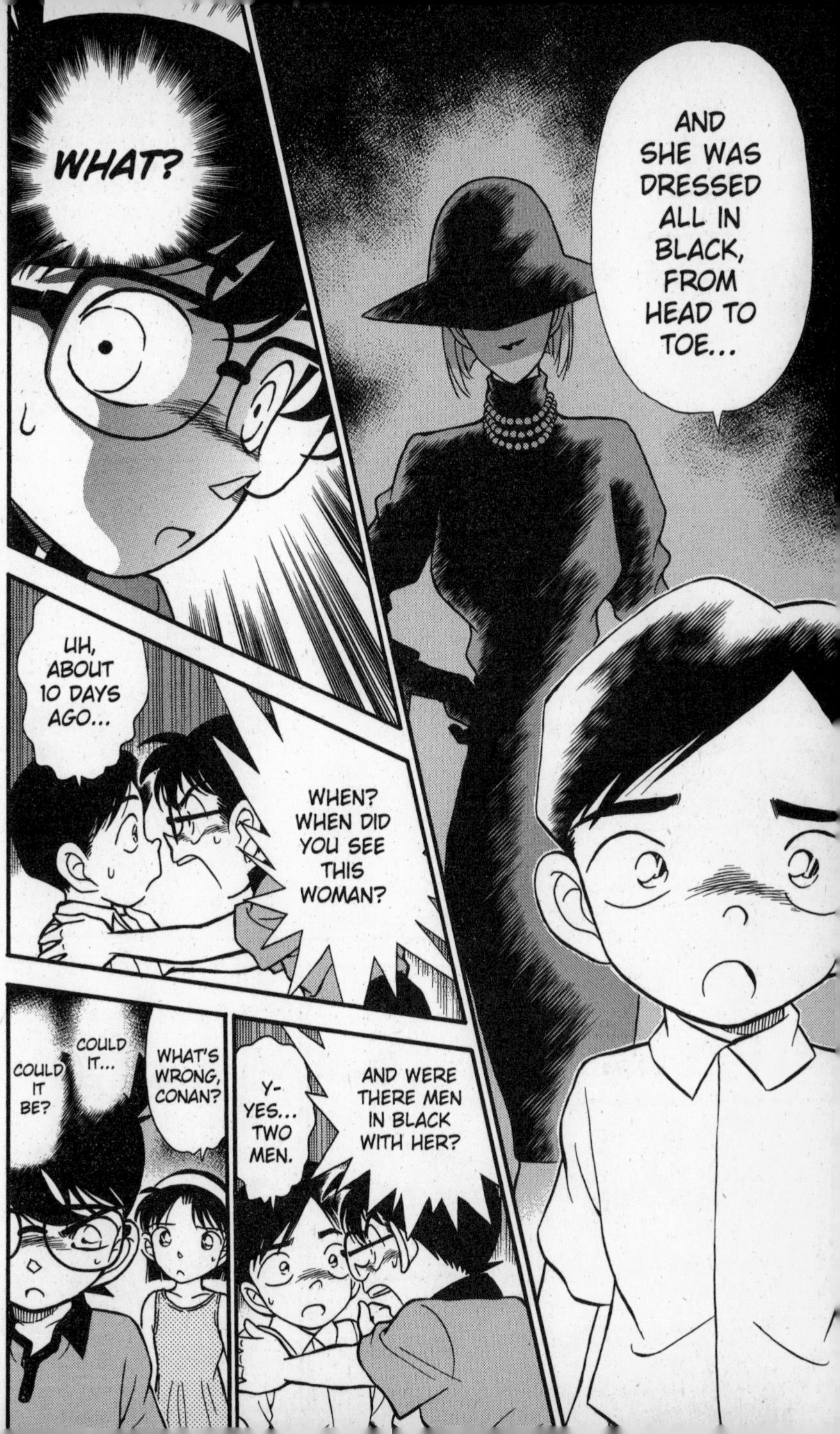
AND SHE WAS DRESSED ALL IN BLACK, FROM HEAD TO TOE...
WHAT?
WHEN? WHEN DID YOU SEE THIS WOMAN?
UH, ABOUT 10 DAYS AGO...
AND WERE THERE MEN IN BLACK WITH HER?
Y- YES... TWO MEN.
WHAT'S WRONG, CONAN?
COULD IT...
COULD IT BE?

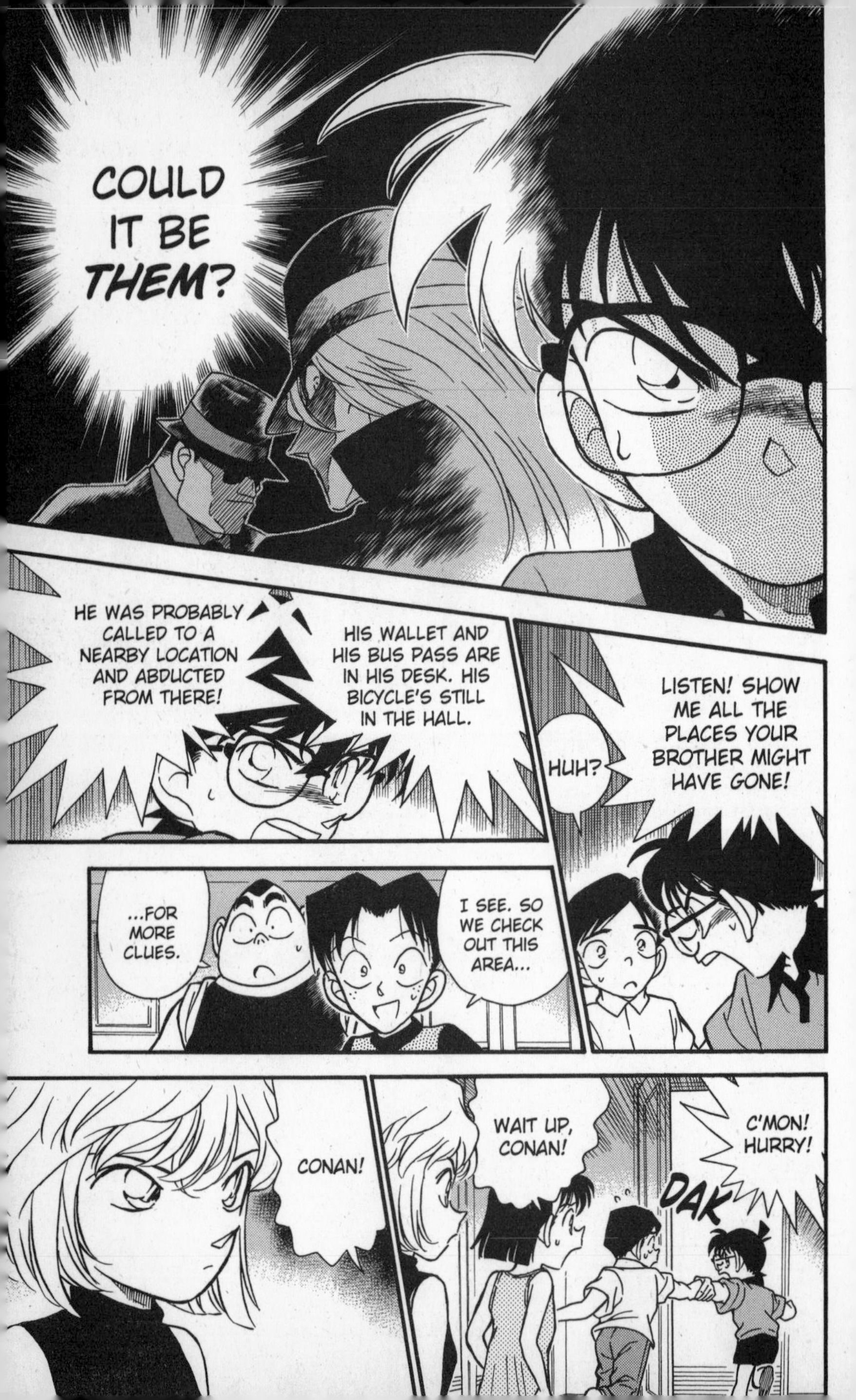
COULD IT BE *THEM*?
LISTEN! SHOW ME ALL THE PLACES YOUR BROTHER MIGHT HAVE GONE!
HUH?
HIS WALLET AND HIS BUS PASS ARE IN HIS DESK. HIS BICYCLE'S STILL IN THE HALL.
HE WAS PROBABLY CALLED TO A NEARBY LOCATION AND ABDUCTED FROM THERE!
I SEE. SO WE CHECK OUT THIS AREA...
...FOR MORE CLUES.
C'MON! HURRY!
DAK
WAIT UP, CONAN!
CONAN!

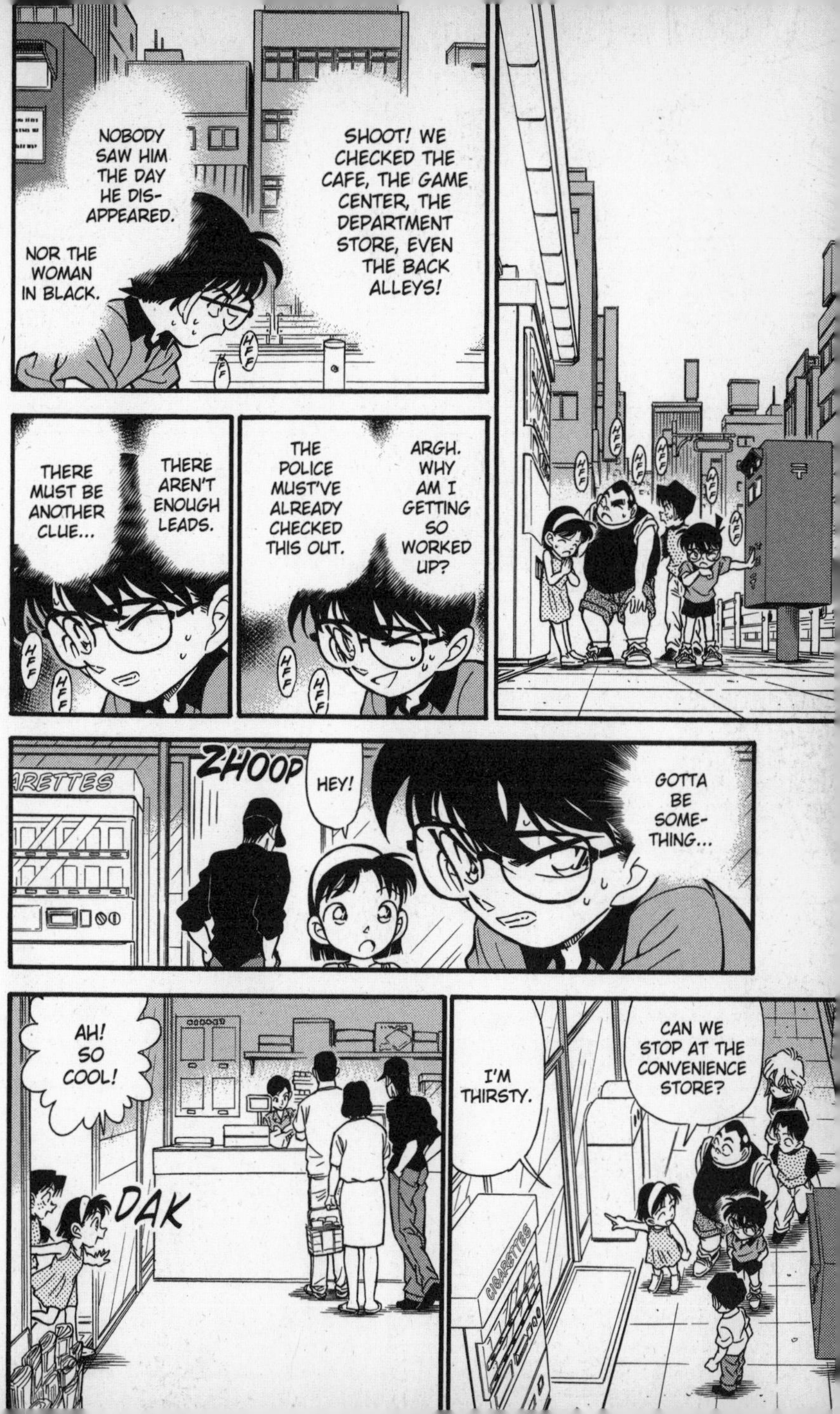

HFF
HFF
HFF
HFF
HFF
SHOOT! WE CHECKED THE CAFE, THE GAME CENTER, THE DEPARTMENT STORE, EVEN THE BACK ALLEYS!
NOBODY SAW HIM THE DAY HE DIS-APPEARED.
NOR THE WOMAN IN BLACK.
HFF
HFF
ARGH. WHY AM I GETTING SO WORKED UP?
THE POLICE MUST'VE ALREADY CHECKED THIS OUT.
HFF
HFF
THERE AREN'T ENOUGH LEADS.
THERE MUST BE ANOTHER CLUE...
HFF
HFF
GOTTA BE SOME-THING...
HEY!
ZHOOP
ARETTES
CAN WE STOP AT THE CONVENIENCE STORE?
I'M THIRSTY.
CIGARETTES
AH! SO COOL!
DAK

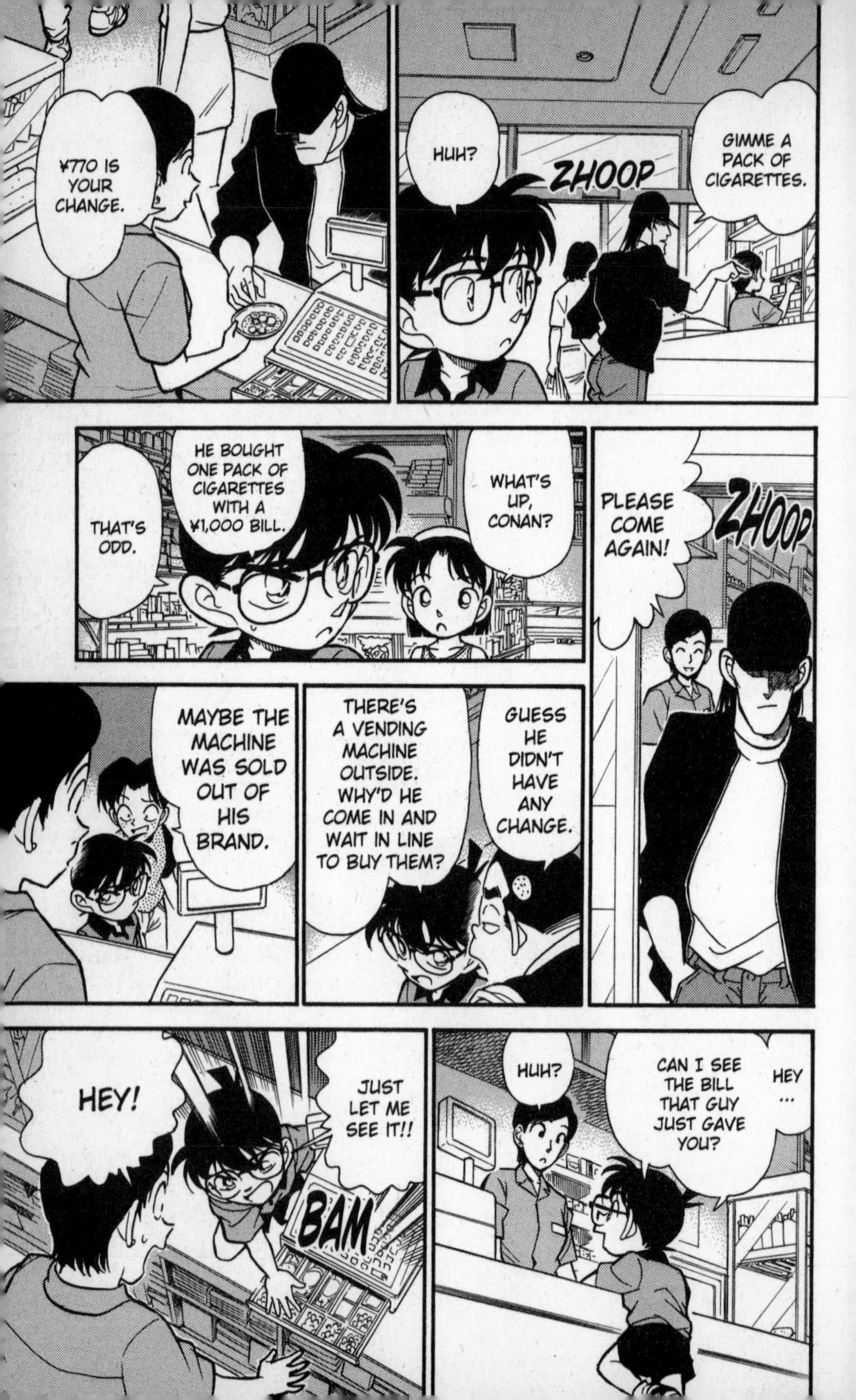
GIMME A PACK OF CIGARETTES.
ZHOOP
HUH?
¥770 IS YOUR CHANGE.
PLEASE COME AGAIN!
ZHOOP
WHAT'S UP, CONAN?
HE BOUGHT ONE PACK OF CIGARETTES WITH A ¥1,000 BILL.
THAT'S ODD.
GUESS HE DIDN'T HAVE ANY CHANGE.
THERE'S A VENDING MACHINE OUTSIDE. WHY'D HE COME IN AND WAIT IN LINE TO BUY THEM?
MAYBE THE MACHINE WAS SOLD OUT OF HIS BRAND.
HEY ...
CAN I SEE THE BILL THAT GUY JUST GAVE YOU?
HUH?
JUST LET ME SEE IT!!
BAM
HEY!

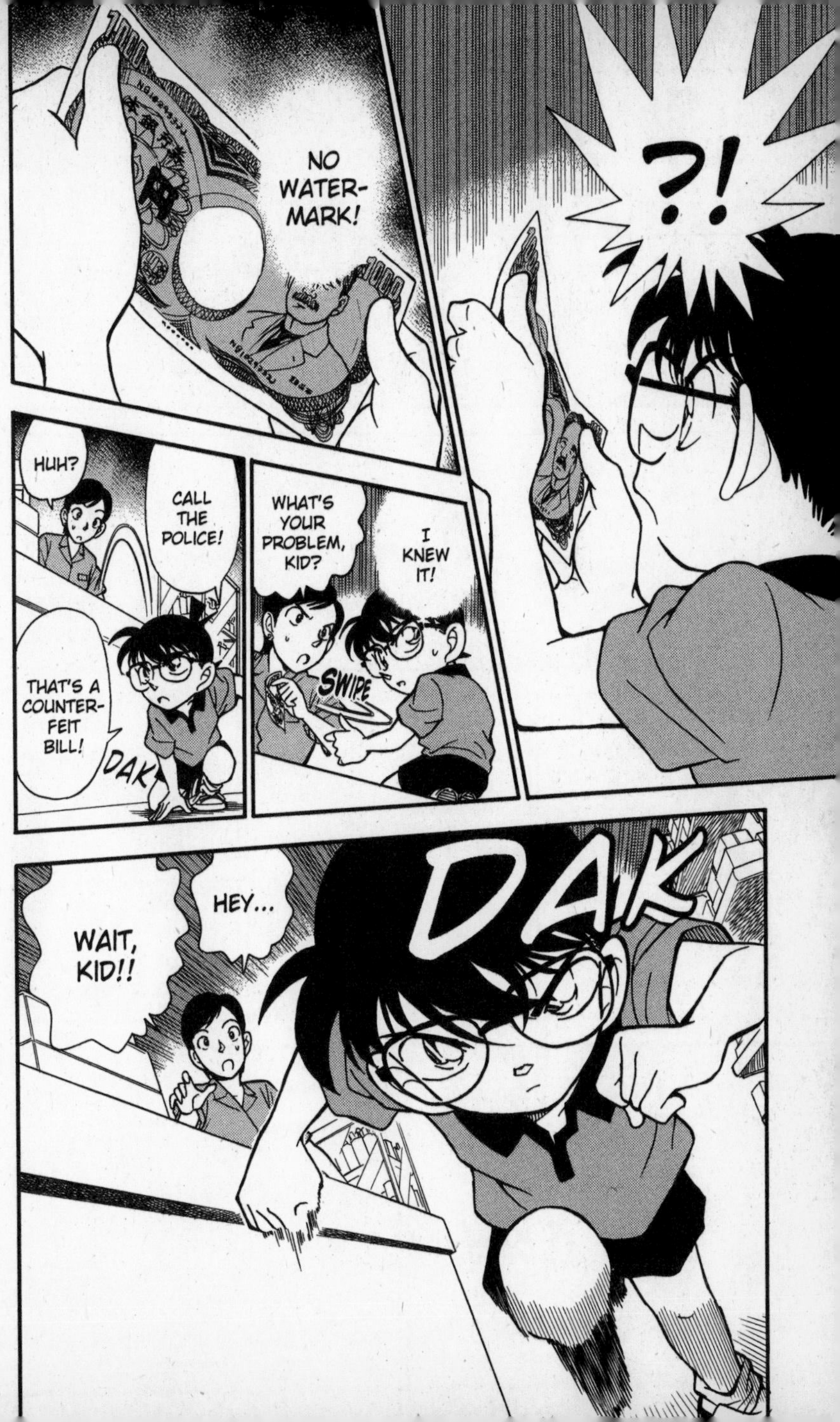
?!
NO WATER-MARK!
I KNEW IT!
WHAT'S YOUR PROBLEM, KID?
SWIPE
CALL THE POLICE!
HUH?
THAT'S A COUNTER-FEIT BILL!
DAK
DAK
HEY...
WAIT, KID!!

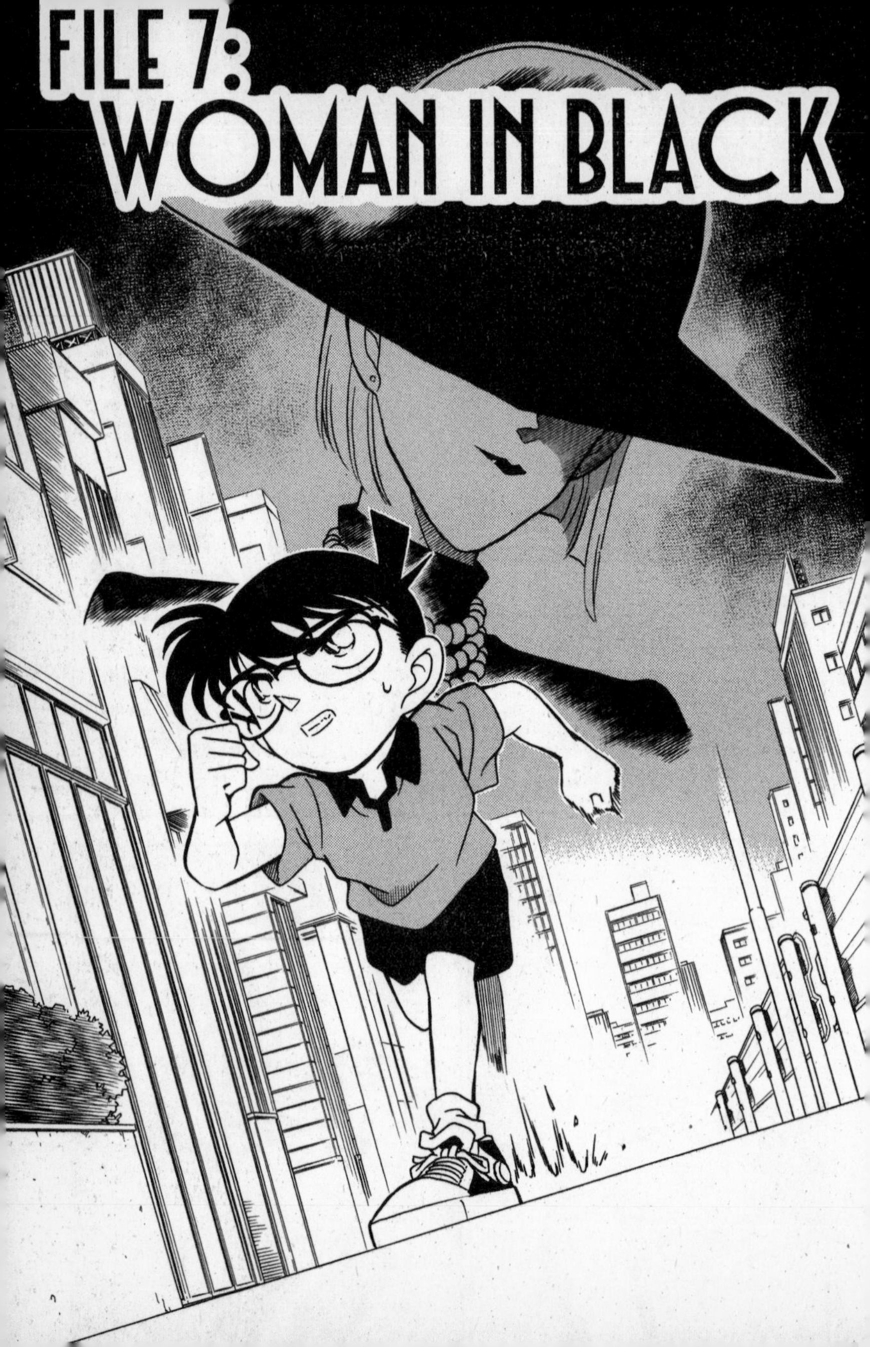
FILE 7:
WOMAN IN BLACK

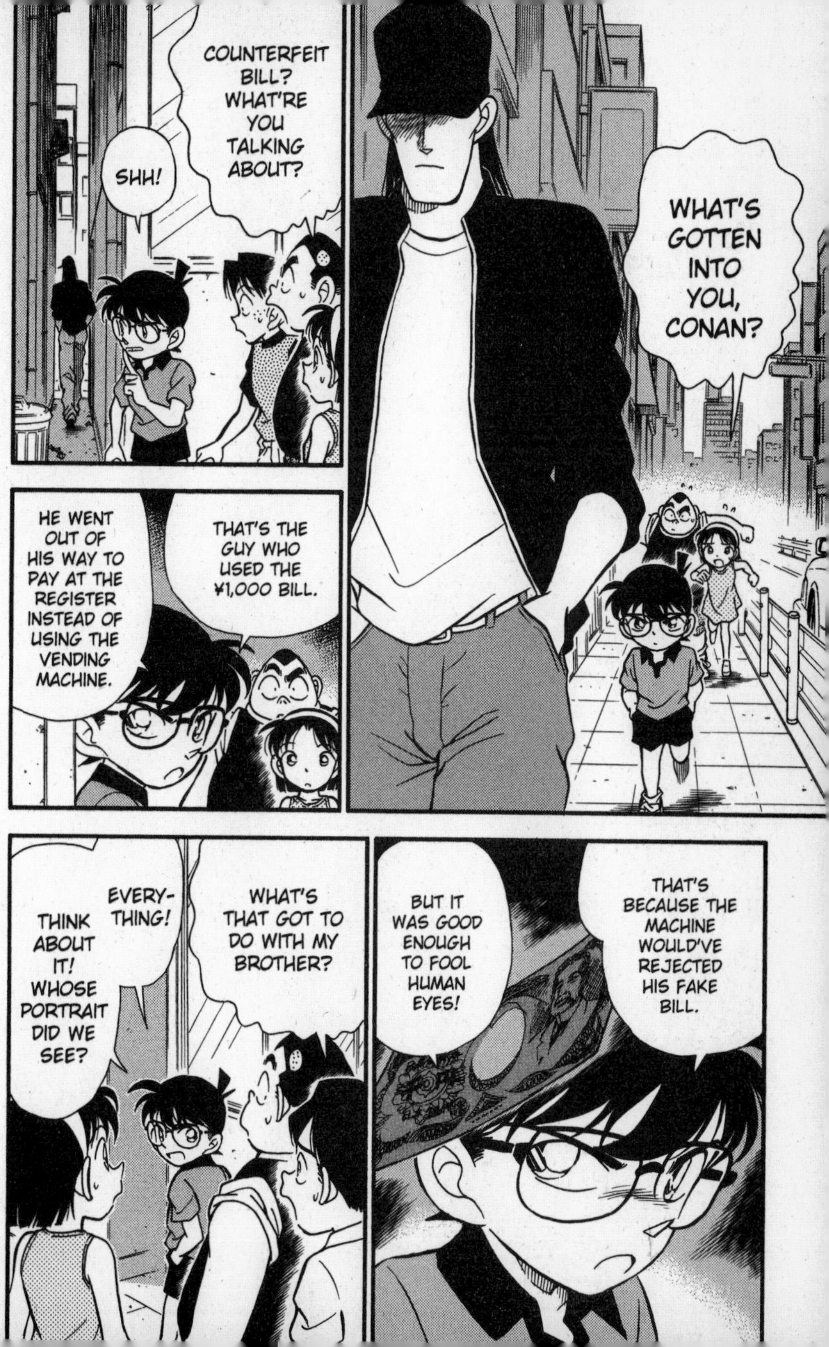
WHAT'S GOTTEN INTO YOU, CONAN?
COUNTERFEIT BILL? WHAT'RE YOU TALKING ABOUT?
SHH!
THAT'S THE GUY WHO USED THE ¥1,000 BILL.
HE WENT OUT OF HIS WAY TO PAY AT THE REGISTER INSTEAD OF USING THE VENDING MACHINE.
THAT'S BECAUSE THE MACHINE WOULD'VE REJECTED HIS FAKE BILL.
BUT IT WAS GOOD ENOUGH TO FOOL HUMAN EYES!
WHAT'S THAT GOT TO DO WITH MY BROTHER?
EVERY-THING!
THINK ABOUT IT! WHOSE PORTRAIT DID WE SEE?

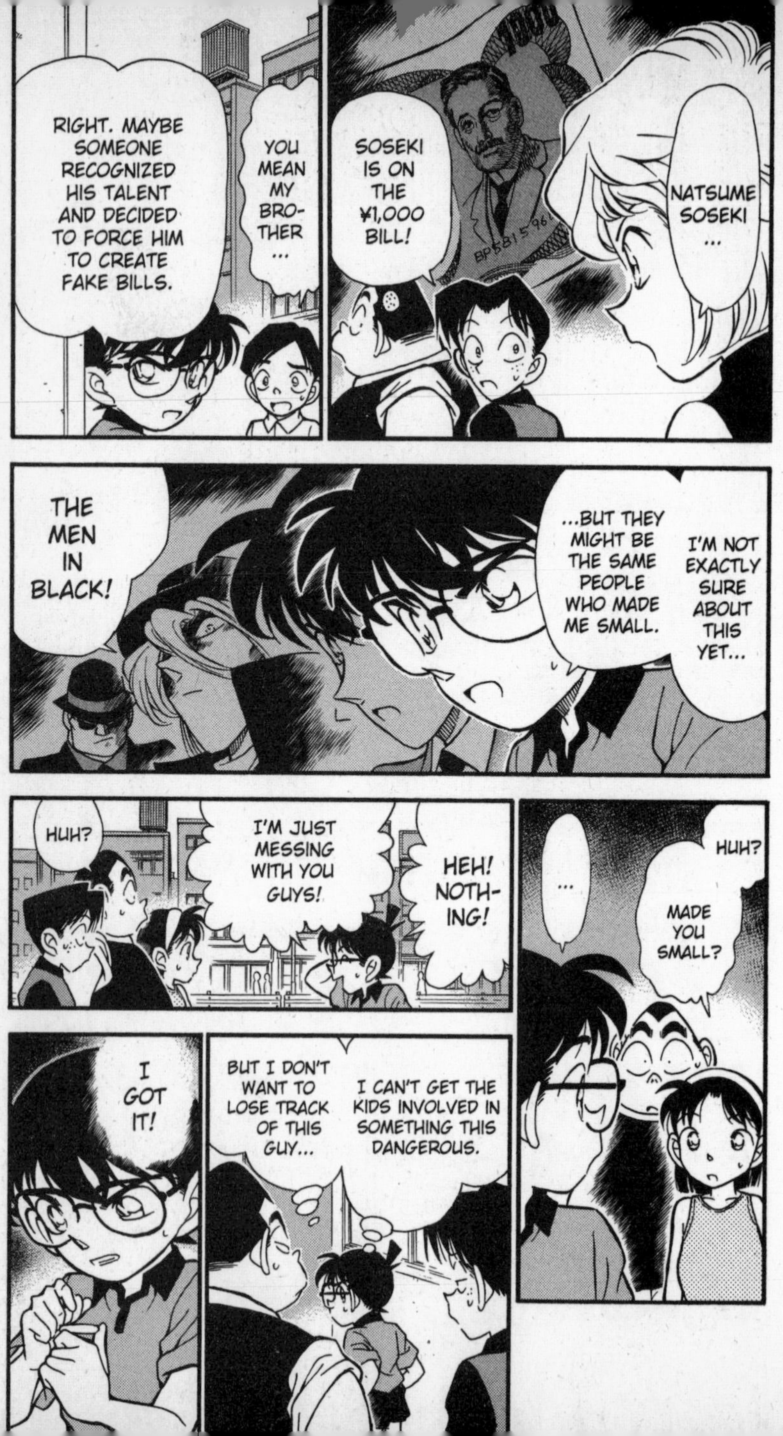
NATSUME SOSEKI...
SOSEKI IS ON THE ¥1,000 BILL!
BP 5815 96
YOU MEAN MY BRO-THER...
RIGHT. MAYBE SOMEONE RECOGNIZED HIS TALENT AND DECIDED TO FORCE HIM TO CREATE FAKE BILLS.
I'M NOT EXACTLY SURE ABOUT THIS YET...
...BUT THEY MIGHT BE THE SAME PEOPLE WHO MADE ME SMALL.
THE MEN IN BLACK!
HUH?
MADE YOU SMALL?
...
HEH! NOTH-ING!
I'M JUST MESSING WITH YOU GUYS!
HUH?
I CAN'T GET THE KIDS INVOLVED IN SOMETHING THIS DANGEROUS.
BUT I DON'T WANT TO LOSE TRACK OF THIS GUY...
I GOT IT!

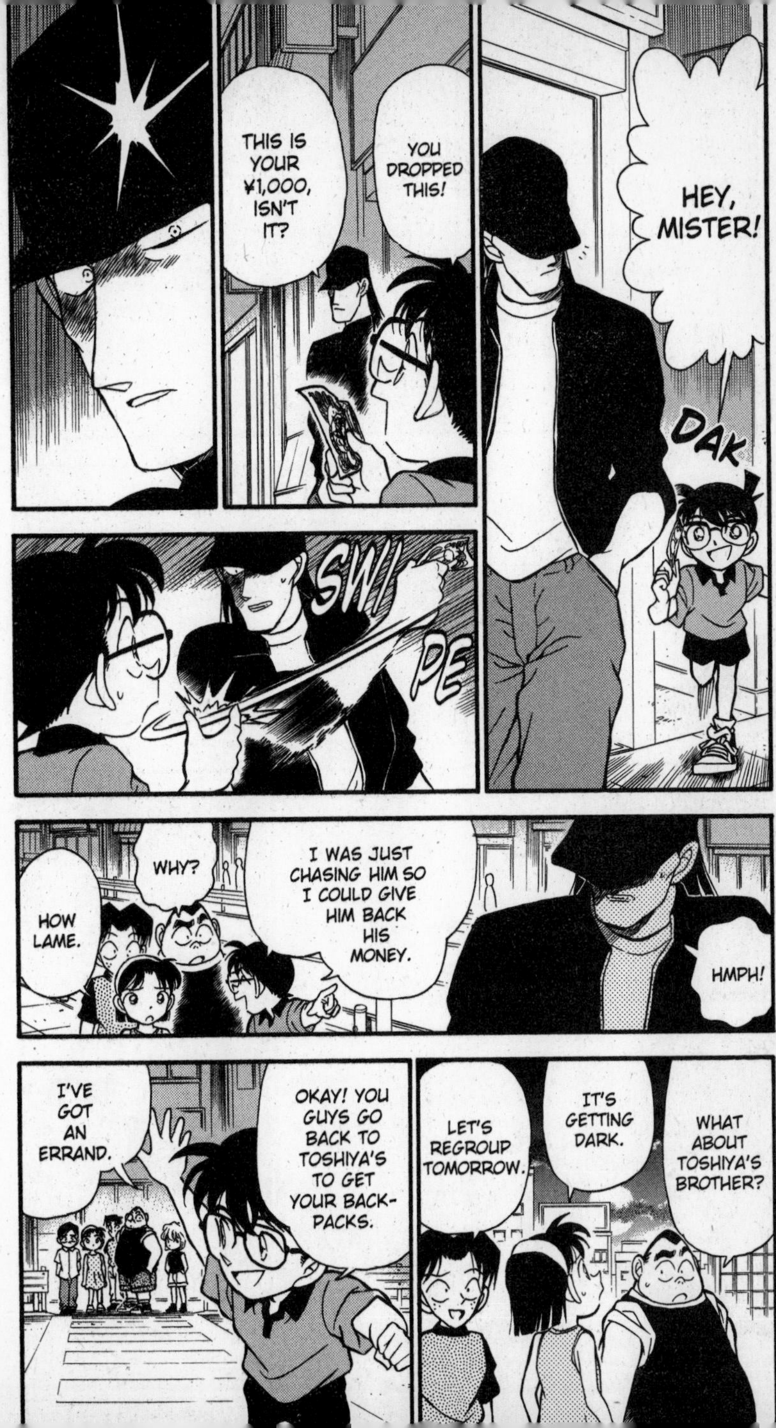
HEY, MISTER!
DAK
YOU DROPPED THIS!
THIS IS YOUR ¥1,000, ISN'T IT?
SWIPE
HMPH!
I WAS JUST CHASING HIM SO I COULD GIVE HIM BACK HIS MONEY.
WHY?
HOW LAME.
WHAT ABOUT TOSHIYA'S BROTHER?
IT'S GETTING DARK.
LET'S REGROUP TOMORROW.
OKAY! YOU GUYS GO BACK TO TOSHIYA'S TO GET YOUR BACKPACKS.
I'VE GOT AN ERRAND.

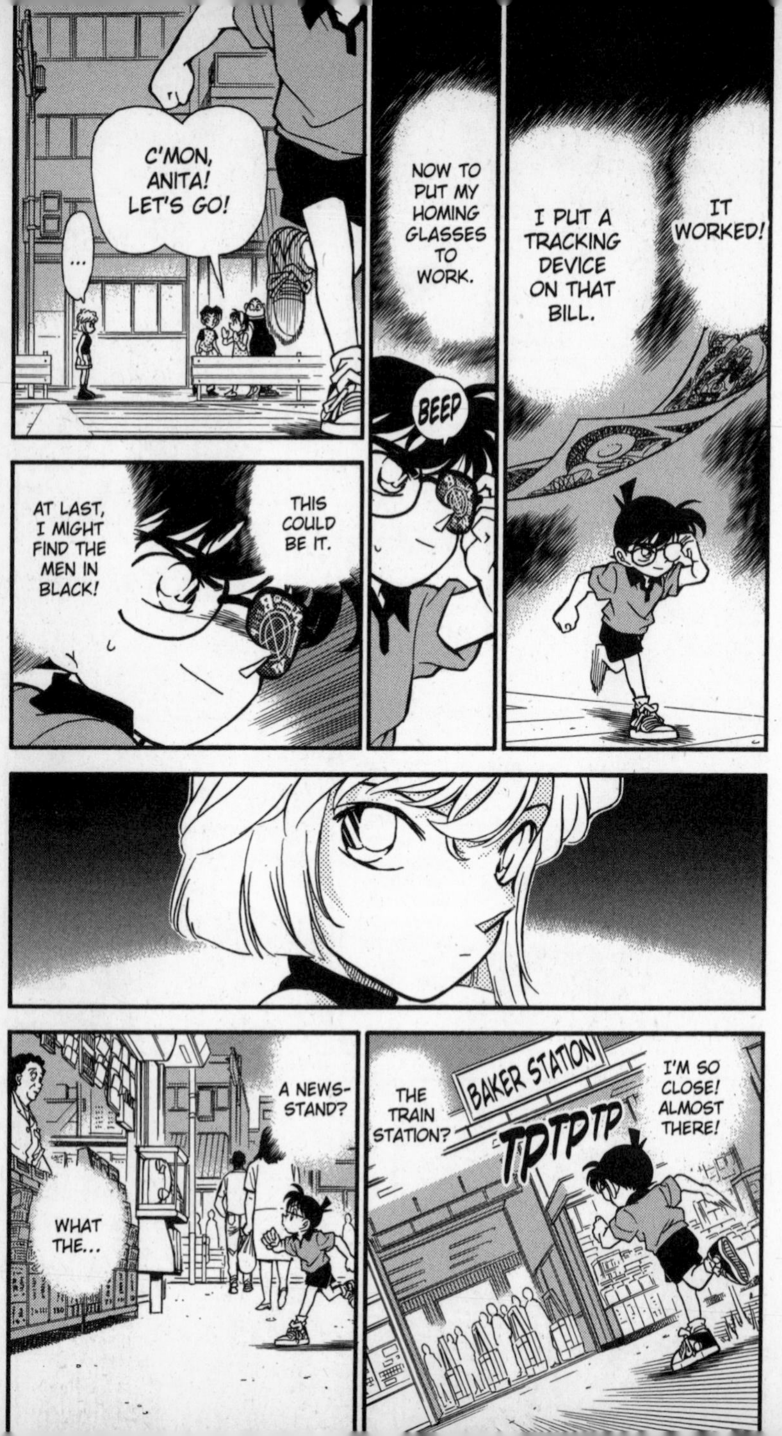
IT WORKED!
I PUT A TRACKING DEVICE ON THAT BILL.
NOW TO PUT MY HOMING GLASSES TO WORK.
BEEP
C'MON, ANITA! LET'S GO!
...
THIS COULD BE IT.
AT LAST, I MIGHT FIND THE MEN IN BLACK!
I'M SO CLOSE! ALMOST THERE!
BAKER STATION
TPTPTP
THE TRAIN STATION?
A NEWS-STAND?
WHAT THE...

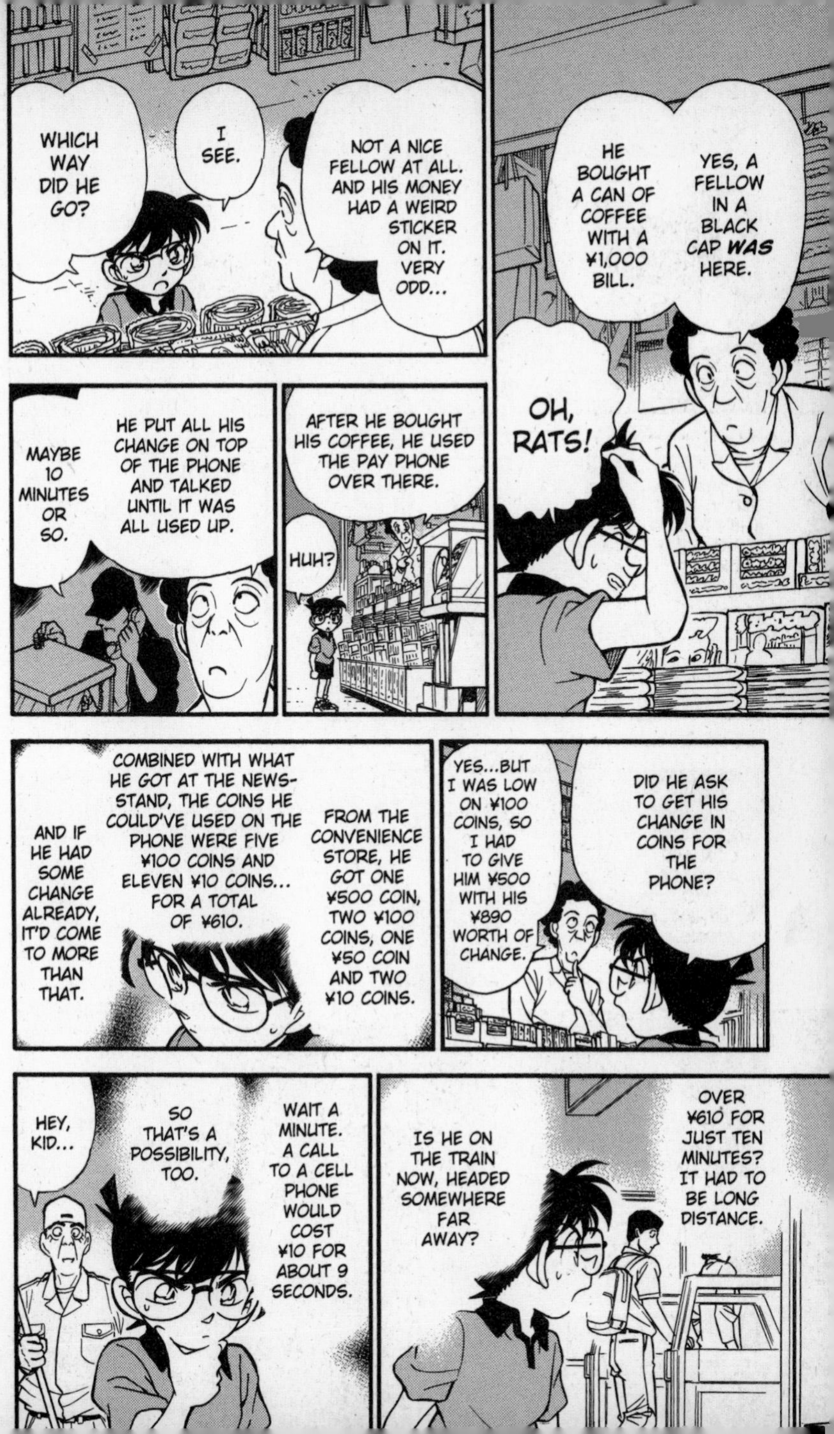
YES, A FELLOW IN A BLACK CAP WAS HERE.
HE BOUGHT A CAN OF COFFEE WITH A ¥1,000 BILL.
OH, RATS!
NOT A NICE FELLOW AT ALL. AND HIS MONEY HAD A WEIRD STICKER ON IT. VERY ODD...
I SEE.
WHICH WAY DID HE GO?
AFTER HE BOUGHT HIS COFFEE, HE USED THE PAY PHONE OVER THERE.
HUH?
HE PUT ALL HIS CHANGE ON TOP OF THE PHONE AND TALKED UNTIL IT WAS ALL USED UP.
MAYBE 10 MINUTES OR SO.
DID HE ASK TO GET HIS CHANGE IN COINS FOR THE PHONE?
YES...BUT I WAS LOW ON ¥100 COINS, SO I HAD TO GIVE HIM ¥500 WITH HIS ¥890 WORTH OF CHANGE.
FROM THE CONVENIENCE STORE, HE GOT ONE ¥500 COIN, TWO ¥100 COINS, ONE ¥50 COIN AND TWO ¥10 COINS.
COMBINED WITH WHAT HE GOT AT THE NEWS-STAND, THE COINS HE COULD'VE USED ON THE PHONE WERE FIVE ¥100 COINS AND ELEVEN ¥10 COINS... FOR A TOTAL OF ¥610.
AND IF HE HAD SOME CHANGE ALREADY, IT'D COME TO MORE THAN THAT.
OVER ¥610 FOR JUST TEN MINUTES? IT HAD TO BE LONG DISTANCE.
IS HE ON THE TRAIN NOW, HEADED SOMEWHERE FAR AWAY?
WAIT A MINUTE. A CALL TO A CELL PHONE WOULD COST ¥10 FOR ABOUT 9 SECONDS.
SO THAT'S A POSSIBILITY, TOO.
HEY, KID...

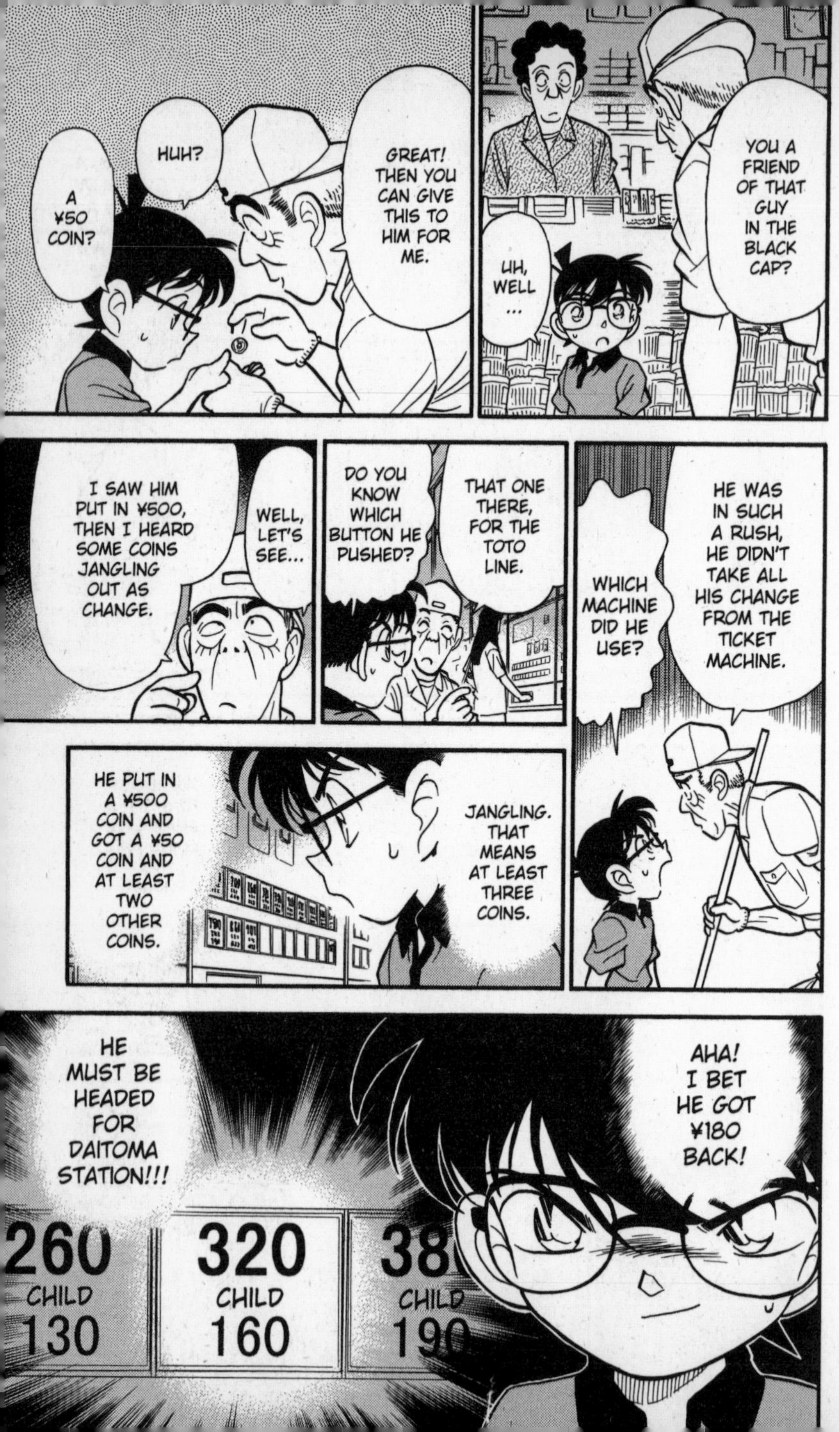
YOU A FRIEND OF THAT GUY IN THE BLACK CAP?
UH, WELL ...
GREAT! THEN YOU CAN GIVE THIS TO HIM FOR ME.
HUH?
A ¥50 COIN?
HE WAS IN SUCH A RUSH, HE DIDN'T TAKE ALL HIS CHANGE FROM THE TICKET MACHINE.
WHICH MACHINE DID HE USE?
THAT ONE THERE, FOR THE TOTO LINE.
DO YOU KNOW WHICH BUTTON HE PUSHED?
WELL, LET'S SEE...
I SAW HIM PUT IN ¥500, THEN I HEARD SOME COINS JANGLING OUT AS CHANGE.
JANGLING. THAT MEANS AT LEAST THREE COINS.
HE PUT IN A ¥500 COIN AND GOT A ¥50 COIN AND AT LEAST TWO OTHER COINS.
AHA! I BET HE GOT ¥180 BACK!
HE MUST BE HEADED FOR DAITOMA STATION!!!
260
CHILD
130
320
CHILD
160
CHILD

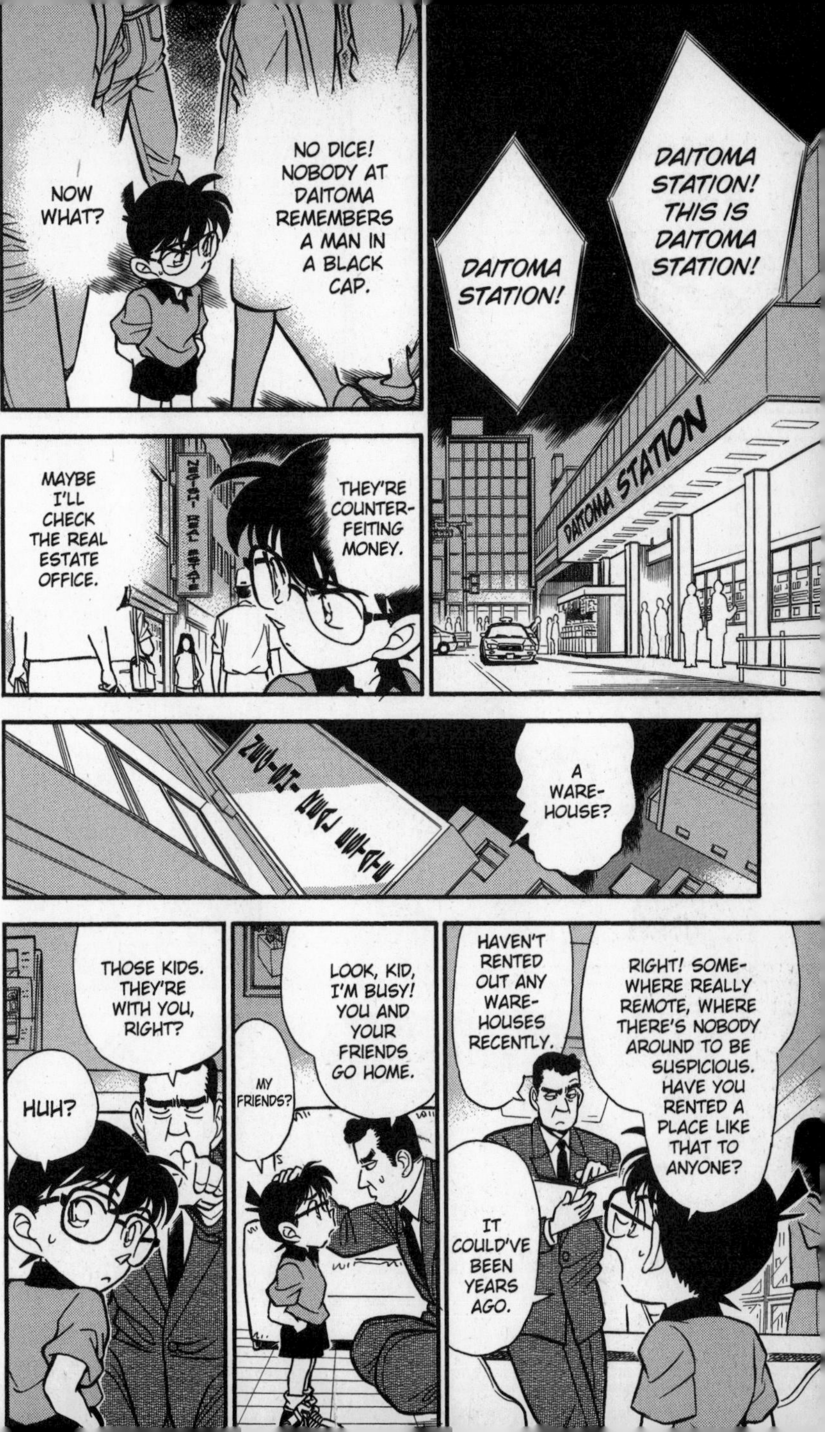
DAITOMA STATION! THIS IS DAITOMA STATION!
DAITOMA STATION!
DAITOMA STATION
NO DICE! NOBODY AT DAITOMA REMEMBERS A MAN IN A BLACK CAP.
NOW WHAT?
THEY'RE COUNTERFEITING MONEY.
MAYBE I'LL CHECK THE REAL ESTATE OFFICE.
A WAREHOUSE?
RIGHT! SOMEWHERE REALLY REMOTE, WHERE THERE'S NOBODY AROUND TO BE SUSPICIOUS. HAVE YOU RENTED A PLACE LIKE THAT TO ANYONE?
HAVEN'T RENTED OUT ANY WAREHOUSES RECENTLY.
IT COULD'VE BEEN YEARS AGO.
LOOK, KID, I'M BUSY! YOU AND YOUR FRIENDS GO HOME.
MY FRIENDS?
THOSE KIDS. THEY'RE WITH YOU, RIGHT?
HUH?

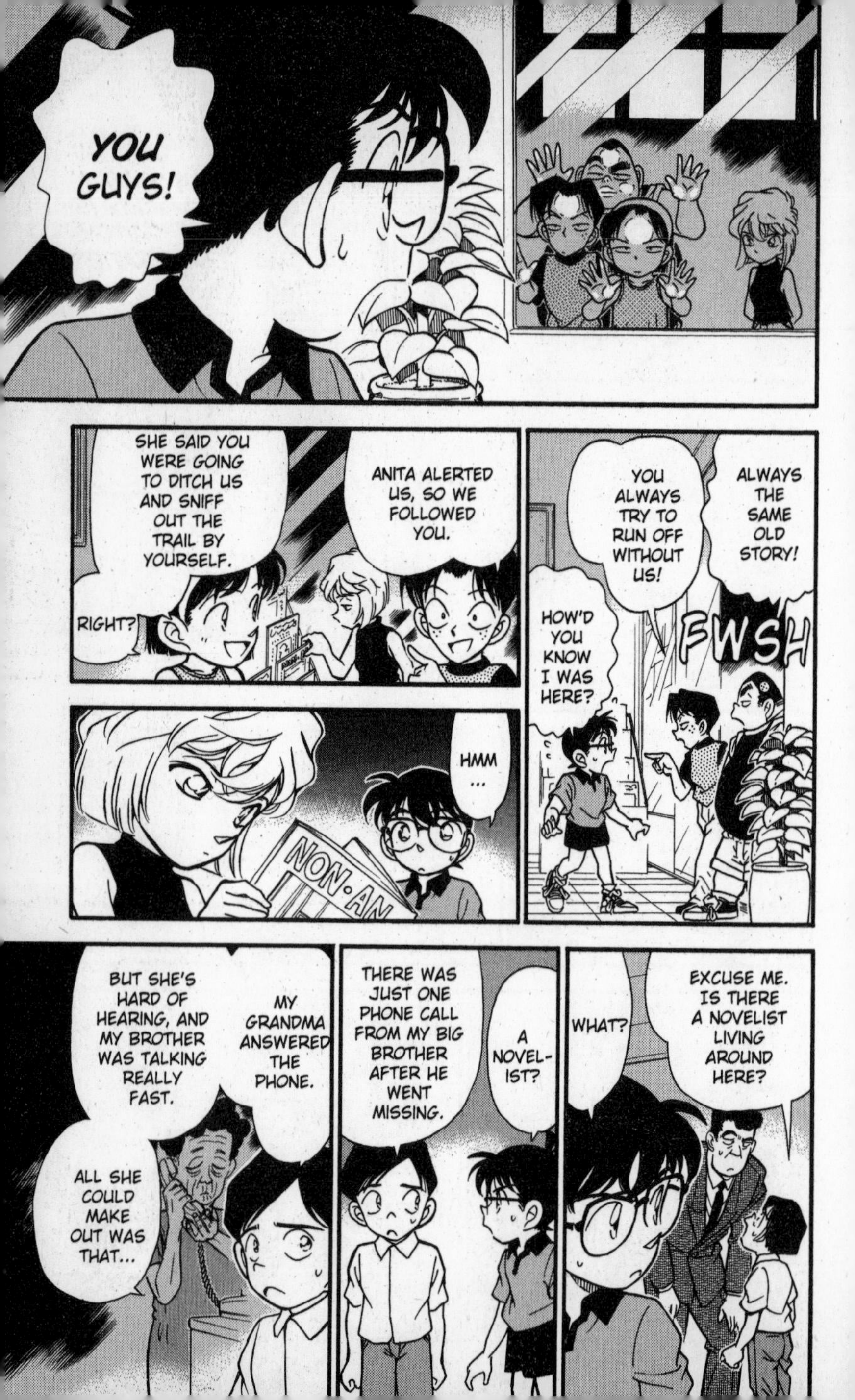
YOU GUYS!
ALWAYS THE SAME OLD STORY!
YOU ALWAYS TRY TO RUN OFF WITHOUT US!
FWSH
HOW'D YOU KNOW I WAS HERE?
ANITA ALERTED US, SO WE FOLLOWED YOU.
SHE SAID YOU WERE GOING TO DITCH US AND SNIFF OUT THE TRAIL BY YOURSELF.
RIGHT?
HMM ...
EXCUSE ME. IS THERE A NOVELIST LIVING AROUND HERE?
WHAT?
A NOVEL-IST?
THERE WAS JUST ONE PHONE CALL FROM MY BIG BROTHER AFTER HE WENT MISSING.
MY GRANDMA ANSWERED THE PHONE.
BUT SHE'S HARD OF HEARING, AND MY BROTHER WAS TALKING REALLY FAST.
ALL SHE COULD MAKE OUT WAS THAT...

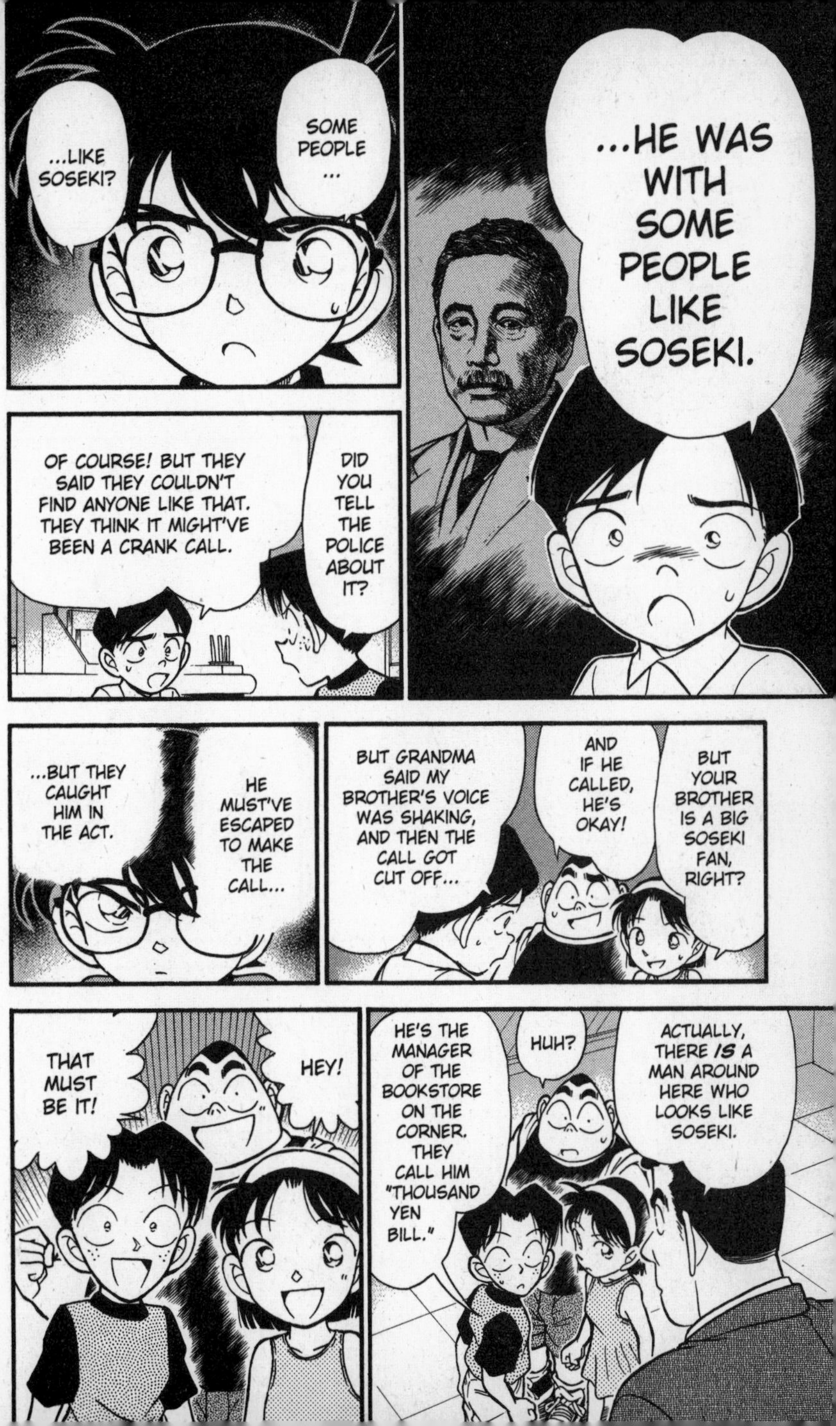
...HE WAS WITH SOME PEOPLE LIKE SOSEKI.
SOME PEOPLE ...
...LIKE SOSEKI?
DID YOU TELL THE POLICE ABOUT IT?
OF COURSE! BUT THEY SAID THEY COULDN'T FIND ANYONE LIKE THAT. THEY THINK IT MIGHT'VE BEEN A CRANK CALL.
BUT YOUR BROTHER IS A BIG SOSEKI FAN, RIGHT?
AND IF HE CALLED, HE'S OKAY!
BUT GRANDMA SAID MY BROTHER'S VOICE WAS SHAKING, AND THEN THE CALL GOT CUT OFF...
HE MUST'VE ESCAPED TO MAKE THE CALL...
...BUT THEY CAUGHT HIM IN THE ACT.
ACTUALLY, THERE *IS* A MAN AROUND HERE WHO LOOKS LIKE SOSEKI.
HUH?
HE'S THE MANAGER OF THE BOOKSTORE ON THE CORNER. THEY CALL HIM "THOUSAND YEN BILL."
HEY!
THAT MUST BE IT!

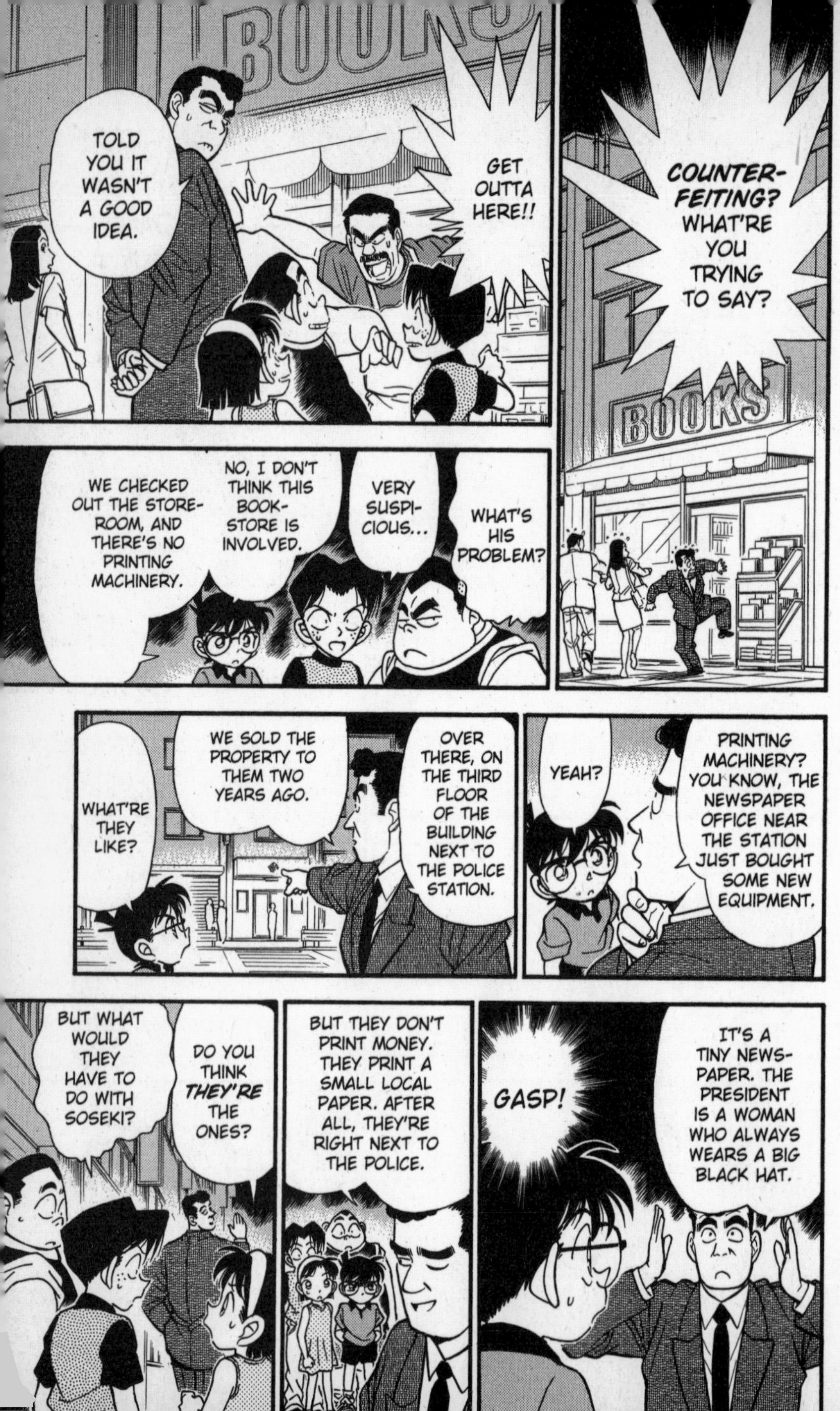
COUNTER-FEITING? WHAT'RE YOU TRYING TO SAY?
BOOKS
BOOKS
GET OUTTA HERE!!
TOLD YOU IT WASN'T A GOOD IDEA.
WHAT'S HIS PROBLEM?
VERY SUSPI-CIOUS...
NO, I DON'T THINK THIS BOOK-STORE IS INVOLVED.
WE CHECKED OUT THE STORE-ROOM, AND THERE'S NO PRINTING MACHINERY.
PRINTING MACHINERY? YOU KNOW, THE NEWSPAPER OFFICE NEAR THE STATION JUST BOUGHT SOME NEW EQUIPMENT.
YEAH?
OVER THERE, ON THE THIRD FLOOR OF THE BUILDING NEXT TO THE POLICE STATION.
WE SOLD THE PROPERTY TO THEM TWO YEARS AGO.
WHAT'RE THEY LIKE?
IT'S A TINY NEWS-PAPER. THE PRESIDENT IS A WOMAN WHO ALWAYS WEARS A BIG BLACK HAT.
GASP!
BUT THEY DON'T PRINT MONEY. THEY PRINT A SMALL LOCAL PAPER. AFTER ALL, THEY'RE RIGHT NEXT TO THE POLICE.
DO YOU THINK *THEY'RE* THE ONES?
BUT WHAT WOULD THEY HAVE TO DO WITH SOSEKI?

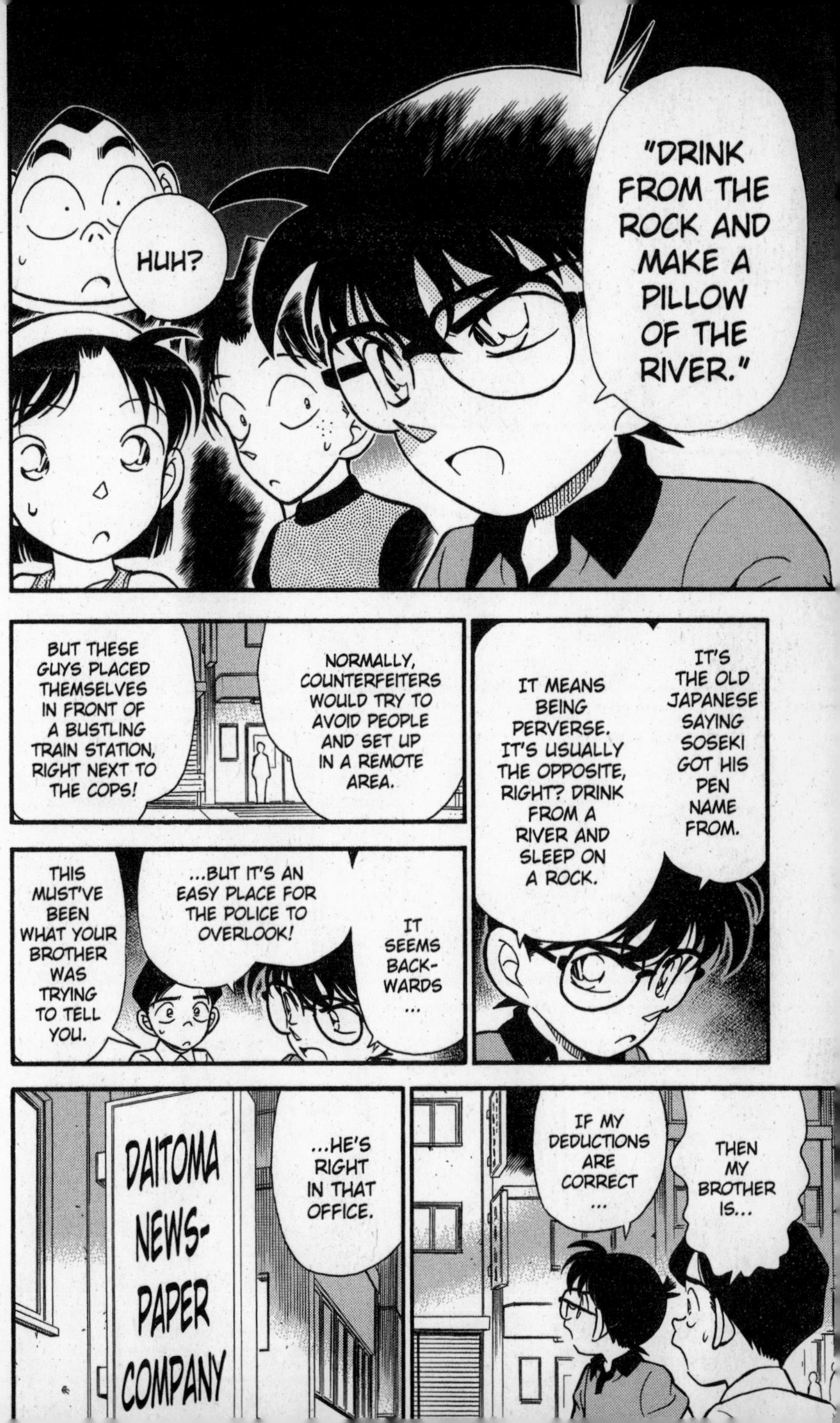
"DRINK FROM THE ROCK AND MAKE A PILLOW OF THE RIVER."
HUH?
IT'S THE OLD JAPANESE SAYING SOSEKI GOT HIS PEN NAME FROM.
IT MEANS BEING PERVERSE. IT'S USUALLY THE OPPOSITE, RIGHT? DRINK FROM A RIVER AND SLEEP ON A ROCK.
NORMALLY, COUNTERFEITERS WOULD TRY TO AVOID PEOPLE AND SET UP IN A REMOTE AREA.
BUT THESE GUYS PLACED THEMSELVES IN FRONT OF A BUSTLING TRAIN STATION, RIGHT NEXT TO THE COPS!
IT SEEMS BACKWARDS...
...BUT IT'S AN EASY PLACE FOR THE POLICE TO OVERLOOK!
THIS MUST'VE BEEN WHAT YOUR BROTHER WAS TRYING TO TELL YOU.
THEN MY BROTHER IS...
IF MY DEDUCTIONS ARE CORRECT...
...HE'S RIGHT IN THAT OFFICE.
DAITOMA NEWS-PAPER COMPANY

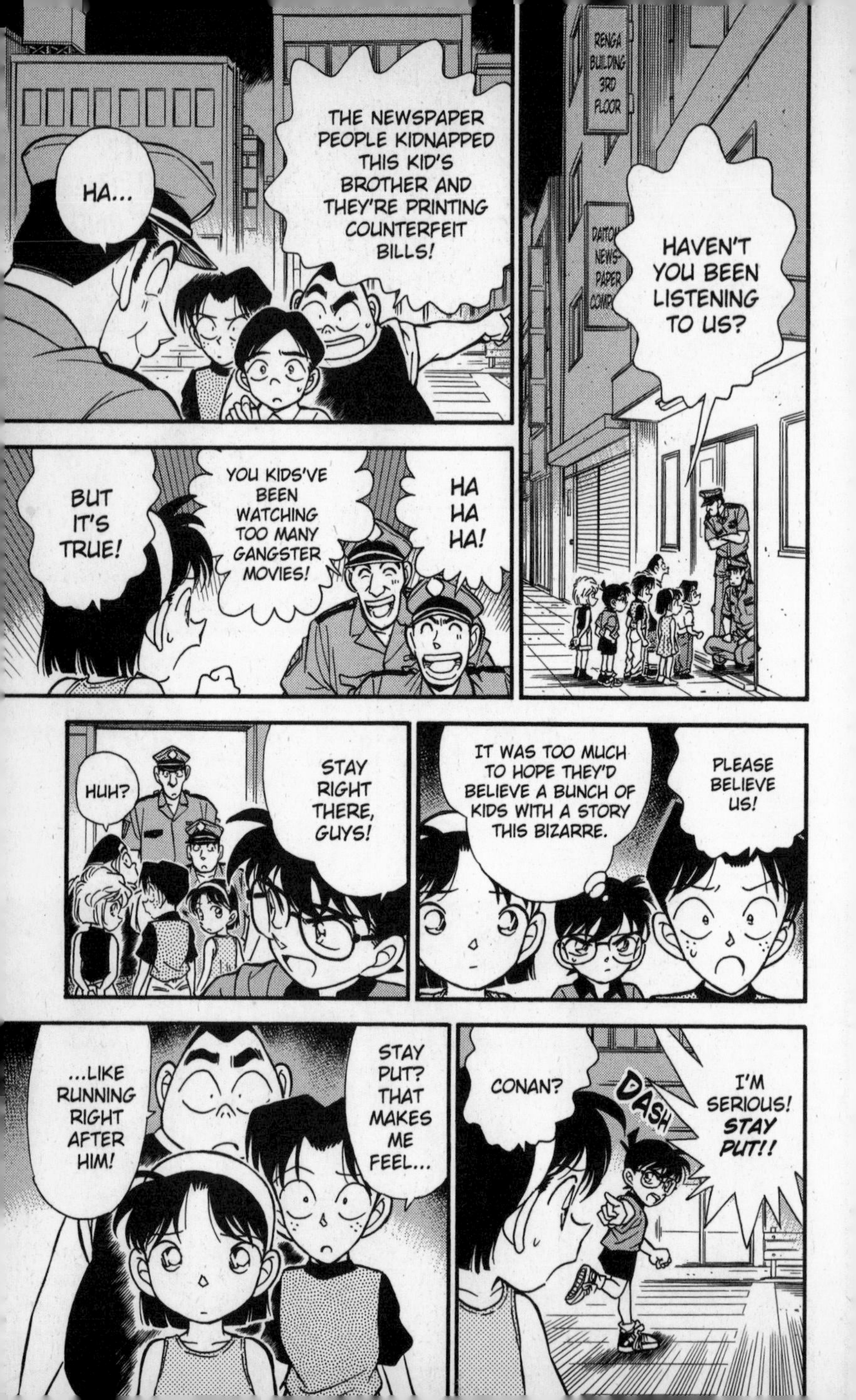

RENGA BUILDING 3RD FLOOR
DAITO NEWS-PAPER COMP
HAVEN'T YOU BEEN LISTENING TO US?
THE NEWSPAPER PEOPLE KIDNAPPED THIS KID'S BROTHER AND THEY'RE PRINTING COUNTERFEIT BILLS!
HA...
HA HA HA!
YOU KIDS'VE BEEN WATCHING TOO MANY GANGSTER MOVIES!
BUT IT'S TRUE!
PLEASE BELIEVE US!
IT WAS TOO MUCH TO HOPE THEY'D BELIEVE A BUNCH OF KIDS WITH A STORY THIS BIZARRE.
STAY RIGHT THERE, GUYS!
HUH?
I'M SERIOUS! STAY PUT!!
DASH
CONAN?
STAY PUT? THAT MAKES ME FEEL...
...LIKE RUNNING RIGHT AFTER HIM!

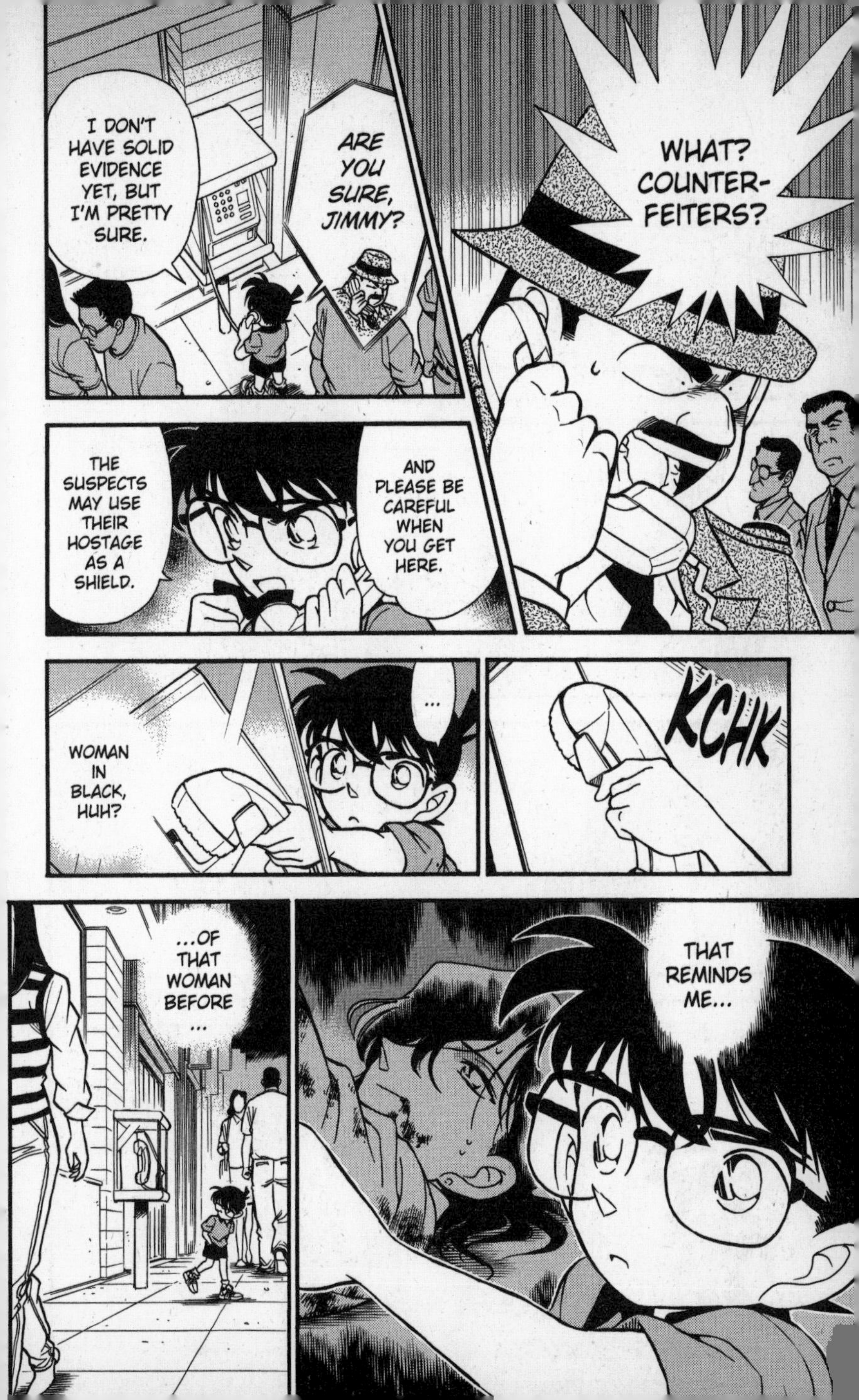
WHAT? COUNTER-FEITERS?
ARE YOU SURE, JIMMY?
I DON'T HAVE SOLID EVIDENCE YET, BUT I'M PRETTY SURE.
AND PLEASE BE CAREFUL WHEN YOU GET HERE.
THE SUSPECTS MAY USE THEIR HOSTAGE AS A SHIELD.
KCHK
...
WOMAN IN BLACK, HUH?
THAT REMINDS ME...
...OF THAT WOMAN BEFORE ...

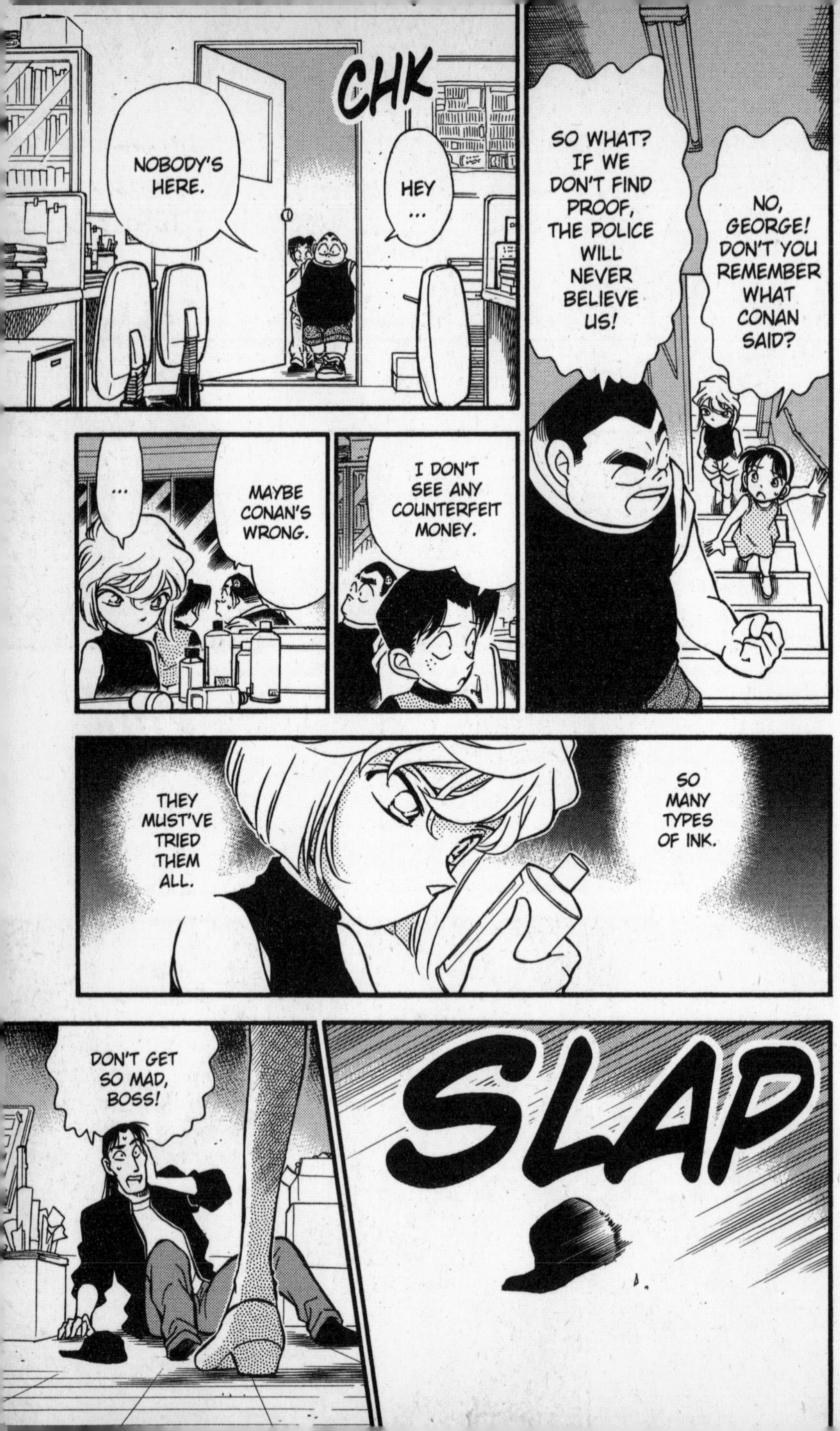
NO, GEORGE! DON'T YOU REMEMBER WHAT CONAN SAID?
SO WHAT? IF WE DON'T FIND PROOF, THE POLICE WILL NEVER BELIEVE US!
CHK
HEY ...
NOBODY'S HERE.
I DON'T SEE ANY COUNTERFEIT MONEY.
MAYBE CONAN'S WRONG.
...
SO MANY TYPES OF INK.
THEY MUST'VE TRIED THEM ALL.
SLAP
DON'T GET SO MAD, BOSS!

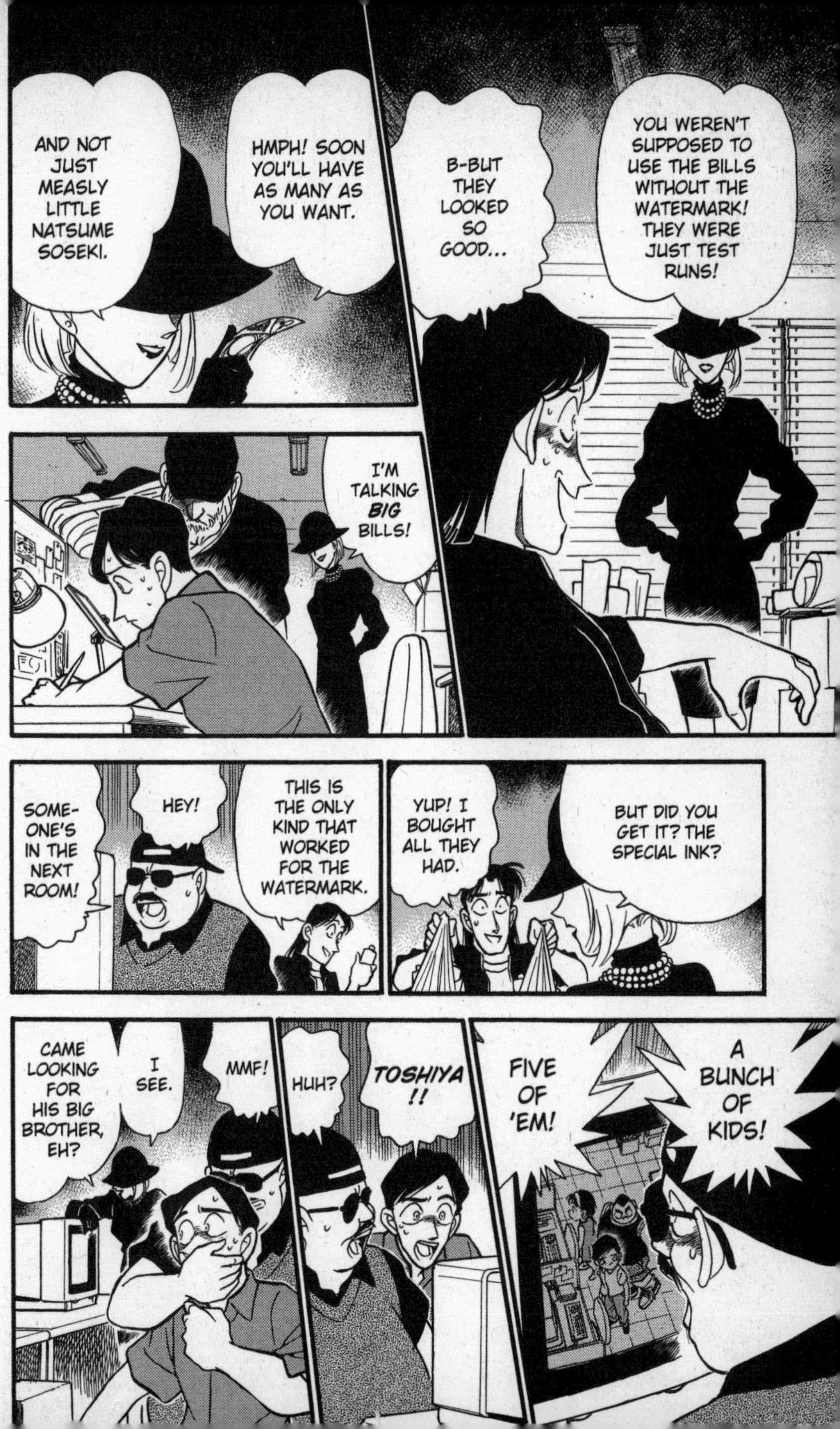
YOU WEREN'T SUPPOSED TO USE THE BILLS WITHOUT THE WATERMARK! THEY WERE JUST TEST RUNS!
B-BUT THEY LOOKED SO GOOD...
HMPH! SOON YOU'LL HAVE AS MANY AS YOU WANT.
AND NOT JUST MEASLY LITTLE NATSUME SOSEKI.
I'M TALKING *BIG* BILLS!
BUT DID YOU GET IT? THE SPECIAL INK?
YUP! I BOUGHT ALL THEY HAD.
THIS IS THE ONLY KIND THAT WORKED FOR THE WATERMARK.
HEY!
SOME-ONE'S IN THE NEXT ROOM!
A BUNCH OF KIDS!
FIVE OF 'EM!
TOSHIYA!!
HUH?
MMF!
I SEE.
CAME LOOKING FOR HIS BIG BROTHER, EH?

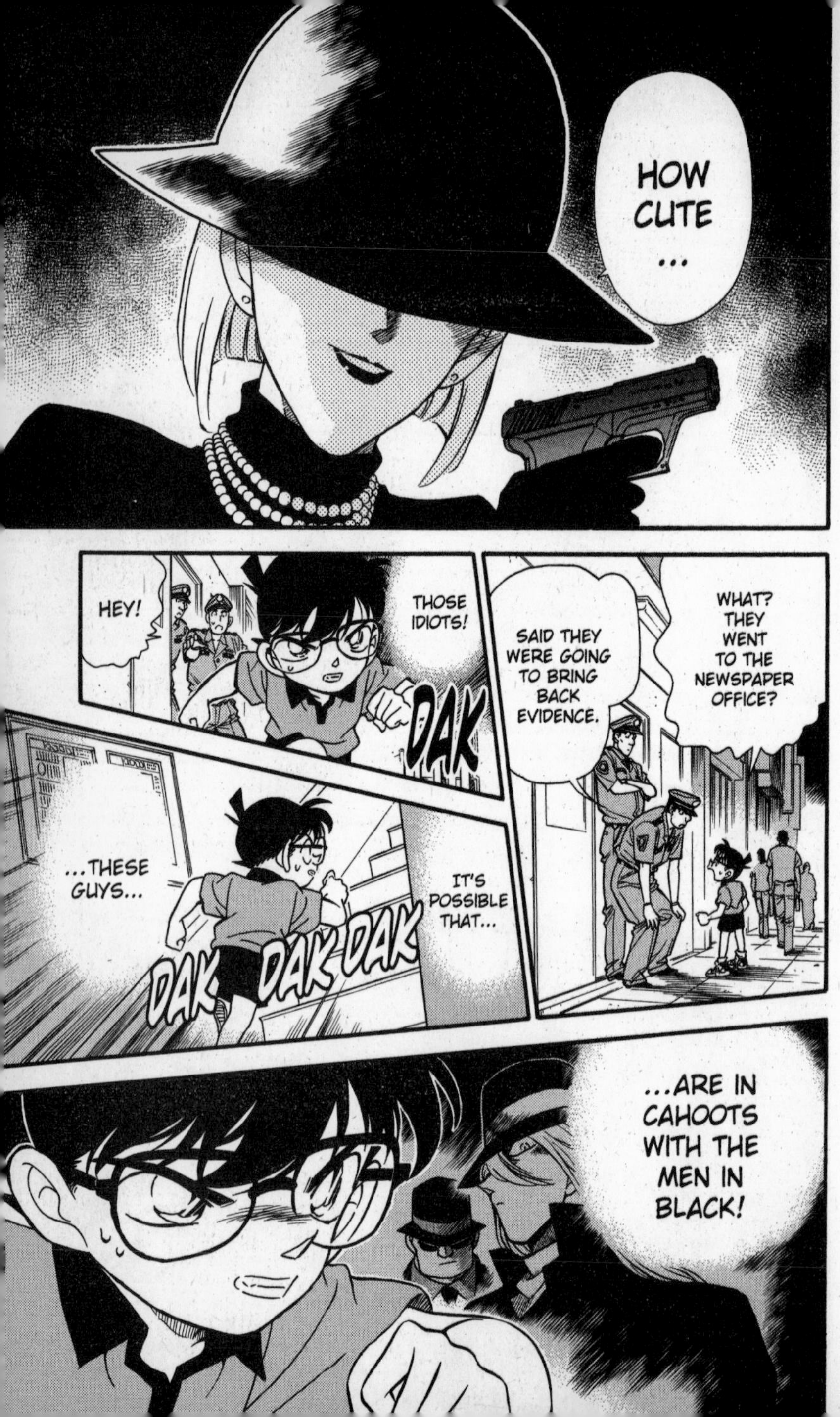
HOW CUTE ...
WHAT? THEY WENT TO THE NEWSPAPER OFFICE?
SAID THEY WERE GOING TO BRING BACK EVIDENCE.
THOSE IDIOTS!
HEY!
DAK
IT'S POSSIBLE THAT...
...THESE GUYS...
DAK DAK DAK
...ARE IN CAHOOTS WITH THE MEN IN BLACK!

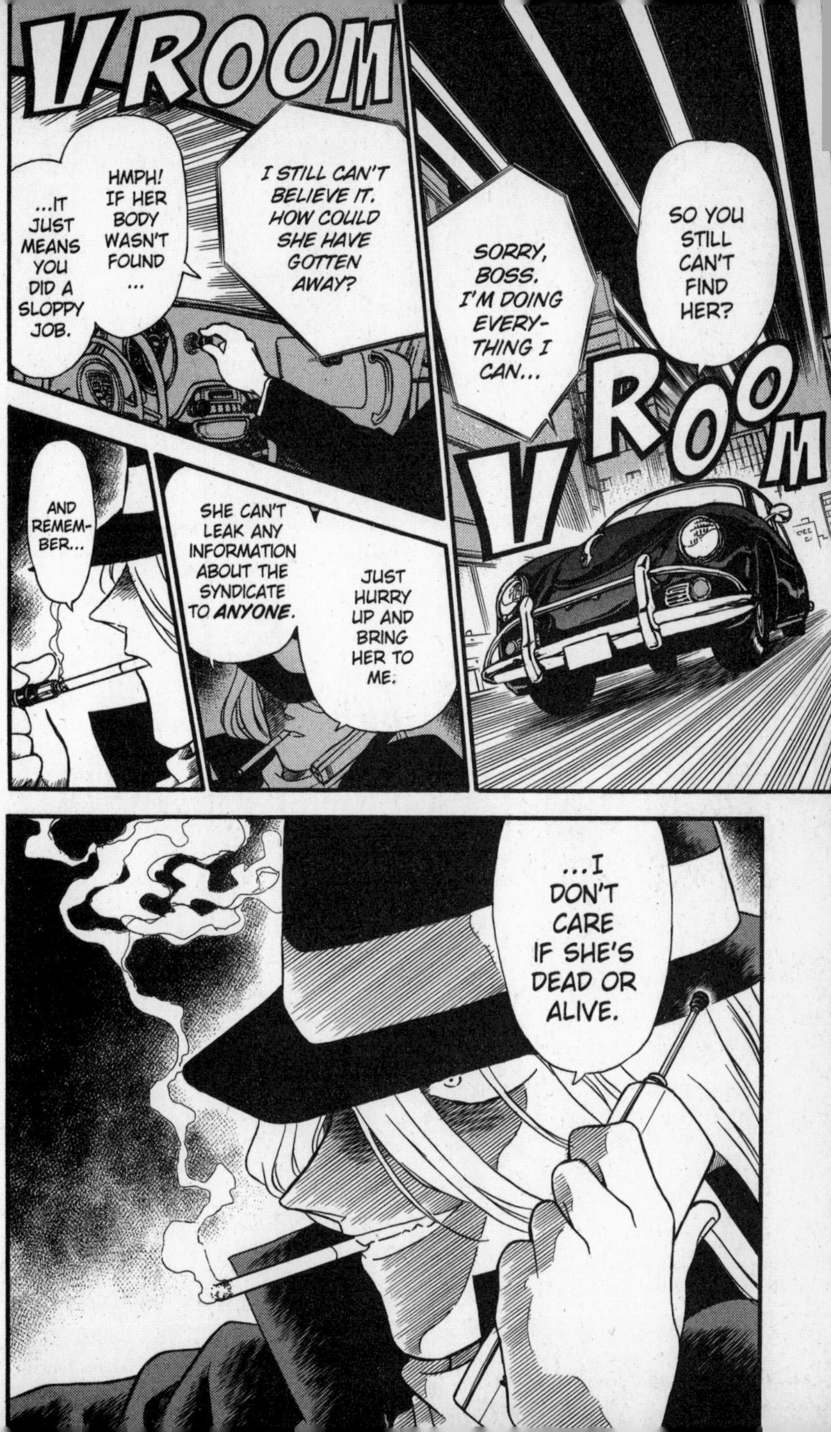
SO YOU STILL CAN'T FIND HER?
SORRY, BOSS. I'M DOING EVERY-THING I CAN...
VROOM
VROOM
I STILL CAN'T BELIEVE IT. HOW COULD SHE HAVE GOTTEN AWAY?
HMPH! IF HER BODY WASN'T FOUND...
...IT JUST MEANS YOU DID A SLOPPY JOB.
SHE CAN'T LEAK ANY INFORMATION ABOUT THE SYNDICATE TO ANYONE.
JUST HURRY UP AND BRING HER TO ME.
AND REMEM-BER...
...I DON'T CARE IF SHE'S DEAD OR ALIVE.

FILE 8: CODENAME: SHERRY

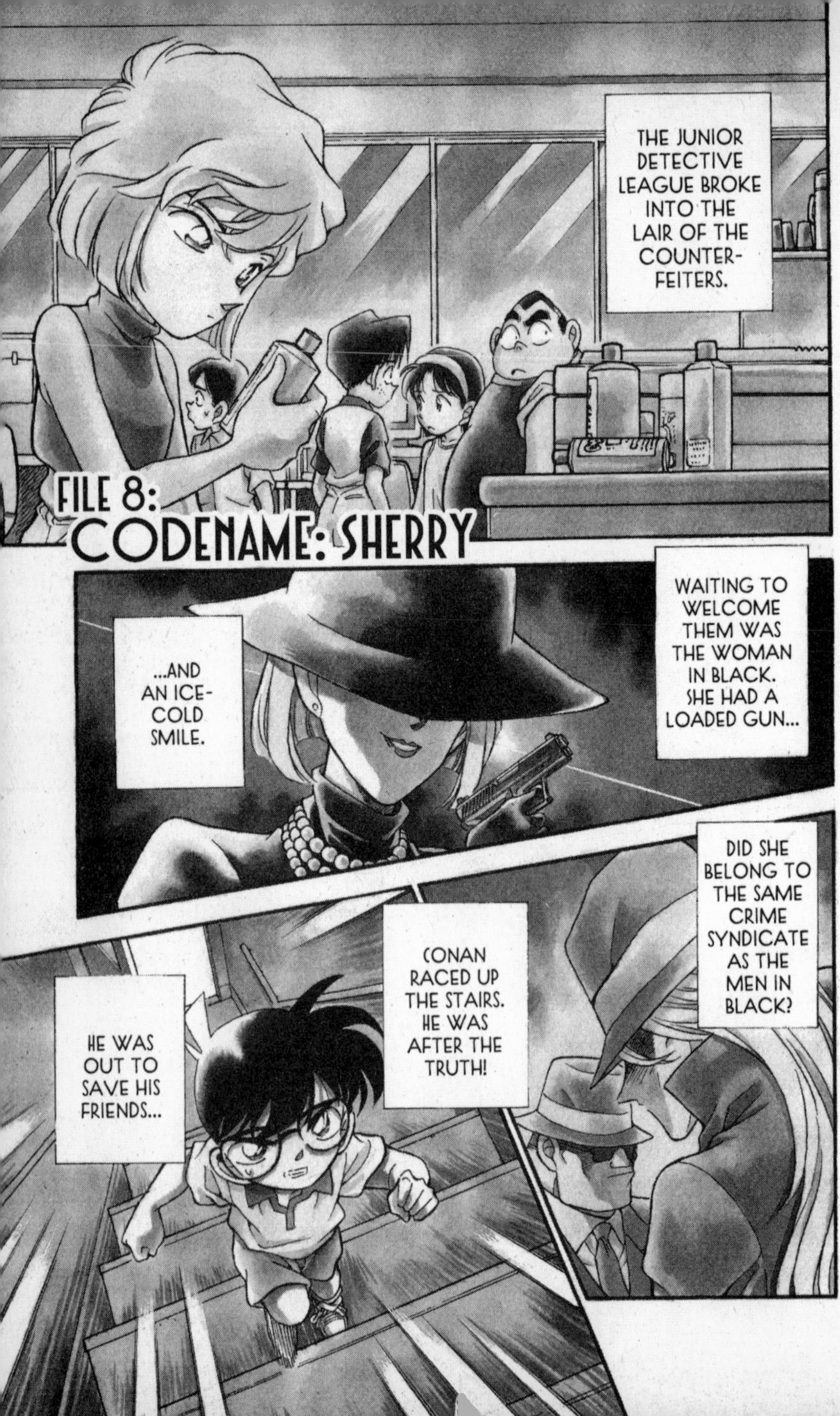
THE JUNIOR DETECTIVE LEAGUE BROKE INTO THE LAIR OF THE COUNTER-FEITERS.
WAITING TO WELCOME THEM WAS THE WOMAN IN BLACK. SHE HAD A LOADED GUN...
...AND AN ICE-COLD SMILE.
DID SHE BELONG TO THE SAME CRIME SYNDICATE AS THE MEN IN BLACK?
CONAN RACED UP THE STAIRS. HE WAS AFTER THE TRUTH!
HE WAS OUT TO SAVE HIS FRIENDS...

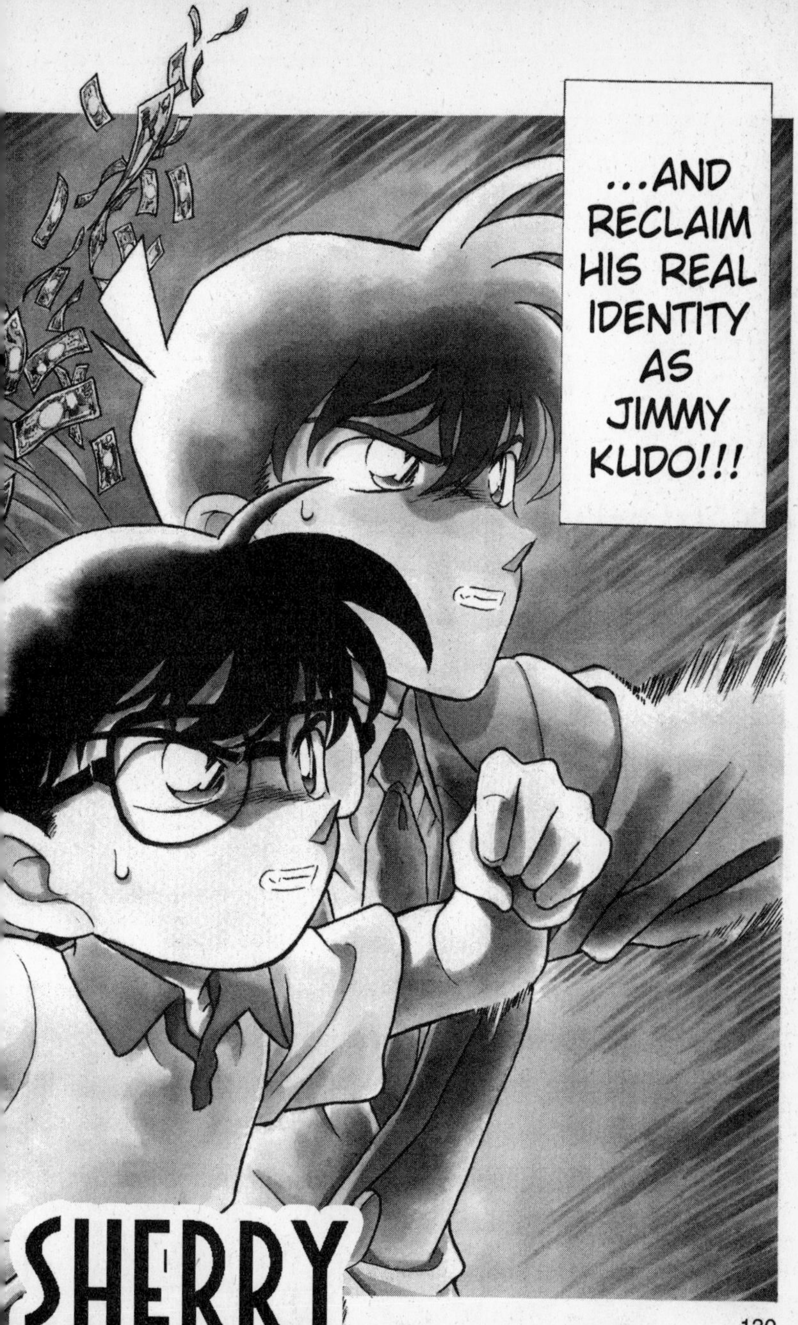
...AND RECLAIM HIS REAL IDENTITY AS JIMMY KUDO!!!
SHERRY

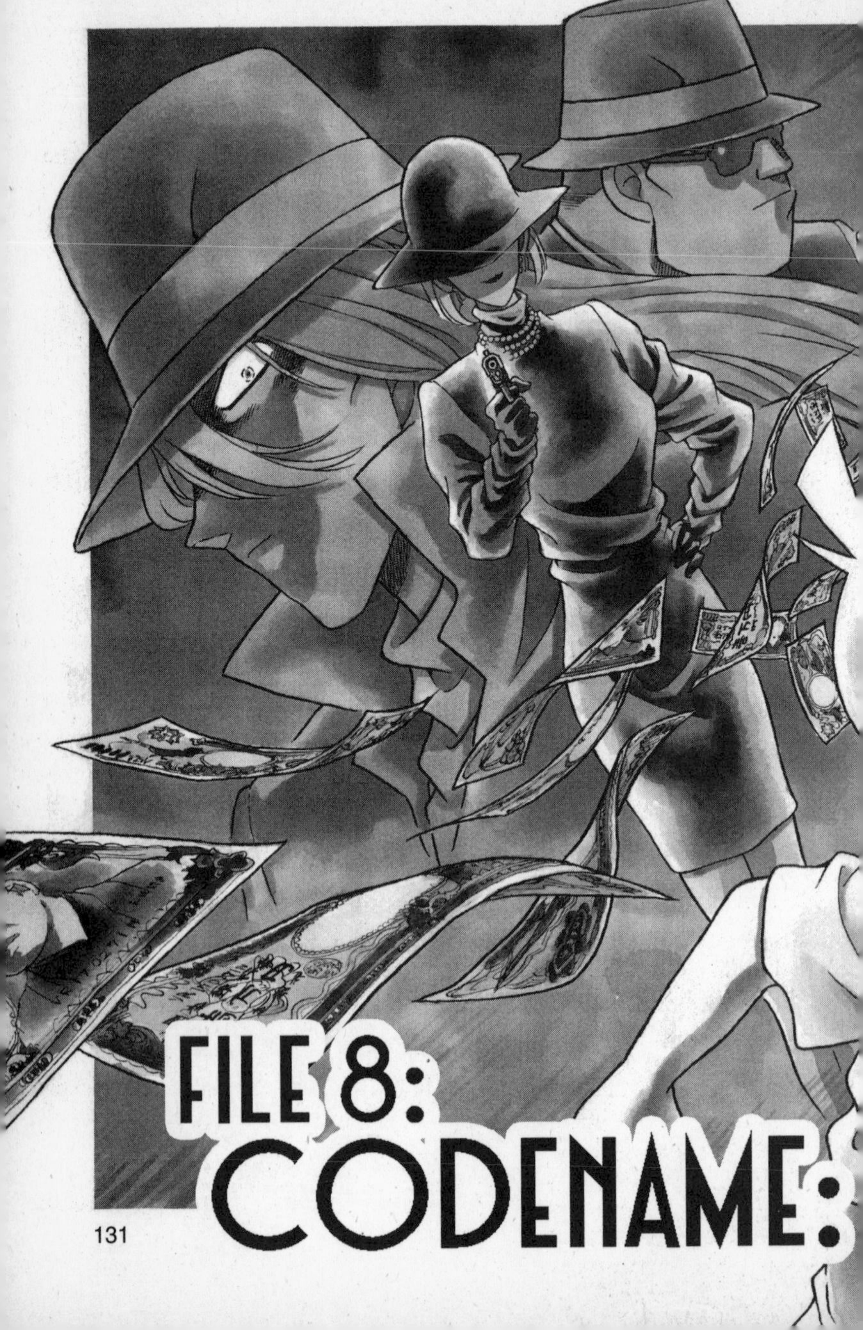
FILE 8:
CODENAME:

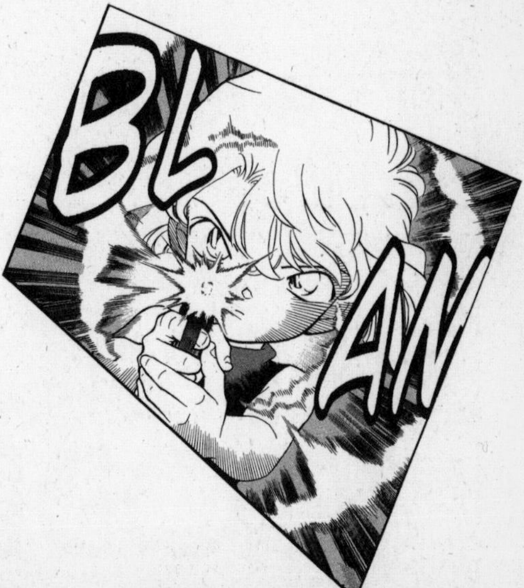
BLAAN

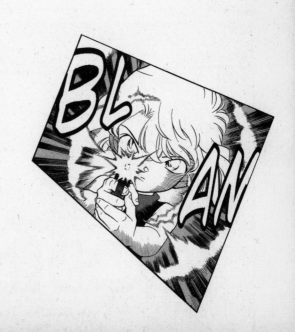

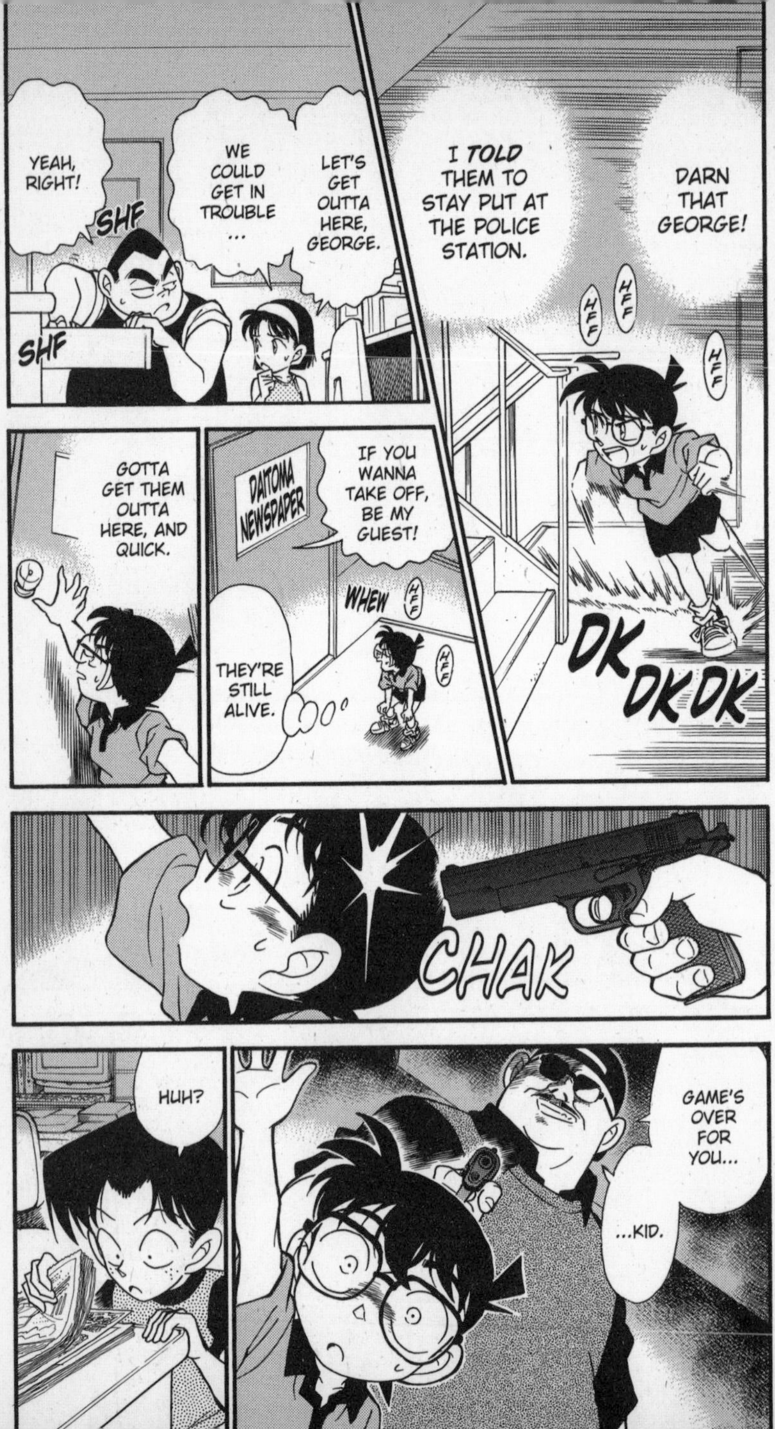
DARN THAT GEORGE!
I TOLD THEM TO STAY PUT AT THE POLICE STATION.
HFF
HFF
HFF
DK DK DK
LET'S GET OUTTA HERE, GEORGE.
WE COULD GET IN TROUBLE ...
YEAH, RIGHT!
SHF
SHF
IF YOU WANNA TAKE OFF, BE MY GUEST!
DAITOMA NEWSPAPER
WHEW
HFF
HFF
THEY'RE STILL ALIVE.
GOTTA GET THEM OUTTA HERE, AND QUICK.
CHAK
GAME'S OVER FOR YOU...
...KID.
HUH?

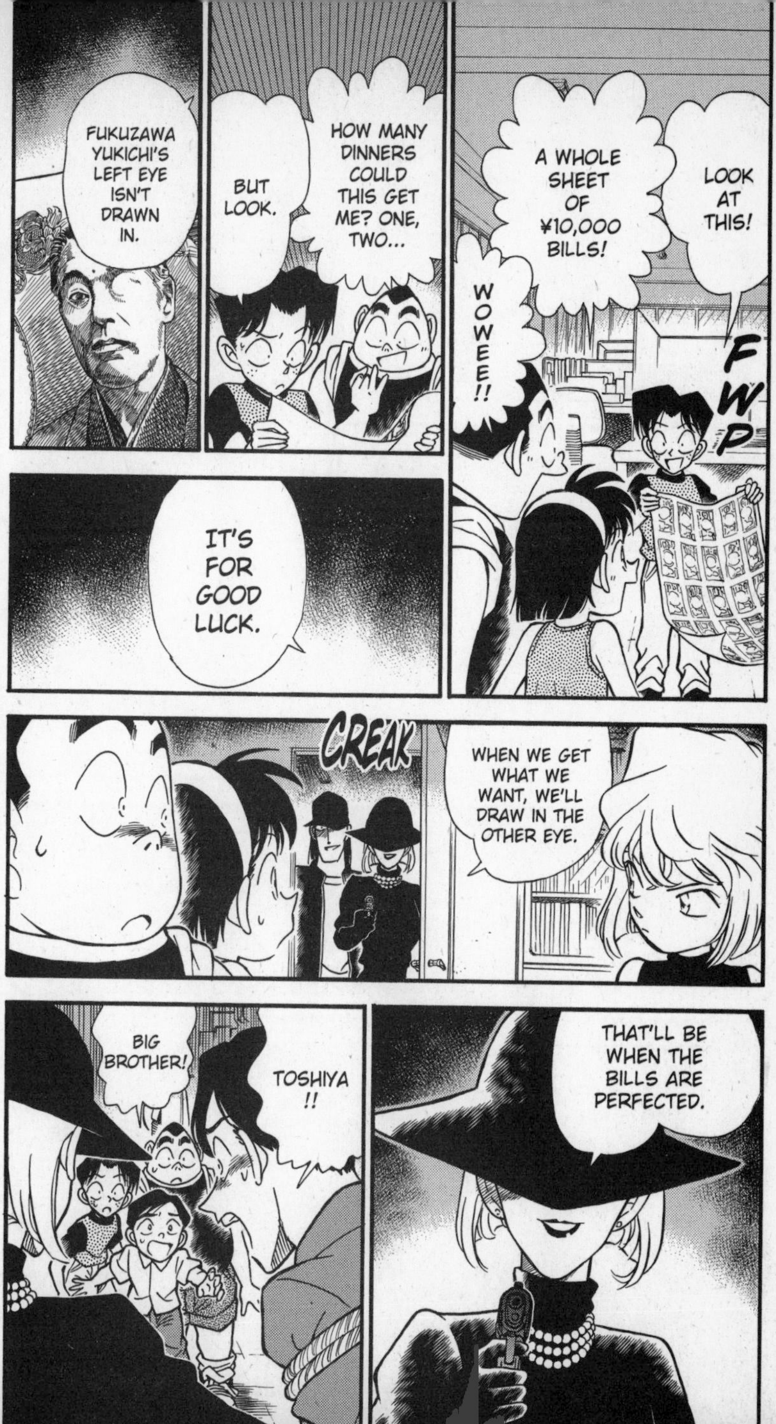
LOOK AT THIS!
A WHOLE SHEET OF ¥10,000 BILLS!
WOWEE!!
FWP
HOW MANY DINNERS COULD THIS GET ME? ONE, TWO...
BUT LOOK.
FUKUZAWA YUKICHI'S LEFT EYE ISN'T DRAWN IN.
IT'S FOR GOOD LUCK.
WHEN WE GET WHAT WE WANT, WE'LL DRAW IN THE OTHER EYE.
CREAK
THAT'LL BE WHEN THE BILLS ARE PERFECTED.
TOSHIYA!!
BIG BROTHER!

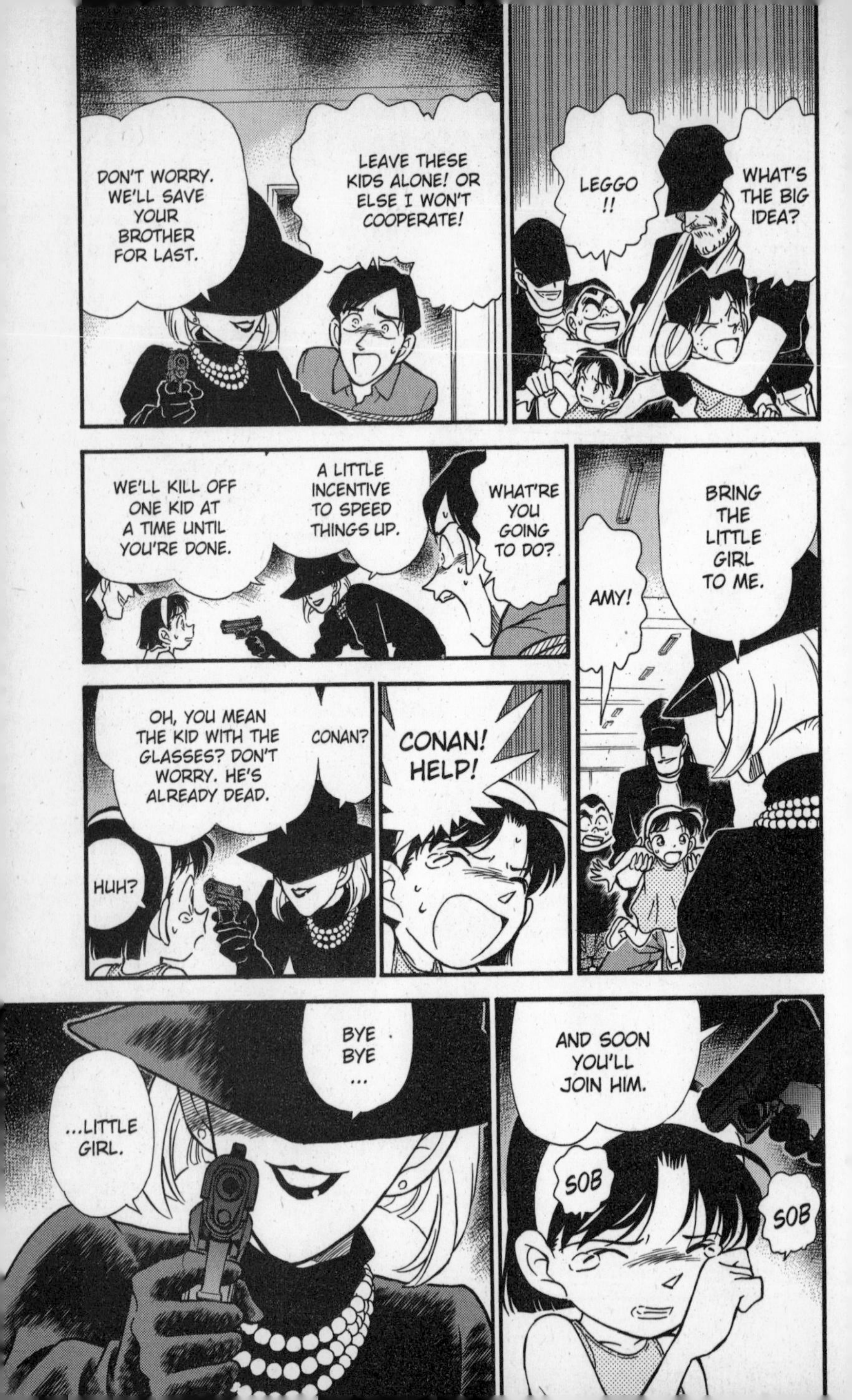
WHAT'S THE BIG IDEA?
LEGGO !!
LEAVE THESE KIDS ALONE! OR ELSE I WON'T COOPERATE!
DON'T WORRY. WE'LL SAVE YOUR BROTHER FOR LAST.
BRING THE LITTLE GIRL TO ME.
AMY!
WHAT'RE YOU GOING TO DO?
A LITTLE INCENTIVE TO SPEED THINGS UP.
WE'LL KILL OFF ONE KID AT A TIME UNTIL YOU'RE DONE.
CONAN! HELP!
CONAN?
OH, YOU MEAN THE KID WITH THE GLASSES? DON'T WORRY. HE'S ALREADY DEAD.
HUH?
AND SOON YOU'LL JOIN HIM.
SOB
SOB
BYE BYE ...
...LITTLE GIRL.

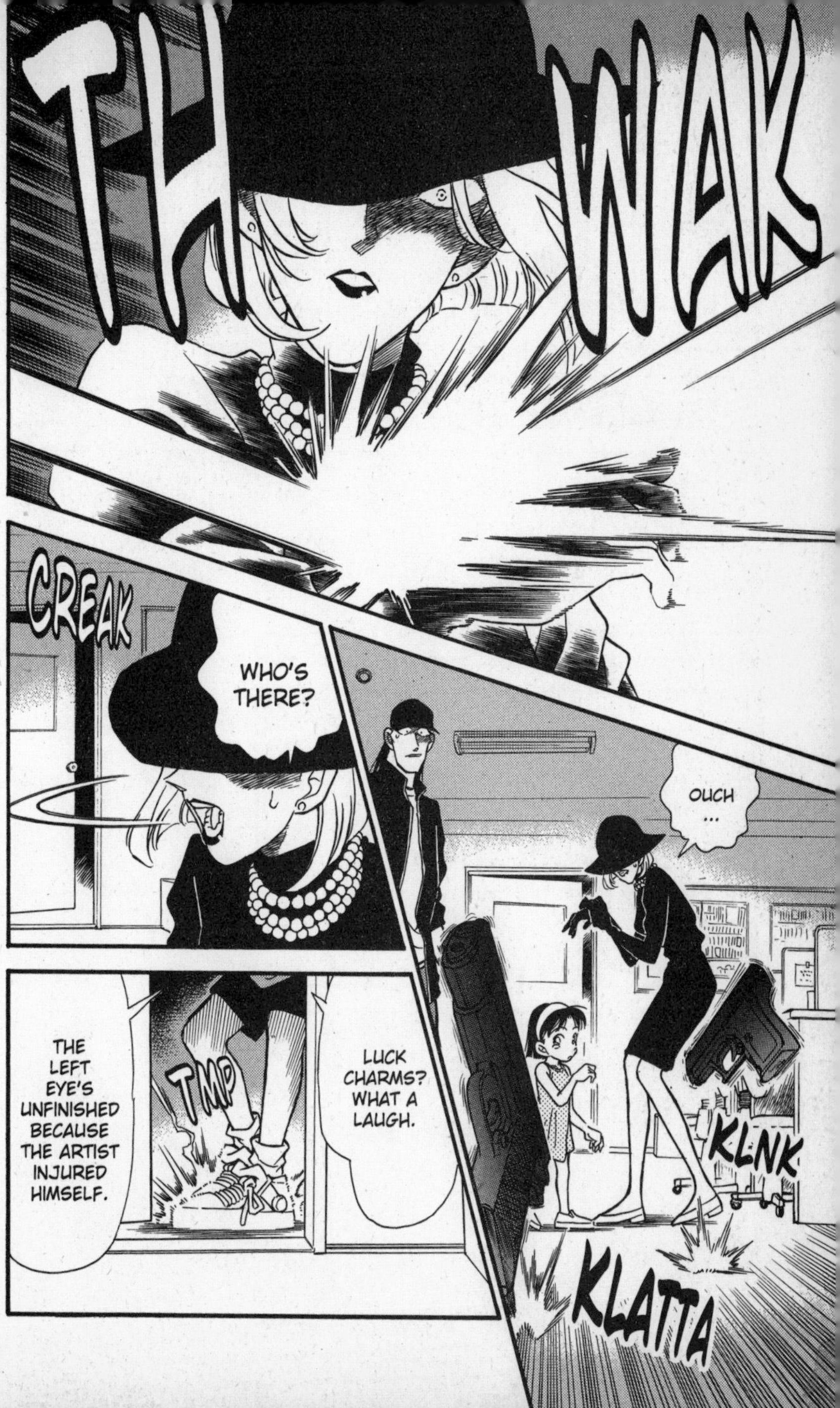
THWAK
OUCH ...
KLNK
KLATTA
CREAK
WHO'S THERE?
LUCK CHARMS? WHAT A LAUGH.
TMP
THE LEFT EYE'S UNFINISHED BECAUSE THE ARTIST INJURED HIMSELF.

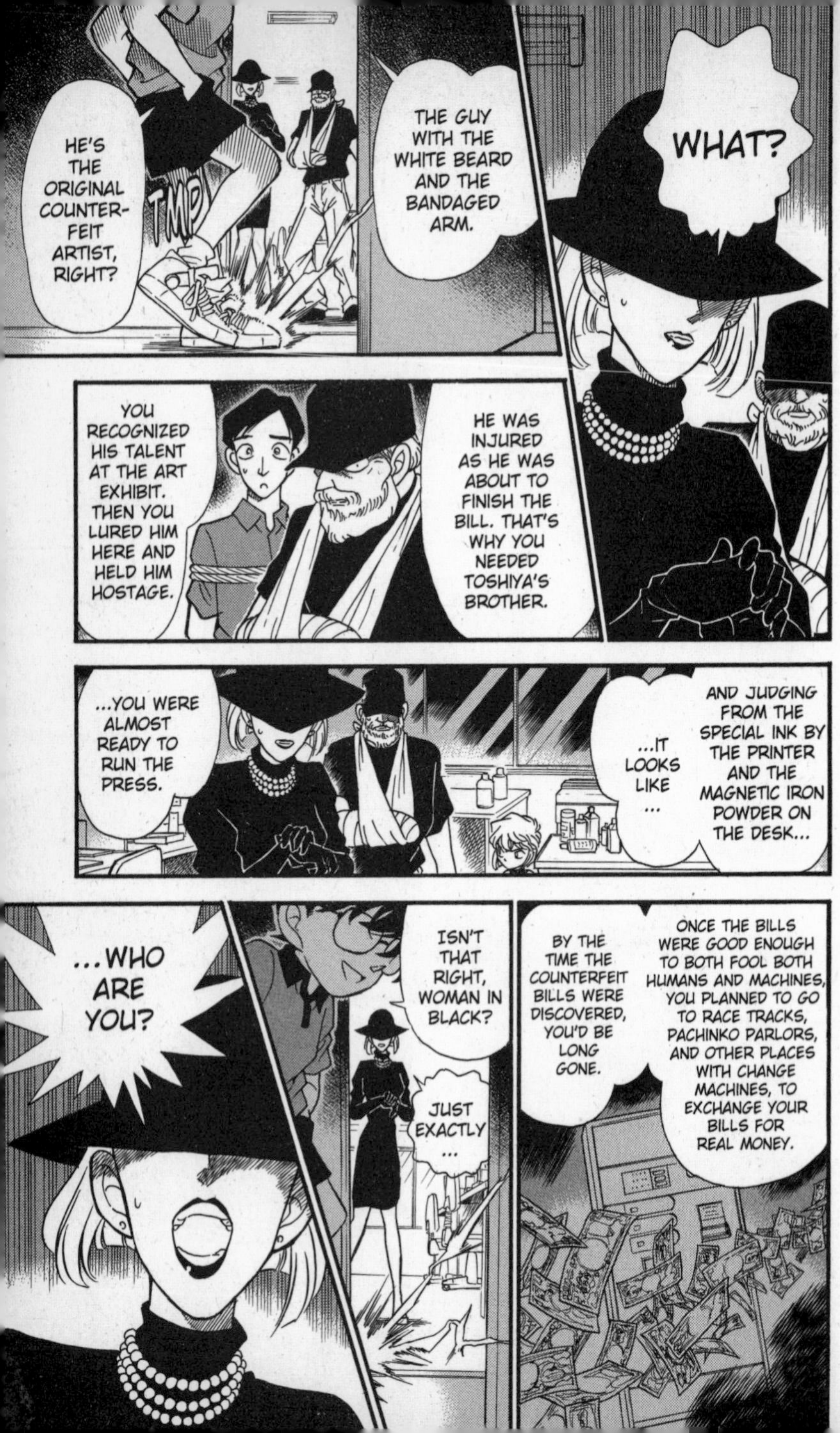
WHAT?
THE GUY WITH THE WHITE BEARD AND THE BANDAGED ARM.
TMP
HE'S THE ORIGINAL COUNTER-FEIT ARTIST, RIGHT?
HE WAS INJURED AS HE WAS ABOUT TO FINISH THE BILL. THAT'S WHY YOU NEEDED TOSHIYA'S BROTHER.
YOU RECOGNIZED HIS TALENT AT THE ART EXHIBIT. THEN YOU LURED HIM HERE AND HELD HIM HOSTAGE.
AND JUDGING FROM THE SPECIAL INK BY THE PRINTER AND THE MAGNETIC IRON POWDER ON THE DESK...
...IT LOOKS LIKE ...
...YOU WERE ALMOST READY TO RUN THE PRESS.
ONCE THE BILLS WERE GOOD ENOUGH TO BOTH FOOL BOTH HUMANS AND MACHINES, YOU PLANNED TO GO TO RACE TRACKS, PACHINKO PARLORS, AND OTHER PLACES WITH CHANGE MACHINES, TO EXCHANGE YOUR BILLS FOR REAL MONEY.
BY THE TIME THE COUNTERFEIT BILLS WERE DISCOVERED, YOU'D BE LONG GONE.
ISN'T THAT RIGHT, WOMAN IN BLACK?
JUST EXACTLY ...
...WHO ARE YOU?

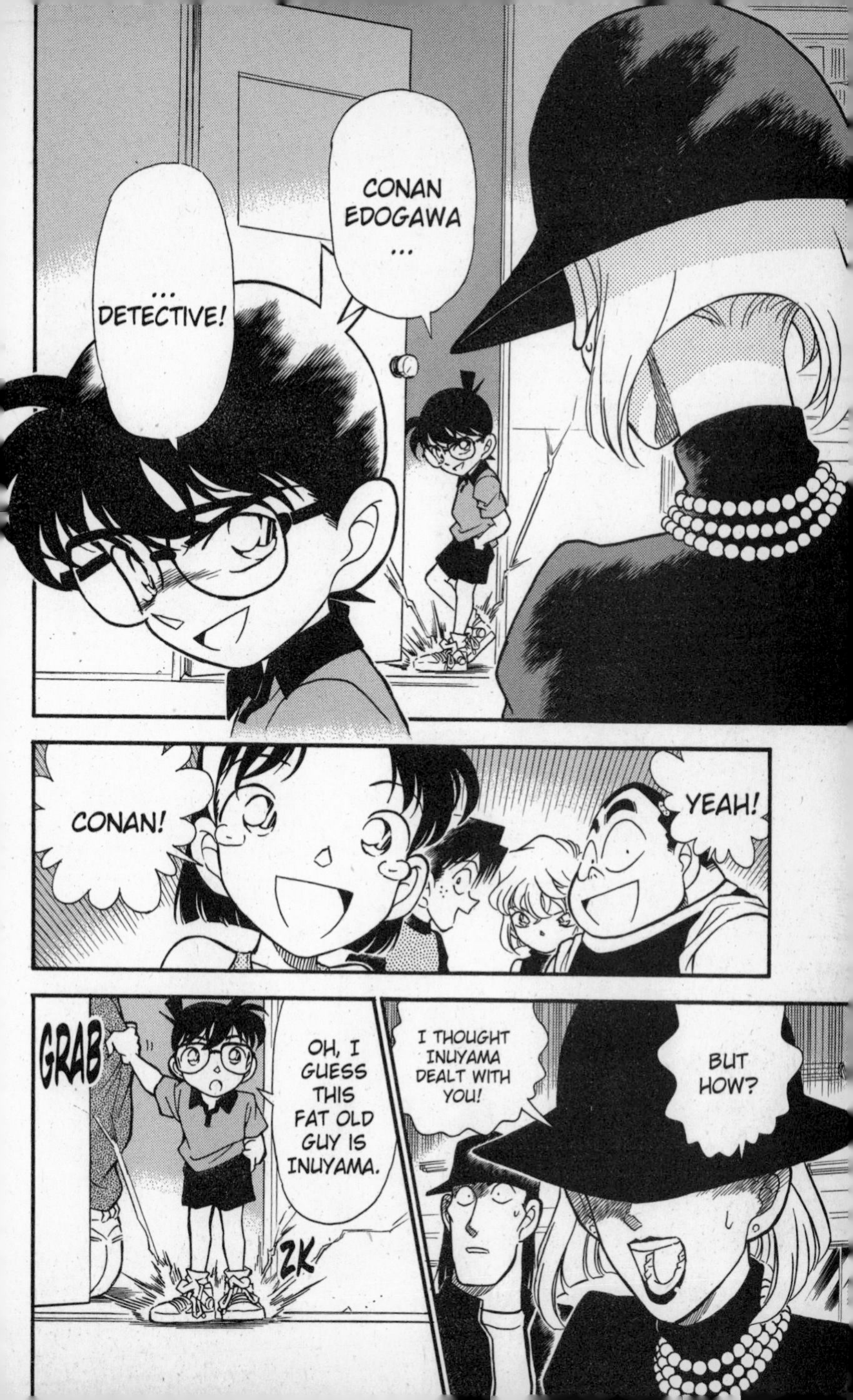
CONAN EDOGAWA ...
... DETECTIVE!
YEAH!
CONAN!
BUT HOW?
I THOUGHT INUYAMA DEALT WITH YOU!
OH, I GUESS THIS FAT OLD GUY IS INUYAMA.
GRAB
ZK

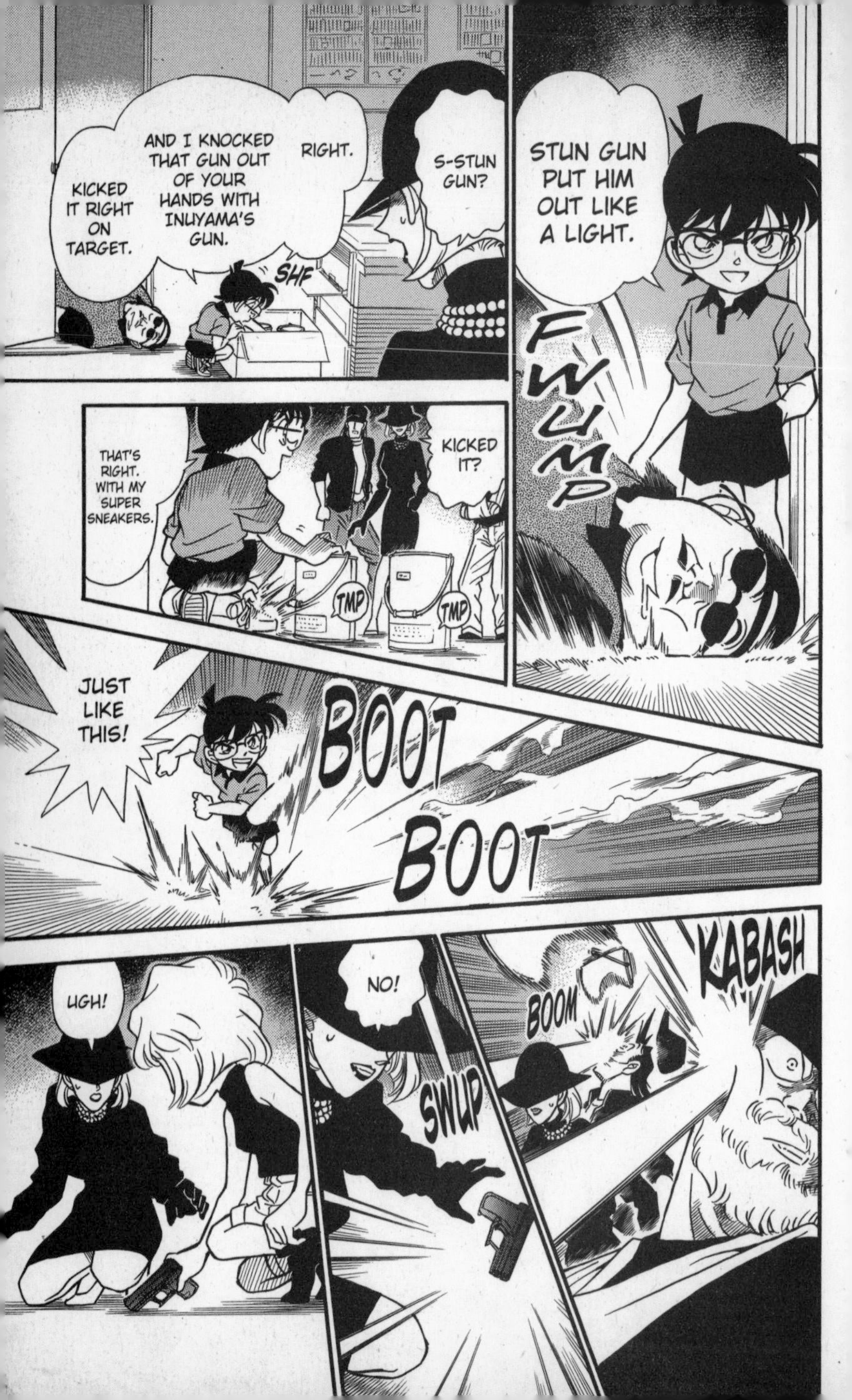
STUN GUN PUT HIM OUT LIKE A LIGHT.
FWUMP
S-STUN GUN?
RIGHT.
AND I KNOCKED THAT GUN OUT OF YOUR HANDS WITH INUYAMA'S GUN.
KICKED IT RIGHT ON TARGET.
SHF
KICKED IT?
TMP
TMP
THAT'S RIGHT. WITH MY SUPER SNEAKERS.
BOOT
BOOT
JUST LIKE THIS!
KABASH
BOOM
NO!
SWUP
UGH!

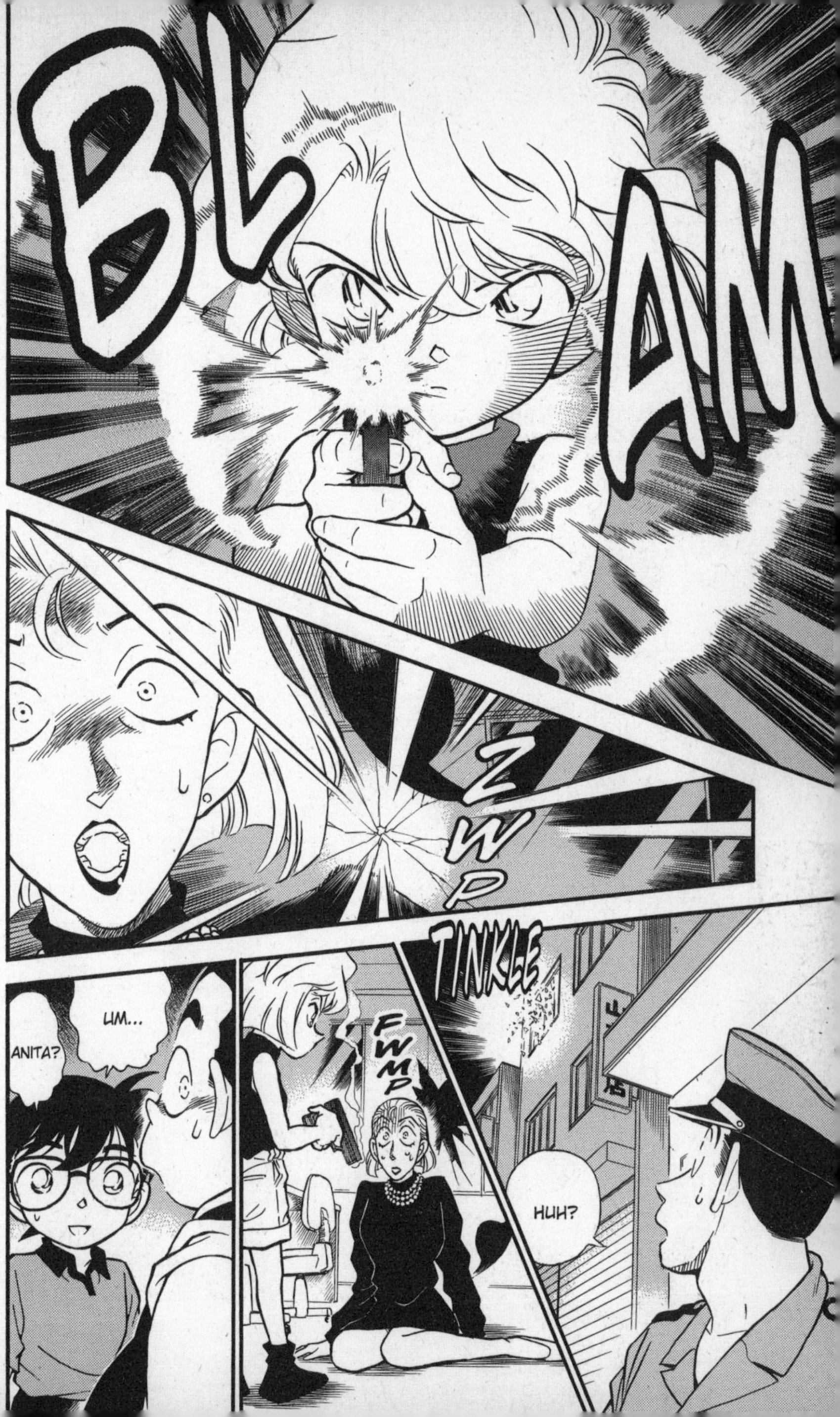
BLAM
ZWP
TINKLE
HUH?
FWMP
UM...
ANITA?

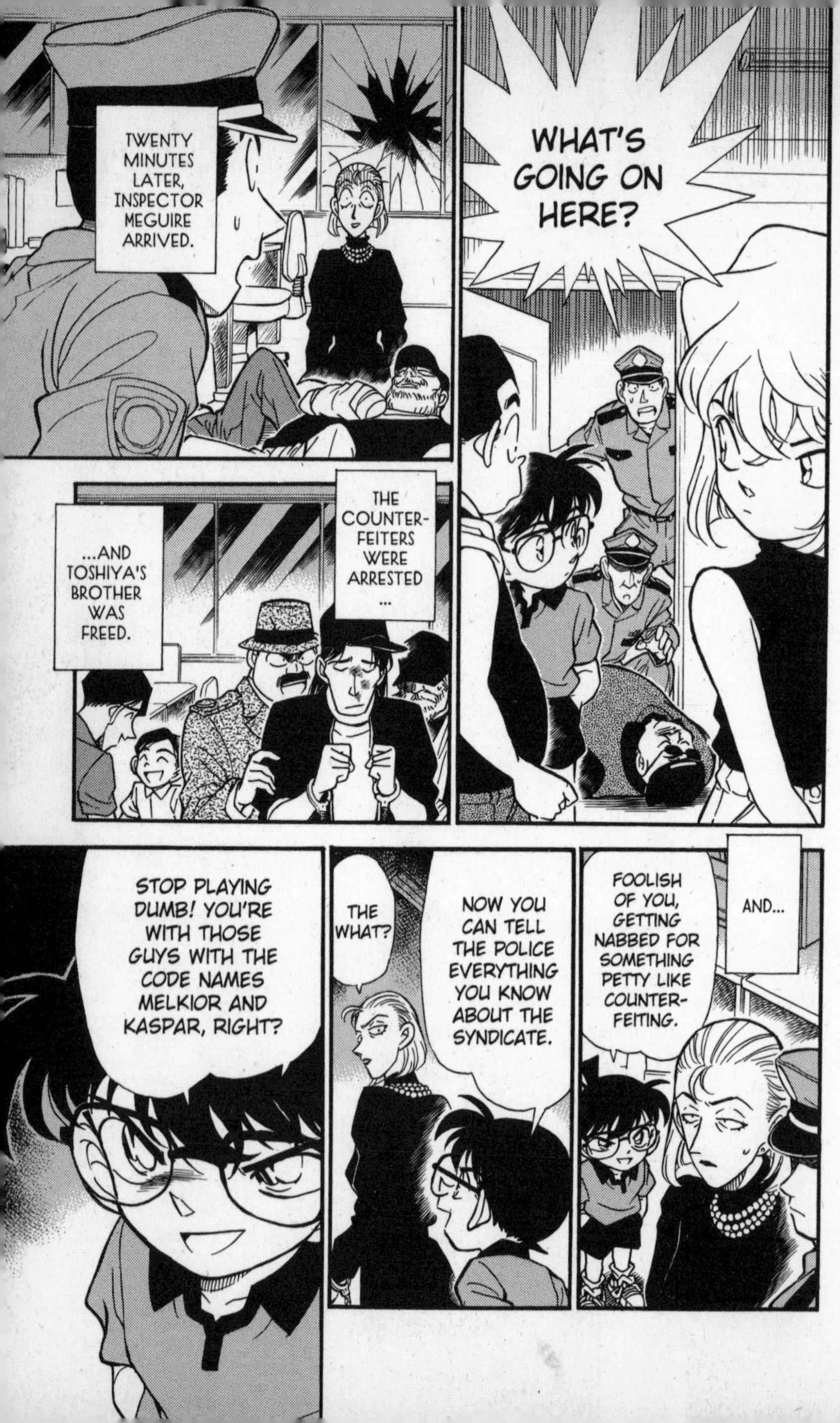
WHAT'S GOING ON HERE?
TWENTY MINUTES LATER, INSPECTOR MEGUIRE ARRIVED.
THE COUNTERFEITERS WERE ARRESTED ...
...AND TOSHIYA'S BROTHER WAS FREED.
AND...
FOOLISH OF YOU, GETTING NABBED FOR SOMETHING PETTY LIKE COUNTER-FEITING.
NOW YOU CAN TELL THE POLICE EVERYTHING YOU KNOW ABOUT THE SYNDICATE.
THE WHAT?
STOP PLAYING DUMB! YOU'RE WITH THOSE GUYS WITH THE CODE NAMES MELKIOR AND KASPAR, RIGHT?

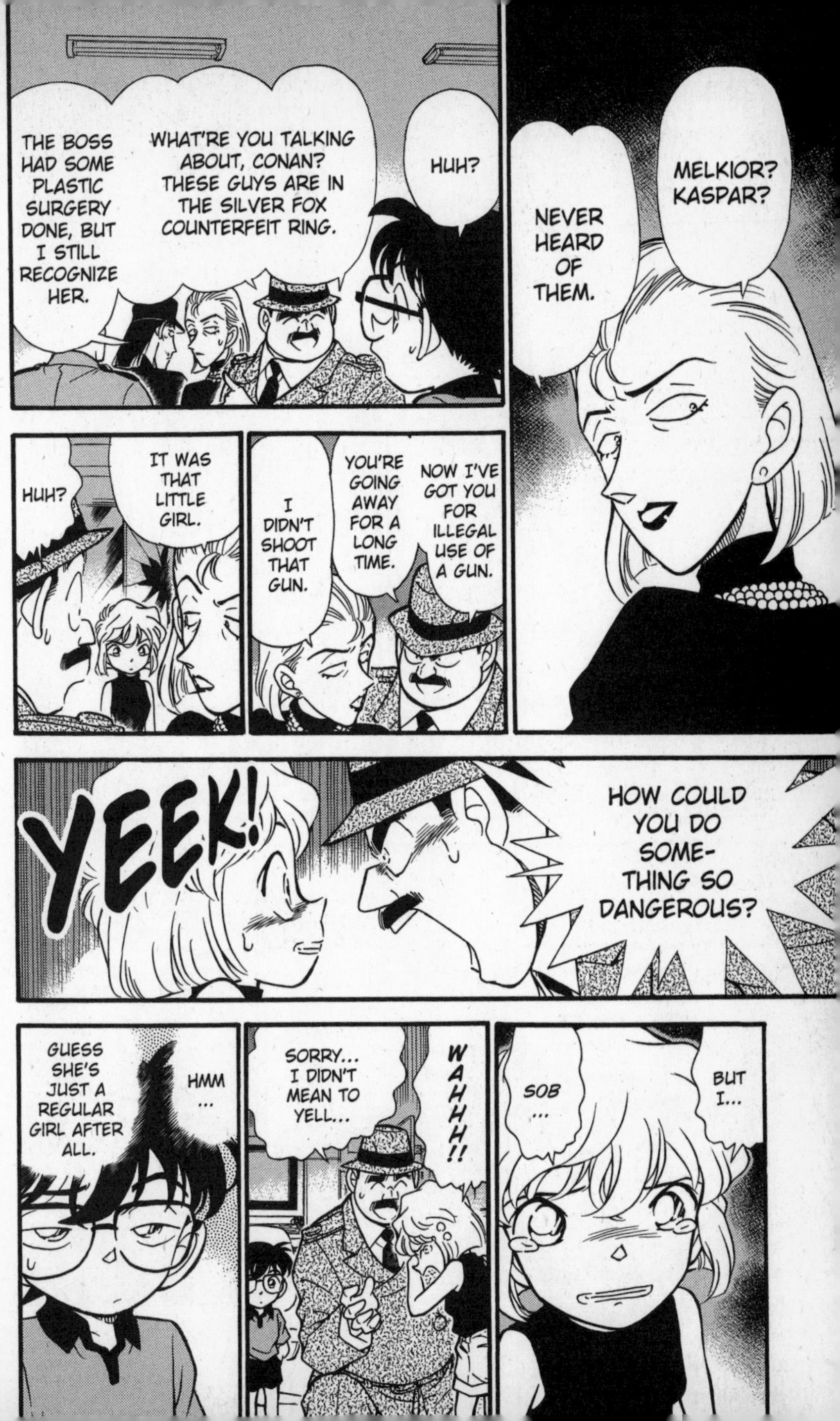
MELKIOR? KASPAR?
NEVER HEARD OF THEM.
HUH?
WHAT'RE YOU TALKING ABOUT, CONAN? THESE GUYS ARE IN THE SILVER FOX COUNTERFEIT RING.
THE BOSS HAD SOME PLASTIC SURGERY DONE, BUT I STILL RECOGNIZE HER.
NOW I'VE GOT YOU FOR ILLEGAL USE OF A GUN.
YOU'RE GOING AWAY FOR A LONG TIME.
I DIDN'T SHOOT THAT GUN.
IT WAS THAT LITTLE GIRL.
HUH?
HOW COULD YOU DO SOME-THING SO DANGEROUS?
YEEK!
BUT I...
SOB...
WAHHH!!
SORRY... I DIDN'T MEAN TO YELL...
HMM...
GUESS SHE'S JUST A REGULAR GIRL AFTER ALL.

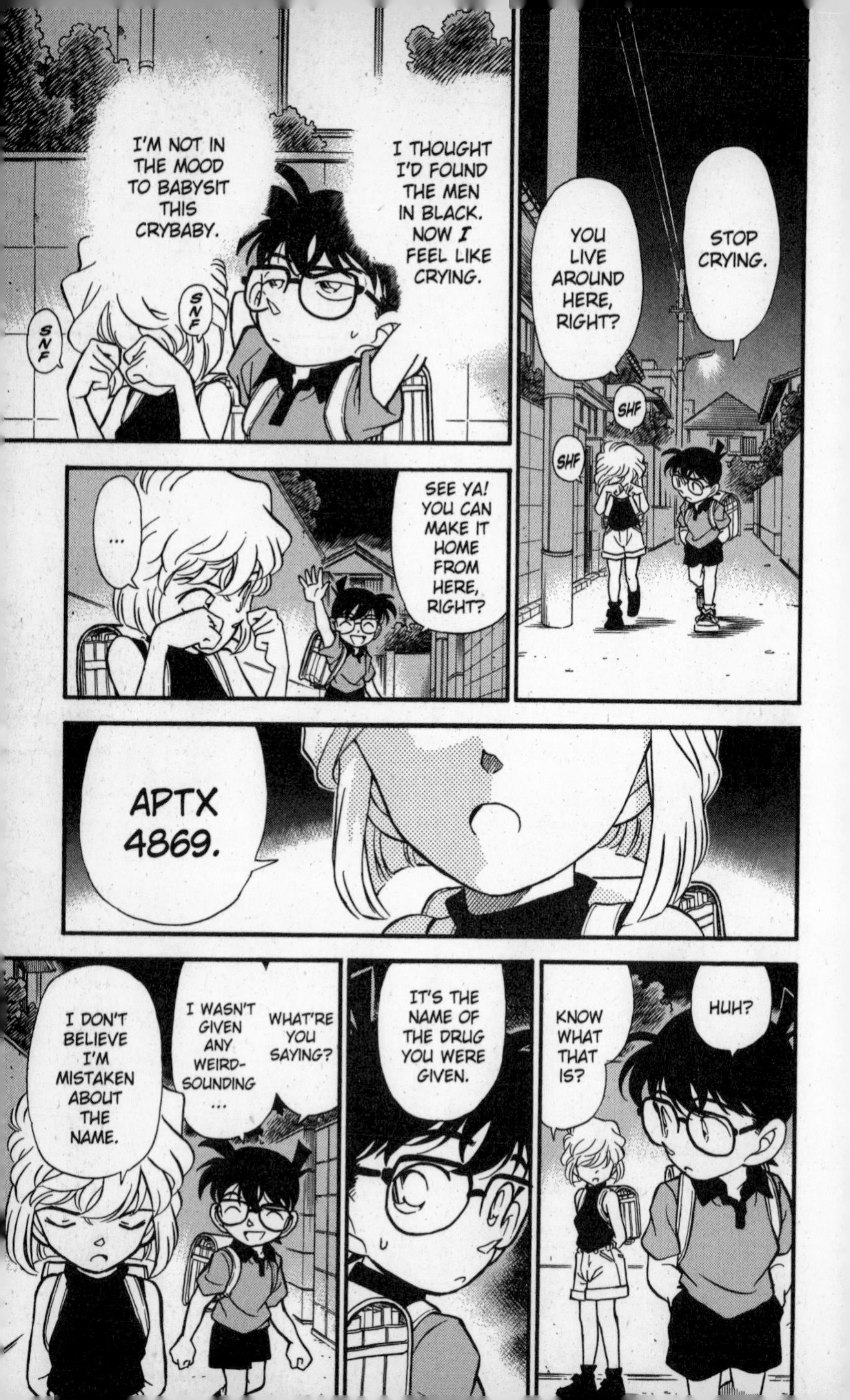
STOP CRYING.
YOU LIVE AROUND HERE, RIGHT?
SHF
SHF
I THOUGHT I'D FOUND THE MEN IN BLACK. NOW I FEEL LIKE CRYING.
I'M NOT IN THE MOOD TO BABYSIT THIS CRYBABY.
SNF
SNF
SEE YA! YOU CAN MAKE IT HOME FROM HERE, RIGHT?
...
APTX 4869.
HUH?
KNOW WHAT THAT IS?
IT'S THE NAME OF THE DRUG YOU WERE GIVEN.
WHAT'RE YOU SAYING?
I WASN'T GIVEN ANY WEIRD-SOUNDING...
I DON'T BELIEVE I'M MISTAKEN ABOUT THE NAME.

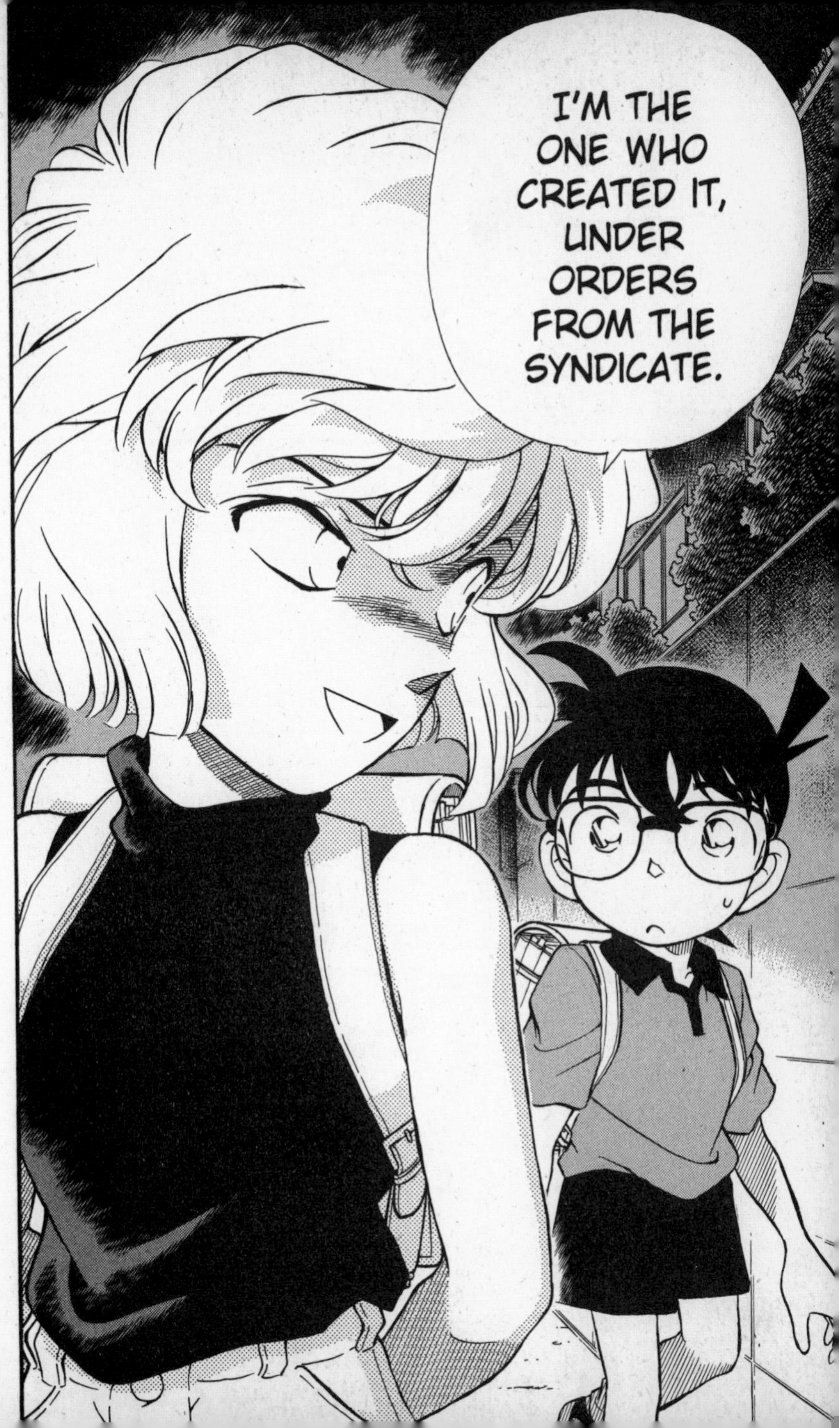
I'M THE ONE WHO CREATED IT, UNDER ORDERS FROM THE SYNDICATE.

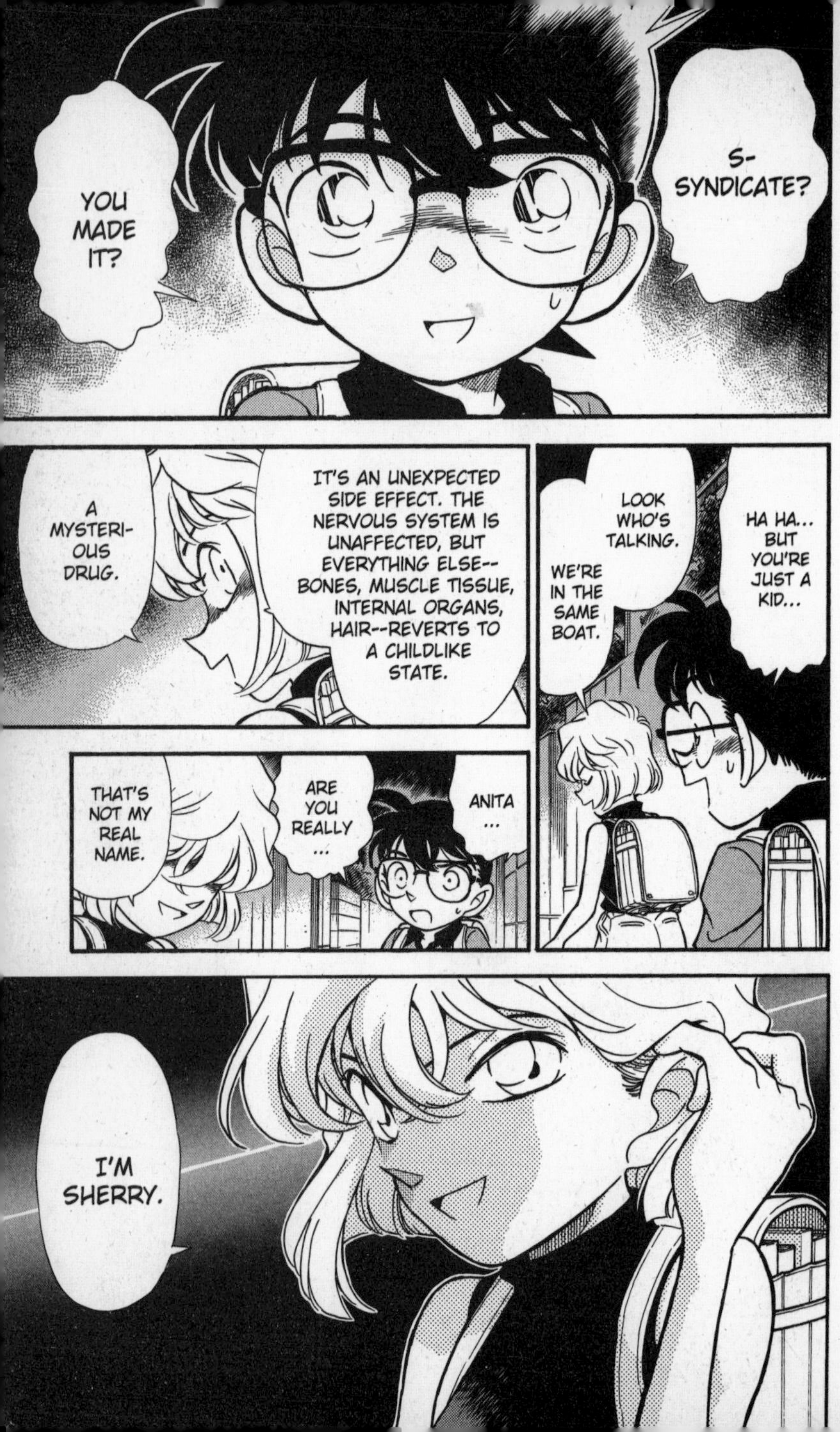
S-SYNDICATE?
YOU MADE IT?
HA HA... BUT YOU'RE JUST A KID...
LOOK WHO'S TALKING.
WE'RE IN THE SAME BOAT.
IT'S AN UNEXPECTED SIDE EFFECT. THE NERVOUS SYSTEM IS UNAFFECTED, BUT EVERYTHING ELSE--BONES, MUSCLE TISSUE, INTERNAL ORGANS, HAIR--REVERTS TO A CHILDLIKE STATE.
A MYSTERIOUS DRUG.
ANITA...
ARE YOU REALLY...
THAT'S NOT MY REAL NAME.
I'M SHERRY.

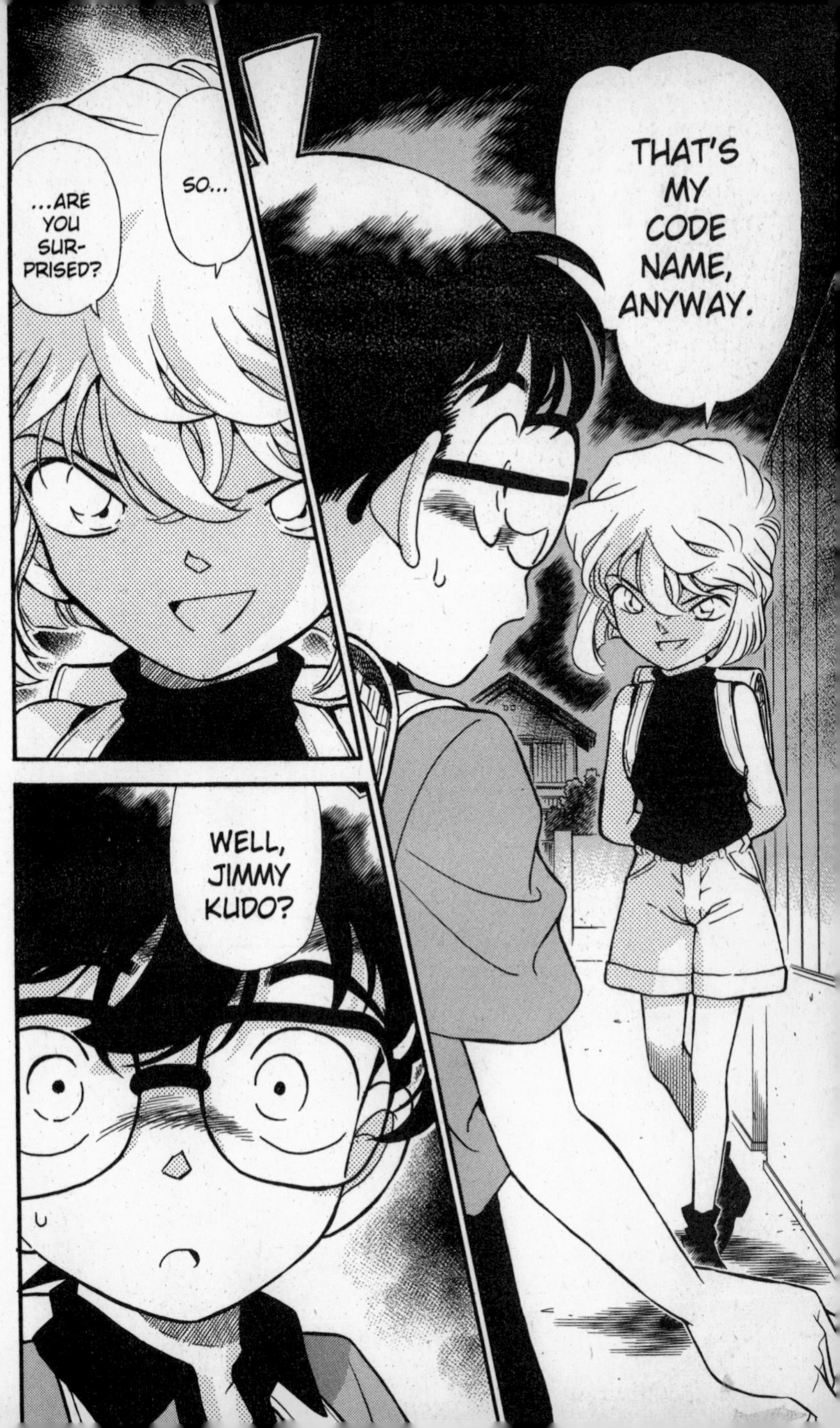
THAT'S MY CODE NAME, ANYWAY.
SO...
...ARE YOU SUR-PRISED?
WELL, JIMMY KUDO?

THE FALSE GIRL

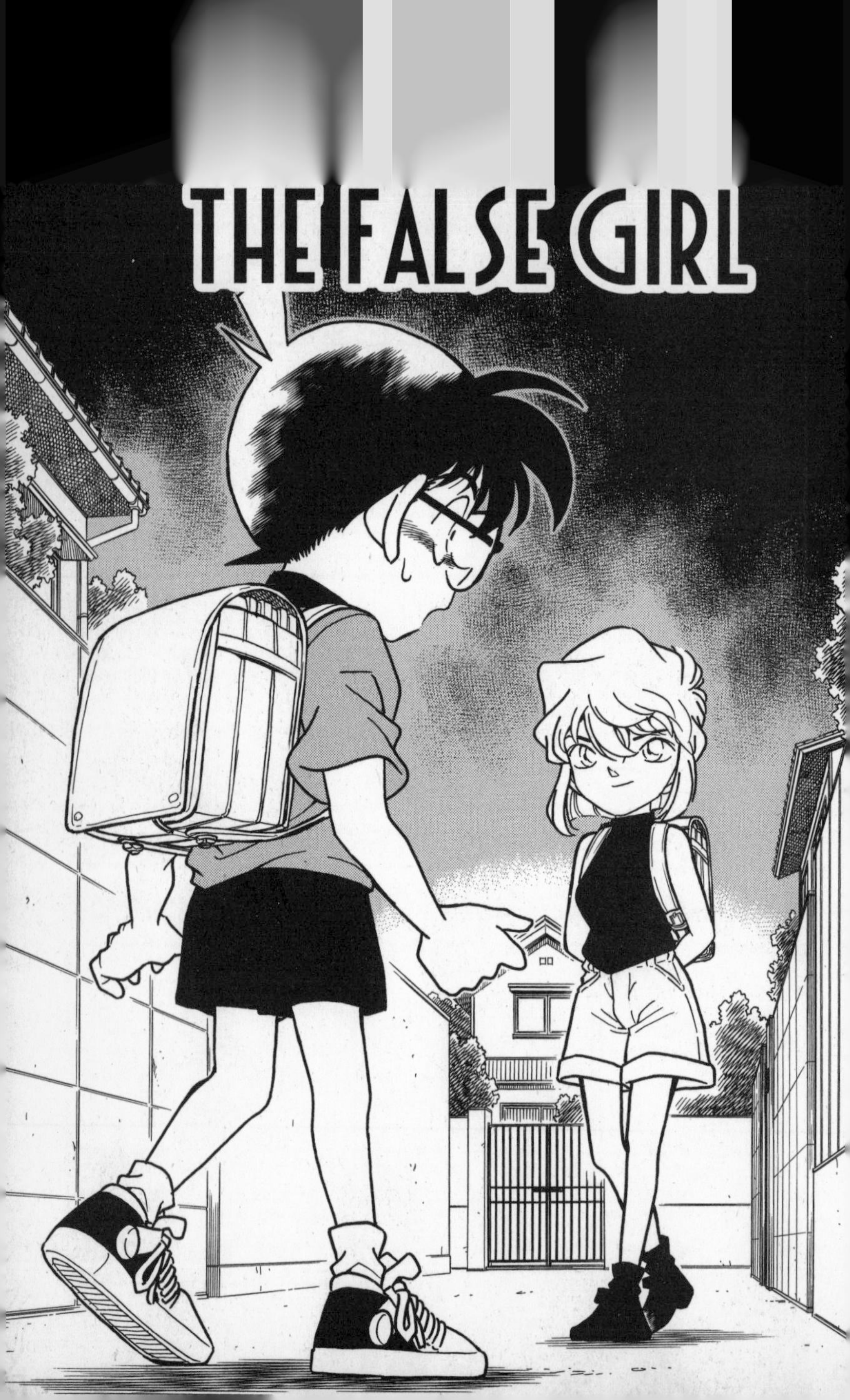

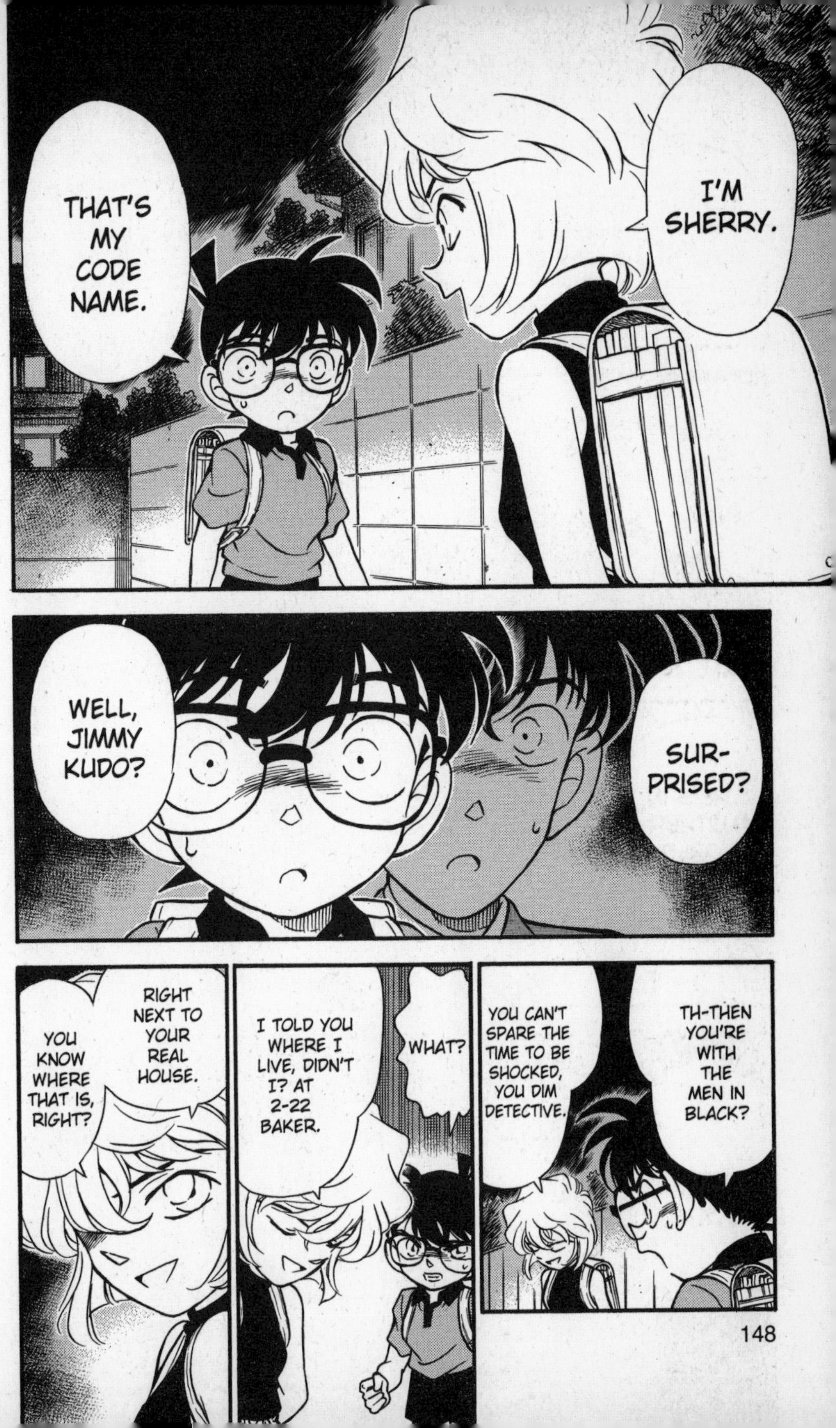
I'M SHERRY.
THAT'S MY CODE NAME.
SUR-PRISED?
WELL, JIMMY KUDO?
TH-THEN YOU'RE WITH THE MEN IN BLACK?
YOU CAN'T SPARE THE TIME TO BE SHOCKED, YOU DIM DETECTIVE.
WHAT?
I TOLD YOU WHERE I LIVE, DIDN'T I? AT 2-22 BAKER.
RIGHT NEXT TO YOUR REAL HOUSE.
YOU KNOW WHERE THAT IS, RIGHT?

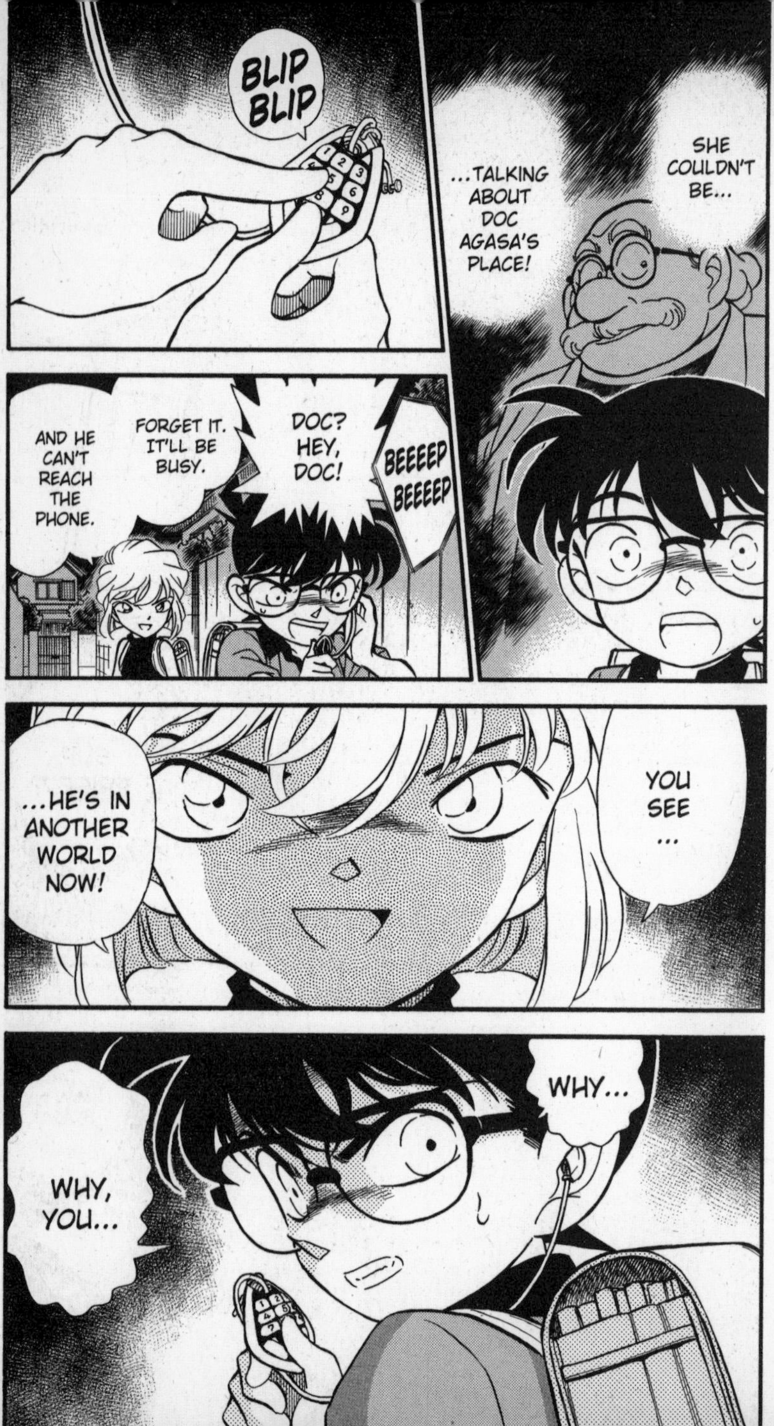
SHE COULDN'T BE...
...TALKING ABOUT DOC AGASA'S PLACE!
BLIP BLIP
BEEEEP BEEEEP
DOC? HEY, DOC!
FORGET IT. IT'LL BE BUSY.
AND HE CAN'T REACH THE PHONE.
YOU SEE...
...HE'S IN ANOTHER WORLD NOW!
WHY...
WHY, YOU...

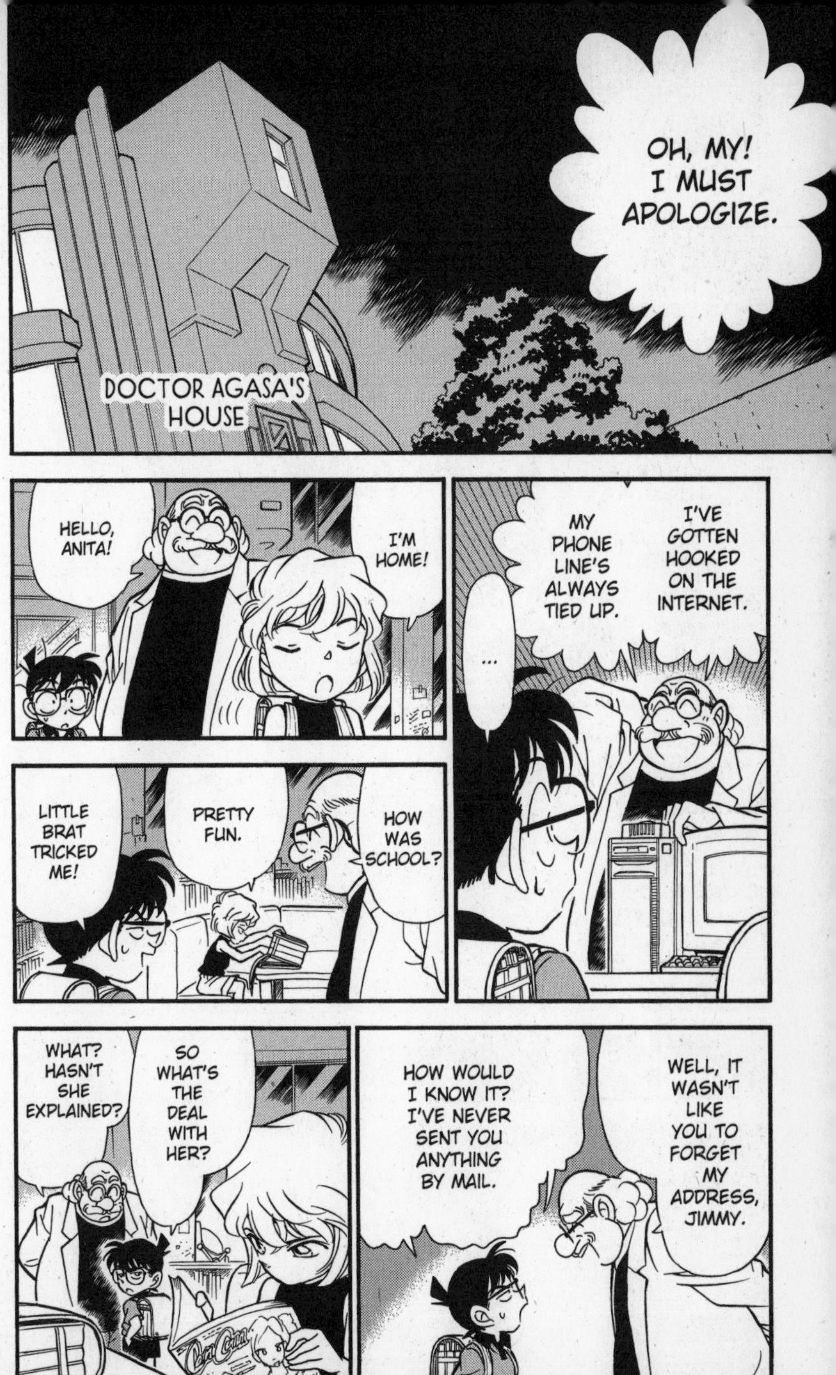
OH, MY! I MUST APOLOGIZE.
DOCTOR AGASA'S HOUSE
I'VE GOTTEN HOOKED ON THE INTERNET.
MY PHONE LINE'S ALWAYS TIED UP.
...
I'M HOME!
HELLO, ANITA!
HOW WAS SCHOOL?
PRETTY FUN.
LITTLE BRAT TRICKED ME!
WELL, IT WASN'T LIKE YOU TO FORGET MY ADDRESS, JIMMY.
HOW WOULD I KNOW IT? I'VE NEVER SENT YOU ANYTHING BY MAIL.
SO WHAT'S THE DEAL WITH HER?
WHAT? HASN'T SHE EXPLAINED?

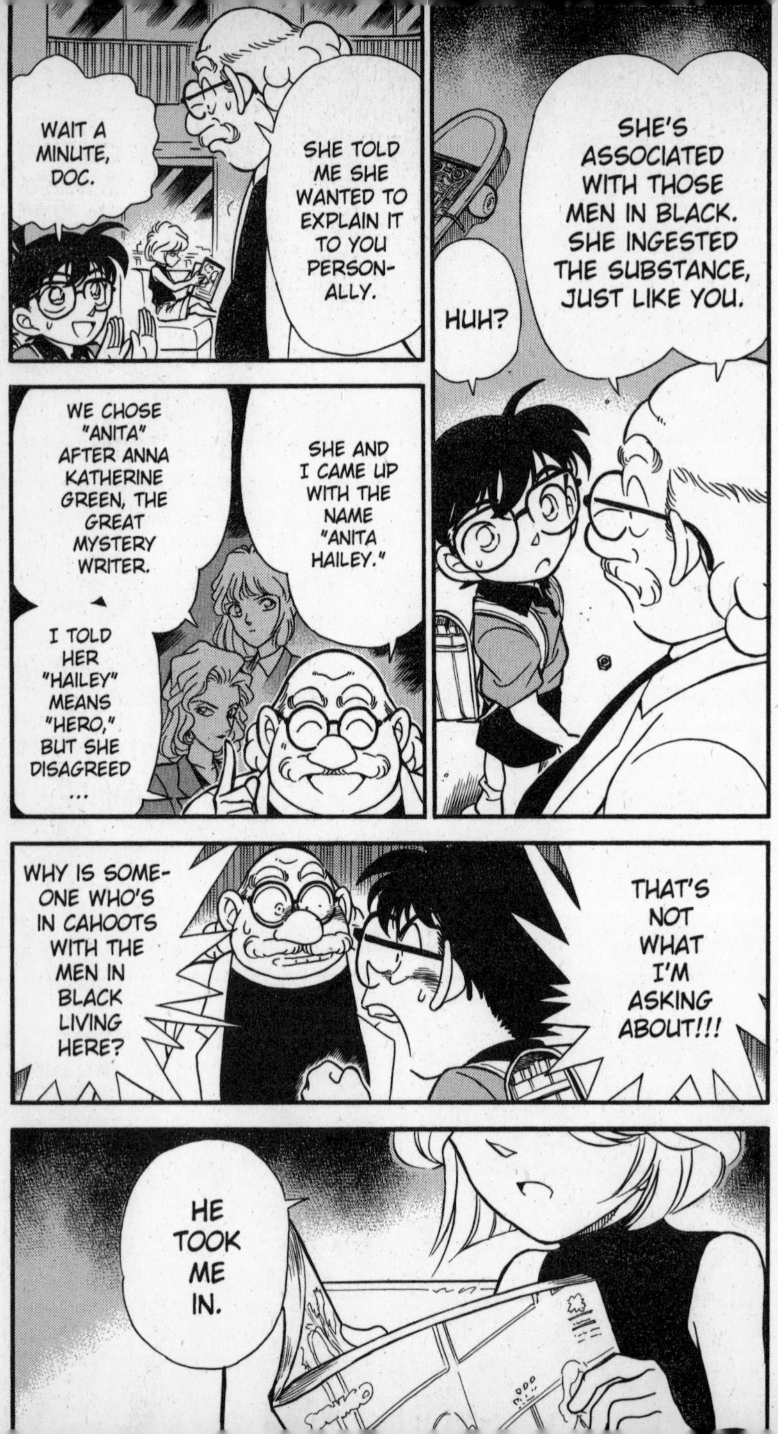
SHE'S ASSOCIATED WITH THOSE MEN IN BLACK. SHE INGESTED THE SUBSTANCE, JUST LIKE YOU.
HUH?
SHE TOLD ME SHE WANTED TO EXPLAIN IT TO YOU PERSON-ALLY.
WAIT A MINUTE, DOC.
SHE AND I CAME UP WITH THE NAME "ANITA HAILEY."
WE CHOSE "ANITA" AFTER ANNA KATHERINE GREEN, THE GREAT MYSTERY WRITER.
I TOLD HER "HAILEY" MEANS "HERO," BUT SHE DISAGREED ...
THAT'S NOT WHAT I'M ASKING ABOUT!!!
WHY IS SOME-ONE WHO'S IN CAHOOTS WITH THE MEN IN BLACK LIVING HERE?
HE TOOK ME IN.

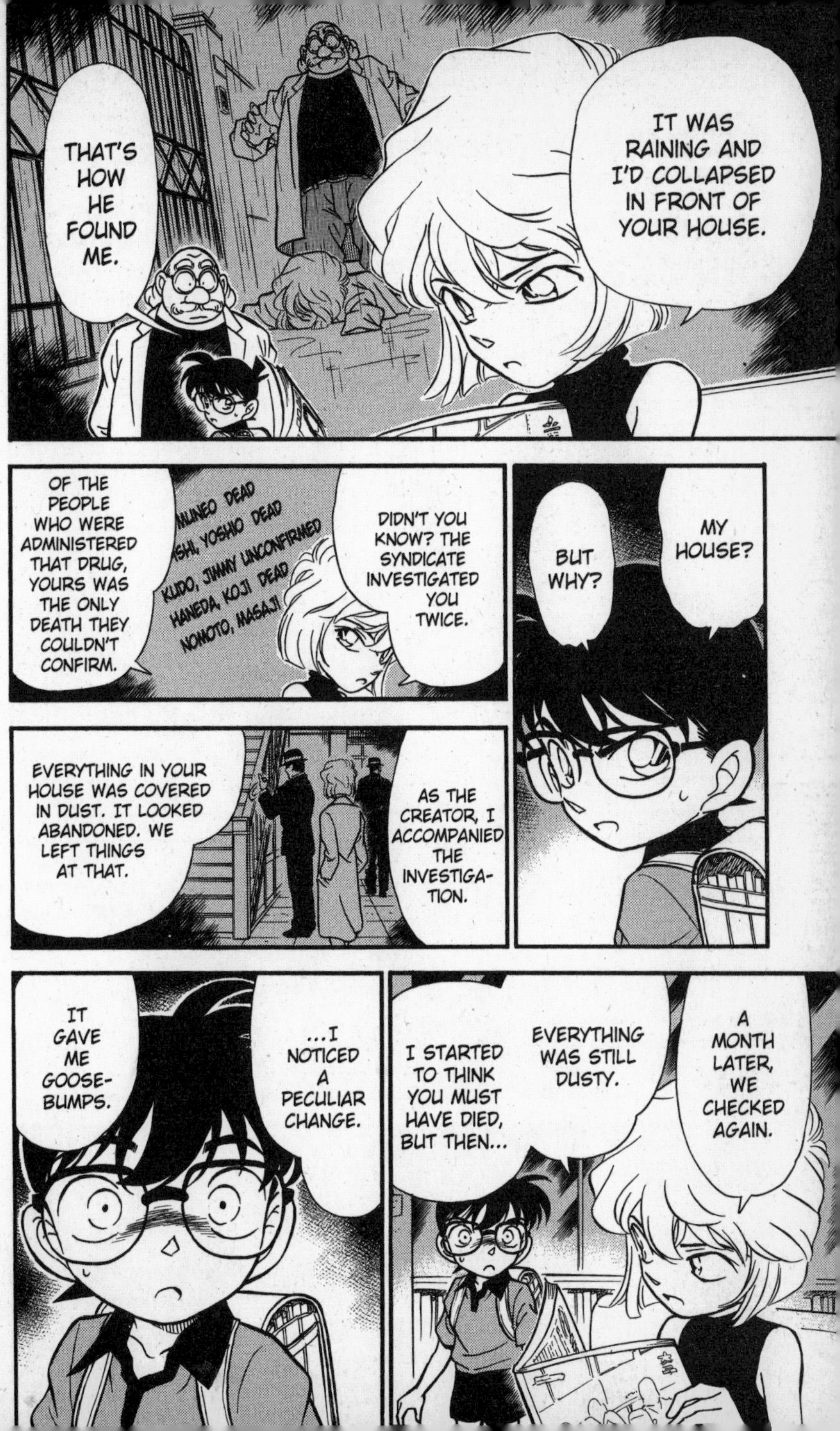
IT WAS RAINING AND I'D COLLAPSED IN FRONT OF YOUR HOUSE.
THAT'S HOW HE FOUND ME.
MY HOUSE?
BUT WHY?
DIDN'T YOU KNOW? THE SYNDICATE INVESTIGATED YOU TWICE.
MUNEO DEAD
SHI, YOSHIO DEAD
KUDO, JIMMY UNCONFIRMED
HANEDA, KOJI DEAD
NOMOTO, MASAJI
OF THE PEOPLE WHO WERE ADMINISTERED THAT DRUG, YOURS WAS THE ONLY DEATH THEY COULDN'T CONFIRM.
AS THE CREATOR, I ACCOMPANIED THE INVESTIGATION.
EVERYTHING IN YOUR HOUSE WAS COVERED IN DUST. IT LOOKED ABANDONED. WE LEFT THINGS AT THAT.
A MONTH LATER, WE CHECKED AGAIN.
EVERYTHING WAS STILL DUSTY.
I STARTED TO THINK YOU MUST HAVE DIED, BUT THEN...
...I NOTICED A PECULIAR CHANGE.
IT GAVE ME GOOSE-BUMPS.

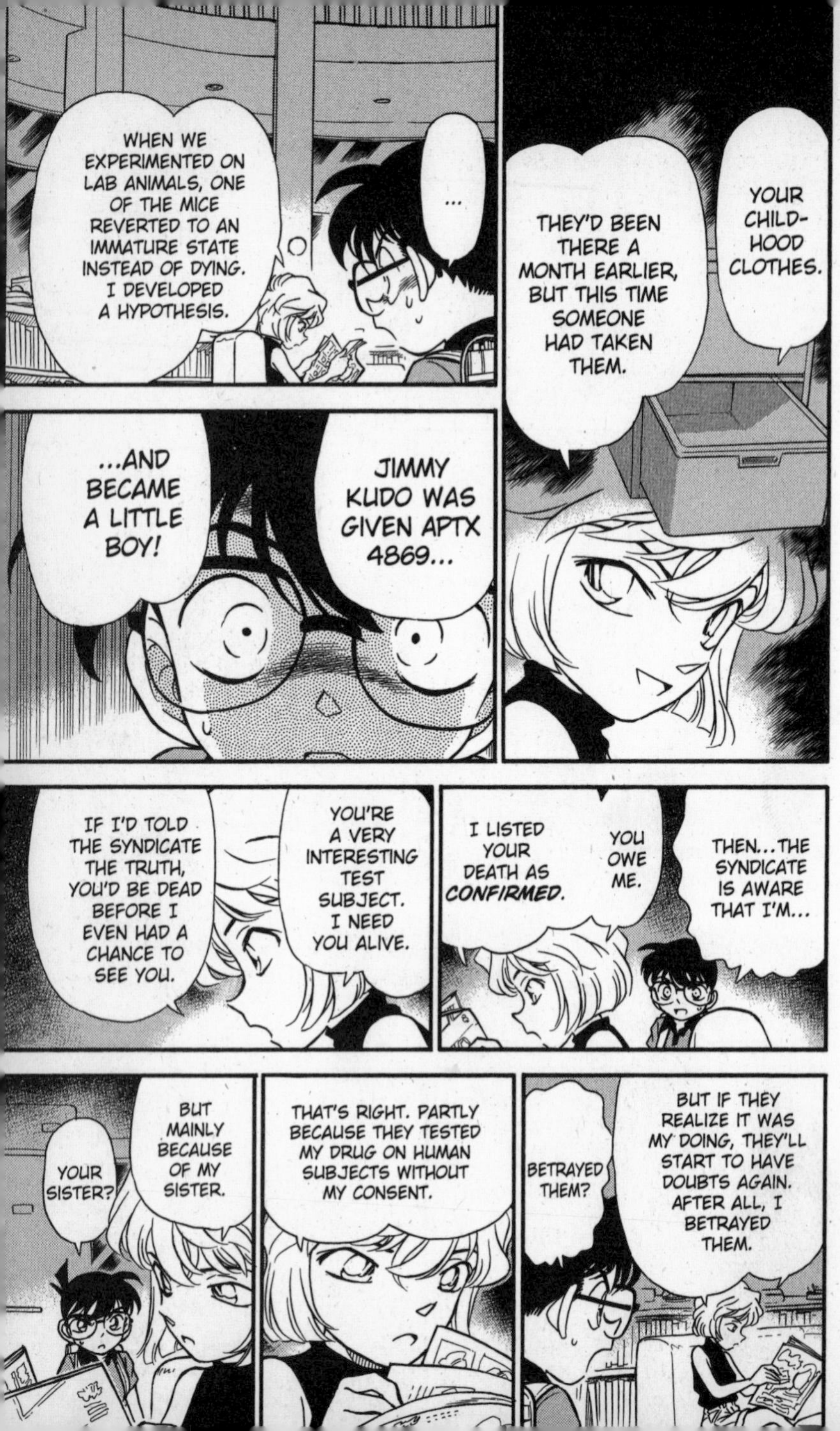
YOUR CHILDHOOD CLOTHES.
THEY'D BEEN THERE A MONTH EARLIER, BUT THIS TIME SOMEONE HAD TAKEN THEM.
...
WHEN WE EXPERIMENTED ON LAB ANIMALS, ONE OF THE MICE REVERTED TO AN IMMATURE STATE INSTEAD OF DYING. I DEVELOPED A HYPOTHESIS.
JIMMY KUDO WAS GIVEN APTX 4869...
...AND BECAME A LITTLE BOY!
THEN...THE SYNDICATE IS AWARE THAT I'M...
YOU OWE ME.
I LISTED YOUR DEATH AS *CONFIRMED*.
YOU'RE A VERY INTERESTING TEST SUBJECT. I NEED YOU ALIVE.
IF I'D TOLD THE SYNDICATE THE TRUTH, YOU'D BE DEAD BEFORE I EVEN HAD A CHANCE TO SEE YOU.
BUT IF THEY REALIZE IT WAS MY DOING, THEY'LL START TO HAVE DOUBTS AGAIN. AFTER ALL, I BETRAYED THEM.
BETRAYED THEM?
THAT'S RIGHT. PARTLY BECAUSE THEY TESTED MY DRUG ON HUMAN SUBJECTS WITHOUT MY CONSENT.
BUT MAINLY BECAUSE OF MY SISTER.
YOUR SISTER?

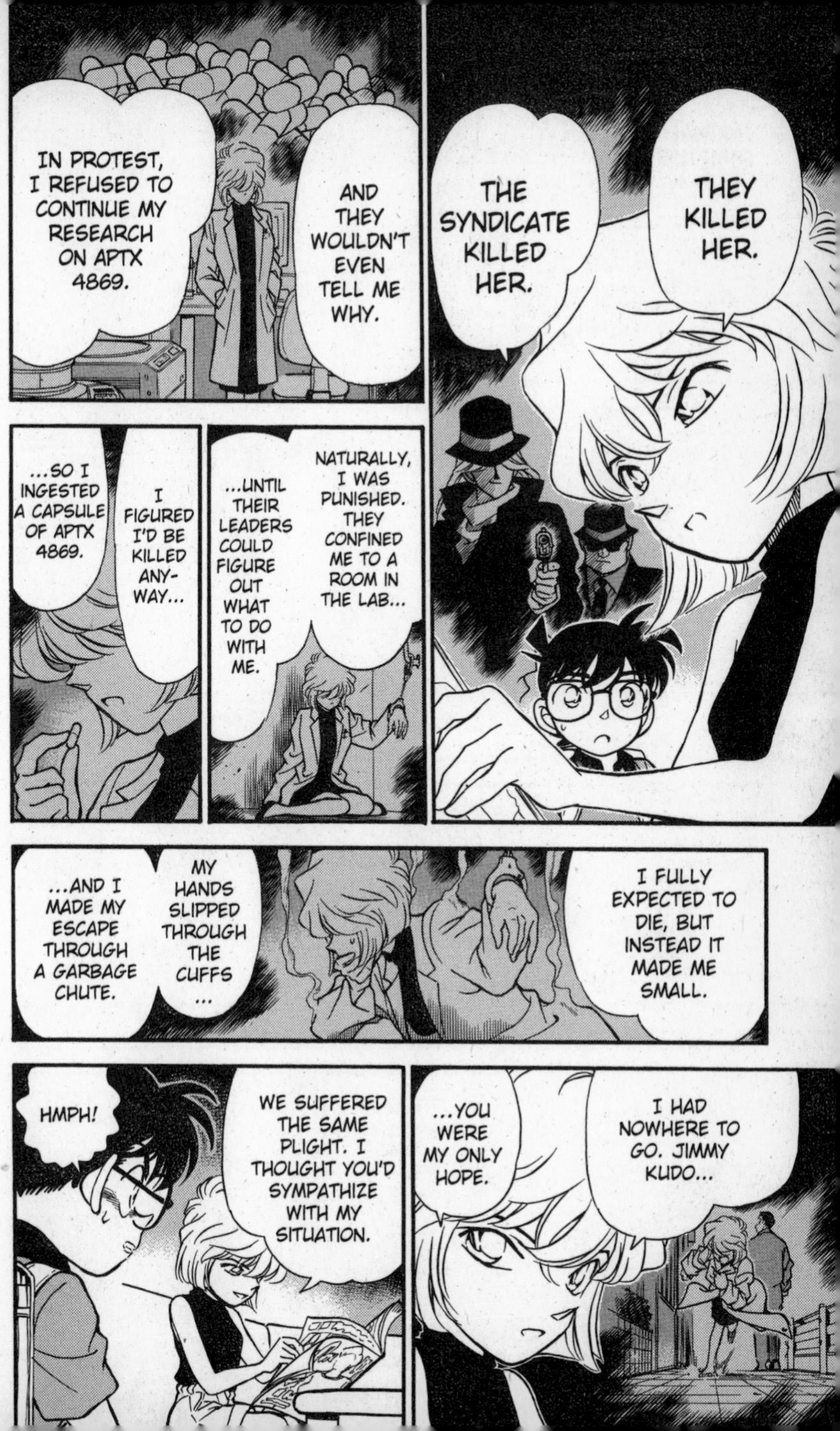
THEY KILLED HER.
THE SYNDICATE KILLED HER.
AND THEY WOULDN'T EVEN TELL ME WHY.
IN PROTEST, I REFUSED TO CONTINUE MY RESEARCH ON APTX 4869.
NATURALLY, I WAS PUNISHED. THEY CONFINED ME TO A ROOM IN THE LAB...
...UNTIL THEIR LEADERS COULD FIGURE OUT WHAT TO DO WITH ME.
I FIGURED I'D BE KILLED ANY-WAY...
...SO I INGESTED A CAPSULE OF APTX 4869.
I FULLY EXPECTED TO DIE, BUT INSTEAD IT MADE ME SMALL.
MY HANDS SLIPPED THROUGH THE CUFFS ...
...AND I MADE MY ESCAPE THROUGH A GARBAGE CHUTE.
I HAD NOWHERE TO GO. JIMMY KUDO...
...YOU WERE MY ONLY HOPE.
WE SUFFERED THE SAME PLIGHT. I THOUGHT YOU'D SYMPATHIZE WITH MY SITUATION.
HMPH!

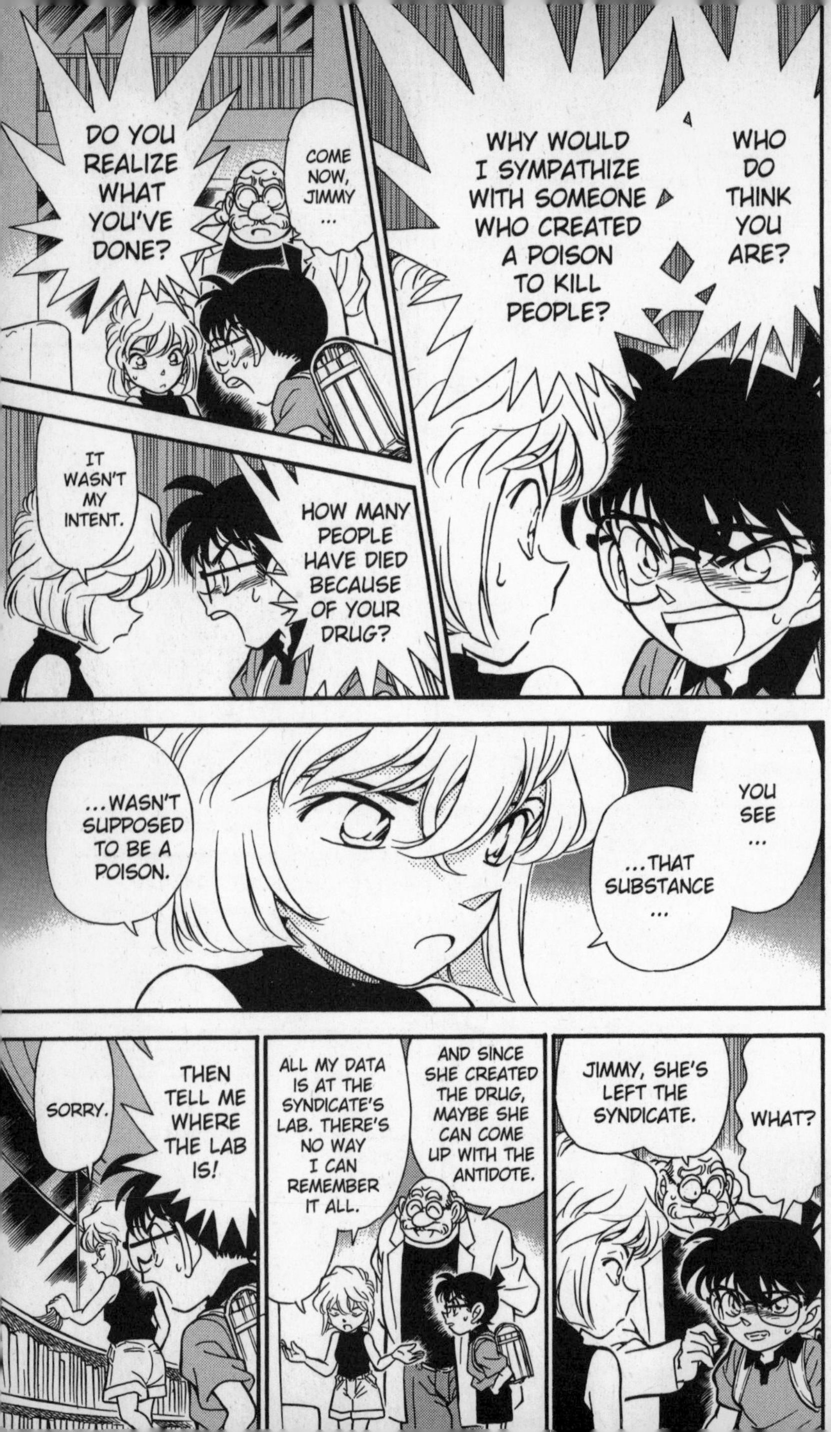
WHO DO THINK YOU ARE?
WHY WOULD I SYMPATHIZE WITH SOMEONE WHO CREATED A POISON TO KILL PEOPLE?
COME NOW, JIMMY ...
DO YOU REALIZE WHAT YOU'VE DONE?
HOW MANY PEOPLE HAVE DIED BECAUSE OF YOUR DRUG?
IT WASN'T MY INTENT.
YOU SEE ...
...THAT SUBSTANCE ...
...WASN'T SUPPOSED TO BE A POISON.
WHAT?
JIMMY, SHE'S LEFT THE SYNDICATE.
AND SINCE SHE CREATED THE DRUG, MAYBE SHE CAN COME UP WITH THE ANTIDOTE.
ALL MY DATA IS AT THE SYNDICATE'S LAB. THERE'S NO WAY I CAN REMEMBER IT ALL.
THEN TELL ME WHERE THE LAB IS!
SORRY.

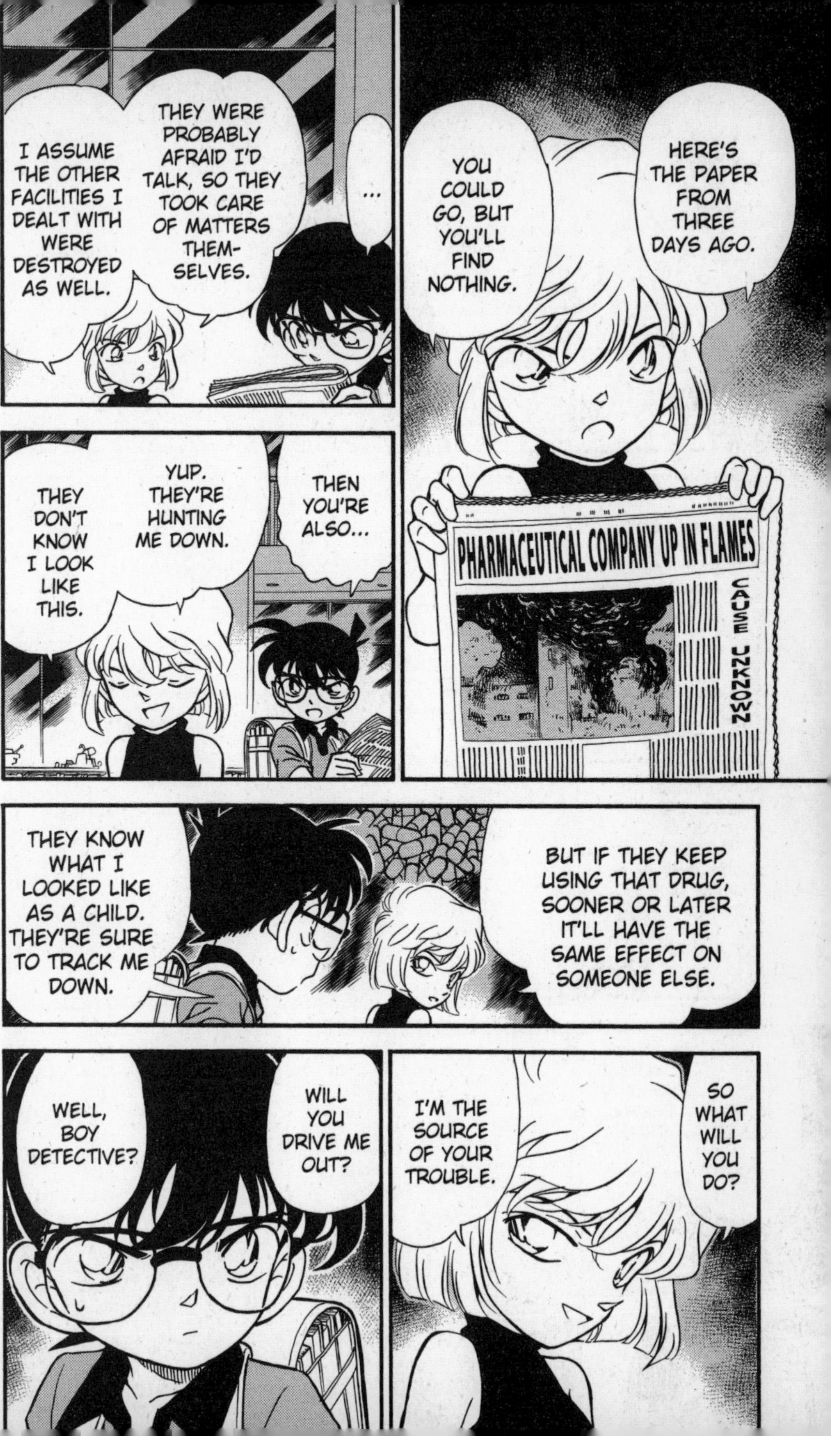
HERE'S THE PAPER FROM THREE DAYS AGO.
YOU COULD GO, BUT YOU'LL FIND NOTHING.
PHARMACEUTICAL COMPANY UP IN FLAMES
CAUSE UNKNOWN
...
THEY WERE PROBABLY AFRAID I'D TALK, SO THEY TOOK CARE OF MATTERS THEM-SELVES.
I ASSUME THE OTHER FACILITIES I DEALT WITH WERE DESTROYED AS WELL.
THEN YOU'RE ALSO...
YUP. THEY'RE HUNTING ME DOWN.
THEY DON'T KNOW I LOOK LIKE THIS.
BUT IF THEY KEEP USING THAT DRUG, SOONER OR LATER IT'LL HAVE THE SAME EFFECT ON SOMEONE ELSE.
THEY KNOW WHAT I LOOKED LIKE AS A CHILD. THEY'RE SURE TO TRACK ME DOWN.
SO WHAT WILL YOU DO?
I'M THE SOURCE OF YOUR TROUBLE.
WILL YOU DRIVE ME OUT?
WELL, BOY DETECTIVE?

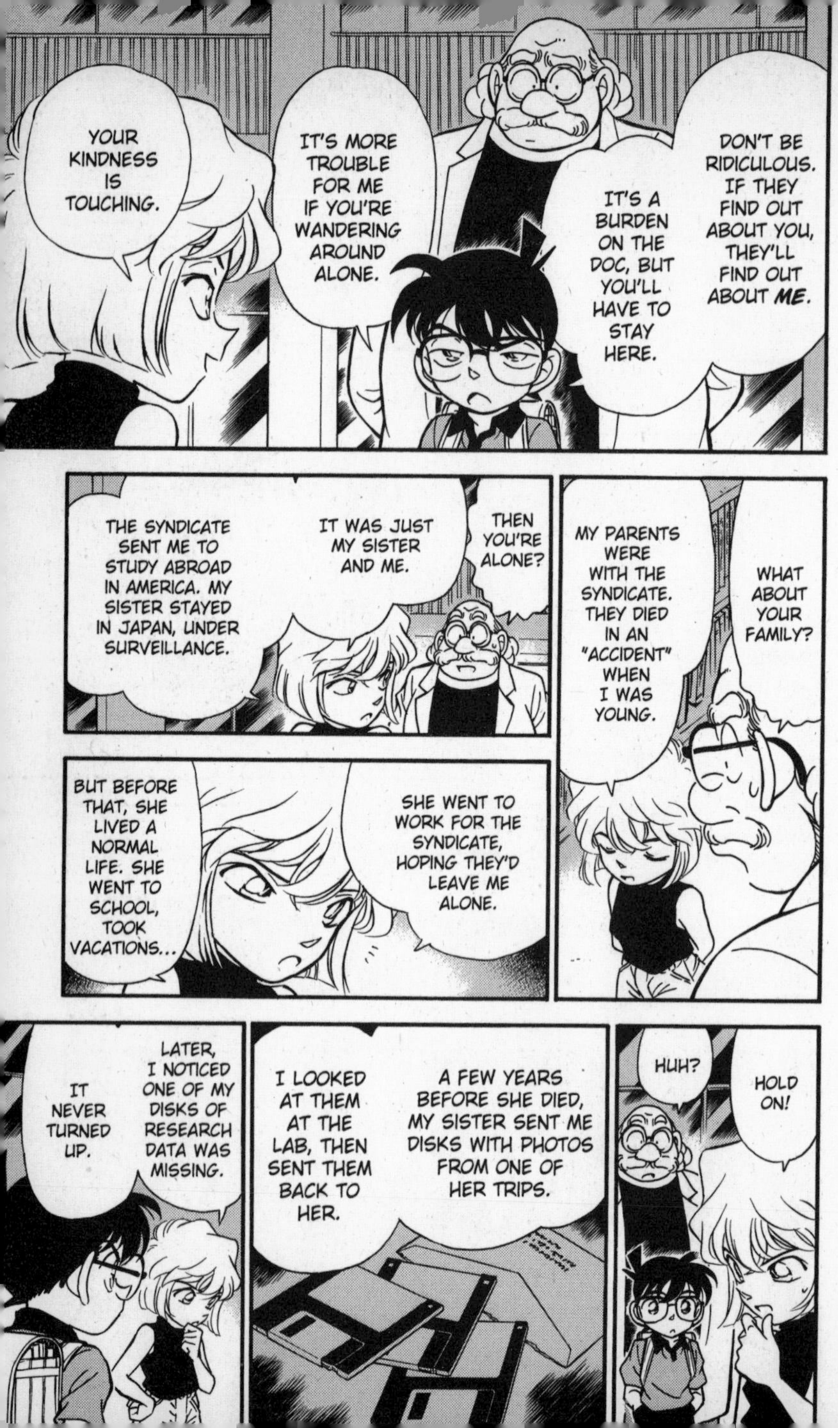
DON'T BE RIDICULOUS. IF THEY FIND OUT ABOUT YOU, THEY'LL FIND OUT ABOUT *ME*.
IT'S A BURDEN ON THE DOC, BUT YOU'LL HAVE TO STAY HERE.
IT'S MORE TROUBLE FOR ME IF YOU'RE WANDERING AROUND ALONE.
YOUR KINDNESS IS TOUCHING.
WHAT ABOUT YOUR FAMILY?
MY PARENTS WERE WITH THE SYNDICATE. THEY DIED IN AN "ACCIDENT" WHEN I WAS YOUNG.
THEN YOU'RE ALONE?
IT WAS JUST MY SISTER AND ME.
THE SYNDICATE SENT ME TO STUDY ABROAD IN AMERICA. MY SISTER STAYED IN JAPAN, UNDER SURVEILLANCE.
SHE WENT TO WORK FOR THE SYNDICATE, HOPING THEY'D LEAVE ME ALONE.
BUT BEFORE THAT, SHE LIVED A NORMAL LIFE. SHE WENT TO SCHOOL, TOOK VACATIONS...
HOLD ON!
HUH?
A FEW YEARS BEFORE SHE DIED, MY SISTER SENT ME DISKS WITH PHOTOS FROM ONE OF HER TRIPS.
I LOOKED AT THEM AT THE LAB, THEN SENT THEM BACK TO HER.
LATER, I NOTICED ONE OF MY DISKS OF RESEARCH DATA WAS MISSING.
IT NEVER TURNED UP.

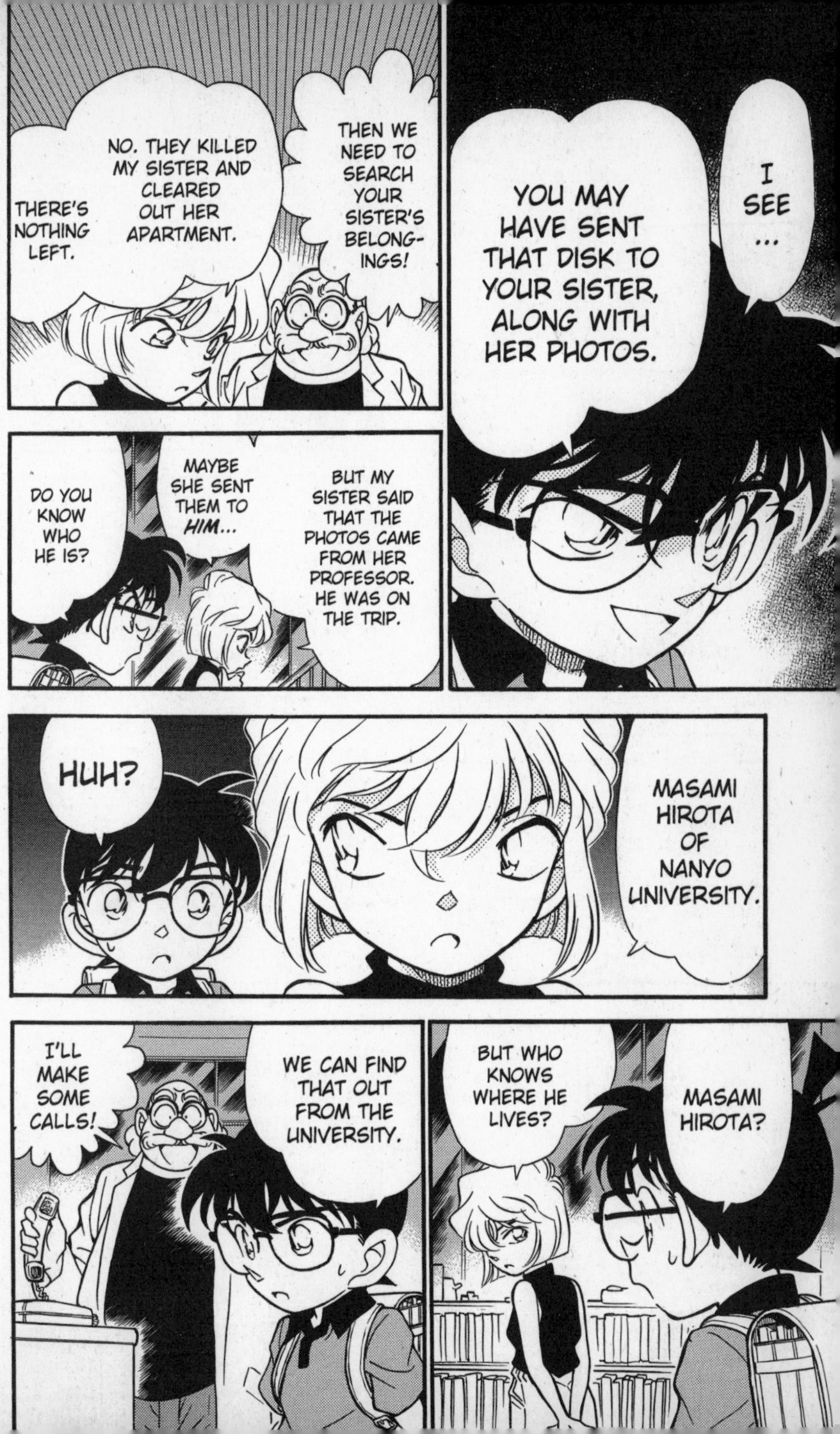
I SEE ...
YOU MAY HAVE SENT THAT DISK TO YOUR SISTER, ALONG WITH HER PHOTOS.
THEN WE NEED TO SEARCH YOUR SISTER'S BELONGINGS!
NO. THEY KILLED MY SISTER AND CLEARED OUT HER APARTMENT.
THERE'S NOTHING LEFT.
BUT MY SISTER SAID THAT THE PHOTOS CAME FROM HER PROFESSOR. HE WAS ON THE TRIP.
MAYBE SHE SENT THEM TO *HIM*...
DO YOU KNOW WHO HE IS?
MASAMI HIROTA OF NANYO UNIVERSITY.
HUH?
MASAMI HIROTA?
BUT WHO KNOWS WHERE HE LIVES?
WE CAN FIND THAT OUT FROM THE UNIVERSITY.
I'LL MAKE SOME CALLS!

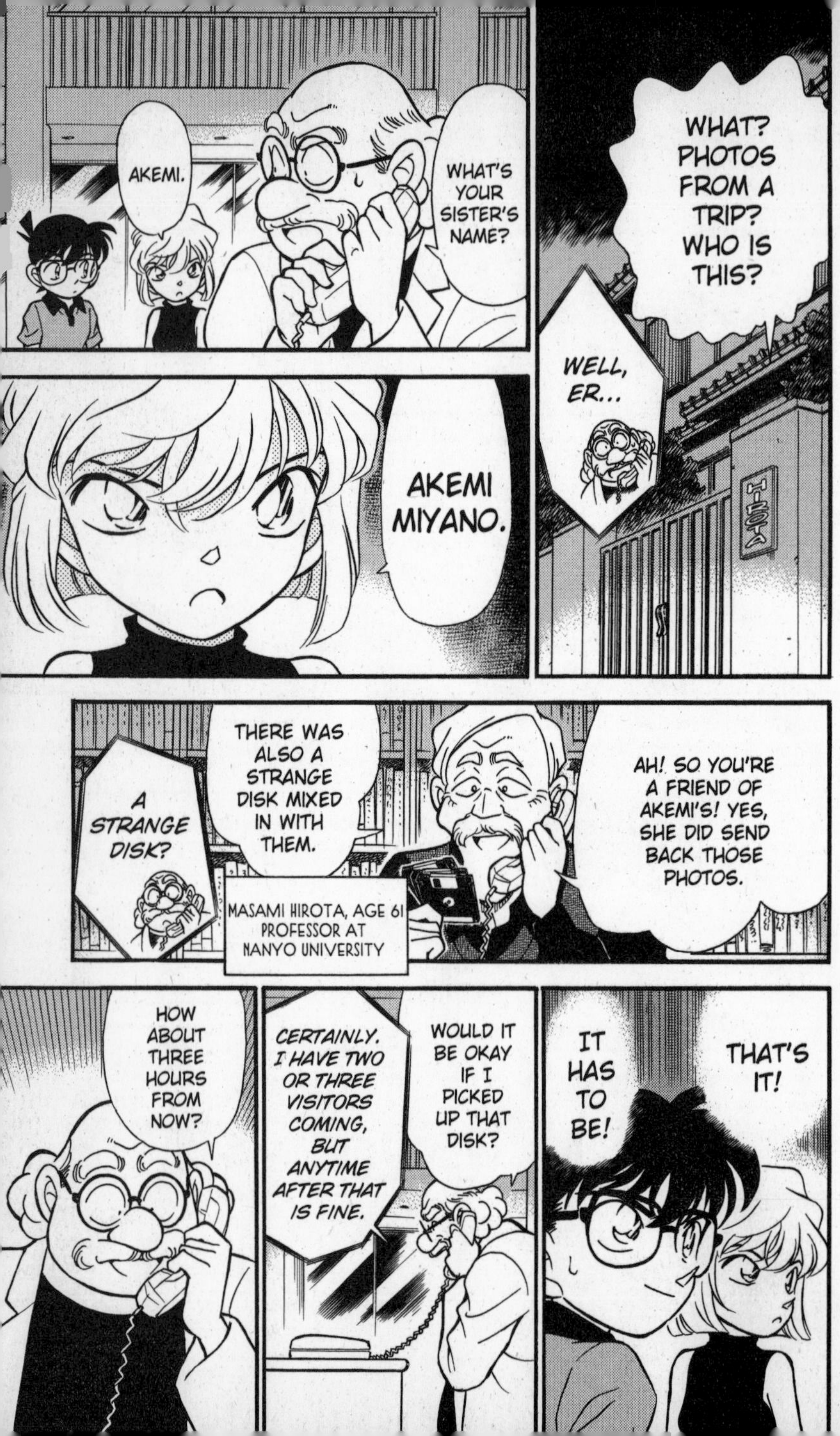
WHAT? PHOTOS FROM A TRIP? WHO IS THIS?
WELL, ER...
WHAT'S YOUR SISTER'S NAME?
AKEMI.
AKEMI MIYANO.
AH! SO YOU'RE A FRIEND OF AKEMI'S! YES, SHE DID SEND BACK THOSE PHOTOS.
THERE WAS ALSO A STRANGE DISK MIXED IN WITH THEM.
A STRANGE DISK?
MASAMI HIROTA, AGE 61 PROFESSOR AT NANYO UNIVERSITY
THAT'S IT!
IT HAS TO BE!
WOULD IT BE OKAY IF I PICKED UP THAT DISK?
CERTAINLY. I HAVE TWO OR THREE VISITORS COMING, BUT ANYTIME AFTER THAT IS FINE.
HOW ABOUT THREE HOURS FROM NOW?

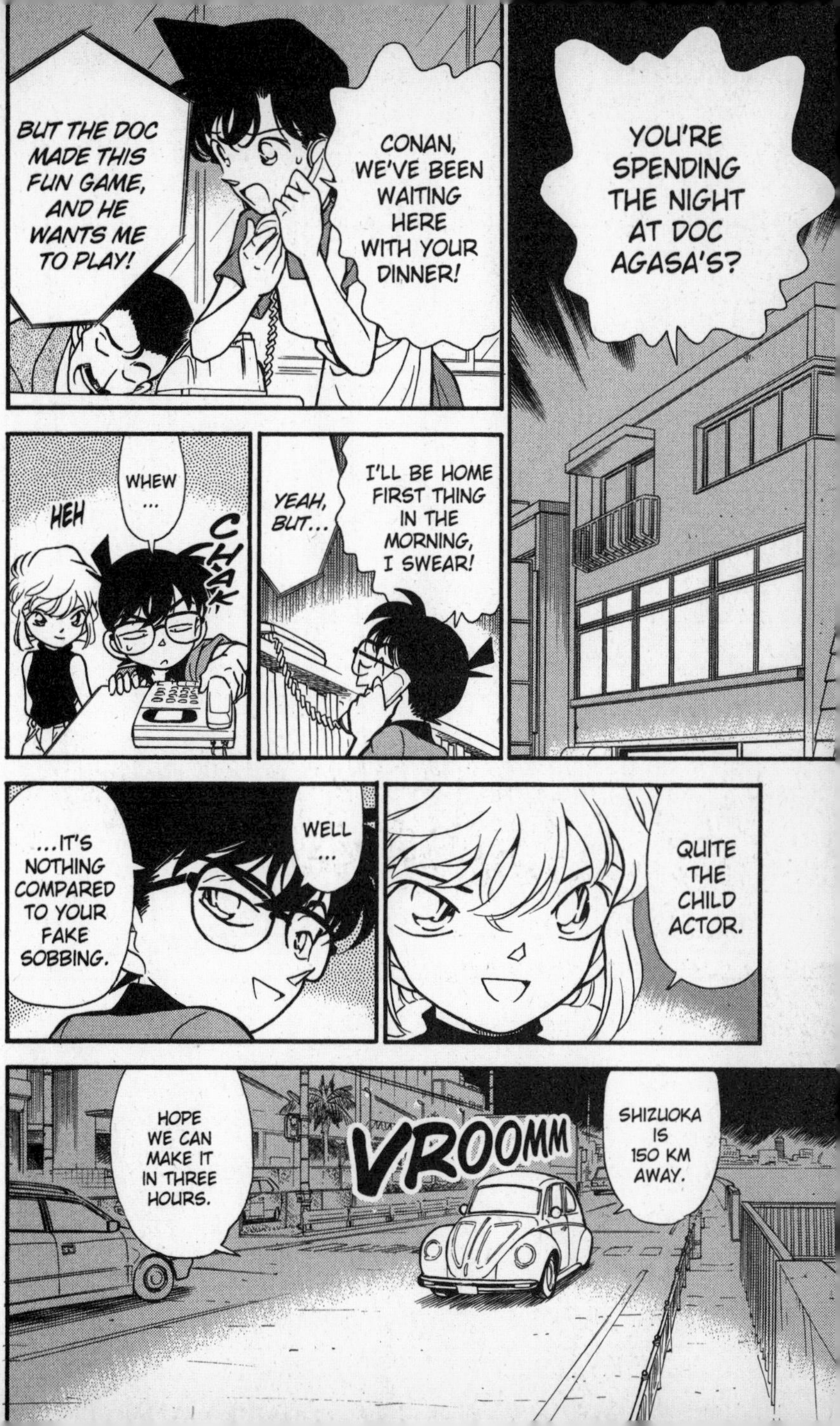
YOU'RE SPENDING THE NIGHT AT DOC AGASA'S?
CONAN, WE'VE BEEN WAITING HERE WITH YOUR DINNER!
BUT THE DOC MADE THIS FUN GAME, AND HE WANTS ME TO PLAY!
I'LL BE HOME FIRST THING IN THE MORNING, I SWEAR!
YEAH, BUT...
CHAK
WHEW ...
HEH
QUITE THE CHILD ACTOR.
WELL ...
...IT'S NOTHING COMPARED TO YOUR FAKE SOBBING.
SHIZUOKA IS 150 KM AWAY.
VROOMM
HOPE WE CAN MAKE IT IN THREE HOURS.

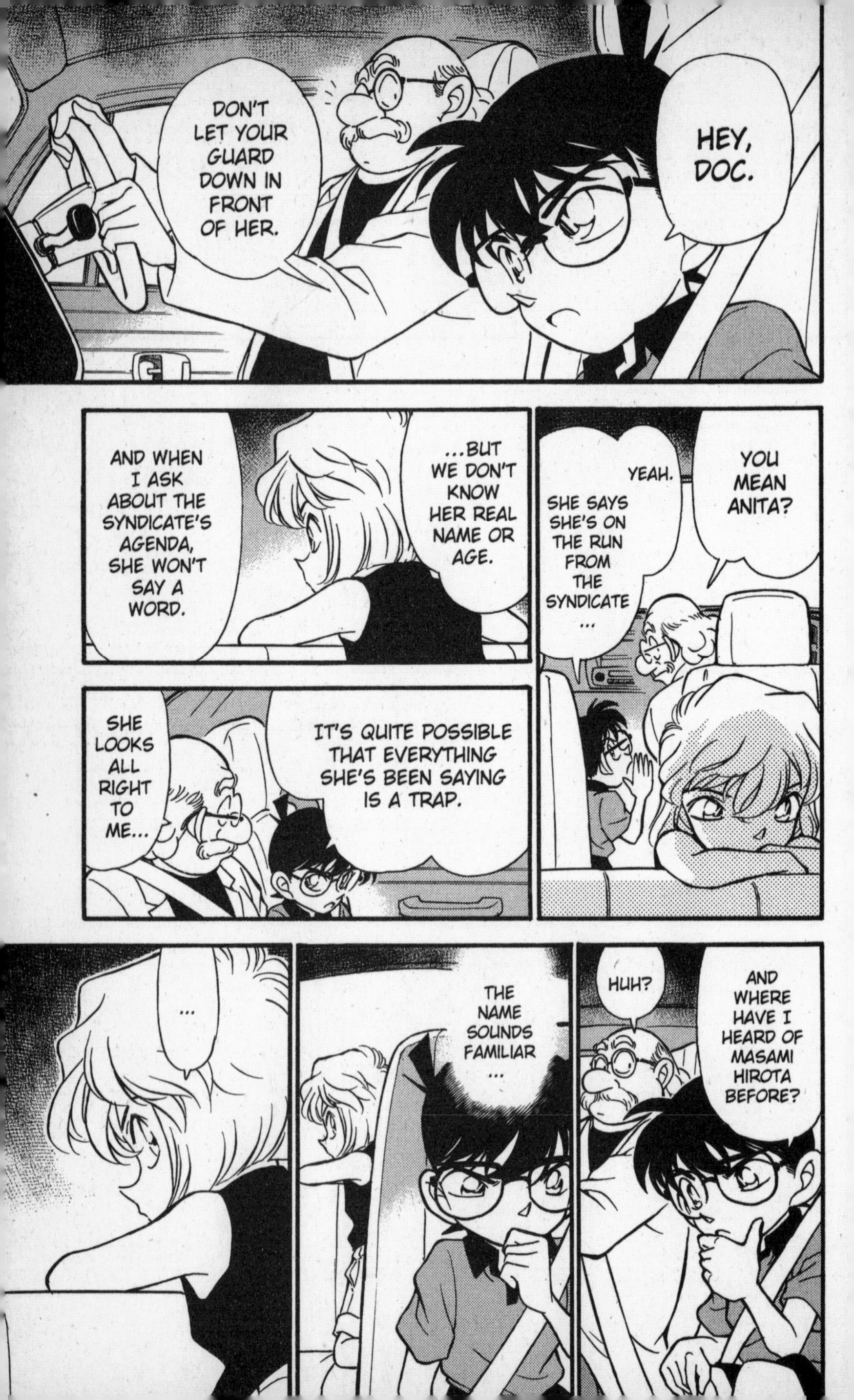
HEY, DOC.
DON'T LET YOUR GUARD DOWN IN FRONT OF HER.
YOU MEAN ANITA?
YEAH.
SHE SAYS SHE'S ON THE RUN FROM THE SYNDICATE ...
...BUT WE DON'T KNOW HER REAL NAME OR AGE.
AND WHEN I ASK ABOUT THE SYNDICATE'S AGENDA, SHE WON'T SAY A WORD.
IT'S QUITE POSSIBLE THAT EVERYTHING SHE'S BEEN SAYING IS A TRAP.
SHE LOOKS ALL RIGHT TO ME...
AND WHERE HAVE I HEARD OF MASAMI HIROTA BEFORE?
HUH?
THE NAME SOUNDS FAMILIAR ...
...

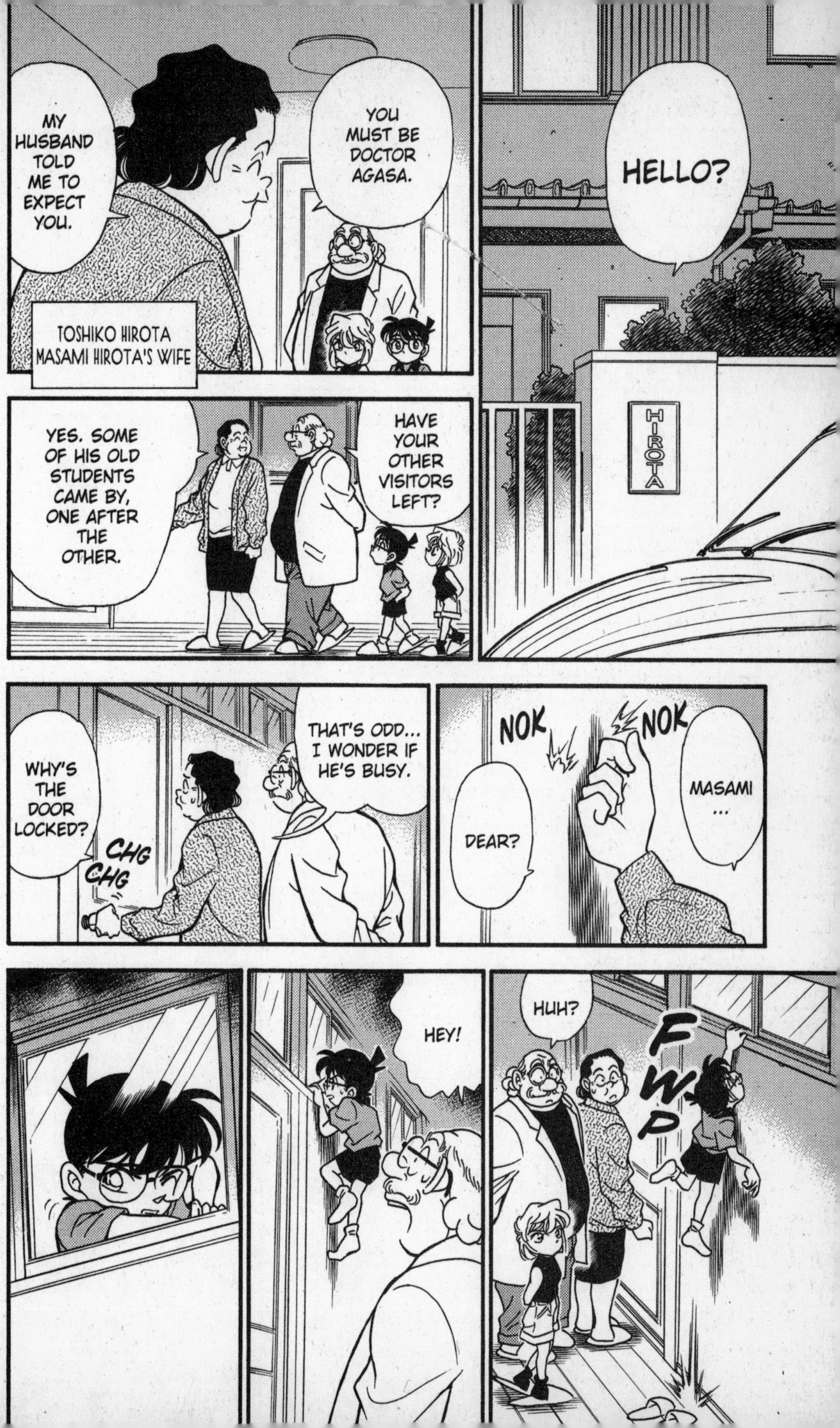
HELLO?
HIROTA
YOU MUST BE DOCTOR AGASA.
MY HUSBAND TOLD ME TO EXPECT YOU.
TOSHIKO HIROTA
MASAMI HIROTA'S WIFE
HAVE YOUR OTHER VISITORS LEFT?
YES. SOME OF HIS OLD STUDENTS CAME BY, ONE AFTER THE OTHER.
NOK
NOK
MASAMI ...
DEAR?
THAT'S ODD... I WONDER IF HE'S BUSY.
WHY'S THE DOOR LOCKED?
CHG CHG
HUH?
FWP
HEY!

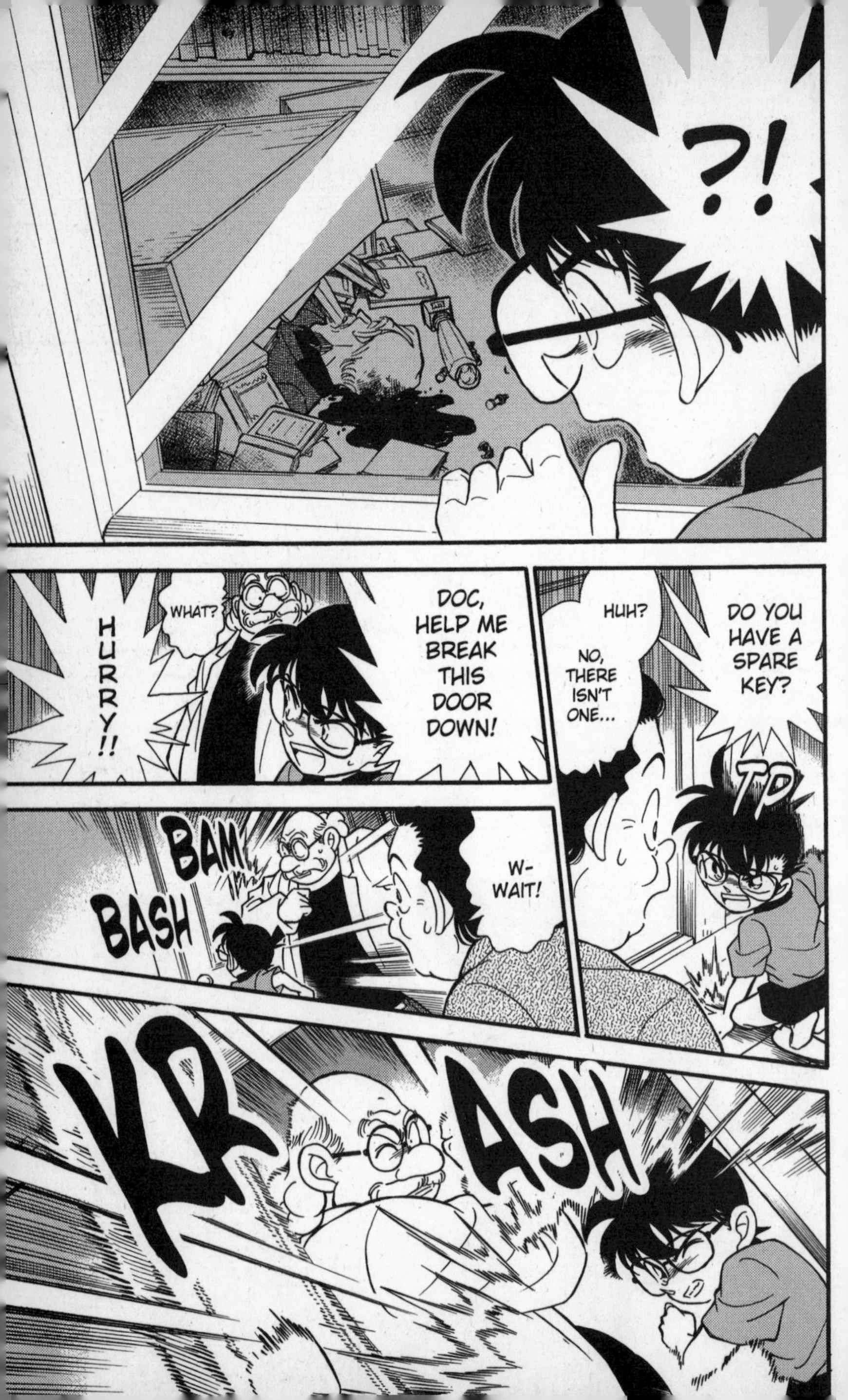
?!
DO YOU HAVE A SPARE KEY?
HUH?
NO, THERE ISN'T ONE...
TP
DOC, HELP ME BREAK THIS DOOR DOWN!
WHAT?
HURRY!!
W-WAIT!
BAM
BASH
KRASH

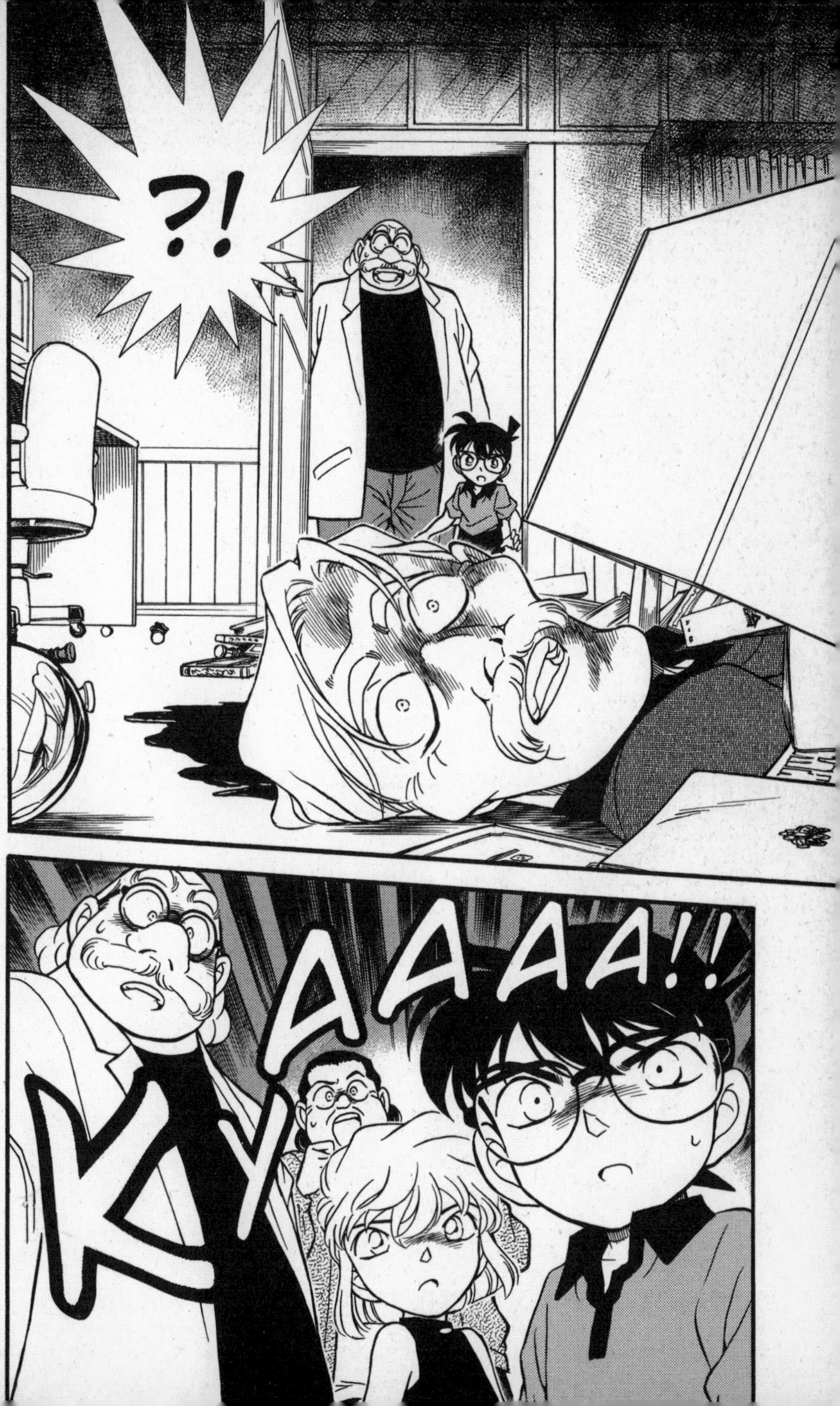
?!
KYAAAA!!

FILE 10: CHECKMATE

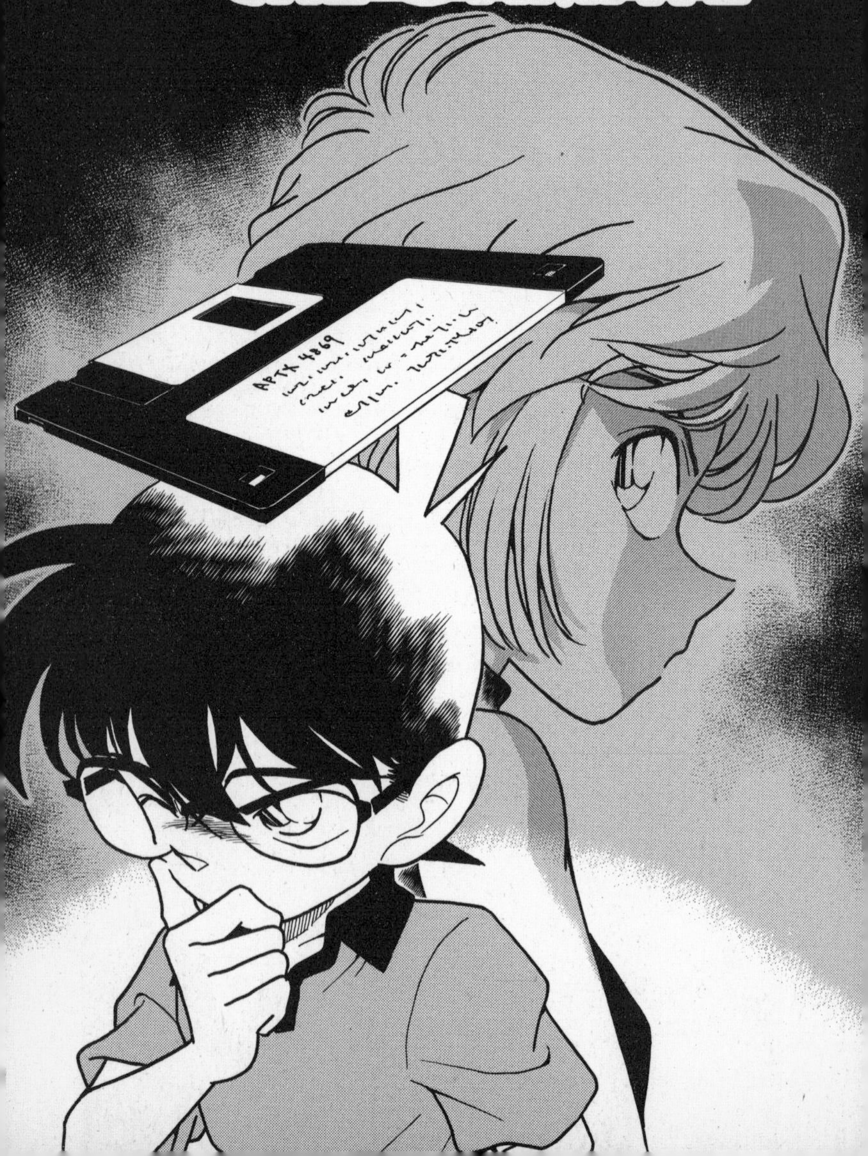
APTX 4869

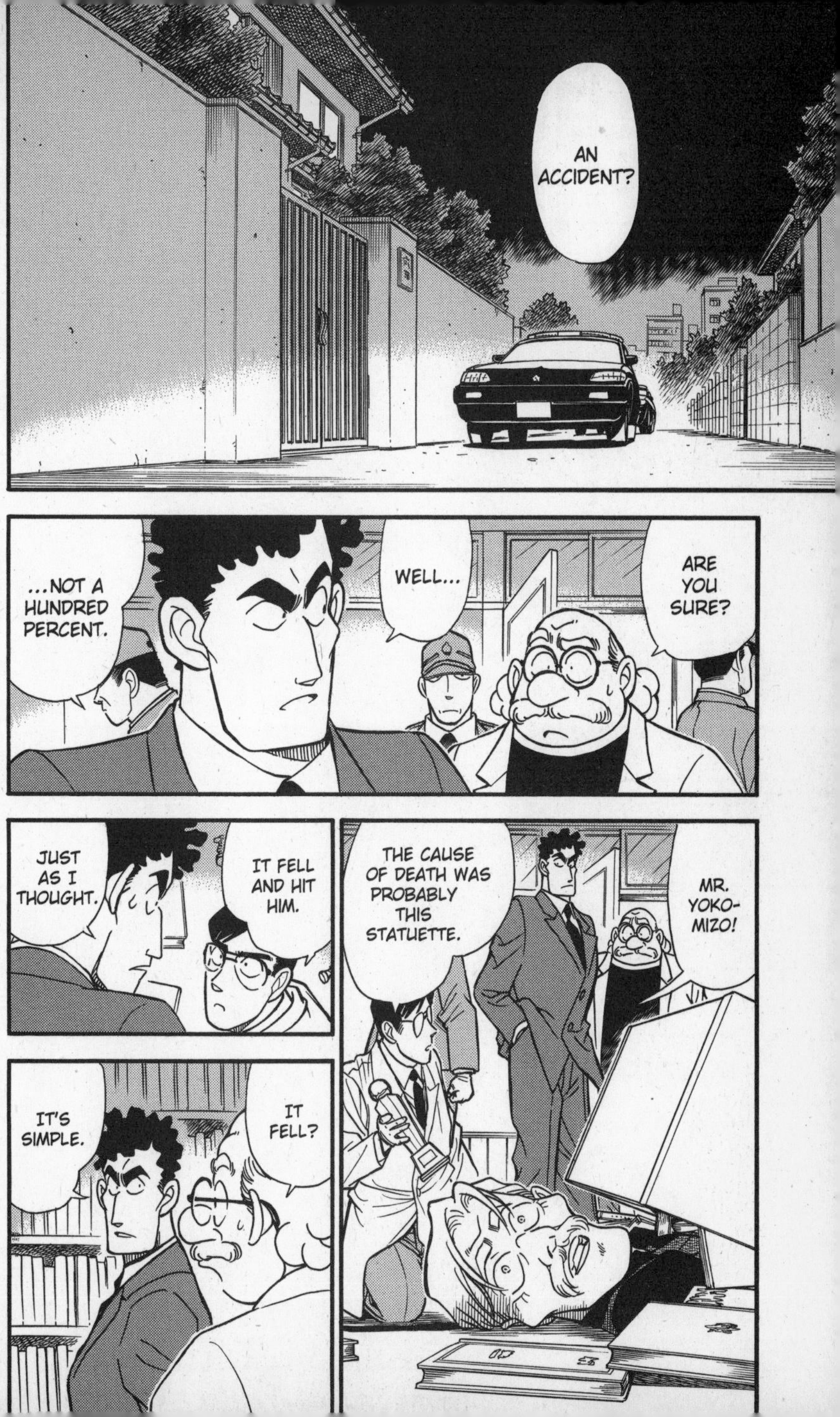
AN ACCIDENT?
ARE YOU SURE?
WELL...
...NOT A HUNDRED PERCENT.
MR. YOKOMIZO!
THE CAUSE OF DEATH WAS PROBABLY THIS STATUETTE.
IT FELL AND HIT HIM.
JUST AS I THOUGHT.
IT FELL?
IT'S SIMPLE.

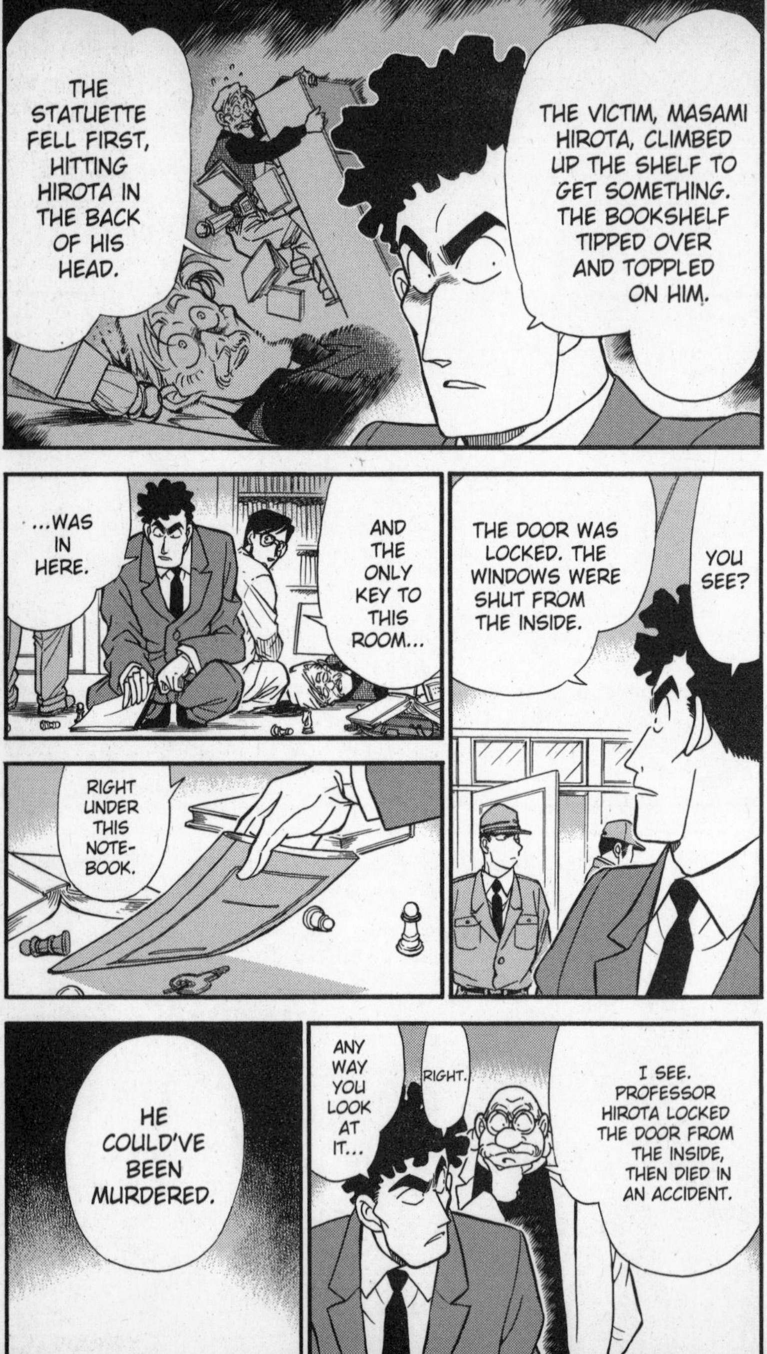
THE VICTIM, MASAMI HIROTA, CLIMBED UP THE SHELF TO GET SOMETHING. THE BOOKSHELF TIPPED OVER AND TOPPLED ON HIM.
THE STATUETTE FELL FIRST, HITTING HIROTA IN THE BACK OF HIS HEAD.
YOU SEE?
THE DOOR WAS LOCKED. THE WINDOWS WERE SHUT FROM THE INSIDE.
AND THE ONLY KEY TO THIS ROOM...
...WAS IN HERE.
RIGHT UNDER THIS NOTE-BOOK.
I SEE. PROFESSOR HIROTA LOCKED THE DOOR FROM THE INSIDE, THEN DIED IN AN ACCIDENT.
RIGHT.
ANY WAY YOU LOOK AT IT...
HE COULD'VE BEEN MURDERED.

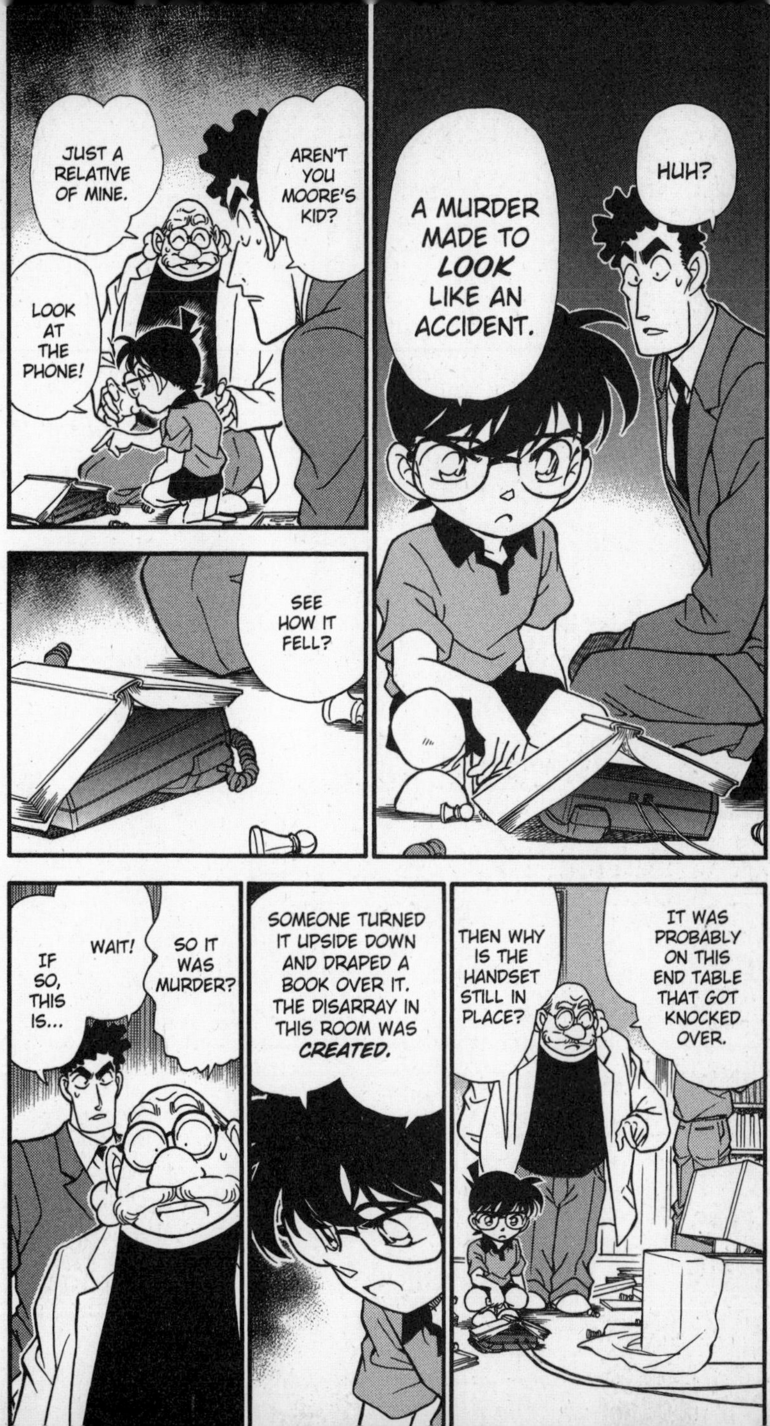
HUH?
A MURDER MADE TO LOOK LIKE AN ACCIDENT.
AREN'T YOU MOORE'S KID?
JUST A RELATIVE OF MINE.
LOOK AT THE PHONE!
SEE HOW IT FELL?
IT WAS PROBABLY ON THIS END TABLE THAT GOT KNOCKED OVER.
THEN WHY IS THE HANDSET STILL IN PLACE?
SOMEONE TURNED IT UPSIDE DOWN AND DRAPED A BOOK OVER IT. THE DISARRAY IN THIS ROOM WAS CREATED.
SO IT WAS MURDER?
WAIT!
IF SO, THIS IS...

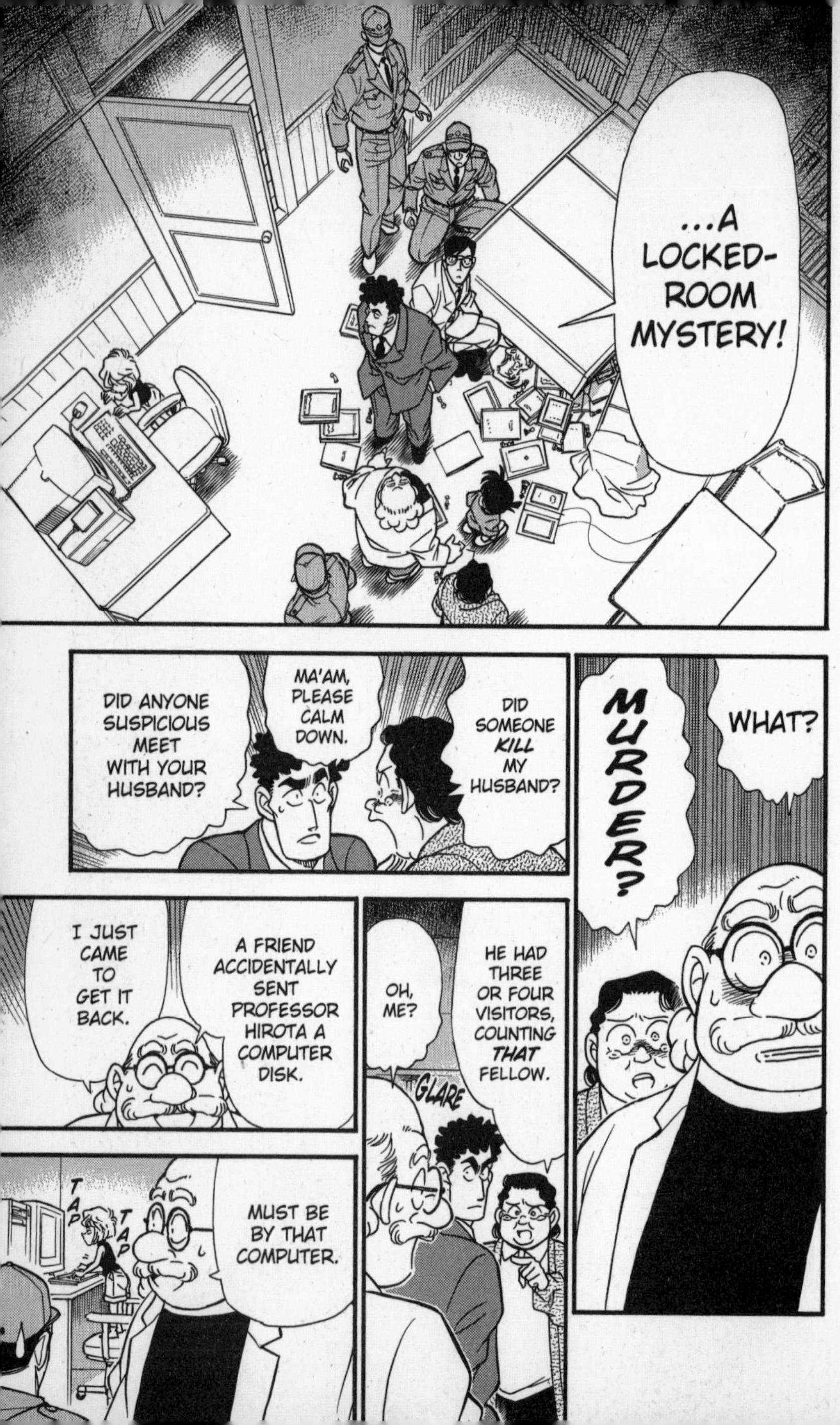
...A LOCKED-ROOM MYSTERY!
WHAT?
MURDER?
DID SOMEONE KILL MY HUSBAND?
MA'AM, PLEASE CALM DOWN.
DID ANYONE SUSPICIOUS MEET WITH YOUR HUSBAND?
HE HAD THREE OR FOUR VISITORS, COUNTING THAT FELLOW.
GLARE
OH, ME?
A FRIEND ACCIDENTALLY SENT PROFESSOR HIROTA A COMPUTER DISK.
I JUST CAME TO GET IT BACK.
TAP TAP
MUST BE BY THAT COMPUTER.

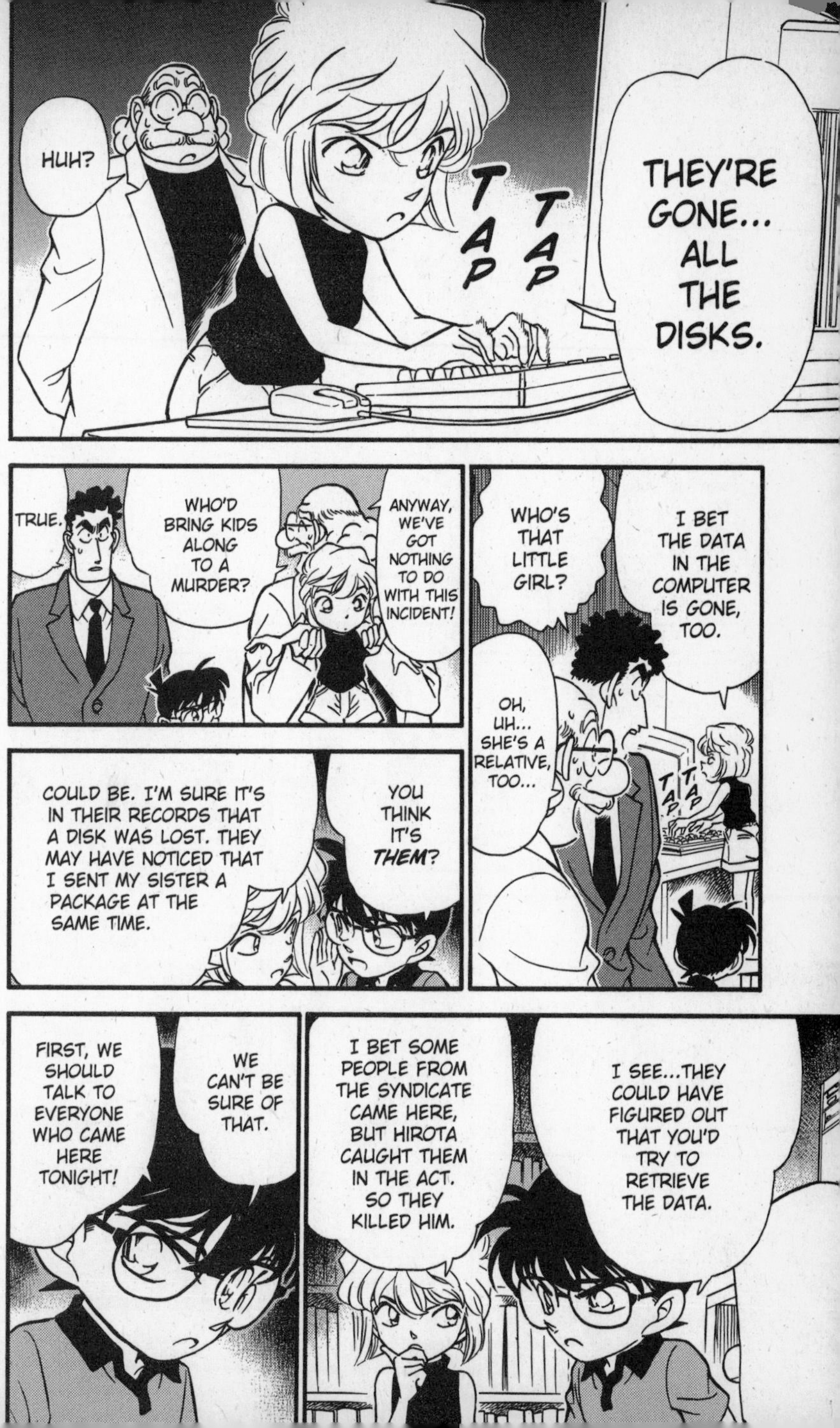
THEY'RE GONE... ALL THE DISKS.
TAP TAP
HUH?
I BET THE DATA IN THE COMPUTER IS GONE, TOO.
WHO'S THAT LITTLE GIRL?
OH, UH... SHE'S A RELATIVE, TOO...
TAP TAP
ANYWAY, WE'VE GOT NOTHING TO DO WITH THIS INCIDENT!
WHO'D BRING KIDS ALONG TO A MURDER?
TRUE.
YOU THINK IT'S *THEM*?
COULD BE. I'M SURE IT'S IN THEIR RECORDS THAT A DISK WAS LOST. THEY MAY HAVE NOTICED THAT I SENT MY SISTER A PACKAGE AT THE SAME TIME.
I SEE...THEY COULD HAVE FIGURED OUT THAT YOU'D TRY TO RETRIEVE THE DATA.
I BET SOME PEOPLE FROM THE SYNDICATE CAME HERE, BUT HIROTA CAUGHT THEM IN THE ACT. SO THEY KILLED HIM.
WE CAN'T BE SURE OF THAT.
FIRST, WE SHOULD TALK TO EVERYONE WHO CAME HERE TONIGHT!

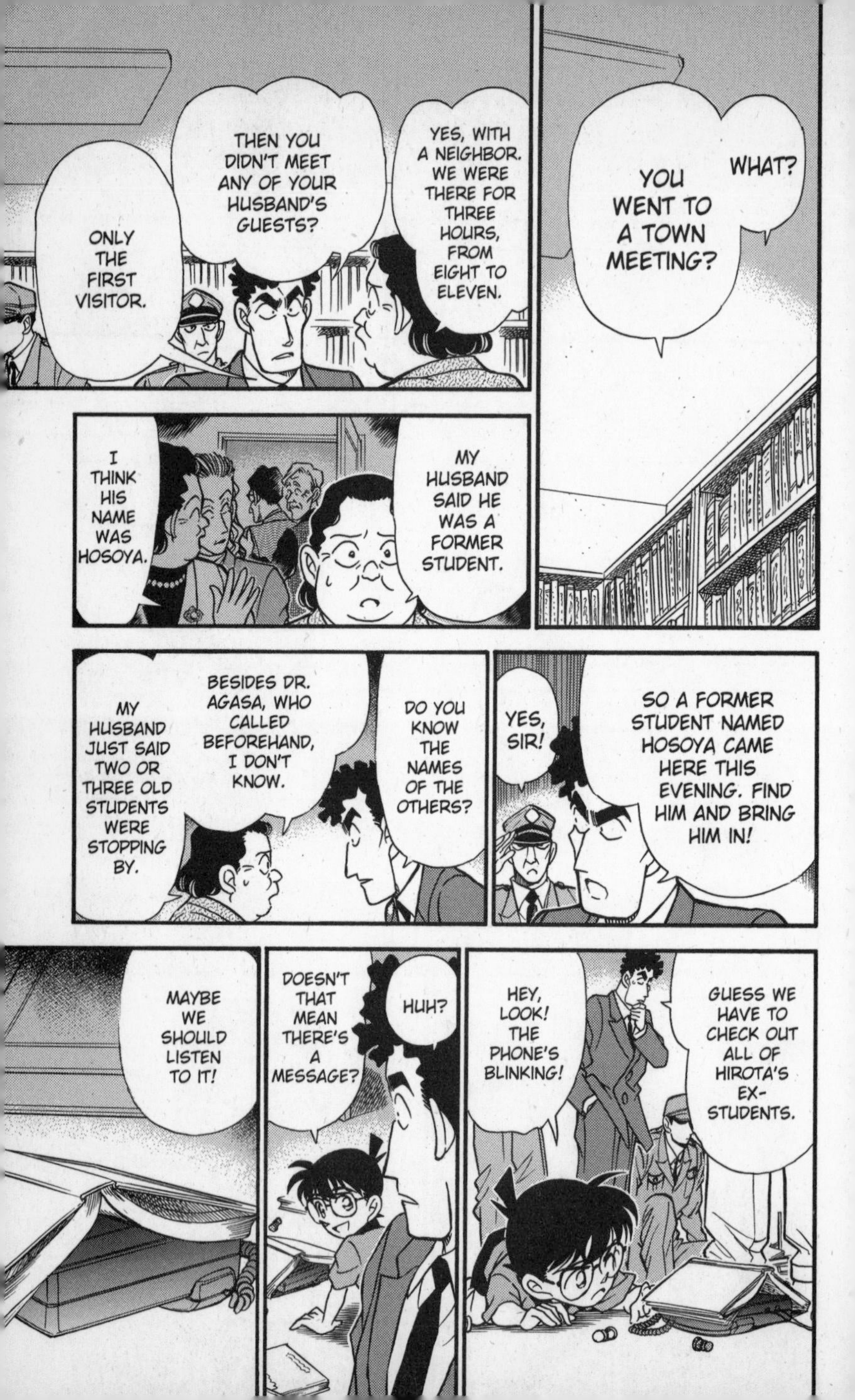
WHAT?
YOU WENT TO A TOWN MEETING?
YES, WITH A NEIGHBOR. WE WERE THERE FOR THREE HOURS, FROM EIGHT TO ELEVEN.
THEN YOU DIDN'T MEET ANY OF YOUR HUSBAND'S GUESTS?
ONLY THE FIRST VISITOR.
MY HUSBAND SAID HE WAS A FORMER STUDENT.
I THINK HIS NAME WAS HOSOYA.
SO A FORMER STUDENT NAMED HOSOYA CAME HERE THIS EVENING. FIND HIM AND BRING HIM IN!
YES, SIR!
DO YOU KNOW THE NAMES OF THE OTHERS?
BESIDES DR. AGASA, WHO CALLED BEFOREHAND, I DON'T KNOW.
MY HUSBAND JUST SAID TWO OR THREE OLD STUDENTS WERE STOPPING BY.
GUESS WE HAVE TO CHECK OUT ALL OF HIROTA'S EX-STUDENTS.
HEY, LOOK! THE PHONE'S BLINKING!
HUH?
DOESN'T THAT MEAN THERE'S A MESSAGE?
MAYBE WE SHOULD LISTEN TO IT!

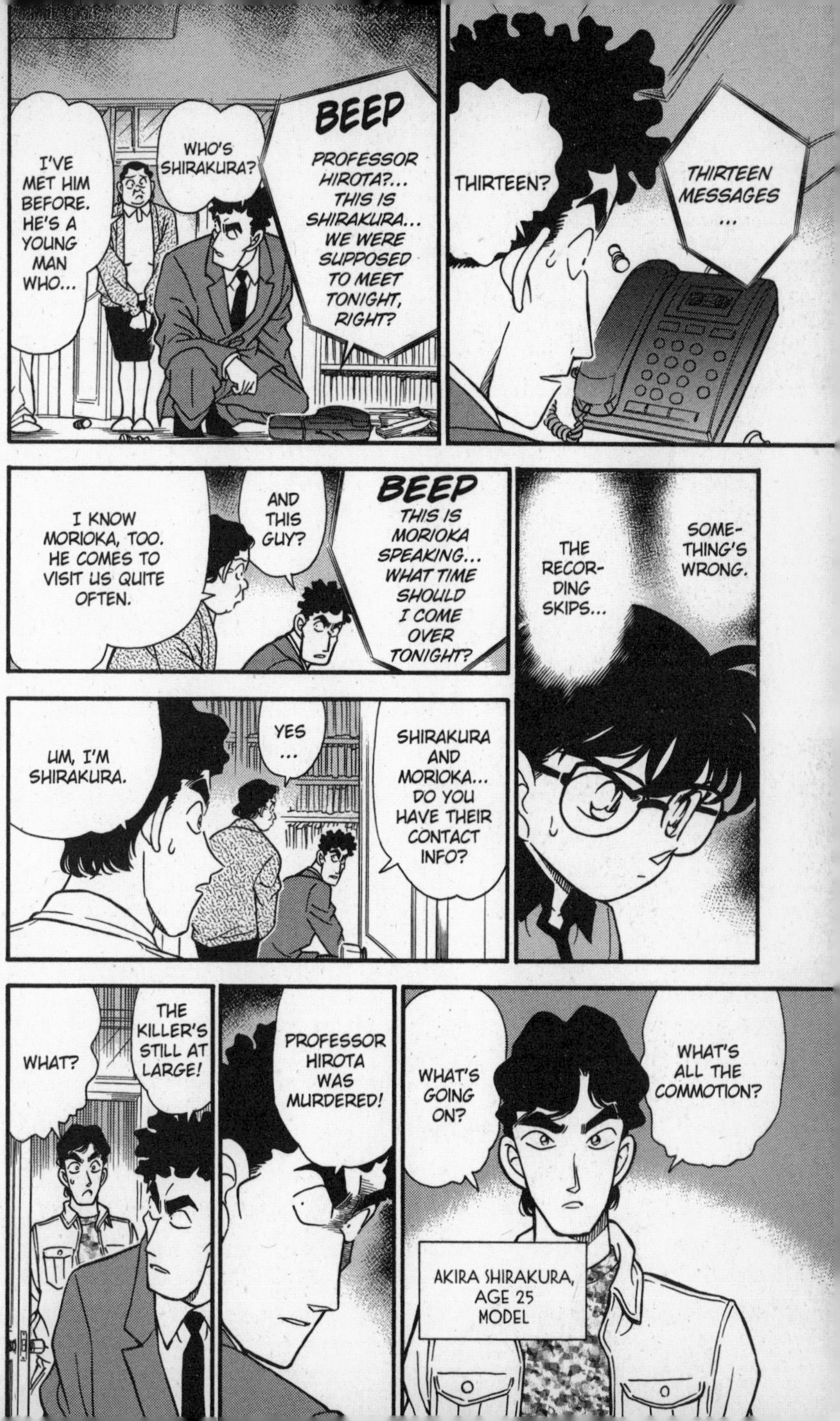
THIRTEEN MESSAGES ...
THIRTEEN?
BEEP
PROFESSOR HIROTA?... THIS IS SHIRAKURA... WE WERE SUPPOSED TO MEET TONIGHT, RIGHT?
WHO'S SHIRAKURA?
I'VE MET HIM BEFORE. HE'S A YOUNG MAN WHO...
SOMETHING'S WRONG.
THE RECORDING SKIPS...
BEEP
THIS IS MORIOKA SPEAKING... WHAT TIME SHOULD I COME OVER TONIGHT?
AND THIS GUY?
I KNOW MORIOKA, TOO. HE COMES TO VISIT US QUITE OFTEN.
SHIRAKURA AND MORIOKA... DO YOU HAVE THEIR CONTACT INFO?
YES ...
UM, I'M SHIRAKURA.
WHAT'S ALL THE COMMOTION?
WHAT'S GOING ON?
AKIRA SHIRAKURA, AGE 25 MODEL
PROFESSOR HIROTA WAS MURDERED!
THE KILLER'S STILL AT LARGE!
WHAT?

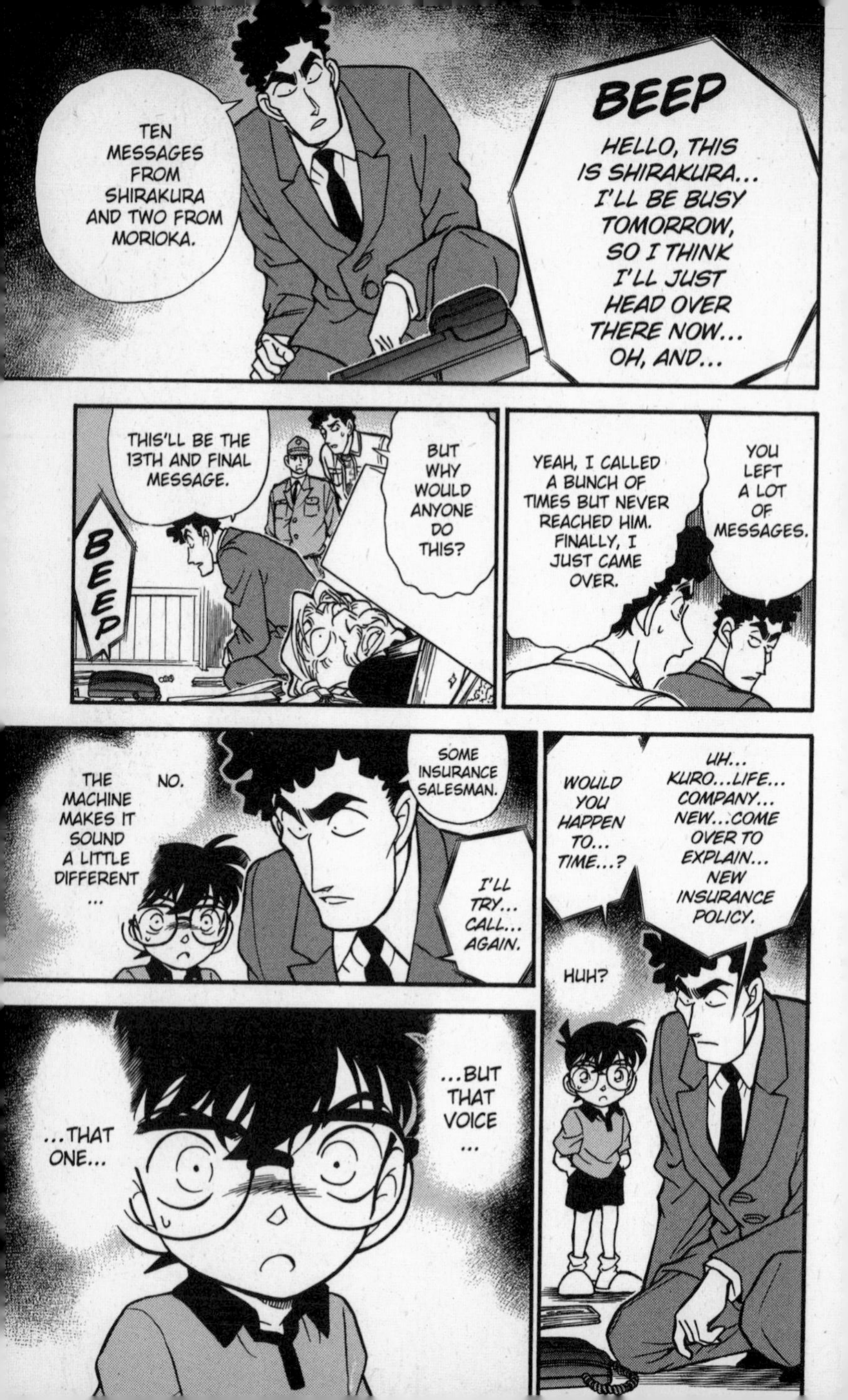
BEEP
HELLO, THIS IS SHIRAKURA... I'LL BE BUSY TOMORROW, SO I THINK I'LL JUST HEAD OVER THERE NOW... OH, AND...
TEN MESSAGES FROM SHIRAKURA AND TWO FROM MORIOKA.
YOU LEFT A LOT OF MESSAGES.
YEAH, I CALLED A BUNCH OF TIMES BUT NEVER REACHED HIM. FINALLY, I JUST CAME OVER.
BUT WHY WOULD ANYONE DO THIS?
THIS'LL BE THE 13TH AND FINAL MESSAGE.
BEEP
UH... KURO...LIFE... COMPANY... NEW...COME OVER TO EXPLAIN... NEW INSURANCE POLICY.
WOULD YOU HAPPEN TO... TIME...?
HUH?
SOME INSURANCE SALESMAN.
I'LL TRY... CALL... AGAIN.
NO.
THE MACHINE MAKES IT SOUND A LITTLE DIFFERENT ...
...BUT THAT VOICE ...
...THAT ONE...

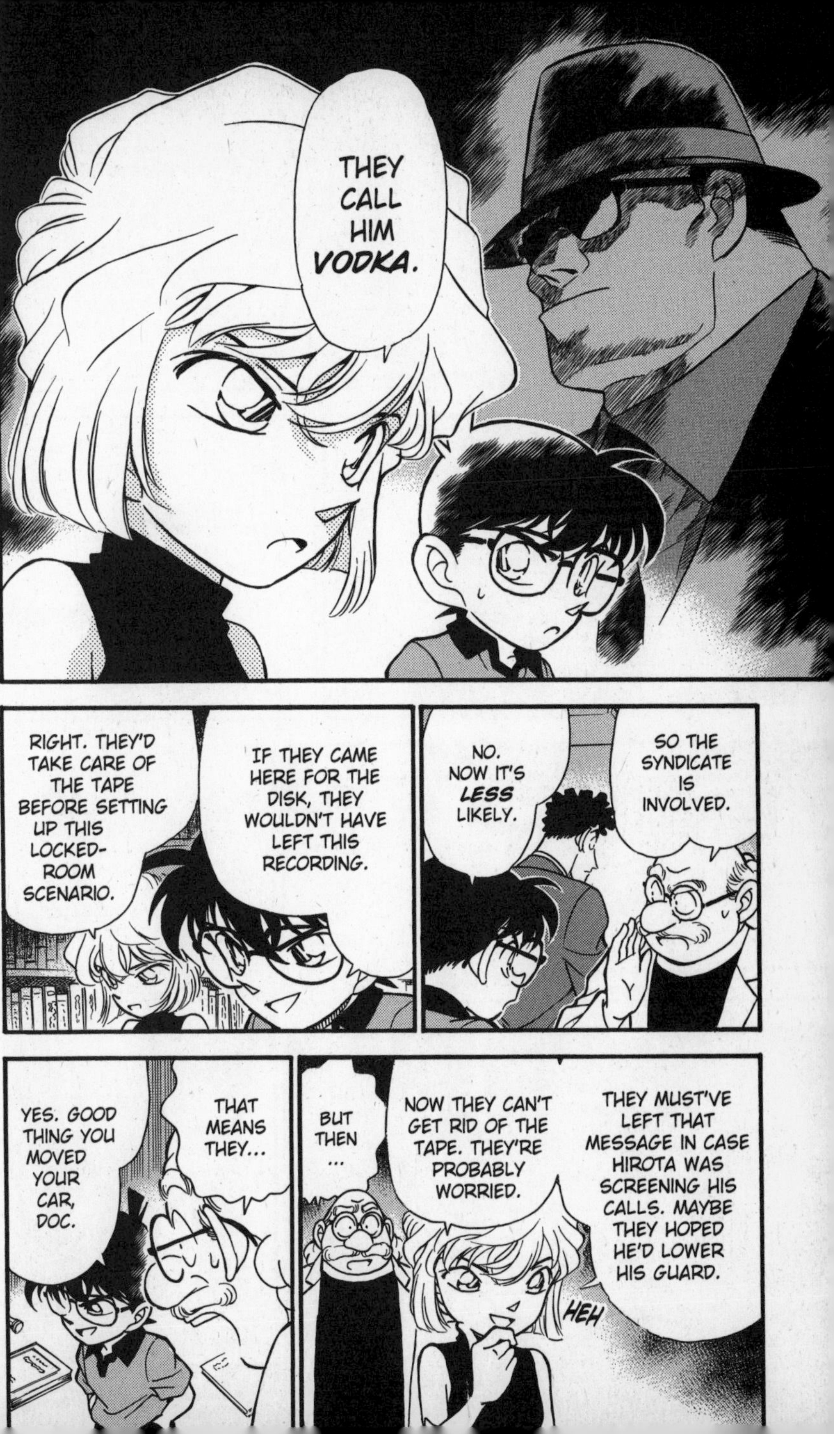
THEY CALL HIM VODKA.
SO THE SYNDICATE IS INVOLVED.
NO. NOW IT'S LESS LIKELY.
IF THEY CAME HERE FOR THE DISK, THEY WOULDN'T HAVE LEFT THIS RECORDING.
RIGHT. THEY'D TAKE CARE OF THE TAPE BEFORE SETTING UP THIS LOCKED-ROOM SCENARIO.
THEY MUST'VE LEFT THAT MESSAGE IN CASE HIROTA WAS SCREENING HIS CALLS. MAYBE THEY HOPED HE'D LOWER HIS GUARD.
NOW THEY CAN'T GET RID OF THE TAPE. THEY'RE PROBABLY WORRIED.
BUT THEN ...
HEH
THAT MEANS THEY...
YES. GOOD THING YOU MOVED YOUR CAR, DOC.

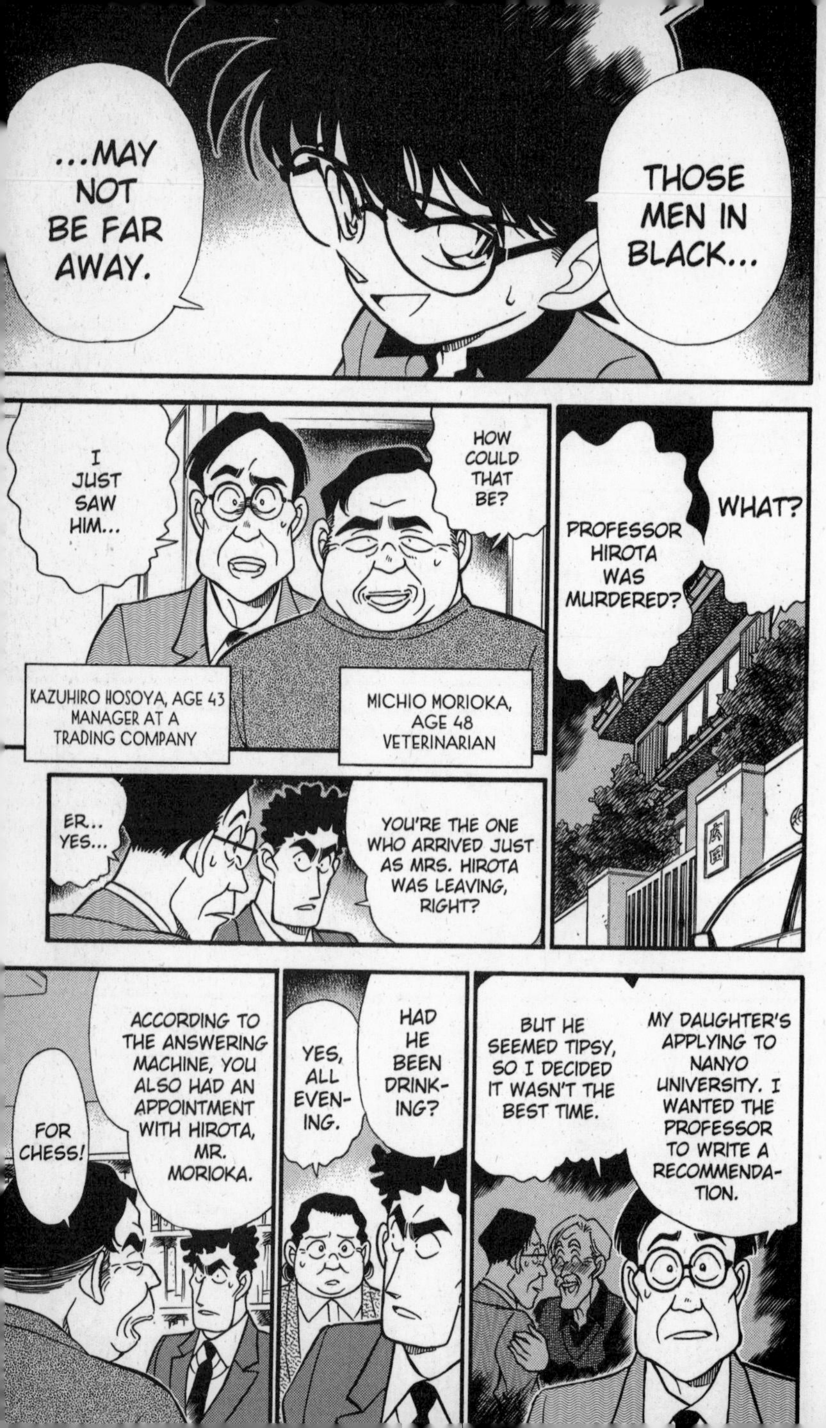
THOSE MEN IN BLACK...
...MAY NOT BE FAR AWAY.
WHAT?
PROFESSOR HIROTA WAS MURDERED?
HOW COULD THAT BE?
I JUST SAW HIM...
MICHIO MORIOKA, AGE 48 VETERINARIAN
KAZUHIRO HOSOYA, AGE 43 MANAGER AT A TRADING COMPANY
YOU'RE THE ONE WHO ARRIVED JUST AS MRS. HIROTA WAS LEAVING, RIGHT?
ER... YES...
MY DAUGHTER'S APPLYING TO NANYO UNIVERSITY. I WANTED THE PROFESSOR TO WRITE A RECOMMENDATION.
BUT HE SEEMED TIPSY, SO I DECIDED IT WASN'T THE BEST TIME.
HAD HE BEEN DRINKING?
YES, ALL EVENING.
ACCORDING TO THE ANSWERING MACHINE, YOU ALSO HAD AN APPOINTMENT WITH HIROTA, MR. MORIOKA.
FOR CHESS!

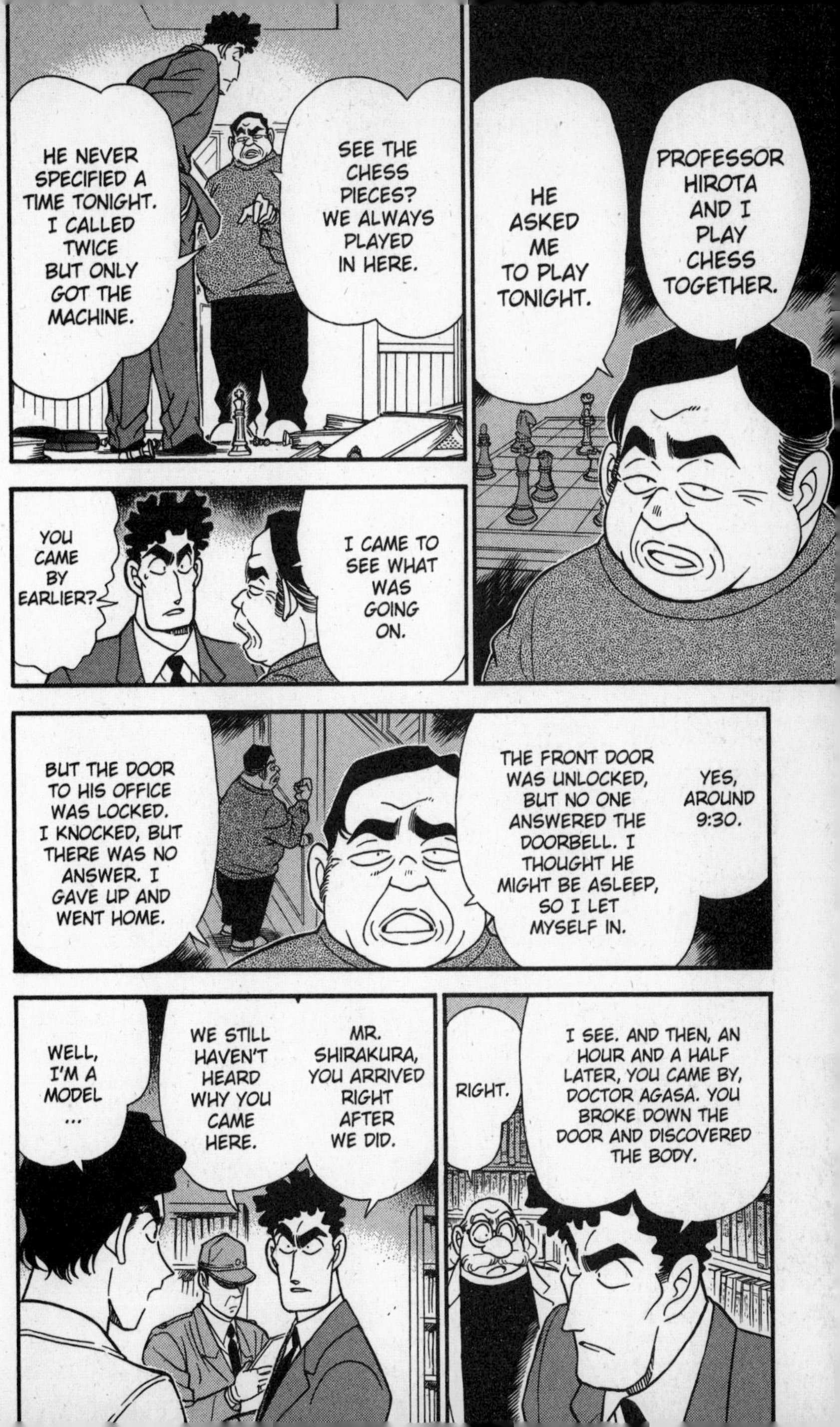
PROFESSOR HIROTA AND I PLAY CHESS TOGETHER.
HE ASKED ME TO PLAY TONIGHT.
SEE THE CHESS PIECES? WE ALWAYS PLAYED IN HERE.
HE NEVER SPECIFIED A TIME TONIGHT. I CALLED TWICE BUT ONLY GOT THE MACHINE.
I CAME TO SEE WHAT WAS GOING ON.
YOU CAME BY EARLIER?
YES, AROUND 9:30.
THE FRONT DOOR WAS UNLOCKED, BUT NO ONE ANSWERED THE DOORBELL. I THOUGHT HE MIGHT BE ASLEEP, SO I LET MYSELF IN.
BUT THE DOOR TO HIS OFFICE WAS LOCKED. I KNOCKED, BUT THERE WAS NO ANSWER. I GAVE UP AND WENT HOME.
I SEE. AND THEN, AN HOUR AND A HALF LATER, YOU CAME BY, DOCTOR AGASA. YOU BROKE DOWN THE DOOR AND DISCOVERED THE BODY.
RIGHT.
MR. SHIRAKURA, YOU ARRIVED RIGHT AFTER WE DID.
WE STILL HAVEN'T HEARD WHY YOU CAME HERE.
WELL, I'M A MODEL ...

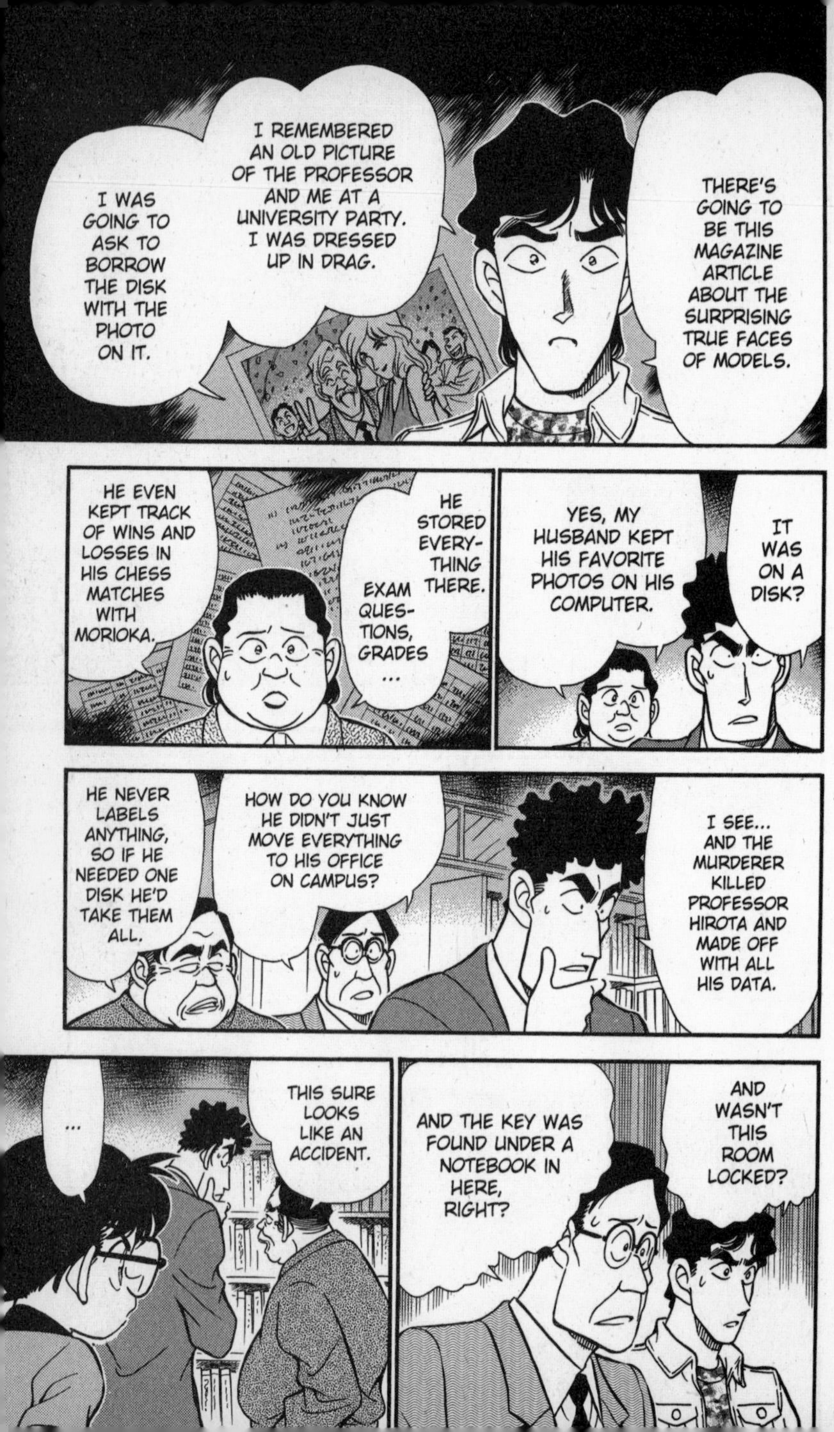
THERE'S GOING TO BE THIS MAGAZINE ARTICLE ABOUT THE SURPRISING TRUE FACES OF MODELS.
I REMEMBERED AN OLD PICTURE OF THE PROFESSOR AND ME AT A UNIVERSITY PARTY. I WAS DRESSED UP IN DRAG.
I WAS GOING TO ASK TO BORROW THE DISK WITH THE PHOTO ON IT.
IT WAS ON A DISK?
YES, MY HUSBAND KEPT HIS FAVORITE PHOTOS ON HIS COMPUTER.
HE STORED EVERY-THING THERE.
EXAM QUES-TIONS, GRADES ...
HE EVEN KEPT TRACK OF WINS AND LOSSES IN HIS CHESS MATCHES WITH MORIOKA.
I SEE... AND THE MURDERER KILLED PROFESSOR HIROTA AND MADE OFF WITH ALL HIS DATA.
HOW DO YOU KNOW HE DIDN'T JUST MOVE EVERYTHING TO HIS OFFICE ON CAMPUS?
HE NEVER LABELS ANYTHING, SO IF HE NEEDED ONE DISK HE'D TAKE THEM ALL.
AND WASN'T THIS ROOM LOCKED?
AND THE KEY WAS FOUND UNDER A NOTEBOOK IN HERE, RIGHT?
THIS SURE LOOKS LIKE AN ACCIDENT.
...

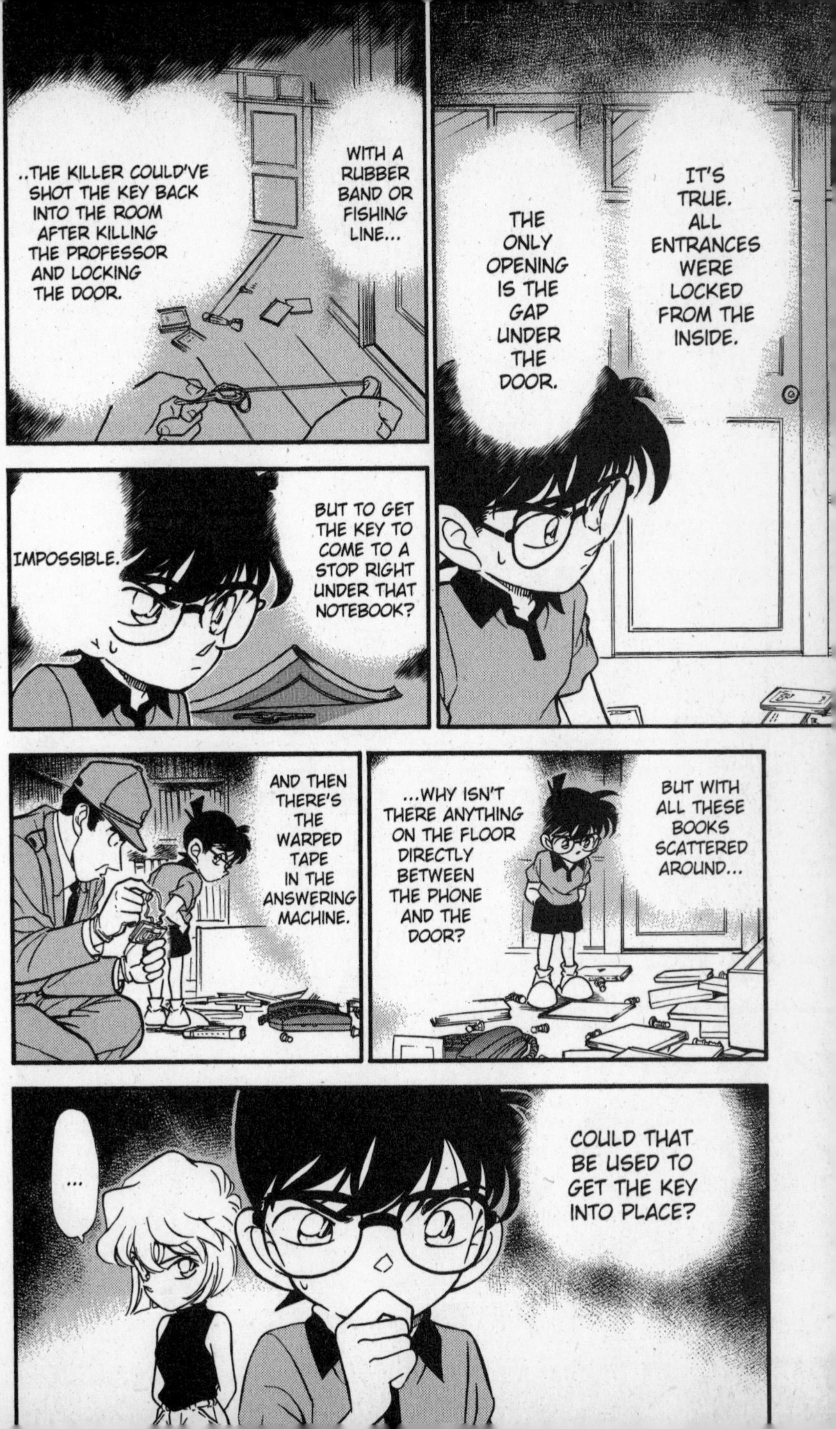
IT'S TRUE. ALL ENTRANCES WERE LOCKED FROM THE INSIDE.
THE ONLY OPENING IS THE GAP UNDER THE DOOR.
WITH A RUBBER BAND OR FISHING LINE...
..THE KILLER COULD'VE SHOT THE KEY BACK INTO THE ROOM AFTER KILLING THE PROFESSOR AND LOCKING THE DOOR.
BUT TO GET THE KEY TO COME TO A STOP RIGHT UNDER THAT NOTEBOOK?
IMPOSSIBLE.
BUT WITH ALL THESE BOOKS SCATTERED AROUND...
...WHY ISN'T THERE ANYTHING ON THE FLOOR DIRECTLY BETWEEN THE PHONE AND THE DOOR?
AND THEN THERE'S THE WARPED TAPE IN THE ANSWERING MACHINE.
COULD THAT BE USED TO GET THE KEY INTO PLACE?
...

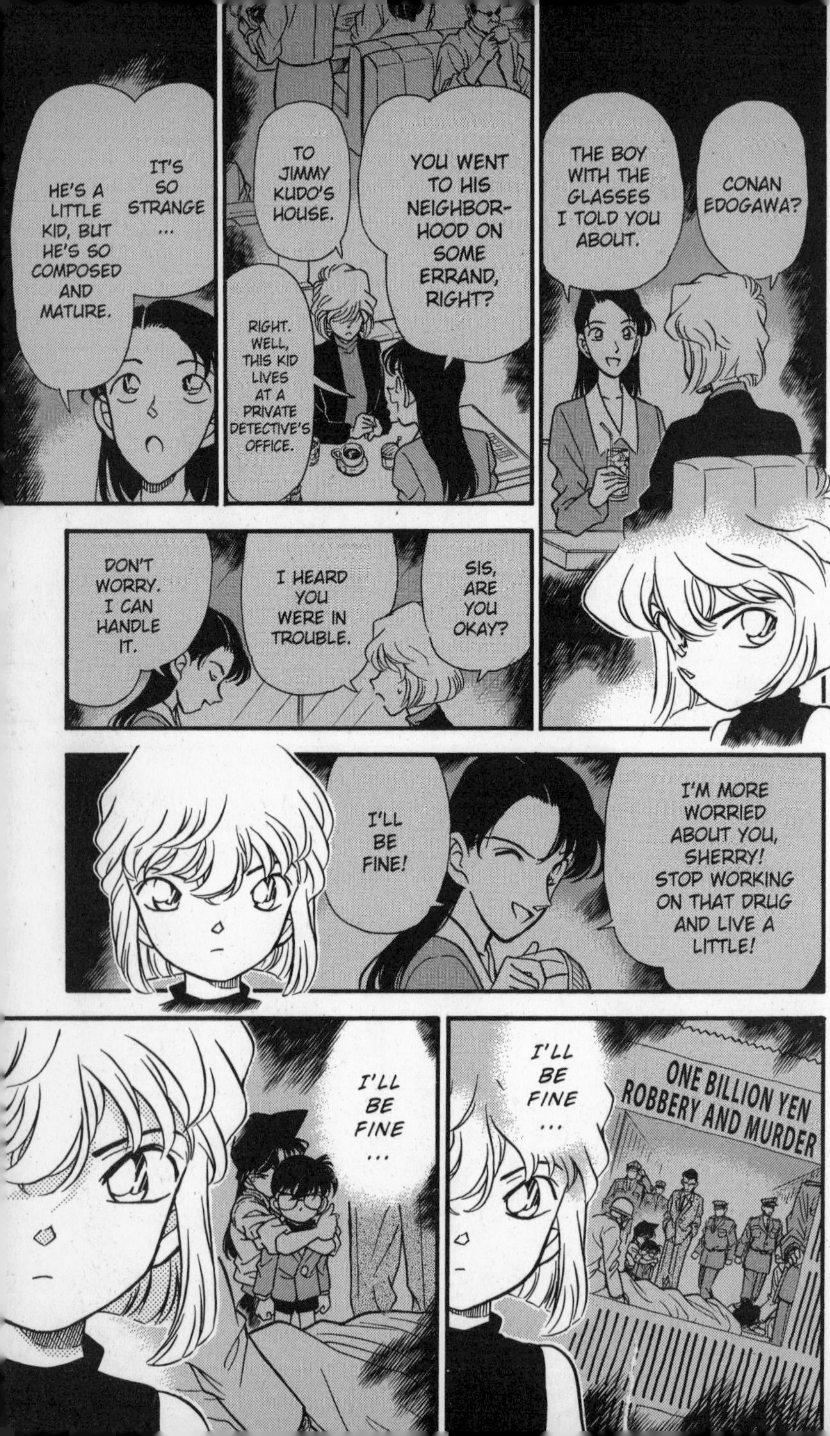
CONAN EDOGAWA?
THE BOY WITH THE GLASSES I TOLD YOU ABOUT.
YOU WENT TO HIS NEIGHBOR-HOOD ON SOME ERRAND, RIGHT?
TO JIMMY KUDO'S HOUSE.
RIGHT. WELL, THIS KID LIVES AT A PRIVATE DETECTIVE'S OFFICE.
IT'S SO STRANGE ...
HE'S A LITTLE KID, BUT HE'S SO COMPOSED AND MATURE.
SIS, ARE YOU OKAY?
I HEARD YOU WERE IN TROUBLE.
DON'T WORRY. I CAN HANDLE IT.
I'M MORE WORRIED ABOUT YOU, SHERRY! STOP WORKING ON THAT DRUG AND LIVE A LITTLE!
I'LL BE FINE!
I'LL BE FINE ...
ONE BILLION YEN ROBBERY AND MURDER
I'LL BE FINE ...

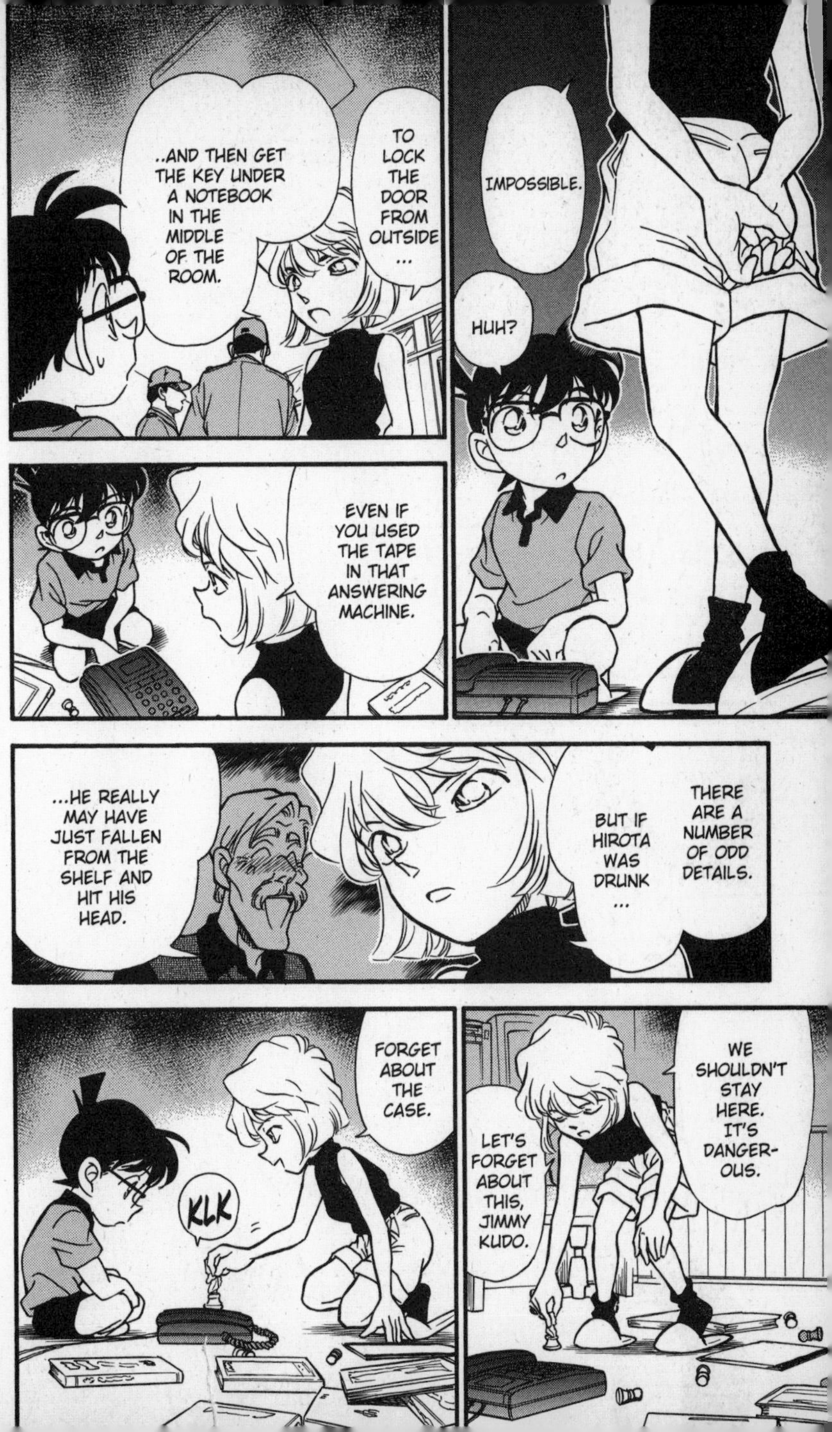
IMPOSSIBLE.
HUH?
TO LOCK THE DOOR FROM OUTSIDE...
..AND THEN GET THE KEY UNDER A NOTEBOOK IN THE MIDDLE OF THE ROOM.
EVEN IF YOU USED THE TAPE IN THAT ANSWERING MACHINE.
THERE ARE A NUMBER OF ODD DETAILS.
BUT IF HIROTA WAS DRUNK...
...HE REALLY MAY HAVE JUST FALLEN FROM THE SHELF AND HIT HIS HEAD.
WE SHOULDN'T STAY HERE. IT'S DANGER-OUS.
LET'S FORGET ABOUT THIS, JIMMY KUDO.
FORGET ABOUT THE CASE.
KLK

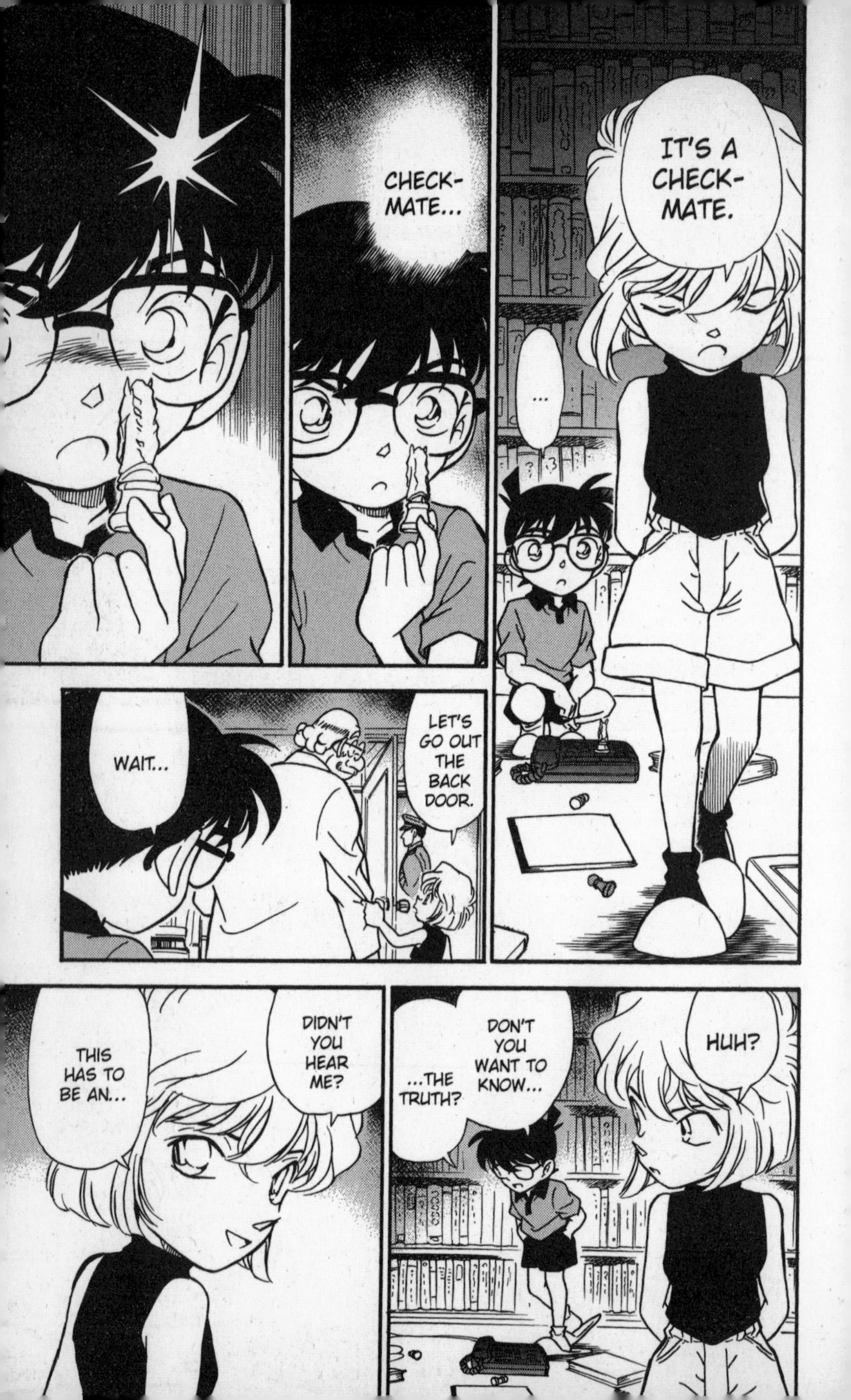
IT'S A CHECK-MATE.
...
CHECK-MATE...
LET'S GO OUT THE BACK DOOR.
WAIT...
HUH?
DON'T YOU WANT TO KNOW...
...THE TRUTH?
DIDN'T YOU HEAR ME?
THIS HAS TO BE AN...

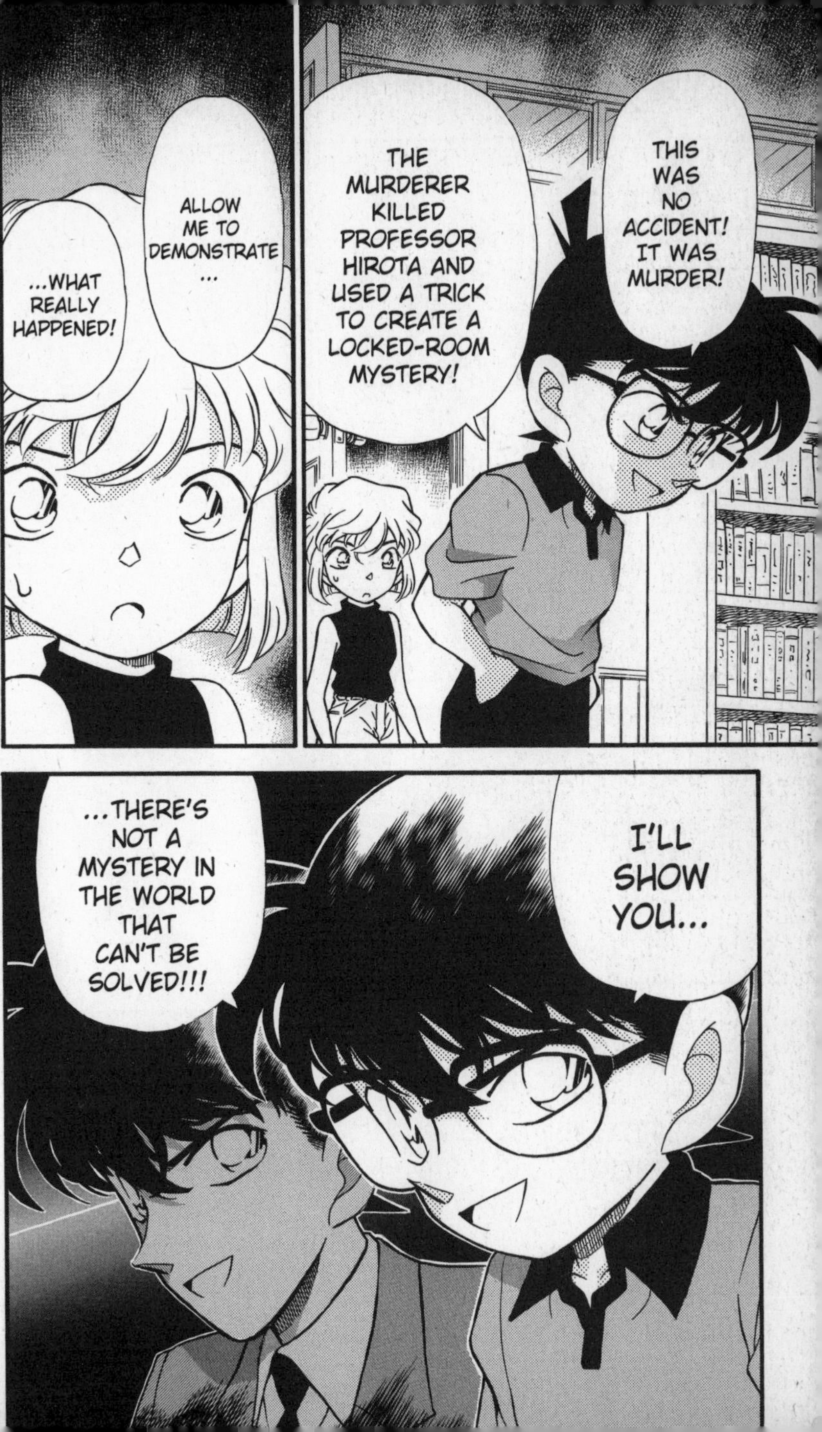
THIS WAS NO ACCIDENT! IT WAS MURDER!
THE MURDERER KILLED PROFESSOR HIROTA AND USED A TRICK TO CREATE A LOCKED-ROOM MYSTERY!
ALLOW ME TO DEMONSTRATE...
...WHAT REALLY HAPPENED!
I'LL SHOW YOU...
...THERE'S NOT A MYSTERY IN THE WORLD THAT CAN'T BE SOLVED!!!

Hello, Aoyama here.

Did you all watch it?

I'm talking about the Japan vs. Iran match in the '98 FIFA World Cup Asia Playoffs, with twists and turns too thrilling to depict in a manga! Oh, that last-minute victory goal by Okano!! That's the loudest I've ever yelled while watching TV. I can't wait for the World Cup to begin!

(Go Japan.)

Gosho Aoyama's
Mystery Library

18

SHUNSAKU KUDO

An urban private eye who's comical one minute and hard-boiled the next...that's Shunsaku Kudo. His office and living quarters are on the roof of an old building. He's lean, has long legs, and wears a black suit, a flashy shirt and a hat pulled over his eyes. Kudo roams the city on an old Vespa. He's particular about his coffee, and his liquor of choice is sherry. When he lights the cigarette dangling from his lips, his lighter always emits a huge flame. He gets wrapped up in trouble every time he accepts a case, but he never loses his cool even in the tightest pinch. Kudo is always able to toss off a joke with a grin. He doesn't get along with the cops, except for Inspector Hattori, veteran of the Metropolitan Homicide Department. Hattori calls him "Kudo-chan," and Kudo responds with, "Gimme a break!" ♥

Of course, Harley Hartwell (Heiji Hattori in the Japanese), the Great Detective of the West, and Jimmy Kudo (Shinichi Kudo in the Japanese), the Great Detective of the East, were inspired by these two!

I recommend *Surf City Blues*.

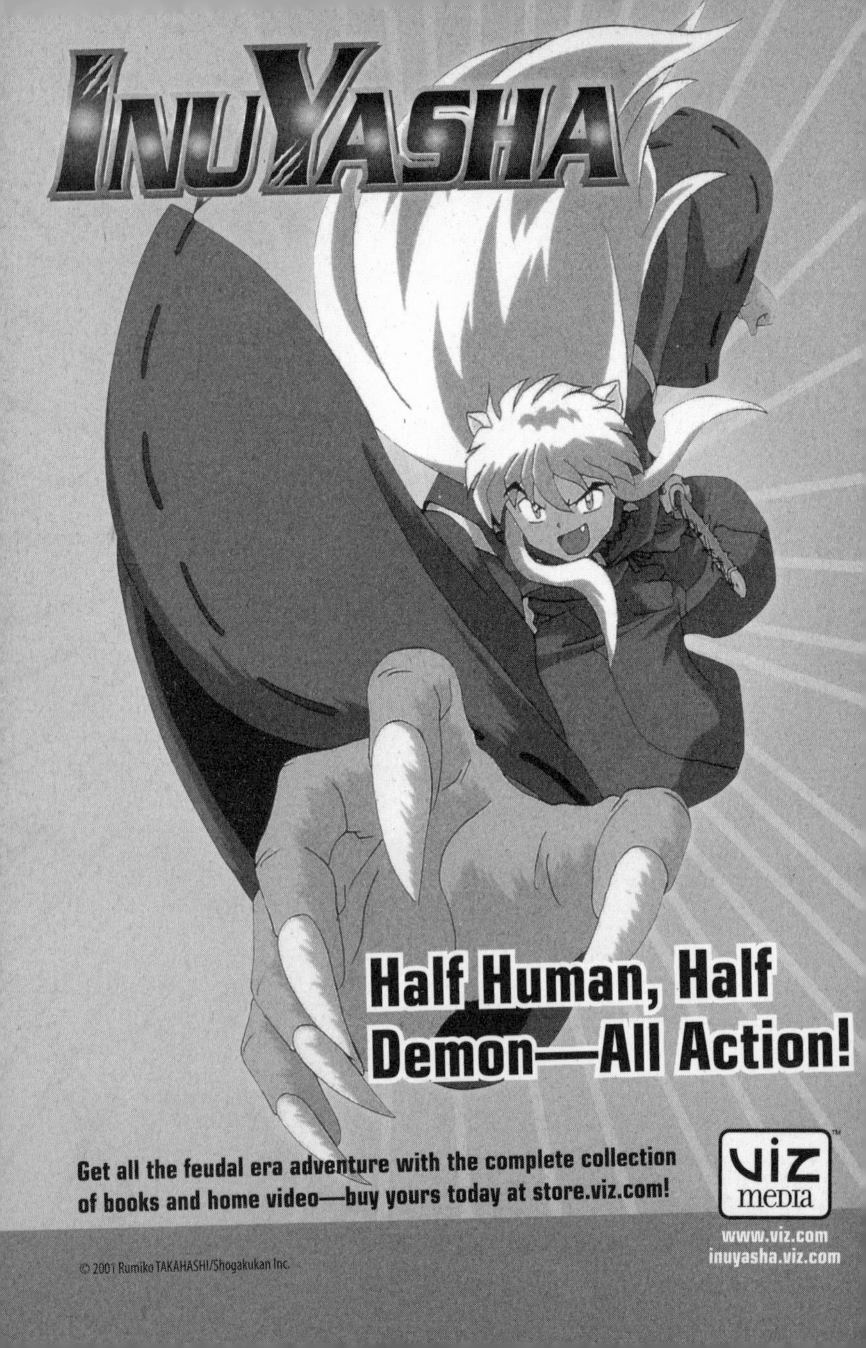
INUYASHA
Half Human, Half Demon—All Action!
Get all the feudal era adventure with the complete collection of books and home video—buy yours today at store.viz.com!
viz media
www.viz.com
inuyasha.viz.com
© 2001 Rumiko TAKAHASHI/Shogakukan Inc.

INUYASHA

Read the action from the start with the original manga series

Full color adaptation of the popular TV series

Art book with cel art, paintings, character profiles and more

TV SERIES & MOVIES ON DVD!

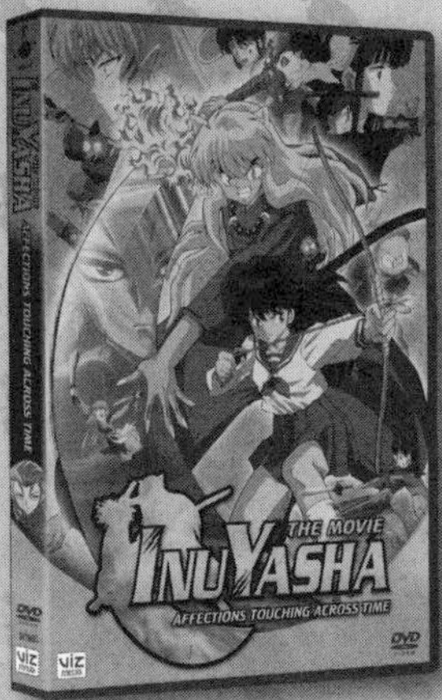
THE MOVIE
INUYASHA
AFFECTIONS TOUCHING ACROSS TIME

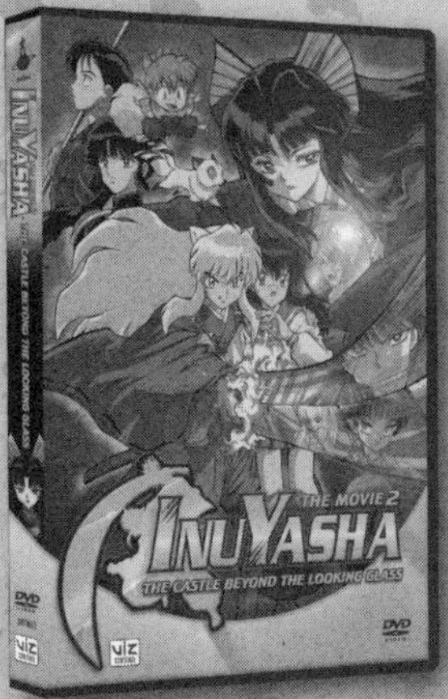
THE MOVIE 2
INUYASHA
THE CASTLE BEYOND THE LOOKING GLASS

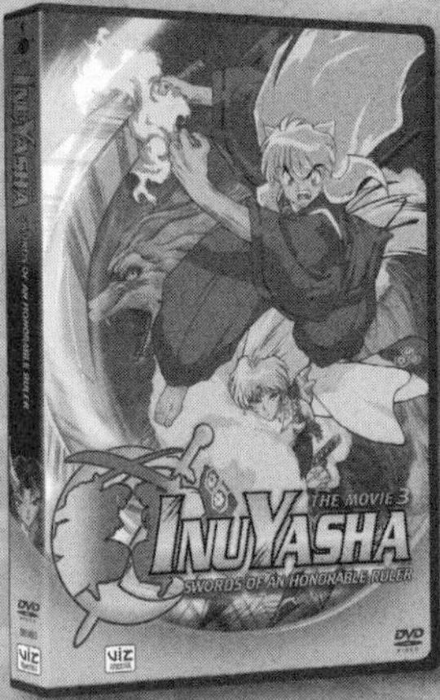
THE MOVIE 3
INUYASHA
SWORDS OF AN HONORABLE RULER

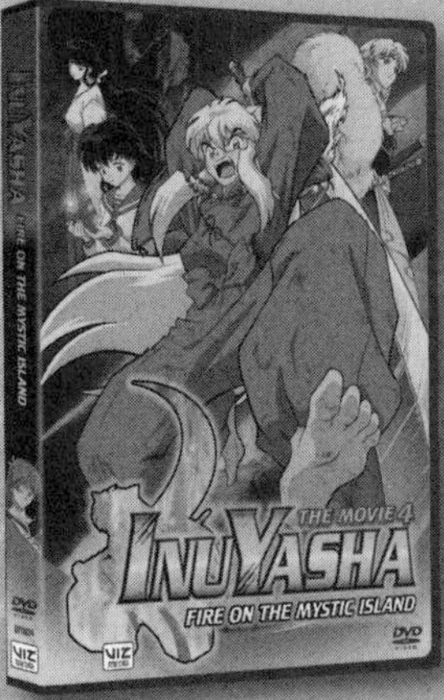
THE MOVIE 4
INUYASHA
FIRE ON THE MYSTIC ISLAND

See more of the action in *Inuyasha* full-length movies

viz media

www.viz.com
inuyasha.viz.com

INUYASHA

The popular anime series now on DVD—each season available in a collectible box set

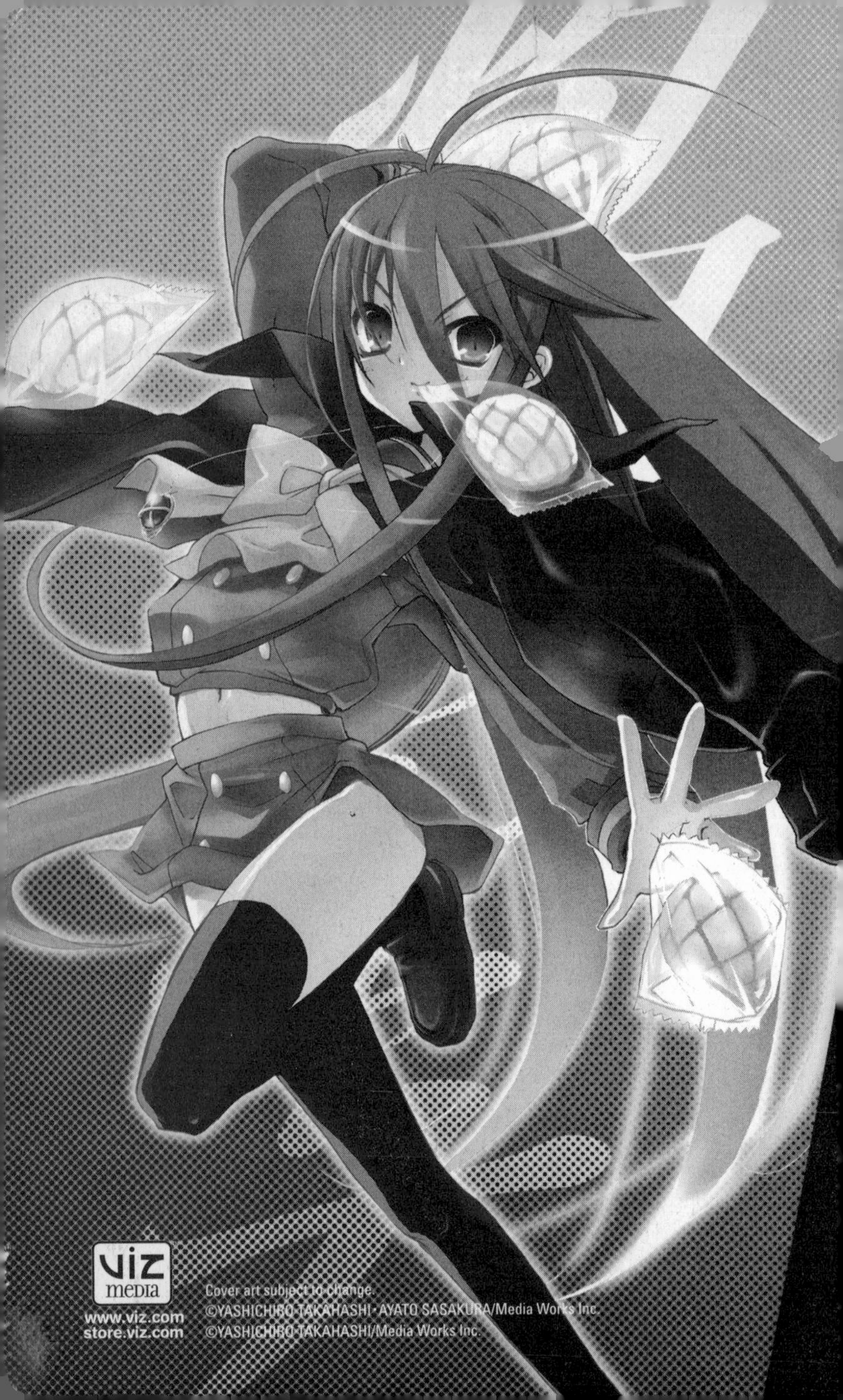

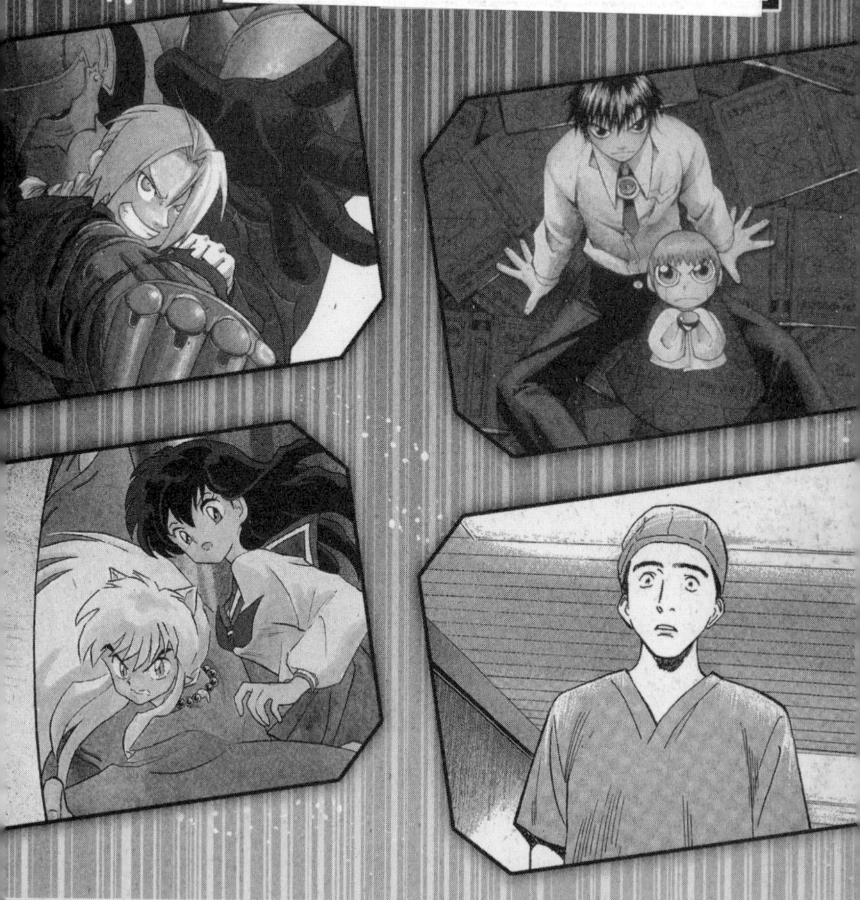